THE *InterActive*
READER™ PLUS
for English Learners

McDougal Littell
A HOUGHTON MIFFLIN COMPANY

Evanston, Illinois • Boston • Dallas

Reading Consultant, *The InterActive Reader™ Plus*

Sharon Sicinski-Skeans, Ph.D. Assistant Professor of Reading, University of Houston-Clear Lake; former K-12 Language Arts Program Director, Spring Independent School District, Houston, Texas
The reading consultant guided the conceptual development of the *InterActive Reader*. She participated in the development of prototype materials, the planning and writing of lessons, and the review of completed materials.

Senior Consultants, *The Language of Literature*

Arthur N. Applebee Professor of Education, State University of New York at Albany; Director, National Research Center on English Learning and Achievements; Senior Fellow, Center for Writing and Literacy

Andrea B. Bermúdez Professor of Studies in Language and Culture; Director, Research Center for Language and Culture; Chair, Foundations and Professional Studies, University of Houston-Clear Lake

Sheridan Blau Senior Lecturer in English and Education and former Director of Composition, University of California at Santa Barbara; Director, South Coast Writing Project; Director, Literature Institute for Teachers; Past President, National Council of Teachers of English

Rebekah Caplan Coordinator, English Language Arts K-12, Oakland Unified School District, Oakland, California; Teacher-Consultant, Bay Area Writing Project, University of California at Berkeley; served on the California State English Assessment Development Team for Language Arts

Peter Elbow Professor of English, University of Massachusetts at Amherst; Fellow, Bard Center for Writing and Thinking

Susan Hynds Professor and Director of English Education, Syracuse University, Syracuse, New York

Judith A. Langer Professor of Education, State University of New York at Albany; Director, National Research Center on English Learning and Achievements; Director, Albany Institute for Research on Education

James Marshall Professor of English and English Education, University of Iowa, Iowa City

Acknowledgments can be found on page 462.

Table of Contents

Test Preparation Strategies 405

Introducing *The InterActive Reader™ Plus*

The InterActive Reader™ Plus is a new kind of literature book. As you will see, this book helps you become an active reader. It is a book to mark on, to write in, and to make your own. You can use it in class *and* take it home.

An Easy-to-Carry Literature Text

This book won't weigh you down—it can fit as comfortably in your hand as it can in your backpack. Yet it contains works by such important authors as . . .

Edgar Allan Poe's classic story "The Cask of Amontillado"

Jack London's unforgettable survival tale "To Build a Fire"

Sandra Cisneros's inspiring essay "On Writing *The House on Mango Street*"

Maya Angelou's touching excerpt from her autobiography *I Know Why the Caged Bird Sings*

You will read these selections and other great literature—plays, poems, stories, and nonfiction. In addition, you will learn how to understand the texts you use in classes, on tests, and in the real world, and you will study and practice specific strategies for taking standardized tests.

Help for Reading

The InterActive Reader™ Plus helps you understand many challenging works of literature. Here's how.

Before-You-Read Activities A prereading page helps you make connections to your everyday life and gives you a key to understanding the selection.

Preview A preview of every selection tells you what to expect.

Reading Tips Reading tips give useful help throughout.

Focus Each longer piece is broken into smaller 'bites' or sections. A focus at the beginning of each section tells you what to look for.

Pause and Reflect At the end of each section, a quick question or two helps you check your understanding.

Read Aloud Specific passages are marked for you to read aloud. You will use your voice and ears to interpret literature.

Reread This feature directs you to passages where a lot of action, change, or meaning is packed in a few lines.

Mark It Up This feature invites you to mark your own notes and questions right on the page.

Vocabulary Support

Words to Know Important new words are underlined. Their definitions appear in a Words to Know section at the bottom of any page where they occur in the selection. You will work with these words in the Words to Know SkillBuilder pages.

Personal Word List As you read, you will want to add some words from the selections to your own vocabulary. Write these words in your Personal Word List on page 444.

SkillBuilder Pages

After each literary selection, you will find these SkillBuilder pages:

   Active Reading SkillBuilder.

   Literary Analysis SkillBuilder.

   Words to Know SkillBuilder (for most selections).

These pages will help you practice and apply important skills.

The InterActive Reader™ Plus for English Learners

The InterActive Reader™ Plus for English Learners provides all of the literature selections and all of the features from the *InterActive Reader™ Plus*. Special additional features include:

Section summaries A brief summary helps get you started with each section or chunk of the text.

More About . . . These notes provide key background information about specific elements of the text such as historical events, scientific concepts, or political situations needed for understanding the selection.

What Does It Mean? These brief notes clearly explain any confusing words, phrases, references, or other constructions.

English Learner Support These notes provide special help with vocabulary, language, and culture issues.

Reading Check These questions at key points in the text help you clarify what is happening in the selection.

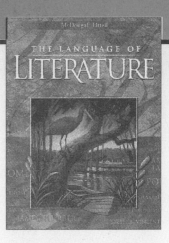

Links to *The Language of Literature*

If you are using McDougal Littell's *The Language of Literature,* you will find *The InterActive Reader™ Plus* to be a perfect companion. The literary selections in the reader can all be found in that book. *The InterActive Reader™ Plus* lets you read certain core selections from *The Language of Literature* more slowly and in greater depth.

Read on to learn more!

Academic and Informational Reading

Here is a special collection of real world examples to help you read every kind of informational material, from textbooks to technical directions. The strategies you learn will help you on tests, in other classes, and in the world outside of school. You will find strategies for the following:

Analyzing Text Features This section will help you read many different types of magazine articles and textbooks. You will learn how titles, subtitles, lists, graphics, many different kinds of visuals, and other special features work in magazines and textbooks. After studying this section you will be ready to read even the most complex material.

Understanding Visuals Tables, charts, graphs, maps, and diagrams all require special reading skills. As you learn the common elements of various visual texts, you will learn to read these materials with accuracy and skill.

Recognizing Text Structures Informational texts can be organized in many different ways. In this section you will study the following structures and learn about special key words that will help you identify the organizational patterns:

- Main idea and supporting details
- Problem and solution
- Sequence
- Cause and Effect
- Comparison and Contrast
- Argument

Reading in the Content Areas You will learn special strategies for reading social studies, science, and mathematics texts.

Reading Beyond the Classroom In this section you will encounter applications, schedules, technical directions, product information, Web pages, and other readings. Learning to analyze these texts will help you in your everyday life and on some standardized tests.

Test Preparation Strategies

In this section, you will find strategies and practice to help you succeed on many different kinds of standardized tests. After closely studying a variety of test formats through annotated examples, you will have an opportunity to practice each format on your own. Additional support will help you think through your answers. You will find strategies for the following:

Successful Test Taking This section provides many suggestions for preparing for and taking tests. The information ranges from analyzing test questions to tips for answering multiple-choice and open-ended test questions.

Reading Tests: Long Selections You will learn how to analyze the structure of a lengthy reading and prepare to answer the comprehension questions that follow it.

Reading Tests: Short Selections These selections may be a paragraph of text, a poem, a chart or graph, or some other item. You will practice the special range of comprehension skills required for these pieces.

Functional Reading These real-world texts present special challenges. You will learn about the various test formats that use applications, product labels, technical directions, Web pages, and more.

Revising and Editing Tests These materials test your understanding of English grammar and usage. You may encounter capitalization and punctuation questions. Sometimes the focus is on usage questions such as verb tenses or pronoun agreement issues. You will become familiar with these formats through the guided practice in this section.

Writing Tests Writing prompts and sample student essays will help you understand how to analyze a prompt and what elements make a successful written response. Scoring rubrics and a prompt for practice will prepare you for the writing tests you will take.

User's Guide

The InterActive Reader™ Plus has an easy-to-follow organization, illustrated by these sample pages from "The Necklace."

The Necklace

Guy de Maupassant

Before You Read

Connect to Your Life

Think of an event that has changed your life. Use the following chart to describe the event and how it affected you.

EVENT	HOW IT CHANGED YOU
My family moved to a new home.	I had to make new friends and adjust to life in a new area.

Key to the Story

WHAT'S THE BIG IDEA? In this story, wealth is very important to the main character, Madame Loisel. Use the word web to show what images come to mind when you think of the word *wealth*. See if your images match those of Madame Loisel.

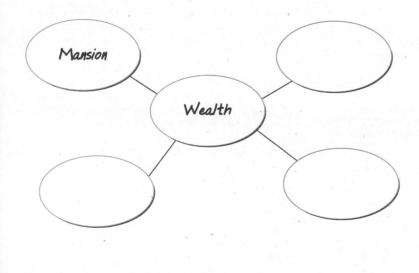

Connect to Your Life

These activities help you see connections between your own life and what happens in the selection.

Key to the Selection

This section provides a "key" to help you unlock the selection so that you can understand and enjoy it. One of these four kinds of keys will appear:

- **What You Need to Know—** important background information.

- **What's the Big Idea?—**an introduction to key words or concepts in the selection.

- **What Do You Think?—** a preview of an important quotation from the selection.

- **What to Listen For—** a chance to examine the sound and rhythm of a piece.

And there's more

User's Guide continued

Reading Tips

1 These practical strategies will help you gain more from your reading.

PREVIEW

2 This feature tells you what the selection is about, so that you'll know what to expect.

FOCUS

3 Every literary work is broken into sections. Each section is introduced by a Focus that tells you what to look for as you read.

MARK IT UP

4 This feature often appears in the Focus. It may ask you to underline or circle key passages in the text or to take notes in the margin as you read.

As the story . . .

5 This feature provides a brief summary to help you get started with each section of the text.

More About . . .

6 These notes give important background information about specific elements of the text to help you understand the selection.

SHORT STORY

1 **Reading Tips**
Try to picture the main character in your mind.
- Look for **details** that tell you what Madame Loisel looks like.
- Look for **details** that help you understand how she feels.

The Necklace
Guy de Maupassant

2 PREVIEW "The Necklace" is set in Paris, France, in the late 1800s. Madame Mathilde Loisel[1] is unhappy with her middle-class life. When her husband gets an invitation to a fancy reception, or party, Madame Loisel gets the chance to experience the life of which she dreams. Then, on the night of the reception, something happens that changes her life and that of her husband forever.

5 **As the story begins . . .**
- Madame Mathilde Loisel is introduced.
- She is unhappy and she wants to be rich.

6 **More About . . .**
PROSPECTS Someone who is likely to become rich or successful has good prospects. In the 1800s, a man with good prospects had family money or a good career. A woman with good prospects had a good chance of marrying a wealthy husband.

3 FOCUS
In this part of the story, you will get to know Madame Mathilde Loisel, the main character.

4 MARK IT UP As you read, circle **details** that help you to understand her and how she feels about her life. Examples are highlighted.

She was one of those pretty and charming girls, born, as if by an accident of fate, into a family of clerks. With no dowry, no prospects, no way of any kind of being met, understood, loved, and married by a man both prosperous and famous, she was finally married to a minor clerk[2] in the Ministry of Education.

She dressed plainly because she could not afford fine clothes, but was as unhappy as a woman who has come down in the world; for women have no family rank

---

1. **Madame Mathilde Loisel** (mə-däm′ mä′tēld lwä-zĕl′): *Madame* is a title of courtesy for a married French woman. The abbreviation for *madame* is *Mme.*
2. **clerk:** office worker who handles routine tasks such as letter writing and record keeping.

7 WORDS TO KNOW
prospects (prŏs′pĕkts′) *n.* chances or possibilities, especially for success or profit

---

7 WORDS TO KNOW Important **Words to Know** are underlined in each selection. Definitions are given at the bottom of the page.

or social class. With them, beauty, grace, and charm take the place of birth and breeding. Their natural poise, their instinctive good taste, and their mental cleverness are the sole guiding principles which make daughters of the common people the equals of ladies in high society.

She grieved incessantly, feeling that she had been born for all the little niceties and luxuries of living. She grieved over the shabbiness of her apartment, the dinginess of the walls, the worn-out appearance of the chairs, the ugliness of the draperies. All these things, which another woman of her class would not even have noticed, gnawed at her and made her furious. The sight of the little Breton³ girl who did her humble housework roused in her disconsolate⁴ regrets and wild daydreams. She would dream of silent chambers, draped with Oriental tapestries and lighted by tall bronze floor lamps, and of two handsome butlers in knee breeches, who, drowsy from the heavy warmth cast by the central stove, dozed in large overstuffed armchairs.

She would dream of great reception halls hung with old silks, of fine furniture filled with priceless curios,⁵ and of small, stylish, scented sitting rooms just right for the four o'clock chat with intimate friends, with distinguished and sought-after men whose attention every woman envies and longs to attract.

When dining at the round table, covered for the third day with the same cloth, opposite her husband, who would raise the cover of the soup tureen, declaring delightedly, "Ah! A good stew! There's nothing I like better . . . ," she would dream of fashionable dinner parties, of gleaming silverware, of tapestries making the walls alive with characters out of history and strange birds in a fairyland forest; she would dream of delicious dishes served on wonderful china, of gallant compliments whispered and listened to with a sphinxlike⁶ smile as one eats the rosy flesh of a trout or nibbles at the wings of a grouse.

She had no evening clothes, no jewels, nothing. But those were the things she wanted; she felt that was the kind of life

---

3. **Breton** (brĕt′n): of or relating to the province of Brittany in northwestern France.
4. **disconsolate:** very unhappy; beyond cheering up.
5. **curios:** rare or unusual ornamental objects.
6. **sphinxlike:** mysterious; from the Greek myth of the sphinx, a winged creature that killed those who could not answer its riddle.

English Learner Support
VOCABULARY

8 **Idiom** *High society* means "wealthy people who belong to the highest social class."

READ ALOUD Lines 18–24

9 Notice the contrast between Madame Loisel's desire for luxury and the ugliness around her.

Reading Check

10 How does Madame Loisel's husband feel about their life? How do you know?

MARK IT UP KEEP TRACK

11 As you read, you can use these marks to keep track of your understanding.

✔ ..... I understand.

? ..... I don't understand this.

! ..... Interesting or surprising idea

The Necklace   **5**

English Learner Support

8 These notes provide help with vocabulary, language, and culture issues.

READ ALOUD Lines 18–24

9 From time to time, you'll be asked to read a passage aloud. That's a great way to increase your understanding —and enjoyment.

Reading Check

10 These questions help you clarify what is happening in the selection.

MARK IT UP KEEP TRACK

11 This easy-to-use marking system will help you track your understanding. Turn to page xiv to see how a model of the system can be used.

And there's more

Student Model

These pages show you how one student made use of *The InterActive Reader Plus*.

MARK IT UP 1. Look at the details you marked as you read. Star the three that best helped you to understand how Madame Loisel feels about her life. **(Evaluate)**

2. If you were Madame Loisel, would you be unhappy? Yes/No, because *I would be jealous of people with more money.*

_____

(Connect)

As the story continues . . .

- Madame Loisel gets an invitation.
- The invitation creates a problem.

English Learner Support

...ighted words
...ppy."

...Check
...me Loisel happy
...ion?

Note how this student used the following symbols:

✓ marks a place where something is made clear or understandable

? marks where something is not understood or is confusing

! marks a surprising or interesting place in the text

Also notice how two words are circled, *distracted* and *dismay*. These are words that the student marked for her Personal Word List.

---

50 for her. She so much longed to please, be envied, be fascinating and sought after. ＊

She had a well-to-do friend, a classmate of convent-school days whom she would no longer go to see, simply because she would feel so distressed on returning home. And she would weep for days on end from vexation, regret, despair, and anguish.

Then one evening, her husband came home proudly holding out a large envelope.

"Look," he said, "I've got something for you."

Pause & Reflect

60 **FOCUS**
Read to find out how Madame Loisel responds to her husband's surprise.

MARK IT UP Underline the words or phrases that describe her response.

She excitedly tore open the envelope and pulled out a printed card bearing these words: "The Minister of Education and Mme. Georges Ramponneau[7] beg M.[8] and Mme. Loisel to do them the honor of attending an evening reception at the Ministerial Mansion on Friday, January 18."

Instead of being delighted, as her husband had hoped, she scornfully tossed the invitation on the table, murmuring,
70 "What good is that to me?"

"But, my dear, I thought you'd be thrilled to death. You never get a chance to go out, and this is a real affair, a wonderful one! I had an awful time getting a card. Everybody wants one; it's much sought after, and not many clerks have a chance at one. You'll see all the most important people there."

! She gave him an irritated glance and burst out impatiently, "What do you think I have to go in?"

He hadn't given that a thought. He stammered, "Why, the dress you wear when we go to the theater. That looks quite
80 nice, I think."

He stopped talking, dazed and distracted to see his wife

---

7. **Mme. Georges Ramponneau** (zhôrzh′ rän-pô-nō′).

8. **M.:** *M.* is an abbreviation for *Monsieur* (mə-syœ′), a title of courtesy for a Frenchman.

WORDS TO KNOW **vexation** (vĕk-sā′shən) *n.* anger or annoyance

burst out weeping. <u>Two large tears slowly rolled from the corners of her eyes to the corners of her mouth;</u> he gasped, "Why, what's the matter? What's the trouble?"

By sheer willpower she overcame her outburst and answered in a calm voice while wiping the tears from her wet cheeks. "Oh, nothing. Only I don't have an evening dress and therefore I can't go to that affair. Give the card to some friend at the office whose wife can dress better than I can."

90   He was stunned. He resumed. "Let's see, Mathilde. How much would a suitable outfit cost—one you could wear for other affairs too—something very simple?"

She thought it over for several seconds, going over her allowance and thinking also of the amount she could ask for without bringing an immediate refusal and an exclamation of (dismay) from the thrifty clerk.

Finally, she answered hesitatingly, "I'm not sure exactly, but I think with four hundred francs[9] I could manage it."

He turned a bit pale, for he had set aside just that amount
100 to buy a rifle so that, the following summer, he could join some friends who were getting up a group to shoot larks on the plain near Nanterre.

However, he said, "All right. I'll give you four hundred francs. But try to get a nice dress."

Pause **&** *Reflect*

FOCUS

Read to find out how an old friend helps Madame Loisel.

As the day of the party approached, Mme. Loisel seemed sad, moody, and ill at ease. Her outfit was ready, however. Her husband said to her one evening, "What's the matter? You've been all out of sorts for three
110 days."

And she answered, "It's embarrassing not to have a jewel or a gem—nothing to wear on my dress. I'll look like a <u>pauper</u>:

---

9. **francs** (frăngks): the franc is the basic monetary unit of France.

WORDS
TO
KNOW

pauper (pô'pər) *n.* a poor person, especially one who depends on public charity

---

English Learner Support
VOCABULARY

Idiom An *evening dress* is a formal dress that is worn to evening social events.

Pause **&** Reflect

1. Look over the words you underlined as you read. In one sentence, **summarize** how Madame Loisel responds to her husband's surprise.

   She was very upset because she didn't have a fancy dress.

2. Do you think Madame Loisel will be happy now? Yes/No, because *Now she has a very pretty dress to wear.*

   (Predict)

As the story continues…
• Madame Loisel has another problem.
• Her husband suggests a solution.

The Necklace   7

THE *InterActive*

READER™ PLUS

for English Learners

The Necklace

Guy de Maupassant

Before You Read

Connect to Your Life

Think of an event that has changed your life. Use the following chart to describe the event and how it affected you.

EVENT	HOW IT CHANGED YOU
My family moved to a new home.	I had to make new friends and adjust to life in a new area.

Key to the Story

WHAT'S THE BIG IDEA? In this story, wealth is very important to the main character, Madame Loisel. Use the word web to show what images come to mind when you think of the word *wealth*. See if your images match those of Madame Loisel.

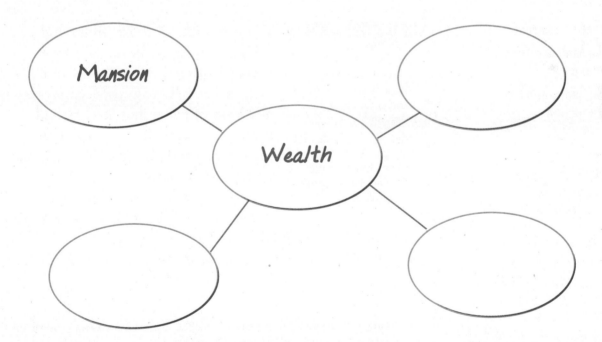

Reading Tips

Try to picture the main character in your mind.

- Look for **details** that tell you what Madame Loisel looks like.

- Look for **details** that help you understand how she feels.

The Necklace

Guy de Maupassant

PREVIEW "The Necklace" is set in Paris, France, in the late 1800s. Madame Mathilde Loisel[1] is unhappy with her middle-class life. When her husband gets an invitation to a fancy reception, or party, Madame Loisel gets the chance to experience the life of which she dreams. Then, on the night of the reception, something happens that changes her life and that of her husband forever.

As the story begins...

- Madame Mathilde Loisel is introduced.

- She is unhappy and she wants to be rich.

More About...

PROSPECTS Someone who is likely to become rich or successful has good prospects. In the 1800s, a man with good prospects had family money or a good career. A woman with good prospects had a good chance of marrying a wealthy husband.

FOCUS
In this part of the story, you will get to know Madame Mathilde Loisel, the main character.

MARK IT UP As you read, circle **details** that help you to understand her and how she feels about her life. Examples are highlighted.

10

She was one of those pretty and charming girls, born, as if by an accident of fate, into a family of clerks. With no dowry, no prospects, no way of any kind of being met, understood, loved, and married by a man both prosperous and famous, she was finally married to a minor clerk[2] in the Ministry of Education.

She dressed plainly because she could not afford fine clothes, but was as unhappy as a woman who has come down in the world; for women have no family rank

1. **Madame Mathilde Loisel** (mə-däm′ mä′tēld lwä-zĕl′): *Madame* is a title of courtesy for a married French woman. The abbreviation for *madame* is *Mme.*

2. **clerk:** office worker who handles routine tasks such as letter writing and record keeping.

WORDS
TO
KNOW

prospects (prŏs′pĕkts′) *n.* chances or possibilities, especially for success or profit

or social class. With them, beauty, grace, and charm take the place of birth and breeding. Their natural poise, their instinctive good taste, and their mental cleverness are the sole guiding principles which make daughters of the common people the equals of ladies in high society.

She grieved incessantly, feeling that she had been born for all the little niceties and luxuries of living. She grieved over the shabbiness of her apartment, the dinginess of the walls, the worn-out appearance of the chairs, the ugliness of the draperies. All these things, which another woman of her class would not even have noticed, gnawed at her and made her furious. The sight of the little Breton[3] girl who did her humble housework roused in her disconsolate[4] regrets and wild daydreams. She would dream of silent chambers, draped with Oriental tapestries and lighted by tall bronze floor lamps, and of two handsome butlers in knee breeches, who, drowsy from the heavy warmth cast by the central stove, dozed in large overstuffed armchairs.

She would dream of great reception halls hung with old silks, of fine furniture filled with priceless curios,[5] and of small, stylish, scented sitting rooms just right for the four o'clock chat with intimate friends, with distinguished and sought-after men whose attention every woman envies and longs to attract.

When dining at the round table, covered for the third day with the same cloth, opposite her husband, who would raise the cover of the soup tureen, declaring delightedly, "Ah! A good stew! There's nothing I like better . . . ," she would dream of fashionable dinner parties, of gleaming silverware, of tapestries making the walls alive with characters out of history and strange birds in a fairyland forest; she would dream of delicious dishes served on wonderful china, of gallant compliments whispered and listened to with a sphinxlike[6] smile as one eats the rosy flesh of a trout or nibbles at the wings of a grouse.

She had no evening clothes, no jewels, nothing. But those were the things she wanted; she felt that was the kind of life

---

3. **Breton** (brĕt′n): of or relating to the province of Brittany in northwestern France.

4. **disconsolate:** very unhappy; beyond cheering up.

5. **curios:** rare or unusual ornamental objects.

6. **sphinxlike:** mysterious; from the Greek myth of the sphinx, a winged creature that killed those who could not answer its riddle.

MARK IT UP **1.** Look at the details you marked as you read. Star the three that best helped you to understand how Madame Loisel feels about her life. **(Evaluate)**

2. If you were Madame Loisel, would you be unhappy? *Yes/No,* because _____

_____

_____ .

(Connect)

As the story continues . . .

- Madame Loisel gets an invitation.

- The invitation creates a problem.

English Learner Support

VOCABULARY

Idiom The highlighted words mean "very happy."

✔ **Reading Check**

Why isn't Madame Loisel happy to get the invitation?

---

⑤⓪ for her. She so much longed to please, be envied, be fascinating and sought after.

She had a well-to-do friend, a classmate of convent-school days whom she would no longer go to see, simply because she would feel so distressed on returning home. And she would weep for days on end from <u>vexation</u>, regret, despair, and anguish.

Then one evening, her husband came home proudly holding out a large envelope.

"Look," he said, "I've got something for you."

⑥⓪ **FOCUS**

Read to find out how Madame Loisel responds to her husband's surprise.

MARK IT UP Underline the words or phrases that describe her response.

She excitedly tore open the envelope and pulled out a printed card bearing these words: "The Minister of Education and Mme. Georges Ramponneau[7] beg M.[8] and Mme. Loisel to do them the honor of attending an evening reception at the Ministerial Mansion on Friday, January 18."

Instead of being delighted, as her husband had hoped, she scornfully tossed the invitation on the table, murmuring, ⑦⓪ "What good is that to me?"

"But, my dear, I thought you'd be thrilled to death. You never get a chance to go out, and this is a real affair, a wonderful one! I had an awful time getting a card. Everybody wants one; it's much sought after, and not many clerks have a chance at one. You'll see all the most important people there."

She gave him an irritated glance and burst out impatiently, "What do you think I have to go in?"

He hadn't given that a thought. He stammered, "Why, the dress you wear when we go to the theater. That looks quite ⑧⓪ nice, I think."

He stopped talking, dazed and distracted to see his wife

---

7. **Mme. Georges Ramponneau** (zhôrzh′ rän-pô-nō′).

8. **M.:** *M.* is an abbreviation for *Monsieur* (mə-syœ′), a title of courtesy for a Frenchman.

WORDS
TO
KNOW

vexation (vĕk-sā′shən) *n.* anger or annoyance

burst out weeping. Two large tears slowly rolled from the corners of her eyes to the corners of her mouth; he gasped, "Why, what's the matter? What's the trouble?"

By sheer willpower she overcame her outburst and answered in a calm voice while wiping the tears from her wet cheeks. "Oh, nothing. Only I don't have an evening dress and therefore I can't go to that affair. Give the card to some friend at the office whose wife can dress better than I can."

90 He was stunned. He resumed. "Let's see, Mathilde. How much would a suitable outfit cost—one you could wear for other affairs too—something very simple?"

She thought it over for several seconds, going over her allowance and thinking also of the amount she could ask for without bringing an immediate refusal and an exclamation of dismay from the thrifty clerk.

Finally, she answered hesitatingly, "I'm not sure exactly, but I think with four hundred francs⁹ I could manage it."

He turned a bit pale, for he had set aside just that amount 100 to buy a rifle so that, the following summer, he could join some friends who were getting up a group to shoot larks on the plain near Nanterre.

However, he said, "All right. I'll give you four hundred francs. But try to get a nice dress."

Pause & Reflect

FOCUS
Read to find out how an old friend helps Madame Loisel.

As the day of the party approached, Mme. Loisel seemed sad, moody, and ill at ease. Her outfit was ready, however. Her husband said to her one evening, "What's the matter? You've been all out of sorts for three 110 days."

And she answered, "It's embarrassing not to have a jewel or a gem—nothing to wear on my dress. I'll look like a pauper:

9. **francs** (frăngks): the franc is the basic monetary unit of France.

WORDS TO KNOW   **pauper** (pô′pər) *n.* a poor person, especially one who depends on public charity

Idiom An *evening dress* is a formal dress that is worn to evening social events.

Pause **&** *Reflect*

1. Look over the words you underlined as you read. In one sentence, **summarize** how Madame Loisel responds to her husband's surprise.

_____

_____

_____

_____

2. Do you think Madame Loisel will be happy now? *Yes/No,* because _____

_____

_____

_____ .

(Predict)

As the story continues...
- Madame Loisel has another problem.
- Her husband suggests a solution.

What Does It Mean?

Humiliating means "shameful," or "embarrassing."

✔ Reading Check

Why does Madame Loisel think she needs jewelry?

Pause **&** *Reflect*

1. Madame Forestier helps Madame Loisel by _____

_____

_____

_____ . (Clarify)

2. Why did Madame Loisel want the diamond necklace and nothing else? **(Infer)**

_____

_____

_____

_____

3. Madame Loisel *will/will not* have a good time at the reception because _____

_____

_____

_____ . (Predict)

I'd almost rather not go to that party."

He answered, "Why not wear some flowers? They're very fashionable this season. For ten francs you can get two or three gorgeous roses."

She wasn't at all convinced. "No. . . . There's nothing more humiliating than to look poor among a lot of rich women."

But her husband exclaimed, "My, but you're silly! Go see your friend Mme. Forestier[10] and ask her to lend you some jewelry. You and she know each other well enough for you to do that."

She gave a cry of joy, "Why, that's so! I hadn't thought of it."

The next day she paid her friend a visit and told her of her predicament.

Mme. Forestier went toward a large closet with mirrored doors, took out a large jewel box, brought it over, opened it, and said to Mme. Loisel, "Pick something out, my dear."

At first her eyes noted some bracelets, then a pearl necklace, then a Venetian cross, gold and gems, of marvelous workmanship. She tried on these adornments in front of the mirror, but hesitated, unable to decide which to part with and put back. She kept on asking, "Haven't you something else?"

"Oh, yes, keep on looking. I don't know just what you'd like."

All at once she found, in a black satin box, a superb diamond necklace; and her pulse beat faster with longing. Her hands trembled as she took it up. Clasping it around her throat, outside her high-necked dress, she stood in ecstasy looking at her reflection.

Then she asked, hesitatingly, pleading, "Could I borrow that, just that and nothing else?"

"Why, of course."

She threw her arms around her friend, kissed her warmly, and fled with her treasure.

Pause **&** *Reflect*

---

10. **Forestier** (fô-rĕs-tyā′).

150 The day of the party arrived. Mme. Loisel was a sensation. She was the prettiest one there, fashionable, gracious, smiling, and wild with joy. All the men turned to look at her, asked who she was, begged to be introduced. All the Cabinet officials wanted to waltz with her. The minister took notice of her.

She danced madly, wildly, drunk with pleasure, giving no thought to anything in the triumph of her beauty, the pride of her success, in a kind of happy cloud composed of all the adulation, of all the admiring glances, of all the awakened longings, of a sense of complete victory that is so sweet to a woman's heart.

160 She left around four o'clock in the morning. Her husband, since midnight, had been dozing in a small empty sitting room with three other gentlemen whose wives were having too good a time.

He threw over her shoulders the wraps he had brought for going home, modest garments of everyday life whose shabbiness clashed with the stylishness of her evening clothes. She felt this and longed to escape, unseen by the other women who were draped in expensive furs.

Loisel held her back.

"Hold on! You'll catch cold outside. I'll call a cab."

170 But she wouldn't listen to him and went rapidly down the stairs. When they were on the street, they didn't find a carriage; and they set out to hunt for one, hailing drivers whom they saw going by at a distance.

They walked toward the Seine,[11] disconsolate and shivering. Finally on the docks they found one of those carriages that one sees in Paris only after nightfall, as if they were ashamed to show their drabness during daylight hours.

It dropped them at their door in the Rue des Martyrs,[12] and they climbed wearily up to their apartment. For her, it was all over. For him, there was the thought that he would 180 have to be at the Ministry at ten o'clock.

Before the mirror, she let the wraps fall from her shoulders to see herself once again in all her glory. Suddenly she gave a cry. The necklace was gone.

---

11. **Seine** (sĕn): the principal river of Paris.

12. **Rue des Martyrs** (rü' dā mär-tēr'): a street in Paris.

WORDS
TO
KNOW   **adulation** (ăj'ə-lā'shən) *n.* excessive praise or flattery

As the story continues...
• Madame Loisel enjoys the party.
• At home, she makes a shocking discovery.

What Does It Mean?
The leaders of governmental departments form the *Cabinet*. The head of the Cabinet is the prime minister.

Reading Check
How does Madame Loisel look when she is at the party?

English Learner Support
VOCABULARY

Idiom *All over* is an idiom meaning "finished."

Her husband, already half-undressed, said, "What's the trouble?"

She turned toward him despairingly, "I . . . I . . . I don't have Mme. Forestier's necklace."

"What! You can't mean it! It's impossible!"

They hunted everywhere, through the folds of the dress, through the folds of the coat, in the pockets. They found nothing.

He asked, "Are you sure you had it when leaving the dance?"

"Yes, I felt it when I was in the hall of the Ministry."

"But if you had lost it on the street, we'd have heard it drop. It must be in the cab."

"Yes. Quite likely. Did you get its number?"

"No. Didn't you notice it either?"

"No."

They looked at each other aghast. Finally Loisel got dressed again.

"I'll retrace our steps on foot," he said, "to see if I can find it."

And he went out. She remained in her evening clothes, without the strength to go to bed, slumped in a chair in the unheated room, her mind a blank.

Her husband came in about seven o'clock. He had had no luck.

He went to the police station, to the newspapers to post a reward, to the cab companies, everywhere the slightest hope drove him.

That evening Loisel returned, pale, his face lined; still he had learned nothing.

Pause & Reflect

Pause & Reflect

1. Think about what happens at the reception. Sketch in two faces below. One should show how Madame Loisel feels during the party. The other should show how she feels after she gets home. **(Infer)**

Party Face   Party's Over

2. The necklace is now lost. **Predict** what might happen next.

_____

_____

_____

_____

As the story continues . . .

• Madame Loisel must decide what to tell her friend.

• Her husband tries to help.

FOCUS
Find out how the Loisels try to replace the necklace.

MARK IT UP In the margins, make a numbered list of the actions they take.

We'll have to write your friend," he said, "to tell her you have broken the catch and are having it repaired. That will give us a little time to turn around."

She wrote to his dictation.

WORDS TO KNOW

aghast (ə-găst′) *adj.* filled with shock or horror

At the end of a week, they had given up all hope.

220 And Loisel, looking five years older, declared, "We must take steps to replace that piece of jewelry."

The next day they took the case to the jeweler whose name they found inside. He consulted his records. "I didn't sell that necklace, madame," he said. "I only supplied the case."

Then they went from one jeweler to another hunting for a similar necklace, going over their recollections, both sick with despair and anxiety.

They found, in a shop in Palais Royal, a string of diamonds which seemed exactly like the one they were seeking. It was 230 priced at forty thousand francs. They could get it for thirty-six.

They asked the jeweler to hold it for them for three days. And they reached an agreement that he would take it back for thirty-four thousand if the lost one was found before the end of February.

Loisel had eighteen thousand francs he had inherited from his father. He would borrow the rest.

He went about raising the money, asking a thousand francs from one, four hundred from another, a hundred here, sixty 240 there. He signed notes, made <u>ruinous</u> deals, did business with loan sharks, ran the whole <u>gamut</u> of moneylenders. He compromised[13] the rest of his life, risked his signature without knowing if he'd be able to honor it, and then, terrified by the outlook for the future, by the blackness of despair about to close around him, by the prospect of all the <u>privations</u> of the body and tortures of the spirit, he went to claim the new necklace with the thirty-six thousand francs which he placed on the counter of the shopkeeper.

When Mme. Loisel took the necklace back, Mme. Forestier 250 said to her frostily, "You should have brought it back sooner; I might have needed it."

She didn't open the case, an action her friend was afraid of. If she had noticed the substitution, what would she have thought? What would she have said? Would she have thought her a thief?

---

13. compromised: exposed to danger.

WORDS TO KNOW	**ruinous** (rōō′ə-nəs) *adj.* bringing ruin or downfall; disastrous **gamut** (găm′ət) *n.* the entire range or series of something **privation** (prī-vā′shən) *n.* lack of basic necessities or comforts of life

Pause & Reflect

1. Review your notes about the Loisels' actions. Do you think the Loisels did the right thing? *Yes/No,* because _____

_____

_____ .

(Evaluate)

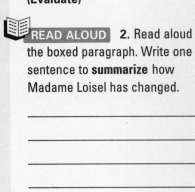

READ ALOUD 2. Read aloud the boxed paragraph. Write one sentence to **summarize** how Madame Loisel has changed.

_____

_____

_____

As the story ends...

• Madame Loisel meets her friend again.

• The story takes an unexpected twist.

Mme. Loisel experienced the horrible life the needy live. She played her part, however, with sudden heroism. That frightful debt had to be paid. She would pay it. She dismissed her maid; they rented a garret[14] under the eaves.

260 She learned to do the heavy housework, to perform the hateful duties of cooking. She washed dishes, wearing down her shell-pink nails scouring the grease from pots and pans; she scrubbed dirty linen, shirts, and cleaning rags, which she hung on a line to dry; she took the garbage down to the street each morning and brought up water, stopping on each landing to get her breath. And, clad like a peasant woman, basket on arm, guarding sou[15] by sou her scanty allowance, she bargained with the fruit dealers, the grocer, the butcher, and was insulted by them.

270 Each month notes had to be paid, and others renewed to give more time.

Her husband labored evenings to balance a tradesman's accounts, and at night, often, he copied documents at five sous a page.

And this went on for ten years.

Pause & Reflect

FOCUS

Read to find out if your prediction is correct.

Finally, all was paid back, everything including the <u>exorbitant</u> rates of the loan sharks and accumulated compound interest.

280 Mme. Loisel appeared an old woman, now. She became heavy, rough, harsh, like one of the poor. Her hair untended, her skirts <u>askew</u>, her hands red, her voice shrill, she even slopped water on her floors and scrubbed them herself. But, sometimes, while her husband was at work, she would sit near the window and think of that long-ago evening when, at the dance, she had been so beautiful and admired.

What would have happened if she had not lost that

---

14. **garret:** room just below the sloping roof of a building; attic.

15. **sou** (sōō): a French coin of small value.

WORDS
TO
KNOW

exorbitant (ĭg-zôr′bĭ-tənt) *adj.* much too high; excessive
askew (ə-skyōō′) *adj.* crooked; to one side

necklace? Who knows? Who can say? How strange and unpredictable life is! How little there is between happiness and misery!

Then one Sunday when she had gone for a walk on the Champs Élysées[16] to relax a bit from the week's labors, she suddenly noticed a woman strolling with a child. It was Mme. Forestier, still young-looking; still beautiful, still charming.

Mme. Loisel felt a rush of emotion. Should she speak to her? Of course. And now that everything was paid off, she would tell her the whole story. Why not?

She went toward her. "Hello, Jeanne."

The other, not recognizing her, showed astonishment at being spoken to so familiarly by this common person. She stammered. "But . . . madame . . . I don't recognize . . . You must be mistaken."

"No, I'm Mathilde Loisel."

Her friend gave a cry, "Oh, my poor Mathilde, how you've changed!"

"Yes, I've had a hard time since last seeing you. And plenty of misfortunes—and all on account of you!"

"Of me . . . How do you mean?"

"Do you remember that diamond necklace you loaned me to wear to the dance at the Ministry?"

"Yes, but what about it?"

"Well, I lost it."

"You lost it! But you returned it."

"I brought you another just like it. And we've been paying for it for ten years now. You can imagine that wasn't easy for us who had nothing. Well, it's over now, and I am glad of it."

Mme. Forestier stopped short, "You mean to say you bought a diamond necklace to replace mine?"

"Yes. You never noticed, then? They were quite alike."

And she smiled with proud and simple joy. Mme. Forestier, quite overcome, clasped her by the hands. "Oh, my poor Mathilde. But mine was only paste.[17] Why, at most it was worth only five hundred francs!"

Pause & Reflect

Pause & Reflect

1. What did Madame Loisel learn about the necklace in the final paragraph? **(Clarify)**

_____

_____

_____

_____

2. How close was the prediction you made on page 12? **(Evaluate)** _____

_____

_____

CHALLENGE

Do you think what happens to Madame Loisel is her own fault, or is she a victim of bad luck? Review the story and circle passages that provide evidence for your opinion. **(Evaluate)**

---

16. **Champs Élysées** (shän zā-lē-zā′): a famous wide street in Paris.

17. **paste:** a hard, glassy material used in making imitations of precious stones.

Active Reading SkillBuilder

Cause and Effect

Events in a plot are sometimes linked causally. One event causes another, which causes another, and so on until the end of the story. A series of events linked in this way is called a chain of **cause and effect.** Use the diagram to connect the major events of "The Necklace" in an unbroken chain of cause and effect. Add links to the diagram if necessary.

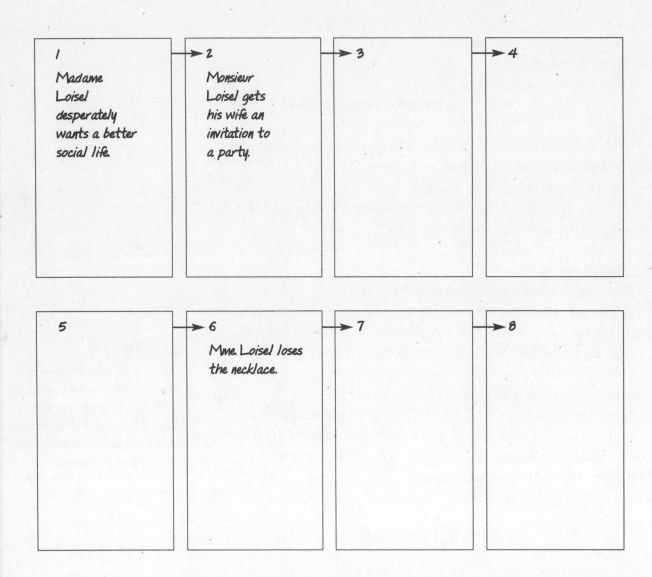

1
Madame Loisel desperately wants a better social life.

2
Monsieur Loisel gets his wife an invitation to a party.

3

4

5

6
Mme. Loisel loses the necklace.

7

8

Literary Analysis SkillBuilder

Plot

The events that make up the **plot** of a story can be divided into rising action and falling action. The rising action consists of the conflicts and complications faced by the main character. Rising action leads to the climax, or turning point, of the story. The falling action, or resolution, occurs at the end of the story and shows how the conflicts are resolved. Use the diagram below to outline events in "The Necklace." Two examples are shown.

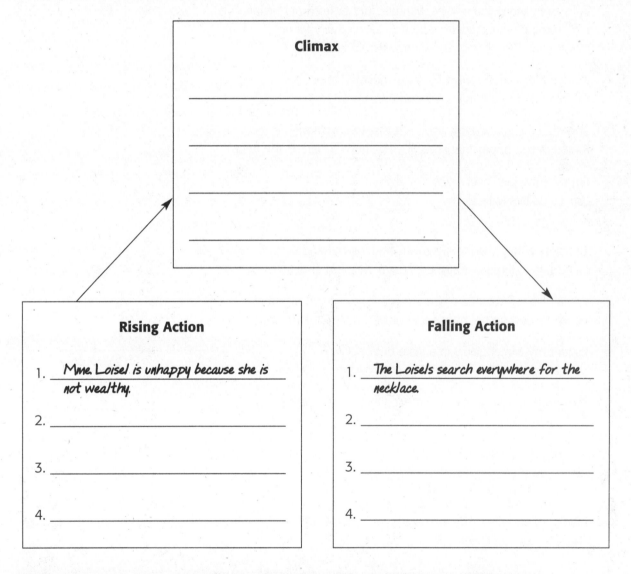

Climax

_____

_____

_____

_____

Rising Action

1. _Mme. Loisel is unhappy because she is_ _not wealthy._

2. _____

3. _____

4. _____

Falling Action

1. _The Loisels search everywhere for the_ _necklace._

2. _____

3. _____

4. _____

Follow Up: Which events that form the rising action of "The Necklace" are conflicts, or struggles between opposing forces? Which are complications that cause difficulties for the characters? Write *conflict* or *complication* next to each event.

Words to Know SkillBuilder

Words to Know

adulation	askew	gamut	privation	ruinous
aghast	exorbitant	pauper	prospects	vexation

A. Decide which word from the word list belongs in each numbered blank.
Then write the word on the blank line on the right.

You tell him, every day, he's perfect. I have one objection.
With every word you say, he wanders further from perfection.
He's turning out conceited, and he's losing every friend.
I wish your (1) of your darling boy would end.

_____ (1)

_____ (2)

If I don't learn that I must be a less devoted shopper,
I'll go so far in debt that I will end up as a (2).

_____ (3)

She read a comic during class. She slept throughout the test.
Although she hopes that she will pass, her (3) aren't the best.

_____ (4)

I'm sure the pie is very nice,
But 15 dollars for a slice
Is too (4) a price.

_____ (5)

The desert that I had to cross was burning hot and vast.
I stood and stared, astonished, feeling helpless and (5).

_____ (6)

I didn't have insurance when the wind blew down the tree,
Which landed on my house and proved quite (6) to me.

_____ (7)

I spent my winter gladly in a state of true (7),
So that I'd have the money for a summertime vacation.

_____ (8)

You promise you will be on time, so that's my expectation;
And when you're late, I must admit to feeling some (8).

_____ (9)

I know your clothes are all brand new,
But I'd be more impressed with you
If your silk necktie weren't (9).

_____ (10)

I looked upon the (10) of the shades of blue, and I
Found many represented in the colors of the sky.

B. Imagine that you are an advice columnist and that *either* M. or Mme. Loisel has
written to you at some point (any point) in the story. Reply, using at least **five** of the
Words to Know.

THE MOST DANGEROUS GAME

RICHARD CONNELL

Before You Read

Connect to Your Life

Sanger Rainsford, one of the characters in "The Most Dangerous Game," says that hunting is "the best sport in the world." Do you agree or disagree with this statement? List two or three reasons for your opinion.

_____

_____

_____

_____

Key to the Story

WHAT'S THE BIG IDEA? The word _game_ in the title of this story has a double meaning. Game can mean "prey that is hunted." A game is also an activity in which players compete with each other according to rules. Complete the word web by writing words that come to mind when you think of the word _game_. Then read to learn about the most dangerous game.

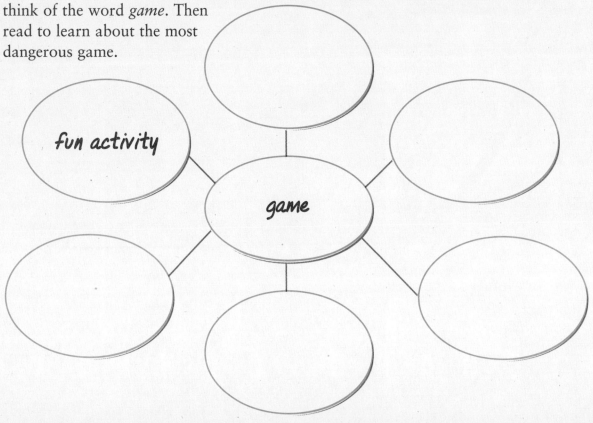

THE MOST DANGEROUS GAME

RICHARD CONNELL

PREVIEW Sanger Rainsford, a famous big game hunter, is sailing on a yacht toward South America when he falls overboard. In order to survive, Rainsford swims to a nearby island. There he encounters the biggest challenge of his life when he becomes a player in "the most dangerous game."

"Off there to the right—somewhere—is a large island," said Whitney. "It's rather a mystery—"

"What island is it?" Rainsford asked. "The old charts call it 'Ship-Trap Island,'" Whitney replied. "A suggestive name, isn't it? Sailors have a curious dread of the place. I don't know why. Some superstition—"

10 "Can't see it," remarked Rainsford, trying to peer through the dank tropical night that was palpable as it pressed its thick warm blackness in upon the yacht.

More About . . .

THE CARIBBEAN The Caribbean Sea is south of Florida and east of Central America. Many tropical islands are found in the Caribbean region. The temperatures in the Caribbean are usually very warm.

English Learner Support
LANGUAGE

Diction The sentence "Great sport, hunting" could be reworded as "Hunting is a great sport."

READ ALOUD **Lines 33–35**

These lines are perhaps the most memorable ones in the story. What do they reveal about Rainsford?

 Reading Check

How are Whitney's views on hunting different from Rainsford's?

English Learner Support
LANGUAGE

Figure of Speech The blue highlighted phrase implies that Captain Nielsen is not afraid of anything.

"You've good eyes," said Whitney, with a laugh, "and I've seen you pick off a moose moving in the brown fall bush at four hundred yards, but even you can't see four miles or so through a moonless Caribbean night."

"Nor four yards," admitted Rainsford. "Ugh! It's like moist black velvet."

"It will be light enough in Rio," promised Whitney. "We 20 should make it in a few days. I hope the jaguar guns have come from Purdey's. We should have some good hunting up the Amazon. Great sport, hunting."

"The best sport in the world," agreed Rainsford.

"For the hunter," amended Whitney. "Not for the jaguar."

"Don't talk rot, Whitney," said Rainsford. "You're a big-game hunter, not a philosopher. Who cares how a jaguar feels?"

"Perhaps the jaguar does," observed Whitney.

"Bah! They've no understanding."

30 "Even so, I rather think they understand one thing—fear. The fear of pain and the fear of death."

"Nonsense," laughed Rainsford. "This hot weather is making you soft, Whitney. Be a realist. The world is made up of two classes—the hunters and the huntees. Luckily, you and I are hunters. Do you think we've passed that island yet?"

"I can't tell in the dark. I hope so."

"Why?" asked Rainsford.

"The place has a reputation—a bad one."

"Cannibals?" suggested Rainsford.

40 "Hardly. Even cannibals wouldn't live in such a Godforsaken place. But it's gotten into sailor lore, somehow. Didn't you notice that the crew's nerves seemed a bit jumpy today?"

"They were a bit strange, now you mention it. Even Captain Nielsen—"

"Yes, even that tough-minded old Swede, who'd go up to the devil himself and ask him for a light. Those fishy blue eyes held a look I never saw there before. All I could get out of him was: 'This place has an evil name among seafaring men, 50 sir.' Then he said to me, very gravely: 'Don't you feel anything?'—as if the air about us was actually poisonous. Now, you mustn't laugh when I tell you this—I did feel something like a sudden chill.

"There was no breeze. The sea was as flat as a plate-glass

window. We were drawing near the island then. What I felt was a—a mental chill; a sort of sudden dread."

"Pure imagination," said Rainsford. "One superstitious sailor can taint the whole ship's company with his fear."

What Does It Mean?
Taint means "stain" or "ruin."

"Maybe. But sometimes I think sailors have an extra sense that tells them when they are in danger. Sometimes I think evil is a <u>tangible</u> thing—with wavelengths, just as sound and light have. An evil place can, so to speak, broadcast vibrations of evil. Anyhow, I'm glad we're getting out of this zone. Well, I think I'll turn in now, Rainsford."

"I'm not sleepy," said Rainsford. "I'm going to smoke another pipe up on the afterdeck."

"Good night, then, Rainsford. See you at breakfast."

"Right. Good night, Whitney."

Reading Check

How does Rainsford feel about the sailors' fear of Ship-Trap Island?

There was no sound in the night as Rainsford sat there but the muffled throb of the engine that drove the yacht swiftly through the darkness, and the swish and ripple of the wash of the propeller.

Rainsford, reclining in a steamer chair, indolently puffed on his favorite brier.[1] The sensuous drowsiness of the night was on him. "It's so dark," he thought, "that I could sleep without closing my eyes; the night would be my eyelids—"

What Does It Mean?
Indolently means "lazily."

An abrupt sound startled him. Off to the right he heard it, and his ears, expert in such matters, could not be mistaken. Again he heard the sound, and again. Somewhere, off in the blackness, someone had fired a gun three times.

Rainsford sprang up and moved quickly to the rail, mystified. He strained his eyes in the direction from which the reports had come, but it was like trying to see through a blanket. He leaped upon the rail and balanced himself there, to get greater elevation; his pipe, striking a rope, was knocked from his mouth. He lunged for it; a short, hoarse cry came from his lips as he realized he had reached too far and had lost his balance. The cry was pinched off short as the blood-warm waters of the Caribbean Sea closed over his head.

He struggled up to the surface and tried to cry out, but the wash from the speeding yacht slapped him in the face, and the salt water in his open mouth made him gag and strangle.

MARK IT UP WORD POWER

Mark words that you'd like to add to your **Personal Word List**. After reading, you can record the words and their meanings beginning on page 402.

---

1. **brier** (brī′ər): a tobacco pipe.

WORDS
TO
KNOW

tangible (tăn′jə-bəl) *adj.* capable of being touched or felt; having actual form and substance

How does Rainsford react
when he falls overboard?

English Learner Support
LANGUAGE

Diction Authors sometimes
vary sentence structure to
make their writing more interesting. The highlighted
sentence near the bottom of
the page can be rewritten as
follows: "Just then, Rainsford
was not concerned about the
perils (dangers) that the tangle
of trees and underbrush (the
jungle) might hold for him."

Pause & **Reflect**

1. In your opinion, what kind of man
is Sanger Rainsford? (**Connect**)

_____
_____
_____

2. What do you **predict** Rainsford
will do now that he is on Ship-
Trap Island?

_____
_____
_____

Desperately he struck out with strong strokes after the
receding lights of the yacht, but he stopped before he had
swum fifty feet. A certain cool-headedness had come to him; it
was not the first time he had been in a tight place. There was
a chance that his cries could be heard by someone aboard the
yacht, but that chance was slender and grew more slender as
the yacht raced on. He wrestled himself out of his clothes and
100 shouted with all his power. The lights of the yacht became
faint and ever-vanishing fireflies; then they were blotted out
entirely by the night.

Rainsford remembered the shots. They had come from the
right, and doggedly he swam in that direction, swimming with
slow, deliberate strokes, conserving his strength. For a
seemingly endless time he fought the sea. He began to count
his strokes; he could do possibly a hundred more and then—

Rainsford heard a sound. It came out of the darkness, a
high, screaming sound, the sound of an animal in an
110 extremity of anguish and terror.

He did not recognize the animal that made the sound; he
did not try to; with fresh vitality he swam toward the sound.
He heard it again; then it was cut short by another noise,
crisp, staccato.

"Pistol shot," muttered Rainsford, swimming on.
Ten minutes of determined effort brought another sound to
his ears—the most welcome he had ever heard—the muttering
and growling of the sea breaking on a rocky shore. He was
almost on the rocks before he saw them; on a night less calm
120 he would have been shattered against them. With his
remaining strength he dragged himself from the swirling
waters. Jagged crags appeared to jut up into the opaqueness;
he forced himself upward, hand over hand. Gasping, his
hands raw, he reached a flat place at the top. Dense jungle
came down to the very edge of the cliffs. What perils that
tangle of trees and underbrush might hold for him did not
concern Rainsford just then. All he knew was that he was safe
from his enemy, the sea, and that utter weariness was on him.
He flung himself down at the jungle edge and tumbled
130 headlong into the deepest sleep of his life.

Pause & **Reflect**

* Rainsford has landed on an island.

* He wakes up hungry from a deep sleep and wants food.

* He finds signs that someone on the island has been hunting.

* He comes upon a large estate with an enormous house.

FOCUS

On the island, Rainsford meets two unusual figures— General Zaroff and his servant Ivan.

✎ **MARK IT UP** As you read, underline details about these men that strike you as unusual or interesting.

When he opened his eyes, he knew from the position of the sun that it was late in the afternoon. Sleep had given him new vigor; a sharp hunger was picking at him. He looked about him, almost cheerfully.

"Where there are pistol shots, there are men. Where there are men, there is food," he thought. But what kind of men, he wondered, in so forbidding a

140 place? An unbroken front of snarled and ragged jungle fringed the shore.

He saw no sign of a trail through the closely knit web of weeds and trees; it was easier to go along the shore, and Rainsford floundered along by the water. Not far from where he had landed, he stopped.

Some wounded thing, by the evidence a large animal, had thrashed about in the underbrush; the jungle weeds were crushed down, and the moss was lacerated; one patch of

150 weeds was stained crimson. A small, glittering object not far away caught Rainsford's eye, and he picked it up. It was an empty cartridge.

"A twenty-two," he remarked. "That's odd. It must have been a fairly large animal, too. The hunter had his nerve with him to tackle it with a light gun. It's clear that the brute put up a fight. I suppose the first three shots I heard was when the hunter flushed[2] his <u>quarry</u> and wounded it. The last shot was when he trailed it here and finished it."

He examined the ground closely and found what he had

160 hoped to find—the print of hunting boots. They pointed along the cliff in the direction he had been going. Eagerly he hurried along, now slipping on a rotten log or a loose stone, but making headway; night was beginning to settle down on the island.

Bleak darkness was blacking out the sea and jungle when Rainsford sighted the lights. He came upon them as he turned a crook in the coastline, and his first thought was that he had come upon a village, for there were many lights. But as he forged along, he saw to his great astonishment that all the

What Does It Mean?

Forbidding means "harsh and threatening."

English Learner Support
LANGUAGE

Diction The highlighted words mean "the evidence shows that the wounded thing was a large animal."

What Does It Mean?

Lacerated means "torn."

Reading Tip

Imagine that you are watching a movie based on this part of the story. Make a mental picture of what Rainsford sees as he explores the island. Then compare your image with that of a classmate.

✔ **Reading Check**

Why is Rainsford happy to find the footprints of hunting boots?

---

2. **flushed:** forced out of a hiding place.

WORDS
TO   **quarry** (kwôr′ē) *n.* the object of a hunt; prey
KNOW

Personification When the author writes "the sea licked greedy lips," he is using personification, or giving human qualities to nonhuman things. The author describes the sea as if it were a hungry person.

More About . . .

(MIRAGES) A *mirage* is an illusion, or something that isn't really there.

What Does It Mean?
Menacing means "threatening."

lights were in one enormous building—a lofty structure with pointed towers plunging upward into the gloom. His eyes made out the shadowy outlines of a palatial château;[3] it was set on a high bluff, and on three sides of it cliffs dived down to where the sea licked greedy lips in the shadows.

"Mirage," thought Rainsford. But it was no mirage, he found, when he opened the tall spiked iron gate. The stone steps were real enough; the massive door with a leering gargoyle[4] for a knocker was real enough; yet about it all hung an air of unreality.

He lifted the knocker, and it creaked up stiffly as if it had never before been used. He let it fall, and it startled him with its booming loudness. He thought he heard steps within; the door remained closed. Again Rainsford lifted the heavy knocker and let it fall. The door opened then, opened as suddenly as if it were on a spring, and Rainsford stood blinking in the river of glaring gold light that poured out. The first thing Rainsford's eyes discerned was the largest man Rainsford had ever seen—a gigantic creature, solidly made and black-bearded to the waist. In his hand the man held a long-barreled revolver, and he was pointing it straight at Rainsford's heart.

Out of the snarl of beard two small eyes regarded Rainsford.

"Don't be alarmed," said Rainsford, with a smile which he hoped was <u>disarming</u>. "I'm no robber. I fell off a yacht. My name is Sanger Rainsford of New York City."

The menacing look in the eyes did not change. The revolver pointed as rigidly as if the giant were a statue. He gave no sign that he understood Rainsford's words, or that he had even heard them. He was dressed in uniform, a black uniform trimmed with gray astrakhan.[5]

"I'm Sanger Rainsford of New York," Rainsford began again. "I fell off a yacht. I am hungry."

The man's only answer was to raise with his thumb the hammer of his revolver. Then Rainsford saw the man's free

---

3. **palatial château** (pə-lā′shəl shă-tō′): palacelike mansion.

4. **gargoyle** (gär′goil): an ornamental figure in the shape of a bizarre, monstrous creature.

5. **astrakhan** (ăs′trə-kăn′): a fur made from skins of young lambs.

WORDS
TO
KNOW

disarming (dĭs-är′mĭng) *adj.* removing or overcoming suspicion; inspiring confidence hand go to his forehead in a military salute, and he saw him click his heels together and stand at attention. Another man was coming down the broad marble steps, an erect, slender man in evening clothes. He advanced to Rainsford and held out his hand.

210   In a cultivated[6] voice marked by a slight accent that gave it added precision and deliberateness, he said: "It is a very great pleasure and honor to welcome Mr. Sanger Rainsford, the celebrated hunter, to my home."

Automatically Rainsford shook the man's hand.

"I've read your book about hunting snow leopards in Tibet, you see," explained the man. "I am General Zaroff."

Rainsford's first impression was that the man was singularly handsome; his second was that there was an original, almost bizarre quality about the general's face. He

220 was a tall man past middle age, for his hair was a vivid white; but his thick eyebrows and pointed military moustache were as black as the night from which Rainsford had come. His eyes, too, were black and very bright. He had high cheekbones, a sharp-cut nose, a spare, dark face, the face of a man used to giving orders, the face of an aristocrat. Turning to the giant in uniform, the general made a sign. The giant put away his pistol, saluted, withdrew.

"Ivan is an incredibly strong fellow," remarked the general, "but he has the misfortune to be deaf and dumb. A simple

230 fellow, but, I'm afraid, like all his race, a bit of a savage."

"Is he Russian?"

"He is a Cossack,"[7] said the general, and his smile showed red lips and pointed teeth. "So am I.

"Come," he said, "we shouldn't be chatting here. We can talk later. Now you want clothes, food, rest. You shall have them. This is a most restful spot."

Ivan had reappeared, and the general spoke to him with lips that moved but gave forth no sound.

"Follow Ivan, if you please, Mr. Rainsford," said the

240 general. "I was about to have my dinner when you came. I'll wait for you. You'll find that my clothes will fit you, I think."

It was to a huge, beam-ceilinged bedroom with a canopied bed big enough for six men that Rainsford followed the silent giant. Ivan laid out an evening suit, and Rainsford, as he put

---

6. **cultivated:** educated and cultured.

7. **Cossack** (kŏs′ăk): a member of a southern Russian people formerly famous as cavalrymen.

English Learner Support
LANGUAGE

Expression *Evening clothes* means that the man is wearing a formal suit.

Reading Tip
What are some of Ivan's characteristics? Fill in the following web with words and phrases that describe him.

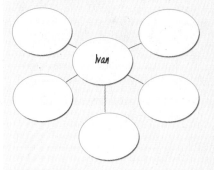
Ivan

More About...
COSSACKS The Cossacks of Russia were free fighting men known for their courage and skill with horses.

What Does It Mean?

A *refectory table* is a long, narrow table. A *score* is twenty, so "two score men could sit down to eat" means that forty people could sit around the table.

✔ **Reading Check**

What is Zaroff's home like?

Pause **&** *Reflect*

Review the details about Zaroff that you marked. What conclusions can you draw about him? **(Draw Conclusions)**

_____

_____

_____

_____

As the story continues . . .

• Rainsford and Zaroff disagree about which animal is the most dangerous to hunt.

• Zaroff tells Rainsford that he is bored with hunting.

• Rainsford is shocked by Zaroff's solution to his boredom.

it on, noticed that it came from a London tailor who ordinarily cut and sewed for none below the rank of duke.

The dining room to which Ivan conducted him was in many ways remarkable. There was a medieval magnificence about it; it suggested a baronial hall of feudal times with its oaken 250 panels, its high ceiling, its vast refectory table where two score men could sit down to eat. About the hall were the mounted heads of many animals—lions, tigers, elephants, moose, bears; larger or more perfect specimens Rainsford had never seen. At the great table the general was sitting, alone.

"You'll have a cocktail, Mr. Rainsford," he suggested. The cocktail was surpassingly good; and, Rainsford noted, the table appointments were of the finest—the linen, the crystal, the silver, the china.

They were eating *borsch*, the rich red soup with whipped 260 cream so dear to Russian palates. Half apologetically General Zaroff said: "We do our best to preserve the amenities of civilization here. Please forgive any lapses. We are well off the beaten track, you know. Do you think the champagne has suffered from its long ocean trip?"

"Not in the least," declared Rainsford. He was finding the general a most thoughtful and affable host, a true cosmopolite.[8] But there was one small trait of the general's that made Rainsford uncomfortable. Whenever he looked up from his plate, he found the general studying him, appraising 270 him narrowly.

Pause **&** *Reflect*

FOCUS

Now Zaroff reveals more about the kind of man he is.

✎ MARK IT UP As you read, circle details that describe how Zaroff feels about hunting. Also circle his opinions about an ideal prey.

"Perhaps," said General Zaroff, "you were surprised that I recognized your name. You see, I read all books on hunting published in English, French, and Russian. I have but one passion in my life, Mr. Rainsford, and it is the hunt."

"You have some wonderful heads

---

8. **cosmopolite** (kŏz-mŏp′ə-līt′): a sophisticated person who can handle any situation well.

WORDS
TO
KNOW

amenity (ə-mĕn′ĭ-tē) *n.* something that adds to one's comfort or convenience

affable (ăf′ə-bəl) *adj.* friendly, pleasant, and easy to talk to

The InterActive Reader PLUS
26 For English Learners

here," said Rainsford as he ate a particularly well cooked filet mignon. "That Cape buffalo is the largest I ever saw."

280 "Oh, that fellow. Yes, he was a monster."

"Did he charge you?"

"Hurled me against a tree," said the general. "Fractured my skull. But I got the brute."

"I've always thought," said Rainsford, "that the Cape buffalo is the most dangerous of all big game."

For a moment the general did not reply; he was smiling his curious red-lipped smile. Then he said slowly: "No. You are wrong, sir. The Cape buffalo is not the most dangerous big game." He sipped his wine. "Here in my preserve on this

290 island," he said, in the same slow tone, "I hunt more dangerous game."

Rainsford expressed his surprise. "Is there (big game) on this island?"

The general nodded. "The biggest."

"Really?"

"Oh, it isn't here naturally, of course. I have to stock the island."

"What have you imported, General?" Rainsford asked. "Tigers?"

300 The general smiled. "No," he said. "Hunting tigers ceased to interest me some years ago. I exhausted their possibilities, you see. No thrill left in tigers, no real danger. I live for danger, Mr. Rainsford."

The general took from his pocket a gold cigarette case and offered his guest a long black cigarette with a silver tip; it was perfumed and gave off a smell like incense.

"We will have some capital hunting, you and I," said the general. "I shall be most glad to have your society."

"But what game—" began Rainsford.

310 "I'll tell you," said the general. "You will be amused, I know. I think I may say, in all modesty, that I have done a rare thing. I have invented a new sensation. May I pour you another glass of port, Mr. Rainsford?"

"Thank you, General."

The general filled both glasses and said: "God makes some men poets. Some he makes kings, some beggars. Me he made a hunter. My hand was made for the trigger, my father said. He was a very rich man with a quarter of a million acres in the Crimea, and he was an ardent sportsman. When I was

More About...

BIG GAME Hunting *big game,* or large animals, was a popular sport among wealthy people in the early twentieth century. They traveled the world to hunt animals such as lions, elephants, and rhinoceroses.

READ ALOUD Lines 300–303

Imagine you are playing the role of Zaroff on a stage. Say these lines to convey his personality.

What Does It Mean?
Here, *capital* means "great" or "first-rate."

What Does It Mean?
Here, *society* means "company."

What Does It Mean?
Ardent means "passionate" or "enthusiastic."

³²⁰ only five years old, he gave me a little gun, specially made in Moscow for me, to shoot sparrows with. When I shot some of his prize turkeys with it, he did not punish me; he complimented me on my marksmanship. I killed my first bear in the Caucasus[9] when I was ten. My whole life has been one prolonged hunt. I went into the army—it was expected of noblemen's sons—and for a time commanded a division of Cossack cavalry, but my real interest was always the hunt. I have hunted every kind of game in every land. It would be impossible for me to tell you how many animals I have ³³⁰ killed."

The general puffed at his cigarette.

"After the debacle[10] in Russia I left the country, for it was imprudent[11] for an officer of the Tsar to stay there. Many noble Russians lost everything. I, luckily, had invested heavily in American securities, so I shall never have to open a tearoom in Monte Carlo or drive a taxi in Paris. Naturally, I continued to hunt—grizzlies in your Rockies, crocodiles in the Ganges,[12] rhinoceroses in East Africa. It was in Africa that the Cape buffalo hit me and laid me up for six months. As soon ³⁴⁰ as I recovered, I started for the Amazon to hunt jaguars, for I had heard they were unusually cunning. They weren't." The Cossack sighed. "They were no match at all for a hunter with his wits about him, and a high-powered rifle. I was bitterly disappointed. I was lying in my tent with a splitting headache one night when a terrible thought pushed its way into my mind. Hunting was beginning to bore me! And hunting, remember, had been my life. I have heard that in America businessmen often go to pieces when they give up the business that has been their life."

³⁵⁰ "Yes, that's so," said Rainsford.

The general smiled. "I had no wish to go to pieces," he said. "I must do something. Now, mine is an analytical mind, Mr. Rainsford. Doubtless that is why I enjoy the problems of the chase."

"No doubt, General Zaroff."

English Learner Support

VOCABULARY

Idiom To *go to pieces* means "to become upset and unable to deal with the situation."

---

9. **Crimea** (krĭ-mē′ə)...**Caucasus** (caucasus): regions in the southern part of the former Russian Empire, near the Black Sea.

10. **debacle** (dĭ-bä′kəl): a disastrous defeat; rout (a reference to the 1917 Russian Revolution that overthrew the czar).

11. **imprudent:** showing poor judgment; unwise.

12. **Ganges** (găn′jēz′): a river in northern India.

"So," continued the general, "I asked myself why the hunt no longer fascinated me. You are much younger than I am, Mr. Rainsford, and have not hunted as much, but you perhaps can guess the answer."

360 "What was it?"

"Simply this: hunting had ceased to be what you call 'a sporting proposition.' It had become too easy. I always got my quarry. Always. There is no greater bore than perfection."

The general lit a fresh cigarette.

"No animal had a chance with me any more. That is no boast; it is a mathematical certainty. The animal had nothing but his legs and his instinct. Instinct is no match for reason. When I thought of this, it was a tragic moment for me, I can tell you."

370 Rainsford leaned across the table, absorbed in what his host was saying.

"It came to me as an inspiration what I must do," the general went on.

"And that was?"

The general smiled the quiet smile of one who has faced an obstacle and surmounted it with success. "I had to invent a new animal to hunt," he said.

"A new animal? You're joking."

"Not at all," said the general. "I never joke about hunting.
380 I needed a new animal. I found one. So I bought this island, built this house, and here I do my hunting. The island is perfect for my purposes—there are jungles with a maze of trails in them, hills, swamps—"

"But the animal, General Zaroff?"

"Oh," said the general, "it supplies me with the most exciting hunting in the world. No other hunting compares with it for an instant. Every day I hunt, and I never grow bored now, for I have a quarry with which I can match my wits."

Rainsford's bewilderment showed in his face.

390 "I wanted the ideal animal to hunt," explained the general. "So I said: 'What are the attributes of an ideal quarry?' And the answer was, of course: 'It must have courage, cunning, and, above all, it must be able to reason.'"

"But no animal can reason," objected Rainsford.

"My dear fellow," said the general, "there is one that can."

"But you can't mean—" gasped Rainsford.

"And why not?"

✏️ **MARK IT UP** 1. Review the details you circled as you read. Star the sentences on page 29 that describe why Zaroff begins hunting human "game." **(Cause and Effect)**

2. If you were in Rainsford's position, what would you be thinking about? **(Connect)**

_____

_____

_____

As the story continues . . .

• Zaroff invites Rainsford to hunt with him.

"I can't believe you are serious, General Zaroff. This is a grisly[13] joke."

400 "Why should I not be serious? I am speaking of hunting."

"Hunting? Good God, General Zaroff, what you speak of is murder."

Pause & Reflect

FOCUS
Now Zaroff explains where he gets his human prey and how he treats them. He also explains the rules of his game. Read to find out how the game is played.

The general laughed with entire good nature. He regarded Rainsford quizzically. "I refuse to believe that so modern and civilized a young man as you seem to be harbors romantic ideas about the value of human life. Surely your experiences in the war—"

410 "Did not make me condone cold-blooded murder," finished Rainsford, stiffly.

Laughter shook the general. "How extraordinarily droll you are!" he said. "One does not expect nowadays to find a young man of the educated class, even in America, with such a naïve, and, if I may say so, mid-Victorian point of view. It's like finding a snuffbox in a limousine. Ah, well, doubtless you had Puritan ancestors. So many Americans appear to have had. I'll wager you'll forget your notions when you go hunting with me. You've a genuine new thrill in store for you, 420 Mr. Rainsford."

"Thank you, I'm a hunter, not a murderer."

"Dear me," said the general, quite unruffled, "again that unpleasant word. But I think I can show you that your scruples are quite ill-founded."

"Yes?"

"Life is for the strong, to be lived by the strong, and, if needs be, taken by the strong. The weak of the world were put here to give the strong pleasure. I am strong. Why should I not use my gift? If I wish to hunt, why should I not? I hunt

---

13. **grisly** (grĭz′lē): horrible; ghastly.

WORDS
TO
KNOW

condone (kən-dōn′) v. to overlook, forgive, or disregard
droll (drōl) adj. amusingly odd or comical
scruple (skrōō′pəl) n. an uneasy feeling arising from one's conscience or principles

430 the scum of the earth—sailors from tramp ships—lascars,[14] blacks, Chinese, whites, mongrels—a thoroughbred horse or hound is worth more than a score of them."

"But they are men," said Rainsford, hotly.

"Precisely," said the general. "That is why I use them. It gives me pleasure. They can reason, after a fashion. So they are dangerous."

"But where do you get them?"

The general's left eyelid fluttered down in a wink. "This island is called Ship Trap," he answered. "Sometimes an angry 440 god of the high seas sends them to me. Sometimes, when Providence is not so kind, I help Providence a bit. Come to the window with me."

Rainsford went to the window and looked out toward the sea.

"Watch! Out there!" exclaimed the general, pointing into the night. Rainsford's eyes saw only blackness, and then, as the general pressed a button, far out to sea Rainsford saw the flash of lights.

The general chuckled. "They indicate a channel," he said, 450 "where there's none: giant rocks with razor edges crouch like a sea monster with wide-open jaws. They can crush a ship as easily as I crush this nut." He dropped a walnut on the hardwood floor and brought his heel grinding down on it. "Oh, yes," he said, casually, as if in answer to a question, "I have electricity. We try to be civilized here."

"Civilized? And you shoot down men?"

A trace of anger was in the general's black eyes, but it was there for but a second, and he said, in his most pleasant manner: "Dear me, what a righteous young man you are! I 460 assure you I do not do the thing you suggest. That would be barbarous. I treat these visitors with every consideration. They get plenty of good food and exercise. They get into splendid physical condition. You shall see for yourself tomorrow."

"What do you mean?"

"We'll visit my training school," smiled the general. "It's in the cellar. I have about a dozen pupils down there now. They're from the Spanish bark Sanlúcar that had the bad luck to go on the rocks out there. A very inferior lot, I regret to say. Poor specimens and more accustomed to the deck than to 470 the jungle."

---

14. **lascars** (lăs′kərz): sailors from India.

What Does It Mean?
Mongrel means "mixed breed." The term is often used for dogs. Zaroff uses it to refer to people, which shows his low opinion of the men he hunts.

What Does It Mean?
Providence is a way of referring to God or to divine direction.

What Does It Mean?
In the highlighted passage, Zaroff explains that he posted lights so that sailors will think the area is a marked channel, but the lights really lead the ships into deadly rocks.

English Learner Support
VOCABULARY

Antonyms The words *civilized* and *barbarous* have opposite meanings. Civilized people are expected to be polite and ethical. Barbarous people are crude and cruel.

What Does It Mean?
A *bark* is a kind of boat.

Reading Check

The boxed passage contains Zaroff's explanation of the rules of his game. What are those rules?

More About . . .

NICOLAS II Nicolas II, (the Great White Tsar,) was a ruler of Russia. He was forced to give up his throne during the Russian Revolution of 1917.

What Does It Mean?

A *braggart* is a person who brags, or boasts.

He raised his hand, and Ivan, who served as waiter, brought thick Turkish coffee. Rainsford, with an effort, held his tongue in check.

"It's a game, you see," pursued the general, blandly. "I suggest to one of them that we go hunting. I give him a supply of food and an excellent hunting knife. I give him three hours' start. I am to follow, armed only with a pistol of the smallest caliber and range. If my quarry <u>eludes</u> me for three whole days, he wins the game. If I find him"—the general smiled—
480 "he loses."

"Suppose he refuses to be hunted?"

"Oh," said the general, "I give him his option, of course. He need not play that game if he doesn't wish to. If he does not wish to hunt, I turn him over to Ivan. Ivan once had the honor of serving as official knouter[15] to (the Great White Tsar,) and he has his own ideas of sport. Invariably, Mr. Rainsford, invariably they choose the hunt."

"And if they win?"

The smile on the general's face widened.

490 "To date I have not lost," he said.

Then he added, hastily: "I don't wish you to think me a braggart, Mr. Rainsford. Many of them afford only the most elementary sort of problem. Occasionally I strike a tartar.[16] One almost did win. I eventually had to use the dogs."

"The dogs?"

"This way, please. I'll show you."

The general steered Rainsford to a window. The lights from the windows sent a flickering illumination that made grotesque patterns on the courtyard below, and Rainsford
500 could see moving about there a dozen or so huge black shapes; as they turned toward him, their eyes glittered greenly. "A rather good lot, I think," observed the general. "They are let out at seven every night. If anyone should try to get into my house—or out of it—something extremely regrettable would occur to him." He hummed a snatch of song from the Folies Bergère.[17]

---

15. **knouter** (nout′ər): a person who whipped criminals in Russia.

16. **strike a tartar:** encounter a fierce opponent.

17. **Folies Bergère** (fô-lē′ bĕr-zhĕr′): a music hall in Paris, famous for its variety shows.

WORDS TO KNOW   **elude** (ĭ-lōod) *v.* to escape, especially by means of daring, cleverness or skill

"And now," said the general, "I want to show you my new collection of heads. Will you come with me to the library?"

"I hope," said Rainsford, "that you will excuse me tonight, General Zaroff. I'm really not feeling at all well."

"Ah, indeed?" the general inquired, <u>solicitously</u>. "Well, I suppose that's only natural, after your long swim. You need a good, restful night's sleep. Tomorrow you'll feel like a new man, I'll wager. Then we'll hunt, eh? I've one rather promising prospect—"

Rainsford was hurrying from the room.

"Sorry you can't go with me tonight," called the general. "I expect rather fair sport—a big, strong black. He looks resourceful—Well, good night, Mr. Rainsford; I hope you have a good night's rest."

Pause & Reflect

Pause & Reflect

1. Where does Zaroff find humans to hunt? **(Clarify)**

_____

_____

_____

2. Review the boxed passage on page 32. Do you think the rules of the game favor Zaroff? *Yes/No,* because _____

_____

_____

_____ .

(Evaluate)

FOCUS
Zaroff expects Rainsford to hunt with him. Read to find out what happens when Rainsford stands up to Zaroff and refuses to hunt.

The bed was good, and the pajamas of the softest silk, and he was tired in every fiber of his being, but nevertheless Rainsford could not quiet his brain with the opiate of sleep. He lay, eyes wide open. Once he thought he heard stealthy steps in the corridor outside his room. He sought to throw open the door; it would not open. He went to the window and looked out. His room was high up in one of the towers. The lights of the château were out now, and it was dark and silent, but there was a fragment of sallow moon, and by its wan light he could see, dimly, the courtyard; there, weaving in and out in the pattern of shadow, were black, noiseless forms; the hounds heard him at the window and looked up, expectantly, with their green eyes. Rainsford went back to the bed and lay down. By many methods he tried to put himself to sleep. He had achieved a doze when, just as morning began to come, he heard, far off in the jungle, the faint report of a pistol.

As the story continues...
• General Zaroff tells Rainsford that he feels his old boredom returning.

• Rainsford refuses to hunt humans and says he is leaving the island.

• Zaroff proposes a contest.

What Does It Mean?
Here, the word *report* means an explosive noise.

WORDS TO KNOW

solicitously (sə-lĭs′ĭ-təs-lē) *adj.* expressing care or concern

The Most Dangerous Game 33

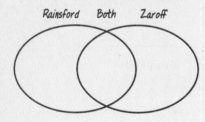
540 General Zaroff did not appear until luncheon. He was dressed faultlessly in the tweeds of a country squire. He was solicitous about the state of Rainsford's health.

"As for me," sighed the general, "I do not feel so well. I am worried, Mr. Rainsford. Last night I detected traces of my old complaint."

To Rainsford's questioning glance the general said: "Ennui. Boredom."

Then, taking a second helping of crêpes suzettes, the general explained: "The hunting was not good last night. The 550 fellow lost his head. He made a straight trail that offered no problems at all. That's the trouble with these sailors; they have dull brains to begin with, and they do not know how to get about in the woods. They do excessively stupid and obvious things. It's most annoying. Will you have another glass of Chablis, Mr. Rainsford?"

"General," said Rainsford, firmly, "I wish to leave this island at once."

The general raised his thickets of eyebrows; he seemed hurt. "But, my dear fellow," the general protested, "you've only just 560 come. You've had no hunting—"

"I wish to go today," said Rainsford. He saw the dead black eyes of the general on him, studying him. General Zaroff's face suddenly brightened.

He filled Rainsford's glass with venerable Chablis from a dusty bottle.

"Tonight," said the general, "we will hunt—you and I."

Rainsford shook his head. "No, General," he said. "I will not hunt."

The general shrugged his shoulders and delicately ate a 570 hothouse grape. "As you wish, my friend," he said. "The choice rests entirely with you. But may I not venture to suggest that you will find my idea of sport more diverting than Ivan's?"

He nodded toward the corner to where the giant stood, scowling, his thick arms crossed on his hogshead of chest.

"You don't mean—" cried Rainsford.

"My dear fellow," said the general, "have I not told you I always mean what I say about hunting? This is really an inspiration. I drink to a foeman worthy of my (steel)—at last."

580 The general raised his glass, but Rainsford sat staring at him.

"You'll find this game worth playing," the general said, enthusiastically. "Your brain against mine. Your woodcraft against mine. Your strength and stamina against mine. Outdoor chess! And the stake is not without value, eh?"

"And if I win—" began Rainsford, huskily.

"I'll cheerfully acknowledge myself defeated if I do not find you by midnight of the third day," said General Zaroff. "My sloop will place you on the mainland near a town."

The general read what Rainsford was thinking.

590 "Oh, you can trust me," said the Cossack. "I will give you my word as a gentleman and a sportsman. Of course, you, in turn, must agree to say nothing of your visit here."

"I'll agree to nothing of the kind," said Rainsford.

"Oh," said the general, "in that case— But why discuss that now? Three days hence we can discuss it over a bottle of Veuve Cliquot, unless—"

The general sipped his wine.

Then a businesslike air animated him. "Ivan," he said to Rainsford, "will supply you with hunting clothes, food, a
600 knife. I suggest you wear moccasins; they leave a poorer trail. I suggest, too, that you avoid the big swamp in the southeast corner of the island. We call it Death Swamp. There's quicksand there. One foolish fellow tried it. The deplorable part of it was that Lazarus followed him. You can imagine my feelings, Mr. Rainsford. I loved Lazarus; he was the finest hound in my pack. Well, I must beg you to excuse me now. I always take a siesta after lunch. You'll hardly have time for a nap, I fear. You'll want to start, no doubt. I shall not follow till dusk. Hunting at night is so much more exciting than by
610 day, don't you think? Au revoir,[18] Mr. Rainsford, au revoir."

General Zaroff, with a deep, courtly bow, strolled from the room.

From another door came Ivan. Under one arm he carried khaki hunting clothes, a haversack of food, a leather sheath containing a long-bladed hunting knife; his right hand rested on a cocked revolver thrust in the crimson sash about his waist. . . .

18. **au revoir** (ō′ rə-vwär′): goodbye; farewell until we meet again

WORDS
TO
KNOW

stamina (stăm′ə-nə) *n.* physical or moral strength; endurance
deplorable (dǐ-plôr′ə-bəl) *adj.* deeply regrettable; unfortunate

 Reading Check
What happens if Rainsford wins the game?

 READ ALOUD Lines 602–606

As you read this passage aloud, use your tone of voice to show what Zaroff cares about more, the human being or the animal.

English Learner Support
VOCABULARY

Bowing Zaroff bows as a polite and formal way of saying goodbye.

 Reading Check
Why has Rainsford agreed to let Zaroff hunt him?

Pause **&** *Reflect*

1. What happens when Rainsford refuses to hunt with Zaroff? **(Cause and Effect)**

_____

_____

_____

✎ MARK IT UP   2. Go back into the story and circle the words that describe the supplies given to Rainsford for the hunt. **(Clarify)**

Rainsford had fought his way through the bush for two hours. "I must keep my nerve. I must keep my nerve," he said,
620 through tight teeth.

He had not been entirely clear-headed when the château gates snapped shut behind him. His whole idea at first was to put distance between himself and General Zaroff, and, to this end, he had plunged along, spurred on by the sharp rowels of something very like panic. Now he had got a grip on himself, had stopped, and was taking stock of himself and the situation.

He saw that straight flight was futile; inevitably it would bring him face to face with the sea. He was in a picture with a
630 frame of water, and his operations, clearly, must take place within that frame.

"I'll give him a trail to follow," muttered Rainsford, and he struck off from the rude path he had been following into the trackless wilderness. He executed a series of intricate loops; he doubled on his trail again and again, recalling all the lore of the fox hunt, and all the dodges of the fox. Night found him leg-weary, with hands and face lashed by the branches, on a thickly wooded ridge. He knew it would be insane to blunder on through the dark, even if he had the
640 strength. His need for rest was <u>imperative</u>, and he thought, "I have played the fox; now I must play the cat of the (fable.)" A big tree with a thick trunk and outspread branches was nearby, and, taking care to leave not the slightest mark, he climbed up into the crotch and, stretching out on one of the broad limbs, after a fashion, rested. Rest brought him new confidence and almost a feeling of security. Even so <u>zealous</u> a hunter as General Zaroff could not trace him there, he told himself; only the devil himself could follow that complicated trail through the jungle after dark. But perhaps the general
650 was a devil—

Pause **&** *Reflect*

WORDS
TO
KNOW

imperative (ĭm-pĕr′ə-tĭv) *adj.* absolutely necessary
zealous (zĕl′əs) *adj.* intensely devoted and enthusiastic

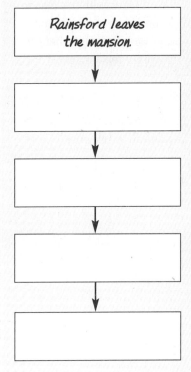

FOCUS

Rainsford is nearly caught by Zaroff. Read to find out what tricks Rainsford uses in his efforts to outsmart his foe.

MARK IT UP As you read, write in the margins a brief description of Rainsford's two tricks.

An apprehensive night crawled slowly by like a wounded snake, and sleep did not visit Rainsford, although the silence of a dead world was on the jungle. Toward morning, when a dingy gray was varnishing the sky, the cry of some startled bird focused Rainsford's attention in that direction. Something was coming through the bush, coming slowly, carefully, coming by the same

660 winding way Rainsford had come. He flattened himself down on the limb, and through a screen of leaves almost as thick as tapestry, he watched. The thing that was approaching was a man.

It was General Zaroff. He made his way along with his eyes fixed in utmost concentration on the ground before him. He paused, almost beneath the tree, dropped to his knees, and studied the ground. Rainsford's impulse was to hurl himself down like a panther, but he saw that the general's right hand

670 held something metallic—a small automatic pistol.

The hunter shook his head several times, as if he were puzzled. Then he straightened up and took from his case one of his black cigarettes; its pungent, incenselike smoke floated up to Rainsford's nostrils.

Rainsford held his breath. The general's eyes had left the ground and were traveling inch by inch up the tree. Rainsford froze there, every muscle tensed for a spring. But the sharp eyes of the hunter stopped before they reached the limb where Rainsford lay; a smile spread over his brown face. Very

680 deliberately he blew a smoke ring into the air; then he turned his back on the tree and walked carelessly away, back along the trail he had come. The swish of the underbrush against his hunting boots grew fainter and fainter.

The pent-up air burst hotly from Rainsford's lungs. His first thought made him feel sick and numb. The general could follow a trail through the woods at night; he could follow an extremely difficult trail; he must have <u>uncanny</u> powers; only by the merest chance had the Cossack failed to see his quarry.

As the story continues...

- Rainsford fights for his life.
- He plays two deadly tricks on Zaroff.

What Does It Mean?

Apprehensive means "fearful" or "uneasy."

Reading Tip

As you read, complete the flow chart below by listing the events of the game that occur from the time Rainsford leaves the mansion to the end of the story.

> Rainsford leaves the mansion.

↓

↓

↓

↓

☑ **Reading Check**

What does General Zaroff do when he arrives at the tree where Rainsford is hiding?

WORDS
TO
KNOW

uncanny (ŭn-kăn′ē) *adj.* so remarkable as to seem supernatural

English Learner Support
VOCABULARY

Idiom The "game of cat and mouse" is being played by Zaroff and Rainsford. Think about the way a cat chases a mouse. The mouse is quick and good at hiding, like Rainsford. When the cat pounces on its prey, it plays with the mouse before killing it. Zaroff, too, plays with Rainsford before he will try to kill him.

What Does It Mean?
Precariously means "unstable and ready to fall over."

Reading Check
How are Zaroff's hunting skills?

690 Rainsford's second thought was even more terrible. It sent a shudder of cold horror through his whole being. Why had the general smiled? Why had he turned back?

Rainsford did not want to believe what his reason told him was true, but the truth was as evident as the sun that had by now pushed through the morning mists. The general was playing with him! The general was saving him for another day's sport! The Cossack was the cat; he was the mouse. Then it was that Rainsford knew the full meaning of terror.

"I will not lose my nerve. I will not."

700 He slid down from the tree and struck off again into the woods. His face was set, and he forced the machinery of his mind to function. Three hundred yards from his hiding place he stopped where a huge dead tree leaned precariously on a smaller, living one. Throwing off his sack of food, Rainsford took his knife from its sheath and began to work with all his energy.

The job was finished at last, and he threw himself down behind a fallen log a hundred feet away. He did not have to wait long. The cat was coming again to play with the mouse.

710 Following the trail with the sureness of a bloodhound came General Zaroff. Nothing escaped those searching black eyes, no crushed blade of grass, no bent twig, no mark, no matter how faint, in the moss. So intent was the Cossack on his stalking that he was upon the thing Rainsford had made before he saw it. His foot touched the protruding bough[19] that was the trigger. Even as he touched it, the general sensed his danger and leaped back with the agility of an ape. But he was not quite quick enough; the dead tree, delicately adjusted to rest on the cut living one, crashed down and struck the

720 general a glancing blow on the shoulder as it fell; but for his alertness, he must have been smashed beneath it. He staggered, but he did not fall; nor did he drop his revolver. He stood there, rubbing his injured shoulder, and Rainsford, with fear again gripping his heart, heard the general's mocking laugh ring through the jungle.

"Rainsford," called the general, "if you are within sound of my voice, as I suppose you are, let me congratulate you. Not many men know how to make a Malay man-catcher. Luckily

19. **protruding bough** (bou): a tree branch that extends or juts out

for me I, too, have hunted in Malacca.[20] You are proving
730 interesting, Mr. Rainsford. I am going now to have my wound
dressed; it's only a slight one. But I shall be back. I shall be
back."

When the general, nursing his bruised shoulder, had gone,
Rainsford took up his flight again. It was flight now, a
desperate, hopeless flight, that carried him on for some hours.
Dusk came, then darkness, and still he pressed on. The
ground grew softer under his moccasins; the vegetation grew
ranker, denser; insects bit him savagely. Then, as he stepped
forward, his foot sank into the ooze. He tried to wrench it
740 back, but the muck sucked viciously at his foot as if it were a
giant leech. With a violent effort he tore his foot loose. He
knew where he was now. Death Swamp and its quicksand.

His hands were tight closed as if his nerve were something
tangible that someone in the darkness was trying to tear from
his grip. The softness of the earth had given him an idea. He
stepped back from the quicksand a dozen feet or so, and like
some huge prehistoric beaver, he began to dig.

Rainsford had dug himself in in France when a second's
delay meant death. That had been a placid pastime compared
750 to his digging now. The pit grew deeper; when it was above
his shoulders, he climbed out and from some hard saplings cut
stakes and sharpened them to a fine point. These stakes he
planted in the bottom of the pit with the points sticking up.
With flying fingers he wove a rough carpet of weeds and
branches, and with it he covered the mouth of the pit. Then,
wet with sweat and aching with tiredness, he crouched behind
the stump of a lightning-charred tree.

He knew his pursuer was coming; he heard the padding
sound of feet on the soft earth, and the night breeze brought
760 him the perfume of the general's cigarette. It seemed to
Rainsford that the general was coming with unusual swiftness;
he was not feeling his way along, foot by foot. Rainsford,
crouching there, could not see the general, nor could he see
the pit. He lived a year in a minute. Then he felt an impulse to
cry aloud with joy, for he heard the sharp crackle of the
breaking branches as the cover of the pit gave way; he heard
the sharp scream of pain as the pointed stakes found their
mark. He leaped up from his place of concealment. Then he

More About . . .

DIGGING IN During World War I,
soldiers dug trenches, or ditches,
to protect themselves from
enemy fire.

English Learner Support
LANGUAGE

Figure of Speech *With flying
fingers* means "with great
speed."

20.**Malay** (mə-lā′)...**Malacca** (mə-lăk′ə): The Malays are a people of southeast
Asia. Malacca is a region they inhabit, just south of Thailand.

Review your descriptions of
Rainsford's tricks. How does
Rainsford try to outsmart Zaroff?
(Clarify)

_____

_____

_____

_____

As the story ends . . .
- The final day of the hunt begins.
- Rainsford tries again to trick Zaroff.

What Does It Mean?

If something is *at bay,* it is held back, or prevented from advancing.

cowered back. Three feet from the pit a man was standing,
with an electric torch in his hand.

"You've done well, Rainsford," the voice of the general
called. "Your Burmese tiger pit has claimed one of my best
dogs. Again you score. I think, Mr. Rainsford, I'll see what
you can do against my whole pack. I'm going home for a rest
now. Thank you for a most amusing evening."

> **FOCUS**
>
> It is now the final day
> of the hunt. Read to
> find out who finally
> wins the game—
> Rainsford or Zaroff.

At daybreak Rainsford, lying near the
swamp, was awakened by a sound that
made him know that he had new things
to learn about fear. It was a distant
sound, faint and wavering, but he knew
it. It was the baying of a pack of hounds.

Rainsford knew he could do one of two things. He could
stay where he was and wait. That was suicide. He could flee.
That was postponing the inevitable. For a moment he stood
there, thinking. An idea that held a wild chance came to him,
and, tightening his belt, he headed away from the swamp.

The baying of the hounds grew nearer, then still nearer,
nearer, ever nearer. On a ridge Rainsford climbed a tree.
Down a watercourse, not a quarter of a mile away, he could
see the bush moving. Straining his eyes, he saw the lean figure
of General Zaroff; just ahead of him, Rainsford made out
another figure whose wide shoulders surged through the tall
jungle weeds; it was the giant Ivan, and he seemed pulled
forward by some unseen force; Rainsford knew that Ivan must
be holding the pack in leash.

They would be on him any minute now. His mind worked
frantically. He thought of a native trick he had learned in
Uganda. He slid down the tree. He caught hold of a springy
young sapling, and to it he fastened his hunting knife, with
the blade pointing down the trail; with a bit of wild grapevine
he tied back the sapling. Then he ran for his life. The hounds
raised their voices as they hit the fresh scent. Rainsford knew
now how an animal at bay feels.

He had to stop to get his breath. The baying of the hounds stopped abruptly, and Rainsford's heart stopped, too. They must have reached the knife.

He shinned excitedly up a tree and looked back. His pursuers had stopped. But the hope that was in Rainsford's brain when he climbed died, for he saw in the shallow valley that General Zaroff was still on his feet. But Ivan was not. The knife, driven by the recoil of the springing tree, had not wholly failed.

Rainsford had hardly tumbled to the ground when the pack took up the cry again.

"Nerve, nerve, nerve!" he panted, as he dashed along. A blue gap showed between the trees dead ahead. Ever nearer drew the hounds. Rainsford forced himself on toward that gap. He reached it. It was the shore of the sea. Across a cove he could see the gloomy gray stone of the château. Twenty feet below him the sea rumbled and hissed. Rainsford hesitated. He heard the hounds. Then he leaped far out into the sea. . . .

When the general and his pack reached the place by the sea, the Cossack stopped. For some minutes he stood regarding the blue-green expanse of water. He shrugged his shoulders. Then he sat down, took a drink of brandy from a silver flask, lit a perfumed cigarette, and hummed a bit from *Madama Butterfly*.[21]

General Zaroff had an exceedingly good dinner in his great paneled dining hall that evening. With it he had a bottle of Pol Roger and half a bottle of Chambertin. Two slight annoyances kept him from perfect enjoyment. One was the thought that it would be difficult to replace Ivan; the other was that his quarry had escaped him; of course the American hadn't played the game—so thought the general as he tasted his after-dinner liqueur. In his library he read, to soothe himself, from the works of Marcus Aurelius.[22] At ten he went up to his bedroom. He was deliciously tired, he said to himself, as he locked himself in. There was a little moonlight, so before turning on his light he went to the window and looked down at the courtyard. He could see the great hounds, and he called "Better luck another time" to them. Then he switched on the light.

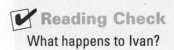
Reading Check
What happens to Ivan?

Reading Check
What does Zaroff think has happened to Rainsford?

---

21. *Madama Butterfly:* a famous opera.

22. **Marcus Aurelius** (mär′kəs ô-rē′lē-əs): an ancient Roman emperor and philosopher.

Pause & *Reflect*

1. Reread the boxed passage. *Rainsford/Zaroff* wins the game when he _____

   _____

   _____

   _____.

   (Cause and Effect)

2. Explain what you think happens to Rainsford and Zaroff at the end of the story. **(Draw Conclusions)**

   _____

   _____

   _____

   _____

A man, who had been hiding in the curtains of the bed, was standing there.

"Rainsford!" screamed the general. "How in God's name did you get here?"

"Swam," said Rainsford. "I found it quicker than walking through the jungle."

The general sucked in his breath and smiled. "I congratulate you," he said. "You have won the game." Rainsford did not smile. "I am still a beast at bay," he said, in a low, hoarse voice. "Get ready, General Zaroff."

The general made one of his deepest bows. "I see," he said. "Splendid! One of us is to furnish a repast[23] for the hounds. The other will sleep in this very excellent bed. On guard, Rainsford. . . ."

He never slept in a better bed, Rainsford decided.

Pause & *Reflect*

---

23. **repast** (rĭ-păst′): meal.

Active Reading SkillBuilder

Predicting

A **prediction** is an attempt to answer the question, "What will happen next?" To make predictions, notice the following in a story:

- interesting details about character, plot, and setting
- unusual statements made by the main characters
- foreshadowing—hints about future plot twists

As you read "The Most Dangerous Game," record three predictions, as well as your reasons for each guess.

Prediction	Reasons
1.	
2.	
3.	

Literary Analysis SkillBuilder

Conflict

Most stories are built around a central **conflict,** or struggle between people, or between people and nature, an obstacle, or society. Sometimes the struggle may go on inside a character. An **external conflict** involves a character pitted against an outside force. An **internal conflict** occurs when the struggle takes place within a character's own mind. List instances of each kind of conflict in the story. Then answer the questions.

Internal Conflict
Zaroff—Bored with hunting and looking for a new "thrill"
Rainsford

External Conflict
Person vs. Person
Person vs. Nature
Person vs. Obstacle

Follow Up: Which conflicts added the most excitement to the story? Which revealed something important about one of the characters? Explain. Why do you think Connell included the other conflicts that you identified?

Words to Know SkillBuilder

Words to Know

affable	deplorable	elude	scruple	tangible
amenity	disarming	imperative	solicitously	uncanny
condone	droll	quarry	stamina	zealous

A. On each blank line, write the word from the word list that the clue describes.

1. This is a word politicians always seem to use to describe the living conditions in slums. _____

2. This is a word you would hope people you want to make friends with would use to describe you. _____

3. This describes the air of confidence that calms your worries about a surgeon's skill. _____

4. This is something that isn't a necessity but is nice to have (like a salt shaker or a telephone). _____

5. This might be the word you'd choose to describe a person who seemed able to read your mind. _____

6. This describes a book but not the ideas in it, a flower but not its smell, a valentine but not the feeling it gives you. _____

7. This is how one says, "Are you sure you're all right? Can I do anything to help?" _____

8. This describes those things you really must have and those things you really must do. _____

B. For each phrase in the first column, find the phrase in the second column that is closest in meaning. Write the letter of that phrase in the blank.

_____ 1. regretful prey	A. elude the rude
_____ 2. zealous protection	B. condone cologne
_____ 3. a droll rabbit	C. a sorry quarry
_____ 4. permit perfume	D. pupils' scruples
_____ 5. students' morals	E. a funny bunny
_____ 6. a fish's endurance	F. intense defense
_____ 7. avoid the unmannerly	G. a salmon's stamina

C. Write a character sketch of General Zaroff using at least **five** of the Words to Know.

MARIGOLDS

Eugenia Collier

Before You Read

Connect to Your Life

Have you ever been so angry that you did something you later regretted?
Fill in the chart below to describe that situation.

EVENT THAT MADE ME ANGRY	HOW I REACTED	WHAT I COULD HAVE DONE DIFFERENTLY

Key to the Story

WHAT YOU NEED TO KNOW "Marigolds" takes place during the Great
Depression. A *depression* is a period of decline in economic activity.
During depressions, people often lose their jobs, and new jobs are hard to
find. In 1929, the government did not provide aid, such as unemployment
insurance, to those who couldn't find work. Although many Americans
suffered, African Americans had a particularly difficult time. Because of
discrimination, they were often the last to be hired and the first to be fired.

Reading Tips

In "Marigolds," the **setting** will help you to understand the **characters,** especially the **narrator,** Lizabeth.

- As you read, try to picture the narrator's home town. How might you feel about living in such a place?

- As a child, the narrator in this story is not always aware of the reasons why she acts as she does. As you read, try to draw conclusions about the narrator and her **motives.**

As the story begins . . .

- Lizabeth recalls growing up in a poor town.

- She remembers Miss Lottie's marigolds.

- She remembers a particular moment when she was fourteen years old.

English Learner Support
VOCABULARY

Shanty-Towns A *shanty* is a poorly built hut or shack. A *shanty-town* is a poor area, usually on the outskirts of a town, where people live in such homes.

What Does It Mean?

Nostalgia means "a longing for the past."

MARIGOLDS

Eugenia Collier

PREVIEW "Marigolds" is set in a poor, rural, African-American community during the early part of the Great Depression (1929–1939). In this story, the narrator, Lizabeth, recalls a turning point in her life. She tells about a childhood encounter with a poor, elderly neighbor named Miss Lottie. This experience changes the narrator in a way she will never forget.

FOCUS

In the first part of the story, you will learn about Lizabeth's home-town and how she felt about growing up there.

MARK IT UP As you read this section, circle details that help you picture the setting. An example is highlighted.

When I think of the home town of my youth, all that I seem to remember is dust—the brown, crumbly dust of late summer—arid, sterile dust that gets into the eyes and makes them water, gets into the throat and between the toes of bare brown feet. I don't know why I should remember only the dust. Surely there must have been lush green lawns and paved streets under leafy shade trees 10 somewhere in town; but memory is an abstract painting—it does not present things as they are, but rather as they *feel*. And so, when I think of that time and that place, I remember only the dry September of the dirt roads and grassless yards of the shanty-town where I lived. And one other thing I remember, another incongruency of memory—a brilliant splash of sunny yellow against the dust—Miss Lottie's marigolds.

Whenever the memory of those marigolds flashes across my mind, a strange nostalgia comes with it and remains long after 20 the picture has faded. I feel again the chaotic emotions of adolescence, illusive as smoke, yet as real as the potted geranium before me now. Joy and rage and wild animal gladness and shame become tangled together in the multicolored skein of 14-going-on-15 as I recall that

<u>devastating</u> moment when I was suddenly more woman than child, years ago in Miss Lottie's yard. I think of those marigolds at the strangest times; I remember them vividly now as I desperately pass away the time waiting for you, who will not come.

30   I suppose that <u>futile</u> waiting was the sorrowful background music of our <u>impoverished</u> little community when I was young. The Depression that gripped the nation was no new thing to us, for the black workers of rural Maryland had always been depressed. I don't know what it was that we were waiting for; certainly not for the prosperity that was "just around the corner," for those were white folks' words, which we never believed. Nor did we wait for hard work and thrift to pay off in shining success as the American Dream[1] promised, for we knew better than that, too. Perhaps

40 we waited for a miracle, <u>amorphous</u> in concept but necessary if one were to have the grit to rise before dawn each day and labor in the white man's vineyard until after dark, or to wander about in the September dust, offering one's sweat in return for some meager share of bread. But God was chary[2] with miracles in those days, and so we waited— and waited.

    We children, of course, were only vaguely aware of the extent of our poverty. Having no radios, few newspapers, and no magazines, we were somewhat unaware of the world

50 outside our community. Nowadays we would be called "culturally deprived" and people would write books and hold conferences about us. In those days everybody we knew was just as hungry and ill-clad as we were. Poverty was the cage in which we all were trapped, and our hatred of it was still the vague, undirected restlessness of the zoo-bred flamingo who knows that nature created him to fly free.

    As I think of those days I feel most <u>poignantly</u> the tag-end of summer, the bright dry times when we began to have a sense of shortening days and the imminence of the cold.

---

1. **American Dream:** the belief that through hard work one will achieve a comfortable and prosperous life.

2. **chary** (châr′ē): sparing or stingy.

WORDS
TO
KNOW

futile (fyōōt′l) *adj.* having no useful result; without effect
impoverished (ĭm-pŏv′ər-ĭsht) *adj.* poor
poignantly (poin′yənt-lē) *adv.* in a profoundly moving manner

Marigolds 49

60 By the time I was 14 my brother Joey and I were the only children left at our house, the older ones having left home for early marriage or the lure of the city, and the two babies having been sent to relatives who might care for them better than we. Joey was three years younger than I, and a boy, and therefore vastly inferior. Each morning our mother and father trudged wearily down the dirt road and around the bend, she to her domestic job, he to his daily unsuccessful quest for work. After our few chores around the tumbledown shanty, Joey and I were free to run wild in the
70 sun with other children similarly situated.

For the most part, those days are ill-defined in my memory, running together and combining like a fresh water-color painting left out in the rain. I remember squatting in the road drawing a picture in the dust, a picture that Joey gleefully erased with one sweep of his dirty foot. I remember fishing for minnows in a muddy creek and watching sadly as they eluded my cupped hands, while Joey laughed uproariously. And I remember, that year, a strange restlessness of body and of spirit, a feeling that something
80 old and familiar was ending, and something unknown and therefore terrifying was beginning.

One day returns to me with special clarity for some reason, perhaps because it was the beginning of the experience that in some inexplicable way marked the end of innocence.

Pause & Reflect

What Does It Mean?

Domestic means "relating to the house." A *domestic job* is a job in which one cleans, cooks, and performs other household chores for an employer.

Pause & Reflect

1. Review the details you marked as you read. What one word or phrase best describes this setting? **(Evaluate)**

   _____

   _____

2. What do you learn about the narrator's childhood? **(Draw Conclusions)**

   _____

   _____

   _____

   _____

3. The narrator will tell about one day that "marked the end of innocence" for her. What do you think happened on that day? **(Predict)**

   _____

   _____

   _____

   _____

FOCUS

The action now moves to an important day in the narrator's past. Read to find out about Miss Lottie.

90

MARK IT UP As you read, circle five key words or phrases that describe Miss Lottie's life and her surroundings.

I was loafing under the great oak tree in our yard, deep in some reverie which I have now forgotten except that it involved some secret, secret thoughts of one of the Harris boys across the yard. Joey and a bunch of kids were bored now with the old tire suspended from an oak limb which had kept them entertained for a while.

"Hey, Lizabeth," Joey yelled. He never talked when he could yell. "Hey, Lizabeth, let's us go somewhere."

I came reluctantly from my private world. "Where you want to go? What you want to do?"

100 The truth was that we were becoming tired of the formlessness of our summer days. The idleness whose prospect had seemed so beautiful during the busy days of spring now had degenerated to an almost desperate effort to fill up the empty midday hours.

"Let's go see can we find some locusts on the hill," someone suggested.

Joey was scornful. "Ain't no more locusts there. Y'all got 'em all while they was still green."

The argument that followed was brief and not really worth 110 the effort. Hunting locust trees wasn't fun any more by now.

"Tell you what," said Joey finally, his eyes sparkling. "Let's go over to Miss Lottie's."

The idea caught on at once, for annoying Miss Lottie was always fun. I was still child enough to scamper along with the group over rickety fences and through bushes that tore our already raggedy clothes, back to where Miss Lottie lived. I think now that we must have made a tragicomic spectacle, five or six kids of different ages, each of us clad in only one garment—the girls in faded dresses that were 120 too long or too short, the boys in patchy pants, their sweaty brown chests gleaming in the hot sun. A little cloud of dust followed our thin legs and bare feet as we tramped over the barren land.

When Miss Lottie's house came into view we stopped, ostensibly to plan our strategy, but actually to reinforce our courage. Miss Lottie's house was the most ramshackle of all

As the story continues . . .

- Lizabeth and her brother Joey are bored.

- With several friends, they decide to annoy their elderly neighbor, Miss Lottie.

- They arrive at Miss Lottie's shack.

Reading Tip

The author of this story has the characters speak in dialect, which is a variety of language spoken by a certain group of people in a certain place. Many words are spelled as they would have been spoken. For example, *y'all*, *git*, and *'long* mean "you all," "get," and "along." Read aloud the words in dialect and use context clues to find their meanings.

What Does It Mean?

Tragicomic is a combination of the words *tragedy* and *comedy*. Something tragicomic is both sad and funny at the same time.

Reading Check

What are the children wearing? What does this tell you about their situation?

What Does It Mean?

The phrase *a monument to decay* means that Miss Lottie's house was a symbol of rot and decay.

Reading Tip

Make a 24-hour time line that begins at 6 A.M. the first day and ends at about the same time the second day. As you read, mark the events of the story on the time line.

What Does It Mean?

Retribution means "punishment" or "payback."

READ ALOUD Lines 151–158

Listen for descriptive details that help you picture Miss Lottie.

English Learner Support
VOCABULARY

Intruders An *intruder* is a person who trespasses or who enters without being wanted or invited.

our ramshackle homes. The sun and rain had long since faded its rickety frame siding from white to a sullen gray. The boards themselves seemed to remain upright not from being nailed together but rather from leaning together like a house that a child might have constructed from cards. A brisk wind might have blown it down, and the fact that it was still standing implied a kind of enchantment that was stronger than the elements. There it stood, and as far as I know is standing yet—a gray rotting thing with no porch, no shutters, no steps, set on a cramped lot with no grass, not even any weeds—a monument to decay.

In front of the house in a squeaky rocking chair sat Miss Lottie's son, John Burke, completing the impression of decay. John Burke was what was known as "queer-headed." Black and ageless, he sat, rocking day in and day out in a mindless stupor, lulled by the monotonous squeak-squawk of the chair. A battered hat atop his shaggy head shaded him from the sun. Usually John Burke was totally unaware of everything outside his quiet dream world. But if you disturbed him, if you intruded upon his fantasies, he would become enraged, strike out at you, and curse at you in some strange enchanted language which only he could understand. We children made a game of thinking of ways to disturb John Burke and then to elude his violent retribution.

But our real fun and our real fear lay in Miss Lottie herself. Miss Lottie seemed to be at least a hundred years old. Her big frame still held traces of the tall, powerful woman she must have been in youth, although it was now bent and drawn. Her smooth skin was a dark reddish-brown, and her face had Indian-like features and the stern stoicism that one associates with Indian faces. Miss Lottie didn't like intruders either, especially children. She never left her yard, and nobody ever visited her. We never knew how she managed those necessities that depend on human interaction—how she ate, for example, or even whether she ate. When we were tiny children, we thought Miss Lottie was a witch and we made up tales, that we half believed ourselves, about her exploits. We were far too sophisticated now, of course, to believe the witch-nonsense. But old fears have a way of

WORDS
TO
KNOW

stoicism (stō′ĭ-sĭz-əm) *n.* indifference to pleasure or pain; not showing emotion

clinging like cobwebs, and so when we sighted the tumbledown shack, we had to stop to reinforce our nerves.

"Look, there she is," I whispered, forgetting that Miss Lottie could not possibly have heard me from that distance. 170 "She's fooling with them crazy flowers."

"Yeh, look at 'er."

Pause **&** *Reflect*

FOCUS

Read to find out what the children do to Miss Lottie and why.

MARK IT UP As you read, circle details that describe how the children feel about the flowers.

Miss Lottie's marigolds were perhaps the strangest part of the picture. Certainly they did not fit in with the crumbling decay of the rest of her yard. Beyond the dusty brown yard, in front of the sorry gray house, rose suddenly and shockingly a dazzling strip of bright blossoms, clumped together in enormous mounds, warm and passionate and sun-180 golden. The old black witch-woman worked on them all summer, every summer, down on her creaky knees, weeding and cultivating and arranging, while the house crumbled and John Burke rocked. For some <u>perverse</u> reason, we children hated those marigolds. They interfered with the perfect ugliness of the place; they were too beautiful; they said too much that we could not understand; they did not make sense. There was something in the vigor with which the old woman destroyed the weeds that intimidated us. It should have been a 190 comical sight—the old woman with the man's hat on her cropped white head, leaning over the bright mounds, her big backside in the air—but it wasn't comical, it was something we could not name. We had to annoy her by whizzing a pebble into her flowers or by yelling a dirty word, then dancing away from her rage, reveling in our youth and mocking her age. Actually, I think it was the flowers we wanted to destroy, but nobody had the nerve to try it, not even Joey, who was usually fool enough to try anything.

Pause **&** Reflect

1. Who is Miss Lottie? **(Clarify)**

_____

_____

2. Review the words and phrases that you circled. What do you learn about Miss Lottie's life and where she lives? **(Draw Conclusions)**

_____

_____

_____

As the story continues . . .

- The children throw stones at Miss Lottie's flowers.

- Lizabeth delights in her power to make Miss Lottie angry.

What Does It Mean?

Intimidated means "frightened."

✔**Reading Check**

How do the children feel about Miss Lottie's marigolds?

WORDS TO KNOW

perverse (pər-vûrs′) *adj.* stubbornly contrary; wrong; harmful

Marigolds **53**

"Y'all git some stones," commanded Joey now, and was met with instant giggling obedience as everyone except me began to gather pebbles from the dusty ground. "Come on, Lizabeth."

I just stood there peering through the bushes, torn between wanting to join the fun and feeling that it was all a bit silly.

"You scared, Lizabeth?"

I cursed and spat on the ground—my favorite gesture of phony bravado. "Y'all children get the stones; I'll show you how to use 'em."

I said before that we children were not consciously aware of how thick were the bars of our cage. I wonder now, though, whether we were not more aware of it than I thought. Perhaps we had some dim notion of what we were, and how little chance we had of being anything else. Otherwise, why would we have been so preoccupied with destruction? Anyway, the pebbles were collected quickly, and everybody looked at me to begin the fun.

"Come on, y'all."

We crept to the edge of the bushes that bordered the narrow road in front of Miss Lottie's place. She was working placidly, kneeling over the flowers, her dark hand plunged into the golden mound. Suddenly "zing"—an expertly-aimed stone cut the head off one of the blossoms.

"Who out there?" Miss Lottie's backside came down and her head came up as her sharp eyes searched the bushes. "You better git!"

We had crouched down out of sight in the bushes, where we stifled the giggles that insisted on coming. Miss Lottie gazed warily across the road for a moment, then cautiously returned to her weeding. "Zing"—Joey sent a pebble into the blooms, and another marigold was beheaded.

Miss Lottie was enraged now. She began struggling to her feet, leaning on a rickety cane and shouting, "Y'all git! Go on home!" Then the rest of the kids let loose with their pebbles, storming the flowers and laughing wildly and senselessly at Miss Lottie's impotent rage. She shook her stick at us and started shakily toward the road crying, "Git 'long! John Burke! John Burke, come help!"

Then I lost my head entirely, mad with the power of

What Does It Mean?
Phony means "fake" or "false."

✔ Reading Check
Why does Lizabeth throw stones at the marigolds?

English Learner Support
VOCABULARY

Idiom To *let loose* means "to let free from restraint." In this case, the children "freed" the stones from their hands and threw the stones at the flowers.

WORDS
TO
KNOW

bravado (brə-vä′dō) *n.* a false show of courage or defiance
impotent (ĭm′pə-tənt) *adj.* powerless; lacking strength or vigor

inciting such rage, and ran out of the bushes in the storm of pebbles, straight toward Miss Lottie chanting madly, "Old witch, fell in a ditch, picked up a penny and thought she was rich!" The children screamed with delight, dropped their pebbles and joined the crazy dance, swarming around Miss Lottie like bees and chanting, "Old lady witch!" while she screamed curses at us. The madness lasted only a moment, for John Burke, startled at last, lurched out of his chair, and we dashed for the bushes just as Miss Lottie's cane went whizzing at my head.

Pause & Reflect

Pause & Reflect

1. Look back at the details you marked. Why do the children hate the marigolds? (**Draw Conclusions**)

_____

_____

_____

_____

2. What is your reaction when the children destroy some of the marigolds? (**Connect**)

_____

_____

_____

FOCUS

Lizabeth is upset by her actions toward Miss Lottie. Then, late that night, she overhears a conversation between her parents. Read to find out how this conversation affects her.

I did not join the merriment when the kids gathered again under the oak in our bare yard. Suddenly I was ashamed, and I did not like being ashamed. The child in me sulked and said it was all in fun, but the woman in me flinched at the thought of the malicious attack that I had led. The mood lasted all afternoon. When we ate the beans and rice that was supper that night, I did not notice my father's silence, for he was always silent these days, nor did I notice my mother's absence, for she always worked until well into evening. Joey and I had a particularly bitter argument after supper; his exuberance got on my nerves. Finally I stretched out upon the palette in the room we shared and fell into a fitful doze.

When I awoke, somewhere in the middle of the night, my mother had returned, and I vaguely listened to the conversation that was audible through the thin walls that separated our rooms. At first I heard no words, only voices. My mother's voice was like a cool, dark room in summer— peaceful, soothing, quiet. I loved to listen to it; it made things seem all right somehow. But my father's voice cut through hers, shattering the peace.

"Twenty-two years, Maybelle, twenty-two years," he was saying, "and I got nothing for you, nothing, nothing."

As the story continues . . .

• Lizabeth is ashamed of herself for damaging some of Miss Lottie's marigolds.

• Late at night, she overhears her parents talking.

Dialect The highlighted words are written in dialect. In standard English, they might be written as, "No man should eat the food his wife buys with money that she earned." This opinion reflects an attitude that the man of the family should be the one who earns the money to buy food.

✔ **Reading Check**

How does Lizabeth feel after hearing her father cry?

READ ALOUD **Lines 303–309**

As you read this passage aloud, try to express the feelings that Lizabeth is experiencing.

What Does It Mean?

Bewilderment means "confusion."

"It's all right, honey, you'll get something. Everybody's out of work now, you know that."

"It ain't right. Ain't no man ought to eat his woman's food year in and year out, and see his children running wild. Ain't nothing right about that."

"Honey, you took good care of us when you had it. Ain't 280 nobody got nothing nowadays."

"I ain't talking about nobody else, I'm talking about *me*. God knows I try." My mother said something I could not hear, and my father cried out louder, "What must a man do, tell me that?"

"Look, we ain't starving. I git paid every week, and Mrs. Ellis is real nice about giving me things. She gonna let me have Mr. Ellis' old coat for you this winter—"

"Damn Mr. Ellis' coat! And damn his money! You think I want white folks' leavings? Damn, Maybelle"—and suddenly 290 he sobbed, loudly and painfully, and cried helplessly and hopelessly in the dark night. I had never heard a man cry before. I did not know men ever cried. I covered my ears with my hands but could not cut off the sound of my father's harsh, painful, despairing sobs. My father was a strong man who would whisk a child upon his shoulders and go singing through the house. My father whittled toys for us and laughed so loud that the great oak seemed to laugh with him, and taught us how to fish and hunt rabbits. How could it be that my father was crying? But the sobs went on, 300 unstifled, finally quieting until I could hear my mother's voice, deep and rich, humming softly as she used to hum to a frightened child.

The world had lost its boundary lines. My mother, who was small and soft, was now the strength of the family; my father, who was the rock on which the family had been built, was sobbing like the tiniest child. Everything was suddenly out of tune, like a broken accordion. Where did I fit into this crazy picture? I do not now remember my thoughts, only a feeling of great bewilderment and fear.

310 Long after the sobbing and the humming had stopped, I lay on the palette, still as stone with my hands over my ears, wishing that I too could cry and be comforted. The night was silent now except for the sound of the crickets and of Joey's

soft breathing. But the room was too crowded with fear to allow me to sleep, and finally, feeling the terrible aloneness of 4 A.M., I decided to awaken Joey.

"Ouch! What's the matter with you? What you want?" he demanded disagreeably when I had pinched and slapped him awake.

320 "Come on, wake up."

"What for? Go 'way."

I was lost for a reasonable reply. I could not say, "I'm scared, and I don't want to be alone," so I merely said, "I'm going out. If you want to come, come on."

The promise of adventure awoke him. "Going out now? Where to, Lizabeth? What you going to do?"

I was pulling my dress over my head. Until now I had not thought of going out. "Just come on," I replied tersely.

I was out the window and halfway down the road before 330 Joey caught up with me.

"Wait, Lizabeth, where you going?"

I was running as if the Furies[3] were after me, as perhaps they were—running silently and furiously until I came to where I had half-known I was headed: to Miss Lottie's yard.

Pause & Reflect

FOCUS
Read to find out what action Lizabeth takes and how the experience changes her.

The half-dawn light was more eerie than complete darkness, and in it the old house was like the ruin that my world had become—foul and crumbling, a grotesque caricature. It looked haunted, 340 but I was not afraid because I was haunted too.

"Lizabeth, you lost your mind?" panted Joey.

I had indeed lost my mind, for all the smoldering emotions of that summer swelled in me and burst—the great need for

---

3. **Furies:** In Greek and Roman mythology, the Furies were three goddesses of vengeance, or revenge.

Pause & Reflect

1. Why is Lizabeth's father so upset? (Draw Conclusions)

_____

_____

_____

_____

2. Lizabeth says she is going to Miss Lottie's yard. What do you suppose she is planning to do now? (Predict)

_____

_____

_____

English Learner Support
VOCABULARY

Caricature A *caricature* is a picture, cartoon, or description that exaggerates the qualities of something. When the narrator describes the house as "a grotesque caricature," she exaggerates the broken-down ugliness of the house.

As the story ends . . .

• Lizabeth's feelings overwhelm her, and she runs back to Miss Lottie's house with Joey.

• She faces Miss Lottie.

What Does It Mean?

The words *smoldering emotions* mean that Lizabeth has been hiding all of her feelings of anger, hopelessness, and confusion.

my mother who was never there, the hopelessness of our poverty and <u>degradation</u>, the bewilderment of being neither child nor woman and yet both at once, the fear unleashed by my father's tears. And these feelings combined in one great impulse toward destruction.

"Lizabeth!"

350 I leaped furiously into the mounds of marigolds and pulled madly, trampling and pulling and destroying the perfect yellow blooms. The fresh smell of early morning and of dew-soaked marigolds spurred me on as I went tearing and mangling and sobbing while Joey tugged my dress or my waist crying, "Lizabeth stop, please stop!"

And then I was sitting in the ruined little garden among the uprooted and ruined flowers, crying and crying, and it was too late to undo what I had done. Joey was sitting beside me, silent and frightened, not knowing what to say. Then,

360 "Lizabeth, look."

I opened my swollen eyes and saw in front of me a pair of large calloused feet; my gaze lifted to the swollen legs, the age-distorted body clad in a tight cotton night dress, and then the shadowed Indian face surrounded by stubby white hair. And there was no rage in the face now, now that the garden was destroyed and there was nothing any longer to be protected.

"M-miss Lottie!" I scrambled to my feet and just stood there and stared at her, and that was the moment when childhood faded and womanhood began. That violent, crazy act was the

370 last act of childhood. For as I gazed at the immobile face with the sad, weary eyes, I gazed upon a kind of reality that is hidden to childhood. The witch was no longer a witch but only a broken old woman who had dared to create beauty in the midst of ugliness and sterility. She had been born in <u>squalor</u> and lived in it all her life. Now at the end of that life she had nothing except a falling-down hut, a wrecked body, and John Burke, the mindless son of her passion. Whatever verve[4] there was left in her, whatever was of love and beauty and joy that had not been squeezed out by life, had been there

380 in the (marigolds) she had so tenderly cared for.

---

4. **verve** (vûrv): vitality, enthusiasm.

What Does It Mean?
To *spur on* means "to encourage."

✔ **Reading Check**
How does Lizabeth feel after she completely destroys the marigolds?

More About . . .
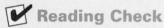 Marigolds are flowering plants with colorful blooms that can range from bright yellow to orange and deep red. They are easy to grow and care for, and they bloom throughout the summer. They can survive in very hot temperatures and can grow well even in poor soil. Think about why Eugenia Collier chose to use marigolds in this story.

Of course I could not express the things that I knew about Miss Lottie as I stood there awkward and ashamed. The years have put words to the things I knew in that moment, and as I look back upon it, I know that that moment marked the end of innocence. People think of the loss of innocence as meaning the loss of virginity, but this is far from true. Innocence involves an unseeing acceptance of things at face value, an ignorance of the area below the surface. In that humiliating moment I looked beyond myself and into the depths of

390 another person. This was the beginning of <u>compassion</u>, and one cannot have both compassion and innocence.

The years have taken me worlds away from that time and that place, from the dust and squalor of our lives and from the bright thing that I destroyed in a blind childish striking out at God-knows-what. Miss Lottie died long ago and many years have passed since I last saw her hut, completely barren at last, for despite my wild contrition she never planted marigolds again. Yet, there are times when the image of those passionate yellow mounds returns with a painful poignancy.

400 For one does not have to be ignorant and poor to find that one's life is barren as the dusty yards of one's town. And I too have planted marigolds.

Pause **Reflect**

What Does It Mean?
Contrition means "sorrow" or "remorse."

What Does It Mean?
Poignancy is "an intense feeling." Here, the narrator is feeling great distress or sorrow.

Pause **Reflect**

1. What did Lizabeth do after leaving her house? **(Clarify)**

_____

_____

READ ALOUD **2.** Slowly read the boxed passage on page 58. What change has taken place in Lizabeth's feelings toward Miss Lottie? **(Draw Conclusions)**

_____

_____

_____

CHALLENGE

How do the children feel about their position in society? Review the selection and box the passages that reveal the children's feelings and attitudes. **(Analyze)**

WORDS
TO
KNOW

compassion (kəm-pǎsh′ən) *n.* deep awareness of the suffering of another coupled with the wish to relieve it

Active Reading SkillBuilder

Drawing Conclusions

Understanding literature requires readers to **draw conclusions** about events, causes of events, characters, and so on. In drawing conclusions, readers combine information from the text with their own prior knowledge. Note places in "Marigolds" where you find yourself drawing a conclusion that helps you understand the story. Use the chart to record your conclusions.

Drawing Conclusions About "Marigolds"		
Text Information	**Prior Knowledge**	**Conclusion**
All the narrator remembers of her hometown is the dust. (p. 48)	People remember pleasant experiences.	The narrator didn't have many pleasant experiences in her hometown.

Literary Analysis SkillBuilder

Setting

The time and place of the action of a story is called the **setting.** The setting often plays an important role in the plot and makes a strong contribution to the story's over-all impact and meaning. In some stories, the setting is simple and straightforward. In others, it can be more complex, taking place in a character's private world of memory or feelings. Locate two passages from "Marigolds" in which the description of the setting seems to express the narrator's feelings.

Passage	Feelings the Setting Expresses
Passage 1 (Lines _____ to _____)	
Passage 2 (Lines _____ to _____)	

Follow Up: Underline vivid descriptive phrases in the passages on your chart. Then use these phrases to create a poem. Share your poem with the class.

Words to Know SkillBuilder

Words to Know

bravado	degradation	impotent	perverse	squalor
compassion	futile	impoverished	poignantly	stoicism

A. Fill in each set of blanks with the correct word from the word list. Then use the boxed letters to complete the sentence below the puzzle.

1. This is shown by a tiny dog who barks madly at a huge dog only when it's on the other side of the fence.
   _ _ _ _ _ □ _

2. People may say, "My hands are tied" when they feel that this describes them.
   _ _ _ _ _ □ _ _

3. This describes someone one who is broke, down and out, and can't make ends meet.
   _ _ □ _ _ _ _ _ _ _ _

4. This is what's going on if you come down in the world or fall into disgrace.
   _ _ _ _ □ _ _ _ _ _

5. People might say this describes someone who argues for the sake of arguing.
   _ _ _ _ □ _ _ _

6. When you want to do something about a sad state of affairs, this is what you are feeling.
   _ _ _ _ _ □ _ _ _

7. This is a quality crybabies do *not* have and that people who lie quietly on a bed of nails do have.
   _ _ _ _ _ _ _ □ _

8. This describes crying over spilled milk, going on a wild goose chase, or trying to empty the sea with a cup.
   _ _ _ □ _ _

9. If your parent says this is the condition your room is in, I hope it's an exaggeration!
   _ _ _ _ _ □ _

10. If a movie presents events this way, it may be described as a "two-hankie movie" or a "tear-jerker." _ _ _ _ _ _ _ □ _ _

Complete the following sentence with the word that the boxed letters spell out.

"Marigolds" takes place during the _____.

B. What might Lizabeth have said to Miss Lottie to try to explain her behavior? Write a short apology that uses at least **five** of the Words to Know.

THE PERFECT

Sebastian Junger

Storm

Before You Read

Connect to Your Life

Think of some times when you had to choose whether to take a risk. Use the chart below to show how you made your decision. A sample answer is provided.

RISK	REASONS TO TAKE IT	REASONS NOT TO TAKE IT	DECISION
Try out for the play	I might get a part	I might forget my lines and get embarrassed	I decided to try out and got a part

Key to the Selection

WHAT YOU NEED TO KNOW In October 1991, several types of weather came together to produce the worst North Atlantic storm in a century. A hurricane, which had been active in the area, was weakening. But at the same time, a cyclone, another type of storm with violent winds, developed over Canada. Moving over warmer waters, the cyclone became a super-storm. Swirling inside another storm, the cyclone produced 100-foot waves and 80-mph winds. This super-storm is now referred to as the "Perfect Storm." The unusual weather pattern finally broke up over Nova Scotia, Canada, on November 2. Storms such as this one are rare, but they can be particularly dangerous.

from
THE PERFECT
Storm

Sebastian Junger

PREVIEW The setting for this excerpt from *The Perfect Storm* is the Atlantic Ocean, off the northeastern coast of Canada. In October of 1991, the sailboat *Satori*, its captain, and two crew members were caught at sea in one of the worst storms of the century. This true account tells about the daring efforts made to rescue the crew.

As the selection begins...

- A sailboat named the *Satori* is in danger of sinking in an extreme storm.

- The crew of the *Satori* radios for help, and the Coast Guard sends another boat, the *Tamaroa*, to help.

More About...

THE COAST GUARD The Coast Guard uses ships, such as the *Tamaroa*, to perform rescues at sea.

English Learner Support
LANGUAGE

Pronouns Here, the word *she* is used to refer to the *Tamaroa*. Female pronouns are always used when referring to boats.

FOCUS
In this section you will get to know the captain and two crew members of the *Satori*. Read to find out what problems the *Satori* faces.

At 11:15 p.m., October 29th, a freighter off Long Island picks up a woman's terrified voice on the VHF:[1] *This is the Satori, the Satori, 39:49 north and 69:52 west. We are three people, this is a mayday.[2] If anyone can hear us, please pass our position on to the coast guard. Repeat. This is a mayday, if anyone can hear us, pass our position on to the coast guard.*

10   The freighter, the *Gold Bond Conveyor*, relays the message to Coast Guard operations in Boston, which in turn contacts the Coast Guard cutter *Tamaroa* in Provincetown Harbor. The *Tamaroa* has just come off Georges Bank, where she was conducting spot checks on the fishing fleet, and now she's waiting out the weather inside Cape Cod's huge flexed arm. A

---

1. **VHF:** a two-way radio that transmits and receives very-high frequency radio waves.

2. **mayday:** a distress signal; call for help.

What Does It Mean?

To *weigh anchor* means "to raise the anchor" so that a ship is ready to move.

Reading Tip

The crew of the *Satori* is made up of three people: Sue Bylander, Karen Stimpson, and Captain Ray Leonard. Choose a different color highlighter for each of the three characters. Then, highlight each crew member's actions in his or her own color.

✎ **MARK IT UP** **WORD POWER**

Mark words that you'd like to add to your **Personal Word List**. After reading, you can record the words and their meanings beginning on page 402.

More About . . .

KNOCKDOWNS A *knockdown* is when a ship is turned on its side with its masts in the water. Thirty-foot waves can knock a boat down, and the *Satori* was fighting 60-foot waves.

What Does It Mean?

To get *broached* means "to move sideways to the wind or waves." Broaching can cause a ship to tip over or fill with water.

☑ **Reading Check**

What problems does the *Satori* face?

small Falcon jet scrambles from Air Station Cape Cod and the *Tamaroa*, 1,600 tons and 205 feet, weighs anchor at midnight and heads down the throat of the storm.

20 The crew of the *Satori* have no way of knowing whether the radio is working, they just have to keep repeating the mayday and hope for the best. And even if the radio is working, they still have to be within two or three miles of another vessel for the signal to be heard. That's a lot to ask for on a night like this. Bylander, wedged behind the nav table,[3] broadcasts their name and position intermittently for half an hour without any response at all; they're alone out there, as far as she can tell. She keeps trying—what else is there to do?—and Stimpson goes back on deck to try to keep the *Satori* pointed into the seas. She's not there 30 long when she hears the sound of an airplane fading in and out through the roar of the storm. She looks around frantically in the darkness, and a minute later a Falcon jet, flying low under the cloud cover, shrieks overhead and raises Bylander on the VHF. "Sue was so excited she was giddy," Stimpson says, "but I wasn't. I remember not feeling elated or relieved so much as like, instantly, I'd rejoined the world of the living."

The Falcon pilot circles just below cloud level and discusses what to do next over the VHF with Bylander. The *Tamaroa* 40 won't be there for another twelve hours, and they've got to keep the boat afloat until then, even if that means burning out the engine. They can't afford to risk any more knockdowns. Bylander, against Leonard's wishes, finally toggles the starter switch, and to her amazement it turns over. With the storm jib up and the prop turning away they can now get a few degrees to the weather.[4] It's not a lot, but it's enough to keep from getting broached by the seas.

Throughout the night the Falcon pilot flies over them, reassuring Bylander that they're going to come out of this 50 alive. Stimpson stays at the helm[5] and Leonard lies on his

---

3. **nav table:** a table for spreading out the charts used in plotting a boat's course.

4. **With the storm jib up...to the weather:** With a small triangular sail raised and the propeller operating, they can turn the *Satori* a bit more toward the direction from which the wind is blowing.

5. **helm:** the steering gear of a boat or ship—usually a tiller or wheel.

WORDS
TO
KNOW

intermittently (ĭn′tər-mĭt′nt-lē) *adv.* at intervals; from time to time

bunk, contemplating the impending loss of his boat. When the *Tamaroa* arrives he'll have to abandon ship, which is an almost unthinkable act for a captain. The *Satori* is his home, his life, and if he allows himself to be taken off by the Coast Guard he'll probably never see her again. Not intact, anyway. At some point that night, lying on his bunk waiting for dawn, Ray Leonard decides he won't get off the boat. The women can leave if they want to, but he'll see the vessel into port.

Pause & Reflect

60 FOCUS

Find out about the plan to rescue the crew of the *Satori*.

MARK IT UP As you read, make notes in the margins about the roles to be played by the *Tamaroa*, the Falcon jet, and the H-3 helicopters.

Throughout that night the *Tamaroa* slugs her way through the storm. She's a bulldog of a vessel, built to salvage crippled battleships in World War Two, and she can "tow anything afloat," according to her literature. The sea state is so high, though, that the most she can make is three or four knots[6]—roughly walking pace. On the larger swells she plunges into the crest, stalls, and

70 launches out the far side, spray streaming off her bridge and greenwater sheeting out her scuppers.[7] She crosses Cape Cod Bay, threads the canal, leaves the Elizabeth Islands to starboard,[8] and finally turns the corner around Martha's Vineyard. Commander Lawrence Brudnicki, chief officer on board, estimates that they'll arrive on-scene late the next afternoon; the *Satori* crew has to stay afloat until then. They have no life raft or survival suits on board, and the nearest helicopter base is an hour away. If the *Satori* goes down, the crew is dead.

80 Brudnicki can't speak directly to the *Satori*, but he can relay messages via the Falcon that's circling above them. Both ship and plane are also in contact with the First District Command Center in Boston—D1 Comcen, as it's referred to in Coast

---

6. **three or four knots:** a speed of three or four nautical miles per hour.

7. **scuppers** (skŭp′ərz): openings in the side of a ship at deck level to allow water to run off.

8. **leaves...to starboard:** passes to the left of the Elizabeth Islands.

Pause & Reflect

Beside each crew member's name, write the letter of the phrase that best describes him or her. (**Clarify**)

___ Sue Bylander

___ Karen Stimpson

___ Captain Ray Leonard

A. operates radio
B. worries about leaving ship
C. stays at helm

As the selection continues...

- The *Tamaroa* moves slowly toward the *Satori*.
- A rescue helicopter arrives.
- Captain Leonard refuses to leave his ship.

More About...

SALVAGE SHIPS The word *salvage* means "to save." Salvage ships are made of steel. They can tow other vessels or lift heavy objects from the ocean floor. Some have special equipment to fight fires and get a disabled ship working again.

What Does It Mean?

Swells is another word for waves.

Reading Tip

Think about where the ships and the jet are in relation to each other. Make a diagram that shows the *Satori*, the Falcon, and the *Tamaroa*.

✔ **Reading Check**

Why doesn't the Falcon airlift the crew off the *Satori*?

More About...

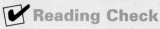

INCIDENT LOGS An *incident log* is a record of what happens during a rescue attempt. The log entries in italic type are based on messages from the planes and ships trying to save the *Satori*'s crew. As these messages come into the Coast Guard command center, they are added to the incident log.

English Learner Support
LANGUAGE

Diction In this context, *screaming* means moving very fast and making a great deal of noise.

Guard reports. D1 Comcen is responsible for coordinating all the Coast Guard vessels and aircraft on the rescue, and developing the safest strategy for taking the people off the boat. Every decision has to be approved by them. Since the *Satori* isn't sinking yet, they decide to have the Falcon fly cover until the *Tamaroa* arrives, and then take the crew off by raft. Air rescue in such conditions can be riskier than actually staying with the boat, so it's used as a last resort. As soon as day breaks, the Falcon will be relieved by an H-3 rescue helicopter, and H-3's will fly cover in shifts until the *Tamaroa* shows up. Helicopters have a limited amount of flying time—generally about four hours—but they can pluck people out of the water if need be. Falcon jets can't do much for people in the water except circle them and watch them drown.

From the incident log, D1 Comcen:

2:30 am—s/v [sailing vessel] is running out of fuel, recommend we try to keep Falcon o/s [on-scene] until Tamaroa arrives.

5:29 am—Falcon has lost comms [communication] with vessel, vessel is low on battery power and taking on water. Pumps are keeping up but are run by ele [electric].

7:07 am—Falcon o/s, vessel has been located. Six hours fuel left. People on board are scared.

The H-3 arrives on scene around 6:30 and spends half an hour just trying to locate the *Satori*. The conditions are so bad that she's vanished from the Falcon's radar, and the H-3 pilot is almost on top of her before spotting her in the foam-streaked seas. The Falcon circles off to the southwest to prepare a life-raft drop while the H-3 takes up a hover directly over the boat. In these conditions the Falcon pilot could never line up on something as small as a sailboat, so the H-3 acts as a stand-in. The Falcon comes back at 140 knots, radar locked onto the helicopter, and at the last moment the H-3 falls away and the jet makes the drop. The pilot comes screaming over the *Satori*'s mast[9] and the copilot pushes two life-raft packages out a hatch in the floorboards. The rafts are linked by a long nylon <u>tether</u>, and as they fall they cartwheel

---

9. **mast:** a vertical pole that supports the sails of a sailing vessel.

WORDS
TO **tether** (tĕth′ər) *n.* a rope or chain connecting two things
KNOW

apart, splashing down well to either side of the *Satori*. The tether, released at two hundred feet into a hurricane-force wind, drops right into Bylander's hand.

The H-3 hovers overhead while the *Satori* crew haul in the packages, but both rafts have exploded on impact. There's nothing at either end of the line. The *Tamaroa* is still five hours away and the storm has retrograded[10] to within a couple of hundred miles of the coast; over the next twenty-four hours it will pass directly over the *Satori*. A daylight

130 rescue in these conditions is difficult, and a nighttime rescue is out of the question. If the *Satori* crew is not taken off in the next few hours, there's a good chance they won't be taken off at all. Late that morning the second H-3 arrives and the pilot, Lieutenant Klosson, explains the situation to Ray Leonard. Leonard radios back that he's not leaving the boat.

It's unclear whether Leonard is serious or just trying to save face. Either way, the Coast Guard is having none of it. Two helicopters, two Falcon jets, a medium-range cutter, and a hundred air- and seamen have already been committed to the

140 rescue; the *Satori* crew are coming off now. "Owner refuses to leave and says he's sailed through hurricanes before," the Comcen incident log records at 12:24 that afternoon. "*Tamaroa* wants manifestly unsafe voyage so that o/o [owner-operator] can be forced off."

A "manifestly unsafe voyage" means that the vessel has been deemed an unacceptable risk to her crew or others, and the Coast Guard has the legal authority to order everyone off. Commander Brudnicki gets on the radio with District One and requests a manifestly unsafe designation for the *Satori*,

150 and at 12:47 it is granted. The *Tamaroa* is just a couple of miles away now, within VHF range of the *Satori*, and Brudnicki raises Leonard on the radio and tells him he has no choice in the matter. Everyone is leaving the boat. At 12:57 in the afternoon, thirteen hours after weighing anchor, the *Tamaroa* plunges into view.

There's a lot of hardware circling the *Satori*. There's the Falcon, the H-3, the *Tamaroa*, and the freighter *Gold Bond Conveyor*, which has been cutting circles around the *Satori* since the first mayday call. Hardware is not the problem,

160 though; it's time. Dark is only three hours away, and the

---

10. **retrograded:** backed up.

from **The Perfect Storm**   **69**

English Learner Support
VOCABULARY

Exploded on Impact *Exploded on impact* means that the rafts exploded as soon as they hit the water.

✔ **Reading Check**
Why does the first attempt to get the crew off the *Satori* fail?

✔ **Reading Check**
Why do the Coast Guards officially classify the *Satori* as a "manifestly unsafe voyage"?

Reading Tip
Add the helicopter and the freighter *Gold Bond Conveyor* to your diagram from page 68.

Pause & Reflect

Review your margin notes. What role does each vehicle below play in the rescue plan? (Summarize)

Tamaroa_____

_____

Falcon jet_____

_____

H-3 helicopters_____

_____

As the selection continues...

- A raft tries to reach the *Satori*.
- The raft rescue has problems.
- The helicopter pilot decides to drop his rescue swimmer.

English Learner Support

VOCABULARY

Lull A *lull* is a quiet, calm interval.

What Does It Mean?

Freefall means "to fall in a rapid, uncontrolled motion from a height."

departing H-3 pilot doesn't think the *Satori* will survive another night. She'll run out of fuel, start getting knocked down, and eventually break apart. The crew will be cast into the sea, and the helicopter pilot will refuse to drop his rescue swimmer because he can't be sure of getting him back. It would be up to the *Tamaroa* to maneuver alongside the swimmers and pull them on board, and in these seas it would be almost impossible. It's now or never.

Pause & Reflect

FOCUS

170 Read to find out what happens when Commander Brudnicki sends in a rescue team on rafts to pick up the *Satori*'s crew.

MARK IT UP   Circle the words and phrases that describe what goes wrong. An example is highlighted on page 71.

The only way to take them off, Brudnicki decides, is to shuttle them back to the *Tamaroa* in one of the little Avons. The Avons are 21-foot inflatable rafts with rigid <u>hulls</u> and outboard engines; one of them could make a run to the *Satori*, drop off survival suits and then come back again to pick up the three crew. If anyone wound up in the water, at least they'd be insulated and afloat. It's not a particularly complicated maneuver, but no one has done it in 180 conditions like this before. No one has even seen conditions like this before. At 1:23 pm the *Tamaroa* crew gathers at the port davits,[11] three men climb aboard the Avon, and they lower away.

It goes badly from the start. What passes for a lull between waves is in fact a crest-to-trough change of thirty or forty feet. Chief bosun[12] Thomas Amidon lowers the Avon half way down, gets lifted up by the next wave, can't keep up with the trough and freefalls to the bottom of the cable. The lifting eye[13] gets ripped out of its mount and Amidon almost pitches

---

11. **port davits:** small cranes on the left side of the ship, used for lowering and raising the inflatable rafts.

12. **bosun**(bō'sən): an officer in charge of a ship's boat crews and maintenance crews.

13. **lifting eye:** a metal ring though which the rope used to lower the boat passes.

WORDS
TO   **hull** (hŭl) *n.* the frame or body of a ship
KNOW

190 overboard. He struggles back into position, finishes lowering the boat, and makes way from the *Tamaroa*.

The seas are twice the size of the Avon raft. With excruciating slowness it fights its way to the *Satori*, comes up bow-to-stern,[14] and a crew member flings the three survival suits on deck. Stimpson grabs them and hands them out, but Amidon doesn't back out in time. The sailboat rides up a sea, comes down on the Avon, and punctures one of her air bladders. Things start to happen very fast now: the Avon's bow collapses, a wave swamps her to the gunwales,[15] the 200 engine dies, and she falls away astern.[16] Amidon tries desperately to get the engine going again and finally manages to, but they're up to their waists in water and the raft is crippled. There's no way they can even get themselves back onto the *Tamaroa*, much less save the crew of the *Satori*. Six people, not just three, now need to be rescued.

The H-3 crew watches all this <u>incredulously.</u> They're in a two o'clock hover[17] with their jump door open, just over the tops of the waves. They can see the raft dragging heavily through the seas, and the *Tamaroa* heaving through 90-degree 210 rolls. Pilot Claude Hessel finally gets on the radio and tells Brudnicki and Amidon that he may have another way of doing this. He can't <u>hoist</u> the *Satori* crew directly off their deck, he says, because the mast is <u>flailing</u> too wildly and might entangle the hoist. That would drag the H-3 right down on top of the boat. But he could drop his rescue swimmer, who could take the people off the boat one at a time and bring them up on the hoist. It's the best chance they've got, and Brudnicki knows it. He consults with District One and then gives the okay.

Pause & Reflect

---

14. **bow-to-stern:** from behind the *Satori*.

15. **swamps her to the gunwales**(gŭn'əlz): fills the boat with water to the top of its sides.

16. **falls away astern:** is left behind by the *Satori*.

17. **in a two o'clock hover:** hovering so that the boat is 60 degrees to the right of straight ahead.

WORDS TO KNOW	**incredulously** (ĭn-krĕj'ə-ləs-lē) *adv.* in a way that expresses disbelief
	hoist (hoist) *v.* to raise or haul up
	flail (flāl) *v.* to move vigorously or erratically; thrash about

What Does It Mean?
Here, *seas* means "waves."

✓ **Reading Check**
Besides the crew of the *Satori,* who else needs to be rescued?

English Learner Support
VOCABULARY

Jump Door A *jump door* is a door on the side of an aircraft that allows people to jump out of the aircraft while it is flying. In this case, the jump door allows the rescue swimmer to jump out of the hovering helicopter and into the water.

What Does It Mean?
During *90-degree rolls,* the *Tamaroa* moves from being upright to lying almost flat on its side.

Pause & Reflect
Review the details you circled as you read. In your own words, tell what went wrong with the Avon team's rescue attempt. **(Summarize)**

_____
_____
_____
_____

from **The Perfect Storm** **71**

As the selection continues…

• Rescue swimmer Dave Moore goes into the water.

• Moore is on his first rescue mission.

• He tries to swim to the *Satori*.

English Learner Support
LANGUAGE

Expressions *Baby-faced* means "young" and *square-jawed* means that Moore's jaw has a square shape.

Reading Check

How has Moore prepared for this rescue?

FOCUS
(220) The next plan calls for a swimmer to be lowered into the water and to swim to the *Satori*. Read to find out whether this plan is successful.

The rescue swimmer on Hessel's helicopter is Dave Moore, a three-year veteran who has never been on a major rescue. ("The good cases don't come along too often—usually someone beats you to them," he says. "If a sailboat gets in trouble far out we usually get a rescue, but otherwise it's just a lot of little stuff.") Moore is handsome in a baby-faced sort of way—square-jawed, blue-eyed, and a big open smile. He has a dense, compact body that (230) is more seal-like than athletic. His profession of rescue swimmer came about when a tanker went down off New York in the mid-1980s. A Coast Guard helicopter was hovering overhead, but it was winter and the tanker crew were too hypothermic to get into the lift basket. They all drowned. Congress decided they wanted something done, and the Coast Guard adopted the Navy rescue program. Moore is 25 years old, born the year Karen Stimpson graduated from high school.

Moore is already wearing a neoprene[18] wetsuit. He puts on socks and hood, straps on swim fins, pulls a mask and snorkel (240) down over his head, and then struggles into his neoprene gloves. He buckles on a life vest and then signals to flight engineer Vriesman that he's ready. Vriesman, who has one arm extended, gate-like, across the jump door, steps aside and allows Moore to crouch by the edge. That means that they're at "ten and ten"—a ten foot hover at ten knots. Moore, who's no longer plugged into the intercom, signals final corrections to Vriesman with his hands, who relays them to the pilot. This is it; Moore has trained three years for this moment. An hour ago he was in the lunch line back on base. Now he's about to (250) drop into the maelstrom.

Hessel holds a low hover with the boat at his two o'clock. Moore can see the crew clustered together on deck and the *Satori* making slow, plunging headway into the seas. Vriesman is seated next to Moore at the hoist controls, and avionicsman[19] Ayres is behind the copilot with the radio and

---

18. **neoprene** (nē′ə-prēn′): a synthetic rubber.

19. **avionicsman** (ā′vē-ŏn′ĭks-mən): the person in charge of an aircraft's electronic equipment.

WORDS
TO
KNOW

hypothermic (hī′pə-thûr′mĭk) *adj.* having an abnormally low body temperature

maelstrom (māl′strəm) *n.* a violent or turbulent situation

search gear. Both wear flightsuits and crash helmets and are plugged into the internal communication system in the wall. The time is 2:07 P.M. Moore picks a spot between waves, takes a deep breath, and jumps.

260 It's a ten-foot fall and he hits feet-first, hands at his side. He comes up, clears his snorkel, settles his mask, and then strikes out for the *Satori*. The water is lukewarm—they're in the Gulf Stream—and the seas are so big they give him the impression he's swimming uphill and downhill rather than over individual waves. Occasionally the wind blows a crest off, and he has to dive under the cascade of whitewater before setting out again. The *Satori* appears and disappears behind the swells and the H-3 thunders overhead, rotors blasting a lily-pad of flattened water into the sea. Vriesman watches anxiously through

270 binoculars from the jump door, trying to gauge the difficulty of getting Moore back into the helicopter. Ultimately, as flight engineer, it's his decision to deploy[20] the swimmer, his job to get everyone safely back into the aircraft. If he has any doubts, Moore doesn't jump.

Moore swims hard for several minutes and finally looks up at Vriesman, shaking his head. The boat's under power and there's no way he's going to catch her, not in these seas. Vriesman sends the basket down and Moore climbs back in. Just as he's about to ride up, the wave hits.

280 It's huge and cresting, fifty or sixty feet. It avalanches over Moore and buries both him and the lift basket. Vriesman counts to ten before Moore finally pops up through the foam, still inside the basket. It's no longer attached to the hoist cable, though; it's been wrenched off the hook and is just floating free. Moore has such tunnel vision[21] that he doesn't realize the basket has come off; he just sits there, waiting to be hoisted. Finally he understands that he's not going anywhere, and swims the basket over to the cable and clips it on. He climbs inside, and Vriesman hauls him up.

Pause & *Reflect*

What Does It Mean?

Lukewarm means "mildly warm." The *Gulf Stream* is a warm ocean current that flows northward off the eastern coast of North America. The conditions of this storm make the water in the Gulf Stream particularly warm.

Pause & Reflect

1. What makes Dave Moore especially well-suited for the job of rescue swimmer? **(Evaluate)**

   _____

   _____

   _____

2. Why do you think the author interrupts the action to tell about Dave Moore? **(Storytelling Elements)**

   _____

   _____

   _____

3. What happens when Dave Moore tries to rescue the *Satori's* crew? **(Clarify)**

   _____

   _____

   _____

   _____

---

20. **deploy:** make use of.
21. **has such tunnel vision:** is so focused on his mission.

- The rescue pilot decides to try a new plan.
- Dave Moore tries to rescue the crew members from the *Satori* and the *Tamaroa*.

What Does It Mean?

Hover means "to hang suspended in the air." Hessel is holding the position of the helicopter just above the surface of the water.

English Learner Support

Figure of Speech To *give the go-ahead* means "to let someone know that it is okay to proceed."

290

> **FOCUS**
> Read to find out how the crew of the *Satori* and the Avon raft are finally rescued.

This time they're going to do things differently. Hessel banks the helicopter to within fifty feet of the *Satori* and shows a chalk board that says, "Channel 16." Bylander disappears below, and when Hessel has her on the VHF, he tells her they're going to do an in-the-water pick-up. They're to get into their survival suits, tie the tiller down,[22] and then jump off the boat. Once they're in the water they are to stay in a group and wait for Moore to swim over to them. He'll 300 put them into the hoist basket and send them up one at a time.

Bylander climbs back up on deck and gives the instructions to the rest of the crew. Moore, looking through a pair of binoculars, watches them pull on their suits and try to will themselves over the gunwale. First, one of them puts a leg over the rail, then another does, and finally all three of them splash into the water. It takes four or five minutes for them to work up the nerve. Leonard has a bag in one hand, and as he goes over he loses his grip and leaves it 310 on deck. It's full of his personal belongings. He claws his way down the length of the hull and finally punches himself in the head when he realizes he's lost it for good. Moore takes this in, wondering if Leonard is going to be a problem in the water.

Moore sheds his hood and gloves because the water's so warm and pulls his mask back down over his face. This is it; if they can't do it now, they can't do it at all. Hessel puts the *Satori* at his six o'clock[23] by lining them up in a little rearview mirror and comes down into a low hover. It's 320 delicate flying. He finally gives Moore the go-ahead, and Moore breathes in deep and pushes off. "They dropped Moore and he just skimmed over the top of the water, flying towards us," says Stimpson. "When he gets there he says, 'Hi, I'm Dave Moore your rescue swimmer, how are you?' And Sue says, 'Fine, how are you?' It was very cordial. Then he asks who's going first, and Sue says, 'I will.' And he

---

22. **tie the tiller down:** tie down the handle used for steering the boat, so that it can't move

23. **puts the *Satori* at his six o'clock:** moves the helicopter so that the *Satori* is directly behind it.

grabbed her by the back of the survival suit and skimmed back across the water."

Moore loads Bylander into the rescue basket, and twenty seconds later she's in the helicopter. Jump to recovery takes five minutes (avionicsman Ayres is writing everything down in the hoist log). The next recovery, Stimpson's, takes two minutes, and Leonard's takes three. Leonard is so <u>despondent</u> that he's deadweight in the water, Moore has to wrestle him into the basket and push his legs in after him. Moore's the last one up, stepping back into the aircraft at 2:29. They've been on-scene barely two hours.

Moore starts stripping off his gear, and he's got his wetsuit half-way off when he realizes the helicopter isn't going anywhere. It's hovering off the *Tamaroa*'s port quarter.[24] He puts his flight helmet on and hears the *Tamaroa* talking to Hessel, telling him to stand by because their Avon crew still needs to be recovered. . . . Moore pulls his gear back on and takes up his position at the jump door. Hessel has decided on another in-the-water rescue, and Moore watches the three Coast Guardsmen grab hands and reluctantly abandon ship. Even from a distance they look nervous. Hessel comes in low and puts them at his six o'clock again, barely able to find such a small target in his rearview mirror. Moore gets the nod and jumps for the third time; he's got the drill down now and the entire rescue takes ten minutes. Each Coast Guardsman that makes it into the aircraft gives Stimpson a thumbs-up. Moore comes up last—"via bare hook," as the report reads—and Vriesman pulls him in through the door. The H-3 banks, drops her nose, and starts for home.

"When I got up into the helicopter I remember everyone looking in my and Sue's faces to make sure we were okay," says Stimpson. "I remember the intensity, it really struck me. These guys were so pumped up, but they were also human— real humanity. They'd take us by the shoulders and look us in the eyes and say, 'I'm so glad you're alive, we were with you

What Does It Mean?

To *abandon ship* means "to leave a ship that is about to sink."

English Learner Support

LANGUAGE

Pronoun Here, the pronoun *her* refers to the helicopter. *Her nose* is the front end of the helicopter.

✔ **Reading Check**

How is the crew of the *Satori* finally rescued?

---

24. **the *Tamaroa*'s port quarter:** the rear part of the *Tamaroa*'s left side.

WORDS
TO   **despondent** (dĭ-spŏn′dənt) *adj.* without hope; dejected
KNOW

Reread the boxed statement. Who do you think was more worried about the rescue—the rescuers or the *Satori*'s crew? Why? **(Infer)**

_____

_____

_____

_____

In this selection, the author uses **primary sources,** or sources that offer direct, firsthand knowledge. The primary sources in this selection include interviews and the Coast Guard incident log. Circle the information that came from primary sources. Why do you think the author included this information? Decide how the primary sources affect the selection. **(Analyze)**

last night, we prayed for you. We were worried about you.' When you're on the rescuing side you're very aware of life and death, and when you're on the rescued side, you just have a sort of numb awareness. At some point I stopped seeing the risk clearly, and it just became an <u>amalgam</u> of experience and observation."

WORDS TO KNOW   **amalgam** (ə-mǎl′gəm) *n.* a mixture of diverse elements

Active Reading SkillBuilder

Identifying Elements of Storytelling

The Perfect Storm is a nonfiction account of a disaster at sea. When reading the selection, pay attention to the way Junger tells the story. Notice how people in the story are like characters in a work of fiction. Look for important moments of action or conflict, and pay close attention to the setting. Record your observations in the chart below.

Storytelling Elements in *The Perfect Storm*

People in the Story
Captain Leonard worried about losing <u>Satori</u>

Action/Conflict

Setting

Literary Analysis SkillBuilder

Narrative Nonfiction

Nonfiction is writing that deals with real people, places, and events. *The Perfect Storm* is an example of **narrative nonfiction.** It uses elements typically found in fiction, such as plot, character, and setting, to present factual information and bring real events to life. Choose a paragraph from the excerpt with details that seem storylike. Record the details in the box below. Then rewrite the paragraph in a way that is strictly informative, without the intensity or dramatic emphasis of a story.

Details from Paragraph_____ (page_____ lines_____)

Rewrite

Follow Up: Did eliminating the elements of fiction affect your enjoyment of the paragraph? Explain.

Words to Know SkillBuilder

Words to Know

amalgam   flail   hull   incredulously   maelstrom

despondent   hoist   hypothermic   intermittently   tether

A. Complete each analogy with one of the words from the word list above. In an analogy, the last two words must be related in the same way that the first two are related.

1. JOYOUS : UNHAPPY : : hopeful : _____

2. BRANCH : LIMB : : frame : _____

3. STOP : MOVE : : lower : _____

4. INGREDIENT : RECIPE : : element : _____

5. STILLNESS : CALM : : turbulence : _____

B. For each phrase in the first column, find the phrase in the second column that is closest in meaning. Write the letter of that phrase in the blank.

_____ 1. an unusual mixture   A. hoist the Stars and Stripes

_____ 2. attach the chain   B. flail furiously

_____ 3. thrash about vigorously   C. disturbingly hypothermic

_____ 4. a good-looking frame   D. interrupt intermittently

_____ 5. examining with disbelief   E. a despondent sailor

_____ 6. temperature way too low   F. tie the tether

_____ 7. a terrifying situation   G. a handsome hull

_____ 8. cut in at intervals   H. an amazing amalgam

_____ 9. raise the flag   I. inspecting incredulously

_____ 10. a discouraged captain   J. a monstrous maelstrom

C. Write a television news bulletin about the plight of the *Satori*. Use at least **four** Words to Know in your bulletin.

O What Is That Sound

W. H. Auden

Before You Read

Connect to Your Life

Suppose a telephone rings suddenly in the night, or perhaps you hear a weird sound outside that you've never heard before. At what point does your curiosity turn to suspense—and then to fear? Describe a situation in which your feelings changed from curiosity to fear.

At first, I was just curious about _____

_____

_____.

Then, _____

_____

_____

_____.

Key to the Poem

WHAT YOU NEED TO KNOW Many details in this poem suggest that it takes place during the American Revolution. The poem was written in the 1930s—a time that W. H. Auden called "the age of anxiety." Auden saw many similarities between the time during the American Revolution and the 1930s. Along with some thrilling events in those days came serious economic depression and a terrible war. Ordinary citizens were never sure when they might be swept away by events beyond their control.

O What Is That Sound

W. H. Auden

PREVIEW This poem is a **ballad,** a poem that tells a story. Like a short story, ballads make use of **plot, character,** and **setting.** They often focus on a single—usually tragic—event. They have an air of mystery about them and suggest more than they actually state. Details in this ballad—drums, horses, and the soldiers' red coats—suggest a New England setting during the American Revolution.

FOCUS
The two speakers are in a house, noticing soldiers moving outside.

MARK IT UP As you read, circle words and phrases that describe the soldiers' actions. One example is highlighted.

O what is that sound which so thrills the ear
    Down in the valley drumming, drumming?
Only the scarlet soldiers,[1] dear,
    The soldiers coming.

5   O what is that light I see flashing so clear
    Over the distance brightly, brightly?
Only the sun on their weapons, dear,
    As they step lightly.

---

1. **scarlet soldiers:** British soldiers, who wore bright red coats.

O what are they doing with all that gear,
        What are they doing this morning, this morning?
Only their usual maneuvers,² dear,
        Or perhaps a warning.

O why have they left the road down there,
        Why are they suddenly wheeling, wheeling?
Perhaps a change in their orders, dear.
        Why are you kneeling?

Pause **&** *Reflect*

FOCUS
The first speaker continues to ask
questions in stanzas 5–8.
MARK IT UP Underline each of the five
questions.

O haven't they stopped for the doctor's care,
        Haven't they reined their horses, their horses?
Why, they are none of them wounded, dear.
        None of these forces.

O is it the parson they want, with white hair,
        Is it the parson, is it, is it?
No, they are passing his gateway, dear,
        Without a visit.

O it must be the farmer who lives so near.
        It must be the farmer so cunning, so cunning?
They have passed the farmyard already, dear,
        And now they are running.

---

2. **maneuvers:** (mə-noō′ vərz) training exercises carried out by troops.

English Learner Support
VOCABULARY

Wheeling Here, *wheeling*
means "turning around." The
soldiers are suddenly turning
toward the speakers.

What Does It Mean?
Most likely, the person is
kneeling to pray. It is also
possible that the person is
kneeling to hide.

As the poem continues . . .
• The speakers keep watching
  the soldiers.
• The soldiers pass by the
  houses of the doctor, the
  parson, and the farmer.

Pause **&** *Reflect*
Review the details you circled
as you read. Then list what the
soldiers do in stanzas 1–4.
(Clarify)

_____

_____

_____

_____

What Does It Mean?
Someone who is *cunning* is
tricky and deceptive.

✔ **Reading Check**
What are the soldiers doing
now?

O where are you going? Stay with me here!
    Were the vows you swore deceiving, deceiving?
No, I promised to love you, dear,
    But I must be leaving.

O it's broken the lock and splintered the door,
    O it's the gate where they're turning, turning;
Their boots are heavy on the floor
    And their eyes are burning.

Pause **&** *Reflect*

30
35

What Does It Mean?

Their eyes are burning means that the soldiers look angry.

Pause **&** *Reflect*

1. Review the five questions you underlined. The first three questions mention people the soldiers might have come for—the doctor, the parson, or the farmer. What are the last two questions about in lines 29–30? **(Infer)**

_____

_____

_____

2. Why do you think the second speaker leaves? **(Infer)**

_____

_____

_____

CHALLENGE

Underline examples of **repetition** in the second line of each stanza. What effect does this technique create? What does the use of repetition reveal about the first speaker?

Active Reading SkillBuilder

Making Inferences About Speakers

An **inference** is a logical guess or conclusion based on facts. Readers normally infer much from dialogue, or what characters say to each other. As you read this poem, use the reactions of the speakers to imagine what is happening. Look for changes in either speaker's attitude as the action takes place. Use the chart below to record information you have inferred about the speakers. Indicate who the two people might be and how they react to the sound—at first and then later in the poem.

	Identity	First Reaction to Sound	Later Reaction to Sound
First Speaker		curious excited	
Second Speaker		calm	

Literary Analysis SkillBuilder

Poetic Form: Ballad

"O What Is That Sound" is a **ballad,** a poem that tells a story and is meant to be sung or recited. Some ballads contain nothing but dialogue. In "O What Is That Sound," one speaker asks a series of questions, and a second speaker gives answers. Make a list of questions to ask the speakers in the poem about the situation described in the poem and the feelings of the speakers.

Questions for First Speaker	Questions for Second Speaker
1. Why did you kneel down after the soldiers left the road ?	

Follow Up: What do you think might be the answers to your questions?

THE CASK OF

EDGAR ALLAN POE

AMONTILLADO

Before You Read

Connect to Your Life

Revenge is a theme that many writers address. Use the word web below to write what you know about revenge.

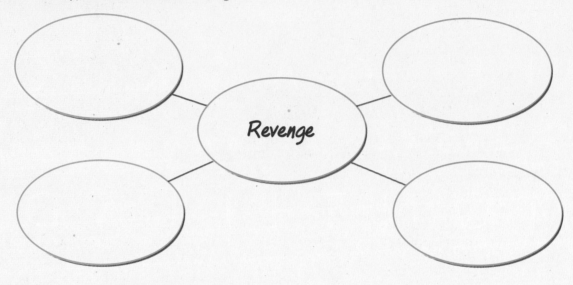

Key to the Story

WHAT YOU NEED TO KNOW This story takes place in a European country, perhaps Italy or France, during carnival. Mainly celebrated in Roman Catholic regions, carnival is a time of festival just before the 40-day period of fasting known as Lent. During carnival, people wear fanciful costumes, attend balls, and participate in feasts. The carnival plays a key role in the narrator's plot for revenge.

THE CASK OF

EDGAR ALLAN POE

AMONTILLADO

PREVIEW "The Cask of Amontillado" is a haunting tale of pride and revenge. When the narrator, Montresor (môn′trĕ-sor′), is insulted by a "friend," he decides on a plan to seek revenge. Using compliments and a cask of wine as bait, Montresor sets his plan in motion on the wildest night of a festival. How far will the narrator go in his efforts to make things right?

SHORT STORY

Reading Tips

Edgar Allan Poe is a master of a suspenseful type of writing called **horror fiction.**

- The vocabulary is difficult, and the diction, or the writer's choice and placement of words, is formal. Read slowly, and "translate" the sentences into modern, everyday language.

- For long or difficult sentences, begin by identifying the simple subject and verb.

FOCUS

The narrator has been insulted.

✎ **MARK IT UP** As you read, circle details that explain the terms he sets up for getting his revenge.

The thousand injuries of Fortunato[1] I had borne as I best could; but when he ventured upon insult, I vowed revenge. You, who so well know the nature of my soul, will not suppose, however, that I gave utterance to a threat. *At length* I would be avenged; this was a point definitively settled—but the very definitiveness with which it was resolved, <u>precluded</u> the idea of risk. I must not only punish, but punish with <u>impunity</u>. A wrong is unredressed when retribution overtakes its redresser. It is equally unredressed when the avenger fails to make himself felt as such to him who has done the wrong.

It must be understood, that neither by word nor deed had I given Fortunato cause to doubt my good-will. I continued, as

As the story begins . . .

- Montresor wants to take revenge on Fortunato.

- For now, Montresor pretends to be Fortunato's friend.

What Does It Mean?

In the highlighted passage the narrator explains that he must take revenge without receiving punishment. He goes on to say that if one were to be punished for trying to correct an injustice, then the injustice would remain uncorrected.

What Does It Mean?

Retribution means "punishment."

---

1. **Fortunato** (fôr′chə-nä′tō).

WORDS TO KNOW
preclude (prĭ-klood′) *v.* to make impossible, especially by taking action in advance; prevent
impunity (ĭm-pyoo′nĭ-tē) *n.* freedom from punishment, penalty or harm

What Does It Mean?

Wont means "habit" or "customary practice."

Reading Tip

Poe uses complex words and long sentences. Use a ruler to help you read slowly and carefully.

What Does It Mean?

Here, *madness* means "wild partying," not "insanity or anger."

MARK IT UP WORD POWER

Mark words that you'd like to add to your **Personal Word List**. After reading, you can record the words and their meanings beginning on page 402.

More About . . .

AMONTILLADO is a dry sherry wine noted for its delicate aroma and nutty flavor. The name comes from Montilla, Spain.

English Learner Support
LANGUAGE

Diction Poe uses many formal words and expressions. You will find definitions for many of these words in the footnotes. You can also break the words apart to see if you recognize any of their parts.

was my wont, to smile in his face, and he did not perceive that my smile *now* was at the thought of his immolation.[2]

20 He had a weak point—this Fortunato—although in other regards he was a man to be respected and even feared. He prided himself on his connoisseurship[3] in wine. Few Italians have the true <u>virtuoso</u> spirit. For the most part their enthusiasm is adopted to suit the time and opportunity—to practice imposture[4] upon the British and Austrian *millionaires*. In painting and gemmary[5] Fortunato, like his countrymen, was a quack—but in the matter of old wines he was sincere. In this respect I did not differ from him materially; I was skillful in the Italian vintages myself, and bought largely whenever I could.

It was about dusk, one evening during the supreme
30 madness of the carnival season, that I encountered my friend. He <u>accosted</u> me with excessive warmth, for he had been drinking much. The man wore motley.[6] He had on a tight-fitting parti-striped dress, and his head was surmounted by the conical cap and bells. I was so pleased to see him, that I thought I should never have done wringing his hand.

I said to him: "My dear Fortunato, you are luckily met. How remarkably well you are looking to-day! But I have received a pipe[7] of what passes for Amontillado,[8] and I have
40 my doubts."

"How?" said he. "Amontillado? A pipe? Impossible! And in the middle of the carnival!"

"I have my doubts," I replied; "and I was silly enough to pay the full Amontillado price without consulting you in the matter. You were not to be found, and I was fearful of losing a bargain."

---

2. **immolation** (ĭm′ə-lā′shən): death or destruction.

3. **connoisseurship** (kŏn′ə-sûr′shĭp): expertise or authority, especially in the fine arts or in matters of taste.

4. **imposture:** deception.

5. **gemmary** (jĕm′ə-rē): knowledge of precious gems.

6. **motley:** the costume of a court jester or clown.

7. **pipe:** a wine barrel with a capacity of 126 gallons.

8. **Amontillado** (ə-mŏn′tl-ä′dō): a pale dry sherry.

WORDS TO KNOW

virtuoso (vûr′chōō-ō′sō) *n.* characteristic of a person with masterly knowledge or skill

accost (ə-kôst′) *v.* to approach and speak to in an aggressive or hostile manner

"Amontillado!"

"I have my doubts."

"Amontillado!"

50 "And I must satisfy them."

"Amontillado!"

"As you are engaged, I am on my way to Luchesi.[9] If anyone has a critical turn, it is he. He will tell me—"

"Luchesi cannot tell Amontillado from Sherry."

"And yet some fools will have it that his taste is a match for your own."

"Come, let us go."

"Whither?"

"To your vaults."

60 "My friend, no; I will not impose upon your good nature. I perceive you have an engagement. Luchesi—"

"I have no engagement;—come."

"My friend, no. It is not the engagement, but the severe cold with which I perceive you are afflicted. The vaults are insufferably damp. They are encrusted with niter."[10]

"Let us go, nevertheless. The cold is merely nothing. Amontillado! You have been imposed upon. And as for Luchesi, he cannot distinguish Sherry from Amontillado."

Thus speaking, Fortunato possessed himself of my arm. 70 Putting on a mask of black silk, and drawing a *roquelaure*[11] closely about my person, I suffered him to hurry me to my palazzo.[12]

Pause & Reflect

English Learner Support
VOCABULARY

Idiom A person with a *critical turn* has a skill for judging the value of something. Here, the word *turn* means "a natural talent" rather than "a physical change of direction."

What Does It Mean?
I suffered him to hurry me to my palazzo means "I allowed him to hurry me to my house."

Pause & Reflect

1. The narrator wants revenge—but on his own terms! Review the details you circled. Then put a check next to the sentences below that reflect Montresor's plan. **(Clarify)**

Montresor's identity must remain a secret, even to Fortunato.

Montresor himself must not get in trouble or caught.

Fortunato must apologize to Montresor in public.

2. Based on the conversation between Montresor and Fortunato, what can you **infer** about each of their characters?

Narrator: _____

_____

Fortunato: _____

_____

_____

9. **Luchesi** (lōō-kā'sē).

10. **niter:** a white, gray, or colorless mineral, consisting of potassium nitrate.

11. *roquelaure* (rôk-lōr') *French:* a man's knee-length cloak, popular during the 18th century.

12. **palazzo** (pə-lät'sō): a palace or mansion.

As the story continues . . .
- Fortunato suspects nothing.
- He follows Montresor into the vaults.

What Does It Mean?
Absconded means "left quickly and secretly."

✔ Reading Check
What orders has the narrator given to his servants? Why has he given the orders?

More About . . .
(CATACOMBS) These are underground burial places that have many narrow passages.

READ ALOUD Lines 103–107
Imagine you are Montresor. Use your voice to convince Fortunato that you care about his health. Saying one thing but meaning another is an example of **verbal irony**.

FOCUS
Read to find out where the narrator leads Fortunato.

MARK IT UP As you read, circle statements that express the narrator's concern for his friend's health.

There were no attendants at home; they had absconded to make merry in honor of the time. I had told them that I should not return until the morning, and had given them explicit orders not to stir from the house. These orders were sufficient, I well knew, to insure their immediate disappearance, one and all, as soon as my back was turned.

I took from their sconces two flambeaux,[13] and giving one to Fortunato, bowed him through several suites of rooms to the archway that led into the vaults. I passed down a long and winding staircase, requesting him to be cautious as he followed. We came at length to the foot of the descent and stood together on the damp ground of the catacombs of the Montresors.

The gait of my friend was unsteady, and the bells upon his cap jingled as he strode.

"The pipe?" said he.

"It is farther on," said I; "but observe the white web-work which gleams from these cavern walls."

He turned toward me, and looked into my eyes with two filmy orbs that distilled the rheum of intoxication.[14]

"Niter?" he asked, at length.

"Niter," I replied. "How long have you had that cough?"

"Ugh! ugh! ugh!—ugh! ugh! ugh!—ugh! ugh! ugh!—ugh! ugh! ugh!—ugh! ugh! ugh!"

My poor friend found it impossible to reply for many minutes.

"It is nothing," he said, at last.

"Come," I said, with decision, "we will go back; your health is precious. You are rich, respected, admired, beloved; you are happy, as once I was. You are a man to be missed. For me it is no matter. We will go back; you will be ill, and I cannot be responsible. Besides, there is Luchesi—"

"Enough," he said; "the cough is a mere nothing; it will not kill me. I shall not die of a cough."

"True—true," I replied; "and, indeed, I had no intention of

---

13. from...flambeaux (flăm′bōz′): from their wall brackets two lighted torches.

14. filmy...intoxication: eyes clouded and watery from drunkenness.

alarming you unnecessarily; but you should use all proper caution. A draft of this Medoc[15] will defend us from the damps."

Here I knocked off the neck of a bottle that I drew from a long row of its fellows that lay upon the mold.

"Drink," I said, presenting him the wine.

He raised it to his lips with a leer. He paused and nodded to me familiarly, while his bells jingled.

"I drink," he said, "to the buried that repose around us."

"And I to your long life."

He again took my arm, and we proceeded.

"These vaults," he said, "are extensive."

"The Montresors," I replied, "were a great and numerous family."

"I forget your arms." [16]

"A huge human foot d'or,[17] in a field azure; the foot crushes a serpent rampant whose fangs are imbedded in the heel."

"And the motto?"

"*Nemo me impune lacessit.*"[18]

"Good!" he said.

Pause & Reflect

FOCUS

The two men continue down through the chambers. Read to find out what happens to Fortunato when they reach the last chamber.

The wine sparkled in his eyes and the bells jingled. My own fancy grew warm with the Medoc. We had passed through walls of piled bones, with casks and puncheons[19] intermingling, into the inmost recesses of the catacombs.

---

15. **Medoc** (mā-dôk′): a red Bordeaux wine.

16. **arms:** coat of arms—a design that represents one's ancestry and family heritage. (In the following paragraph, Montresor describes his family's coat of arms.)

17. **d'or** (dôr) *French:* gold colored.

18. *Nemo me impune lacessit* (nä′mō mā ĭm-pōō′nĕ lä-kĕs′ĭt) *Latin:* Nobody provokes me with impunity.

19. **casks and puncheons:** large containers for storing wine.

WORDS
TO
KNOW
    repose (rĭ-pōz′) *v.* to lie dead or at rest

What Does It Mean?
Here, *draft* means "drink," or "swallow."

Pause & Reflect

1. Review the statements you circled. Why is the narrator acting so concerned about Fortunato's health? **(Infer)**

_____

_____

_____

2. If you were Fortunato, would you be suspicious of the narrator? *Yes/No,* because _____

_____

_____.

(Connect)

As the story continues . . .
• Fortunato reaches the last chamber of the catacombs.
• Montresor begins to act out his plan of revenge.

What Does It Mean?
Fancy means "imagination."

I paused again, and this time I made bold to seize Fortunato
by an arm above the elbow.

"The niter!" I said; "see, it increases. It hangs like moss
140 upon the vaults. We are below the river's bed. The drops of
moisture trickle among the bones. Come, we will go back ere
it is too late. Your cough—"

"It is nothing," he said; "let us go on. But first, another
draft of the Medoc."

I broke and reached him a flagon of De Grâve.[20] He
emptied it at a breath. His eyes flashed with a fierce light. He
laughed and threw the bottle upward with a gesticulation[21] I
did not understand.

I looked at him in surprise. He repeated the movement—a
150 grotesque one.

"You do not comprehend?" he said.

"Not I," I replied.

"Then you are not of the brotherhood."

"How?"

"You are not of the masons."[22]

"Yes, yes," I said; "yes, yes."

"You? Impossible! A mason?"

"A mason," I replied.

"A sign," he said.

160 "It is this," I answered, producing a trowel from beneath
the folds of my *roquelaure*.

"You jest," he exclaimed, recoiling a few paces. "But let us
proceed to the Amontillado."

"Be it so," I said, replacing the tool beneath the cloak, and
again offering him my arm. He leaned upon it heavily. We
continued our route in search of the Amontillado. We passed
through a range of low arches, descended, passed on, and
descending again, arrived at a deep crypt,[23] in which the
foulness of the air caused our flambeaux rather to glow
170 than flame.

At the most remote end of the crypt there appeared another
less spacious. Its walls had been lined with human remains,
piled to the vault overhead, in the fashion of the great
catacombs of Paris. Three sides of this interior crypt were still

English Learner Support
LANGUAGE

Diction The highlighted
phrase means "another
crypt appeared that was
less spacious."

---

20. De Grâve (də gräv'): a red Bordeaux wine.

21. gesticulation (jə-stĭk'yə-lā'shən): a vigorous motion or gesture.

22. of the masons: a Freemason, a member of a social organization with secret
    rituals and signs.

23. crypt: an underground chamber serving as a burial place.

ornamented in this manner. From the fourth the bones had been thrown down, and lay promiscuously[24] upon the earth, forming at one point a mound of some size. Within the wall thus exposed by the displacing of the bones, we perceived a still interior recess, in depth about four feet, in width three, in height six or seven. It seemed to have been constructed for no especial use within itself, but formed merely the interval between two of the colossal supports of the roof of the catacombs, and was backed by one of their circumscribing walls of solid granite.

It was in vain that Fortunato, uplifting his dull torch, endeavored to pry into the depth of the recess. Its termination the feeble light did not enable us to see.

"Proceed," I said; "herein is the Amontillado. As for Luchesi—"

"He is an ignoramus," interrupted my friend, as he stepped unsteadily forward, while I followed immediately at his heels. In an instant he had reached the extremity of the niche, and finding his progress arrested by the rock, stood stupidly bewildered. A moment more and I had fettered him to the granite. In its surface were two iron staples, distant from each other about two feet, horizontally. From one of these depended a short chain, from the other a padlock. Throwing the links about his waist, it was but the work of a few seconds to secure it. He was too much astounded to resist. Withdrawing the key I stepped back from the recess.

"Pass your hand," I said, "over the wall; you cannot help feeling the niter. Indeed it is very damp. Once more let me *implore* you to return. No? Then I must positively leave you. But I must first render you all the little attentions in my power."

Pause **&** *Reflect*

---
24. **promiscuously** (prə-mĭs′kyōō-əs-lē): randomly.

WORDS TO KNOW	**termination** (tûr′mə-nā′shən) *n.* the end of something; limit or edge
	fetter (fĕt′ər) *v.* to restrain with chains or shackles
	implore (ĭm-plôr′) *v.* to beg, earnestly ask for

As the story ends . . .

- Montresor chains Fortunato to the wall.
- Montresor carries out his plan.

English Learner Support

Tier A *tier* is one in a series of rows that are placed one above the other. Montresor lays stones in rows one on top of the other to make a wall.

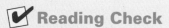

Reading Check

Describe how Montresor gets his revenge on Fortunato.

FOCUS

The story now takes a bizarre turn. Read to find out if the narrator succeeds in getting his revenge.

210

"The Amontillado!" ejaculated my friend, not yet recovered from his astonishment.

"True," I replied; "the Amontillado."

As I said these words I busied myself among the pile of bones of which I have before spoken. Throwing them aside, I soon uncovered a quantity of building stone and mortar. With these materials and with the aid of my trowel, I began vigorously to wall up the entrance of the niche.

I had scarcely laid the first tier of the masonry[25] when I discovered that the intoxication of Fortunato had in a great measure worn off. The earliest indication I had of this was a low moaning cry from the depth of the recess. It was *not* the 220 cry of a drunken man. There was then a long and obstinate silence. I laid the second tier, and the third, and the fourth; and then I heard the furious vibrations of the chain. The noise lasted for several minutes, during which, that I might hearken to it with the more satisfaction, I ceased my labors and sat down upon the bones. When at last the clanking subsided, I resumed the trowel, and finished without interruption the fifth, the sixth, and the seventh tier. The wall was now nearly upon a level with my breast. I again paused, and holding the flambeaux over the mason-work, threw a few feeble rays 230 upon the figure within.

A succession of loud and shrill screams, bursting suddenly from the throat of the chained form, seemed to thrust me violently back. For a brief moment I hesitated—I trembled. Unsheathing my rapier,[26] I began to grope with it about the recess; but the thought of an instant reassured me. I placed my hand upon the solid fabric of the catacombs, and felt satisfied. I reapproached the wall. I replied to the yells of him who clamored. I re-echoed—I aided—I surpassed them in volume and in strength. I did this, and the clamorer grew still.

240 It was now midnight, and my task was drawing to a close. I had completed the eighth, the ninth, and the tenth tier. I had

---

25. **masonry:** stonework.

26. **rapier** (rā′pē-ər): a long, slender sword.

WORDS
TO
KNOW

subside (səb-sīd′) *v.* to become less agitated or active; lessen

finished a portion of the last and the eleventh; there remained but a single stone to be fitted and plastered in. I struggled with its weight; I placed it partially in its <u>destined</u> position. But now there came from out the niche a low laugh that erected the hairs upon my head. It was succeeded by a sad voice, which I had difficulty in recognizing as that of the noble Fortunato. The voice said—

"Ha! ha! ha!—he! he!—a very good joke indeed—an excellent jest. We will have many a rich laugh about it at the palazzo—he! he! he! —over our wine—he! he! he!"

"The Amontillado!" I said.

"He! he! he!—he! he! he!—yes, the Amontillado. But is it not getting late? Will not they be awaiting us at the palazzo, the Lady Fortunato and the rest? Let us be gone."

"Yes," I said, "let us be gone."

"For the love of God, Montresor!"

"Yes," I said, "for the love of God!"

But to these words I hearkened in vain for a reply. I grew impatient. I called aloud,

"Fortunato!"

No answer. I called again,

"Fortunato!"

No answer still. I thrust a torch through the remaining aperture[27] and let it fall within. There came forth in return only a jingling of the bells. My heart grew sick—on account of the dampness of the catacombs. I hastened to make an end of my labor. I forced the last stone into its position; I plastered it up. Against the new masonry I re-erected the old rampart[28] of bones. For the half of a century no mortal has disturbed them. *In pace requiescat!*[29]

Pause & Reflect

---

27. **aperture** (ăp′ər-chər): an opening, such as a hole or a gap.
28. **rampart**: fortification, protective barrier.
29. *In pace requiescat* (ĭn pä′kĕ rĕ-kwē-ĕs′kät) *Latin:* May he rest in peace.

WORDS
TO
KNOW

destined (dĕs′tĭnd) *adj.* determined beforehand; fated
destine *v.*

English Learner Support
LANGUAGE

Diction The highlighted phrase could be rewritten as "But now a low laugh came out of the small hole."

More About . . .

BELLS The jingling of the bells on Fortunato's cap reminds you that he is wearing the costume of a court jester—a fool. Only a fool would have allowed himself to be so tricked.

Pause & Reflect

1. What is Fortunato's fate? **(Infer)**

_____

_____

MARK IT UP 2. Do you think Montresor ever hesitated in carrying out his plan for revenge? *Yes/No.* Underline passages in the text to support your opinion. **(Evaluate)**

CHALLENGE

What words and images does Poe use to build suspense and horror? Circle phrases that you thought were particularly effective. **(Author's Craft)**

The Cask of Amontillado **97**

Active Reading SkillBuilder

Making Inferences

Making an **inference** is figuring something out on the basis of evidence. Readers usually infer by combining clues in the text with what they already know from their own experiences or other reading. Think about the actions, thoughts, and feelings of the narrator in "The Cask of Amontillado." Look for insights into his motivation. Record any observations that provide clues about the narrator's state of mind.

What the Narrator Says	What I Can Infer
The thousand injuries of Fortunato I had borne as I best could; but when he ventured upon insult, I vowed revenge.	The narrator is a sensitive person who feels that he has been injured by Fortunato's insults.

Literary Analysis SkillBuilder

Mood

The overall feeling or atmosphere that a writer creates for the reader is called **mood.** Descriptive words, the setting, and figurative language, as well as the sound and rhythm of the language the writer uses, contribute to the mood of a work. On the chart below, list examples of passages that help create the mood of the story. Identify the kind of mood that is created and explain how the mood is developed.

Passage	Mood that Is Created	How Mood Is Developed
"We are below the river's bed. The drops of moisture trickle among the bones."	gloomy, creepy, chilly, dark and damp	descriptive words, setting

Follow Up: How do you react to the overall mood of this story? Discuss your thoughts and feelings with a group of classmates.

Words to Know SkillBuilder

Words to Know

accost	fetter	impunity	repose	termination
destined	implore	preclude	subside	virtuoso

A. Each of the following sentences suggests a word in the word list. The word itself is hidden in the sentence. Underline the hidden word and then write it on the line. An example, using another word from the story, has been done for you.

Example: Using a tool like a shovel, I dug the first row. Ellen came along behind me, putting the seeds in place.

_____*trowel*_____

The guy in the monster outfit stopped me with a paw and snarled right in my face. I said, "Back off, Mac. Costume party or no costume party, I'm not putting up with this."

_____
(1)

We'll scoop up the money and take off in the blimp. Unity is the key here. If we stick together, we'll get away with it for sure!

_____
(2)

Oh, no! An all-you-can-eat buffet! Terrible things will happen to my diet if you don't handcuff me and chain me to my chair!

_____
(3)

It has a certain poetic sound, but don't say, "He was bound from birth to be the baddest." In educated speech, that would be "Fated to be the worst," even if doesn't sound as good.

_____
(4)

In the book's drawings, cats of all kinds are posed on chairs and sofas, sleeping soundly and dreaming of mice.

_____
(5)

B. For each phrase in the first column, find the phrase in the second column that is closest in meaning. Write the letter of that phrase in the blank.

_____ 1. to ask again	A. virtuoso, better than so-so
_____ 2. to snugly rest	B. to implore some more
_____ 3. to decline everywhere	C. to fetter better
_____ 4. the end of a holiday	D. to cozily repose
_____ 5. highly skilled, above average	E. to subside worldwide
_____ 6. to more effectively restrain	F. to preclude a brooding mood
_____ 7. to prevent a sad frame of mind	G. an opportunity for impunity
_____ 8. the chance to avoid consequences	H. the termination of a vacation

C. Describe Montresor's crime in a statement that could be used to support a charge of murder against him. Use at least **five** of the Words to Know.

from

Angela's Ashes

Frank McCourt

Before You Read

Connect to Your Life

Cards, flowers, balloons—can any of these "get-well" gifts really make you feel better? Think about the last time you were sick. What cheered you or helped you pass the time? Write your answers in the web below.

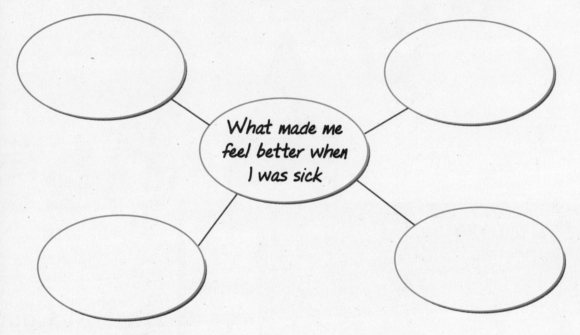

What made me feel better when I was sick

Key to the Memoir

WHAT YOU NEED TO KNOW A *memoir* describes an author's personal experience. In this excerpt, Frank McCourt recalls his childhood in Ireland. Frank's mother, Angela, struggled constantly to keep the family clothed and fed. She got help from local charities and the Irish welfare program, known as the *dole*. Three of Frank's siblings died from childhood diseases that might have been prevented with better living conditions and proper medical care.

from

Angela's Ashes

Frank McCourt

PREVIEW In this excerpt from his memoir, Frank McCourt recalls the time he spent in the hospital as a young boy. While Frank is there, he gets to know a girl named Patricia Madigan who gets him in trouble but also enriches his life in unexpected ways.

FOCUS
Young Frank is sent to the hospital with typhoid fever. Read to find out about his first days in the hospital.

MARK IT UP As you read, underline details that help you understand the seriousness of his illness. An example is highlighted.

Mam comes with Dr. Troy. He feels my forehead, rolls up my eyelids, turns me over to see my back, picks me up and runs to his motor car. Mam runs after him and he tells her I have typhoid fever. Mam cries, . . . am I to lose the whole family? Will it ever end? She gets into the car, holds me in her lap and moans all the way to the Fever Hospital at the City Home.

The bed has cool white sheets. The nurses have clean white uniforms and the nun, Sister Rita, is all in white.

Reading Tips

A **memoir** is a recollection of important events in the writer's life. Here is a strategy that can help you read this account.

• Although the events in this memoir happened to the author when he was a boy, he writes in the present tense—as if the events are happening now. Notice how this technique helps you see the events from young Frank's **point of view.**

MARK IT UP KEEP TRACK

As you read, you can use these marks to keep track of your understanding.

✔ ..... I understand.

? ..... I don't understand this.

! ..... Interesting or surprising idea

As the memoir begins . . .

• Frank is rushed to the hospital with typhoid fever.

• His mother is worried that Frank will die.

What Does It Mean?

Mam is what Frank calls his mother.

More About . . .

(FRANCIS) Throughout the story, Frank is also called Francis and Frankie. Francis is his given name, and Frank and Frankie are nicknames.

More About . . .

If typhoid is not treated with antibiotics, victims can develop a very high fever about a week after becoming ill. Those who survive this (crisis,) or danger point, have a good chance of recovery.

English Learner Support
VOCABULARY

Idiom To *drift off* means "to fall asleep."

English Learner Support
LANGUAGE

Grammar The author does not use quotation marks when he writes dialogue. To keep track of who is talking, write each speaker's name in the margin.

What Does It Mean?

Sister is a title given to a nun, or a Catholic woman who is devoted to religious service. A *habit* is the dress and head-piece a nun wears.

Dr. Humphrey and Dr. Campbell have white coats and things hanging from their necks which they stick against my chest and all over. I sleep and sleep but I'm awake when they bring in jars of bright red stuff that hang from tall poles above my bed and they stick tubes into my ankles and the back of my right hand. Sister Rita says, You're getting blood, (Francis.)
20 Soldier's blood from the Sarsfield Barracks.

Mam is sitting by the bed and the nurse is saying, You know, missus, this is very unusual.

No one is ever allowed into the Fever Hospital for fear they'd catch something but they made an <u>exception</u> for you with his (crisis) coming. If he gets over this he'll surely recover.

I fall asleep. Mam is gone when I wake but there's movement in the room and it's the priest, Father Gorey, from the Confraternity[1] saying Mass at a table in the corner. I drift off again and now they're waking me and pulling down the
30 bedclothes. Father Gorey is touching me with oil and praying in Latin. I know it's Extreme Unction[2] and that means I'm going to die and I don't care. They wake me again to receive Communion. I don't want it, I'm afraid I might get sick. I keep the wafer on my tongue and fall asleep and when I wake up again it's gone.

It's dark and Dr. Campbell is sitting by my bed. He's holding my wrist and looking at his watch. He has red hair and glasses and he always smiles when he talks to me. He sits now and hums and looks out the window. His eyes close and
40 he snores a little. . . .

Sister Rita's white habit is bright in the sun that comes in the window. She's holding my wrist, looking at her watch, smiling. Oh, she says, we're awake, are we? Well, Francis, I think we've come through the worst. Our prayers are answered and all the prayers of those hundreds of little boys at the Confraternity. Can you imagine that? Hundreds of boys saying the rosary[3] for you and offering up their communion.

---

1. **Confraternity:** (kŏn′frə-tûr′nĭ-tē) a religious society or association.
2. **Extreme Unction** (ŭngk′shən): in the Roman Catholic faith, the sacrament given to a person who is in danger of dying.
3. **rosary** (rō′zə-rē): a series of prayers repeated by Roman Catholics as a form of devotion to the Virgin Mary—usually counted off on a string of beads as they are said.

WORDS TO KNOW

exception (ĭk-sĕp′shən) *n.* a case in which a rule does not apply

My ankles and the back of my hand are throbbing from the tubes bringing in the blood and I don't care about boys praying for me. I can hear the swish of Sister Rita's habit and the click of her rosary beads when she leaves the room. I fall asleep and when I wake it's dark and Dad is sitting by the bed with his hand on mine.

Son, are you awake?

I try to talk but I'm dry, nothing will come out and I point to my mouth. He holds a glass of water to my lips and it's sweet and cool. He presses my hand and says I'm a great old soldier and why wouldn't I? Don't I have the soldier's blood in me?

The tubes are not in me anymore and the glass jars are gone.

Sister Rita comes in and tells Dad he has to go. I don't want him to go because he looks sad. When he looks sad it's the worst thing in the world and I start crying. Now what's this? says Sister Rita. Crying with all that soldier blood in you? There's a big surprise for you tomorrow, Francis. You'll never guess. Well, I'll tell you, we're bringing you a nice biscuit[4] with your tea in the morning. Isn't that a treat? And your father will be back in a day or two, won't you, Mr. McCourt?

Dad nods and puts his hand on mine again. He looks at me, steps away, stops, comes back, kisses me on the forehead for the first time in my life and I'm so happy I feel like floating out of the bed.

The other two beds in my room are empty. The nurse says I'm the only typhoid patient and I'm a miracle for getting over the crisis.

Pause & *Reflect*

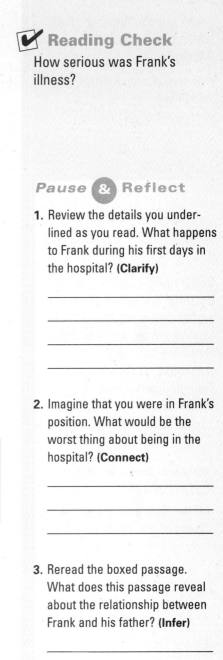

✔ **Reading Check**

How serious was Frank's illness?

Pause & **Reflect**

1. Review the details you underlined as you read. What happens to Frank during his first days in the hospital? **(Clarify)**

   _____

   _____

   _____

   _____

2. Imagine that you were in Frank's position. What would be the worst thing about being in the hospital? **(Connect)**

   _____

   _____

   _____

3. Reread the boxed passage. What does this passage reveal about the relationship between Frank and his father? **(Infer)**

   _____

   _____

   _____

4. biscuit: cookie.

As the memoir
continues . . .

- Frank talks to the only other patient near him, Patricia Madigan.

- The two young patients get in trouble.

More About . . .

DIPHTHERIA *Diphtheria* is a bacterial disease that causes a gray coating to form in the victim's throat. It can result in breathing difficulties, high fever, weakness, and even death. Though diphtheria is rare in the United States, it still affects people in developing countries.

English Learner Support
LANGUAGE

Idiom *Foreign parts* means "parts of the world other than Ireland," or "other countries."

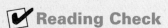 **Reading Check**

What does Patricia want to know about Frank?

English Learner Support
LANGUAGE

Figure of Speech *Put in the soldier's blood* means that the doctors gave Frank a blood transfusion because he needed more blood.

FOCUS
Read to find out about Frank's fellow patient, Patricia Madigan.
MARK IT UP As you read, circle details that help you get to know her.

The room next to me is empty till one morning a girl's voice says, Yoo hoo, who's there?

I'm not sure if she's talking to me or someone in the room beyond.

Yoo hoo, boy with the typhoid, are you awake?

I am.

Are you better?

I am.

Well, why are you here?

I don't know. I'm still in the bed. They stick needles in me and give me medicine.

What do you look like?

I wonder, What kind of a question is that? I don't know what to tell her.

Yoo hoo, are you there, typhoid boy?

I am.

What's your name?

Frank.

That's a good name. My name is Patricia Madigan. How old are you?

Ten.

Oh. She sounds disappointed.

But I'll be eleven in August, next month.

Well, that's better than ten. I'll be fourteen in September. Do you want to know why I'm in the Fever Hospital?

I do.

I have diphtheria and something else.

What's something else?

They don't know. They think I have a disease from foreign parts because my father used to be in Africa. I nearly died. Are you going to tell me what you look like?

I have black hair.

You and millions.

I have brown eyes with bits of green that's called hazel.

You and thousands.

I have stitches on the back of my right hand and my two feet where they put in the soldier's blood.

Oh, . . . did they?

They did.

You won't be able to stop marching and saluting.

120 There's a swish of habit and click of beads and then Sister Rita's voice. Now, now, what's this? There's to be no talking between two rooms especially when it's a boy and a girl. Do you hear me, Patricia?

I do, Sister.

Do you hear me, Francis?

I do, Sister.

You could be giving thanks for your two remarkable recoveries. You could be saying the rosary. You could be reading *The Little Messenger of the Sacred Heart*[5] that's
130 beside your beds. Don't let me come back and find you talking. She comes into my room and wags her finger at me. Especially you, Francis, after thousands of boys prayed for you at the Confraternity. Give thanks, Francis, give thanks.

She leaves and there's silence for awhile. Then Patricia whispers, Give thanks, Francis, give thanks, and say your rosary, Francis, and I laugh so hard a nurse runs in to see if I'm all right. She's a very stern nurse from the County Kerry and she frightens me. What's this, Francis? Laughing? What
140 is there to laugh about? Are you and that Madigan girl talking? I'll report you to Sister Rita. There's to be no laughing for you could be doing serious damage to your internal apparatus.[6]

She plods out and Patricia whispers again in a heavy Kerry accent, No laughing, Francis, you could be doin' serious damage to your internal apparatus. Say your rosary, Francis, and pray for your internal apparatus.

Mam visits me on Thursdays, I'd like to see my father, too, but I'm out of danger, crisis time is over, and I'm
150 allowed only one visitor. Besides, she says, he's back at work at Rank's Flour Mills and please God this job will last a while with the war on and the English desperate for flour. She brings me a chocolate bar and that proves Dad is working. She could never afford it on the dole.[7] He sends me notes. He tells me my brothers are all praying for me, that I should be a good boy, obey the doctors, the nuns, the

READ ALOUD Lines 121–134
Use your voice to express Sister Rita's personality.

More About...

COUNTY KERRY The Republic of Ireland has twenty-six counties, or territorial divisions. The people from these different counties may each speak with distinct accents and dialects. County Kerry is located in southwest Ireland.

✔ **Reading Check**
Why does Frank laugh when Patricia says, "Give thanks, Francis"?

English Learner Support
LANGUAGE

Dialect *Doin'* is short for "doing."

✔ **Reading Check**
How does Patricia help Frank pass the time?

---

5. **The Little...Heart:** a Roman Catholic magazine.

6. **internal apparatus** (ăp′ə-rā′təs): the internal organs of the body.

7. **on the dole:** receiving government unemployment payments.

Pause **&** Reflect

Look back at the details you circled as you read. Is Patricia Madigan the kind of person you'd like to get to know? *Yes/No*, because_____

_____

_____.

(Connect)

As the memoir continues . . .

- Patricia starts teaching Frank a poem.

- Frank thinks "The Highwayman" is almost as good as Shakespeare.

- The nurse is upset to find Patricia and Frank talking together.

What Does It Mean?

The highlighted words mean that Seamus will need to beg for money if he loses his job at the hospital.

✔ **Reading Check**

How would you describe Sister Rita?

nurses, and don't forget to say my prayers. He's sure St. Jude pulled me through the crisis because he's the patron saint of desperate cases and I was indeed a desperate case.

Pause **&** Reflect

160 **FOCUS**

Patricia lends Frank a book about English history. She also reads "The Highwayman," a poem about a daring robber who falls in love with a woman named Bess. Read to find out how this exchange gets the patients in trouble.

Patricia says she has two books by her bed. One is a poetry book and that's the one she loves. The other is a short history of England and do I want it? She gives it to Seamus, the man who mops the floors every day, and he brings it to me. He says, I'm not supposed to be bringing anything from a diphtheria room to a typhoid room with all the germs flying around and hiding between 170 the pages and if you ever catch diphtheria on top of the typhoid they'll know and I'll lose my good job and be out on the street singing patriotic songs with a tin cup in my hand, which I could easily do because there isn't a song ever written about Ireland's sufferings I don't know. . . .

Oh, yes, he knows Roddy McCorley. He'll sing it for me right enough but he's barely into the first verse when the Kerry nurse rushes in. What's this, Seamus? Singing? Of all the people in this hospital you should know the rules against singing. I have a good mind to report you to Sister Rita.

180 Ah, . . . don't do that, nurse.

Very well, Seamus. I'll let it go this one time. You know the singing could lead to a <u>relapse</u> in these patients.

When she leaves he whispers he'll teach me a few songs because singing is good for passing the time when you're by yourself in a typhoid room. He says Patricia is a lovely girl the way she often gives him sweets from the parcel her mother sends every fortnight.[8] He stops mopping the floor and calls to

---

8. **fortnight:** two weeks.

WORDS
TO
KNOW

relapse (rē'lăps) *n.* a worsening of an illness after a partial recovery

Patricia in the next room, I was telling Frankie you're a lovely girl, Patricia, and she says, You're a lovely man, Seamus. He smiles because he's an old man of forty and he never had children but the ones he can talk to here in the Fever Hospital. He says, Here's the book, Frankie. Isn't it a great pity you have to be reading all about England after all they did to us, that there isn't a history of Ireland to be had in this hospital.

The book tells me all about King Alfred and William the Conqueror and all the kings and queens down to Edward, who had to wait forever for his mother, Victoria, to die before he could be king. The book has the first bit of Shakespeare I ever read.

> I do believe, <u>induced</u> by <u>potent</u> circumstances
> That thou art mine enemy.

The history writer says this is what Catherine, who is a wife of Henry the Eighth, says to Cardinal Wolsey, who is trying to have her head cut off. I don't know what it means and I don't care because it's Shakespeare and it's like having jewels in my mouth when I say the words. If I had a whole book of Shakespeare they could keep me in the hospital for a year.

Patricia says she doesn't know what induced means or potent circumstances and she doesn't care about Shakespeare, she has her poetry book and she reads to me from beyond the wall a poem about an owl and a pussycat that went to sea in a green boat with honey and money[9] and it makes no sense and when I say that Patricia gets huffy and says that's the last poem she'll ever read to me. She says I'm always <u>reciting</u> the lines from Shakespeare and they make no sense either. Seamus stops mopping again and tells us we shouldn't be fighting over poetry because we'll have enough to fight about when we grow up and get married. Patricia says she's sorry and I'm sorry too so she reads me part of another poem which I have to remember so I can say it back to her

---

9. **a poem...money:** "The Owl and the Pussycat," a humorous poem by the 19th-century British poet and artist Edward Lear.

WORDS
TO
KNOW

induced (rē'lăps) *adj.* persuaded, influenced **induce** *v.*
potent (pōt'nt) *adj.* powerful
recite (rĭ-sīt') *v.* to say out loud something memorized

from **Angela's Ashes** **109**

More About . . .
ENGLAND AND IRELAND
England and Ireland fought about land and religion for hundreds of years. England continually tried to control Ireland's land, government, and religion.

MARK IT UP WORD POWER

Remember to mark words that you'd like to add to your **Personal Word List.** Later, you can record the words and their meanings beginning on page 402.

✔ **Reading Check**
Describe Frank's reaction to reading Shakespeare for the first time.

English Learner Support
VOCABULARY

Huffy means "annoyed" or "offended."

What Does It Mean?

A *highwayman* is a person who robs travelers on public roads. To Frank, the poem is exciting and romantic.

What Does It Mean?

British soldiers were nick-named *redcoats* because of the bright red jackets they wore.

English Learner Support
LANGUAGE

Dialect *Ye* is a shortened version of "you." *'Tis* is a shortened version of "it is," and *o'* is a shortened version of "of."

 **Reading Check**

What does Frank like about "The Highwayman"?

---

early in the morning or late at night when there are no nuns or nurses about,

> *The wind was a <u>torrent</u> of darkness among the gusty trees,*
> *The moon was a ghostly galleon tossed upon cloudy seas,*
> *The road was a ribbon of moonlight over the purple moor,*
> *And the highwayman came riding*
> *Riding riding*
> 230 *The highwayman came riding, up to the old inn-door.*
> *He'd a French cocked-hat on his forehead, a bunch of lace*
>   *at his chin,*
> *A coat of the claret velvet, and breeches of brown doe-skin,*
> *They fitted with never a wrinkle, his boots were up*
>   *to the thigh.*
> *And he rode with a jeweled twinkle,*
> *His pistol butts a-twinkle,*
> *His rapier hilt a-twinkle, under the jeweled sky.*[10]

Every day I can't wait for the doctors and nurses to leave
240 me alone so I can learn a new verse from Patricia and find out what's happening to the highwayman and the landlord's red-lipped daughter. I love the poem because it's exciting and almost as good as my two lines of Shakespeare. The redcoats are after the highwayman because they know he told her, I'll come to thee by moonlight, . . .

I'd love to do that myself, come by moonlight for Patricia in the next room. . . . She's ready to read the last few verses when in comes the nurse from Kerry shouting at her, shouting at me, I told ye there was to be no talking between rooms.
250 Diphtheria is never allowed to talk to typhoid and visa versa. I warned ye. And she calls out, Seamus, take this one. Take the by.[11] Sister Rita said one more word out of him and upstairs with him. We gave ye a warning to stop the blathering but ye wouldn't. Take the by, Seamus, take him.

Ah, now, nurse, sure isn't he harmless. 'Tis only a bit o' poetry.

Take that by, Seamus, take him at once.

---

10. **The wind...jeweled sky:** the opening lines of "The Highwayman," a narrative poem by the 20th-century British writer Alfred Noyes.

11. **by:** boy (spelled thus to indicate the nurse's dialectical pronunciation).

WORDS TO KNOW   **torrent** (tôr′ənt) *n.* a rushing stream

He bends over me and whispers, Ah, . . . I'm sorry, Frankie. Here's your English history book. He slips the book under my shirt and lifts me from the bed. He whispers that I'm a feather. I try to see Patricia when we pass through her room but all I can make out is a blur of dark head on a pillow.

Sister Rita stops us in the hall to tell me I'm a great disappointment to her, that she expected me to be a good boy after what God had done for me, after all the prayers said by hundreds of boys at the Confraternity, after all the care from the nuns and nurses of the Fever Hospital, after the way they let my mother and father in to see me, a thing rarely allowed, and this is how I repaid them lying in the bed reciting silly poetry back and forth with Patricia Madigan knowing very well there was a ban on all talk between typhoid and diphtheria. She says I'll have plenty of time to reflect on my sins in the big ward upstairs and I should beg forgiveness for my disobedience reciting a <u>pagan</u> English poem about a thief on a horse and a maiden with red lips who commits a terrible sin when I could have been praying or reading the life of a saint. She made it her business to read that poem so she did and I'd be well advised to tell the priest in confession.

The Kerry nurse follows us upstairs gasping and holding on to the banister. She tells me I better not get the notion she'll be running up to this part of the world every time I have a little pain or a twinge.

Pause & Reflect

FOCUS

Frank is now separated from his new friend. Read to find out what happens to Patricia.

There are twenty beds in the ward, all white, all empty. The nurse tells Seamus put me at the far end of the ward against the wall to make sure I don't talk to anyone who might be passing the door, which is very unlikely since there isn't another soul on this whole floor. She tells Seamus this was the fever ward

Pause & Reflect

1. What trouble results from the reading of "The Highwayman"? **(Cause and Effect)**

_____

_____

_____

_____

2. Sister Rita is quite upset by the sharing of the poem. Circle two statements that tell why. **(Infer)**

She thinks the poem is sinful.

She fears that the poetry will tire the children.

She is annoyed that the children broke the rules.

She doesn't know how to read.

3. Seamus is the janitor, the man who mops the floors. How would you describe his feelings about Patricia and Frank? **(Draw Conclusions)**

_____

_____

_____

_____

As the memoir continues . . .

• Frank is moved into a room by himself.

• Seamus is worried about Patricia.

WORDS
TO
KNOW

pagan (pā′gən) *adj.* non-Christian

More About . . .

(THE GREAT FAMINE) During the Great Famine (1845–1849), a plant disease ruined Ireland's potato crop. Potatoes were the main food of the Irish people. Hundreds of thousands of people died from hunger and disease. More than a million people emigrated to the United States. By 1851, the Irish population had dropped from about 8.5 million to 6.5 million.

during (the Great Famine[12]) long ago and only God knows how many died here brought in too late for anything but a wash before they were buried and there are stories of cries and moans in the far reaches of the night. She says 'twould break your heart to think of what the English did to us, that if they didn't put the blight[13] on the potato they didn't do much to take it off. No pity. No feeling at all for the people that died in this very ward, children suffering and dying here while the English feasted on roast beef and guzzled the best of wine in their big houses, little children with their mouths all green from trying to eat the grass in the fields beyond, God bless us and save us and guard us from future famines.

Seamus says 'twas a terrible thing indeed and he wouldn't want to be walking these halls in the dark with all the little green mouths gaping at him. The nurse takes my temperature, 'Tis up a bit, have a good sleep for yourself now that you're away from the chatter with Patricia Madigan below who will never know a gray hair.[14]

She shakes her head at Seamus and he gives her a sad shake back.

Nurses and nuns never think you know what they're talking about. If you're ten going on eleven you're supposed to be simple like my uncle Pat Sheehan who was dropped on his head. You can't ask questions. You can't show you understand what the nurse said about Patricia Madigan, that she's going to die, and you can't show you want to cry over this girl who taught you a lovely poem which the nun says is bad.

The nurse tells Seamus she has to go and he's to sweep the lint from under my bed and mop up a bit around the ward. Seamus tells me . . . that you can't catch a disease from . . . he never heard the likes of it, a little fella shifted upstairs for saying a poem and he has a good mind to go to the *Limerick Leader*[15] and tell them print the whole thing except he has this job and he'd lose it if ever Sister Rita found out. Anyway,

---

12. **Great Famine** (făm′ĭn): a devastating food shortage in Ireland in the late 1840s, caused by a failure of the potato crop. Almost a million Irish people died of starvation during the famine, and about 1.5 million emigrated, mainly to the United States.

13. **blight:** a plant disease—in this case, the one that destroyed the Irish potato crop.

14. **never know a gray hair:** won't live to be old.

15. *Limerick Leader:* a newspaper published in the Irish city of Limerick.

Frankie, you'll be outa here one of these fine days and you can read all the poetry you want though I don't know about Patricia below, I don't know about Patricia. . . .

He knows about Patricia in two days because she got out of the bed to go to the lavatory when she was supposed to use a bedpan and collapsed and died in the lavatory. Seamus is mopping the floor and there are tears on his cheeks and he's saying, 'Tis a dirty rotten thing to die in a lavatory when you're lovely in yourself. She told me she was sorry she had you reciting that poem and getting you shifted from the room, Frankie. She said 'twas all her fault.

It wasn't, Seamus.

I know and didn't I tell her that.

Pause & Reflect

FOCUS
Read to find out how Frank finally learns the ending of "The Highwayman."

Patricia is gone and I'll never know what happened to the highwayman and Bess, the landlord's daughter. I ask Seamus but he doesn't know any poetry at all especially English poetry. He knew an Irish poem once but it was about fairies and had no sign of a highwayman in it. Still he'll ask the men in his local pub where there's always someone reciting something and he'll bring it back to me. Won't I be busy meanwhile reading my short history of England and finding out all about their perfidy. That's what Seamus says, perfidy, and I don't know what it means and he doesn't know what it means but if it's something the English do it must be terrible.

He comes three times a week to mop the floor and the nurse is there every morning to take my temperature and pulse. The doctor listens to my chest with the thing hanging from his neck. They all say, And how's our little soldier today? A girl with a blue dress brings meals three times a day and never talks to me. Seamus says she's not right in the head so don't say a word to her.

What Does It Mean?
A *lavatory* is a bathroom.

Pause & Reflect

1. What happens to Patricia? **(Clarify)**

_____

_____

2. Reread the boxed passage on page 112. Underline the clues that hint at Patricia's fate. **(Infer)**

As the memoir ends . . .

• Frank thinks he'll never know how the poem ends.

• He begins learning how to walk again.

More About . . .

PUBS Ireland is famous for its public houses, or *pubs.* These neighborhood gathering places serve alcohol and light meals. Before the invention of radio and television, reciting poetry and singing songs was a form of entertainment in many Irish homes. The tradition extended to the local pubs.

WORDS
TO
KNOW

perfidy (pŭr′fĭ-dē) *n.* dishonesty; treachery

The July days are long and I fear the dark. There are only two ceiling lights in the ward and they're switched off when the tea tray is taken away and the nurse gives me pills. The nurse tells me go to sleep but I can't because I see people in the nineteen beds in the ward all dying and green around their mouths where they tried to eat grass and moaning for soup Protestant soup[16] any soup and I cover my face with the pillow hoping they won't come and stand around the bed clawing at me and howling for bits of the chocolate bar my mother brought last week.

No, she didn't bring it. She had to send it in because I can't have any more visitors. Sister Rita tells me a visit to the Fever Hospital is a <u>privilege</u> and after my bad behavior with Patricia Madigan and that poem I can't have the privilege anymore. She says I'll be going home in a few weeks and my job is to concentrate on getting better and learn to walk again after being in bed for six weeks and I can get out of bed tomorrow after breakfast. I don't know why she says I have to learn how to walk when I've been walking since I was a baby but when the nurse stands me by the side of the bed I fall to the floor and the nurse laughs, See, you're a baby again.

I practice walking from bed to bed back and forth back and forth. I don't want to be a baby. I don't want to be in this empty ward with no Patricia and no highwayman and no red-lipped landlord's daughter. I don't want the ghosts of children with green mouths pointing bony fingers at me and <u>clamoring</u> for bits of my chocolate bar.

Seamus says a man in his pub knew all the verses of the highwayman poem and it has a very sad end. Would I like him to say it because he never learned how to read and he had to carry the poem in his head? He stands in the middle of the ward leaning on his mop and recites,

Tlot-tlot, in the frosty silence! Tlot-tlot in the echoing
    night!
Nearer he came and nearer! Her face was like a light!
Her eyes grew wide for a moment, she drew one last deep
    breath,

Reading Check

In line 376, Frank says that he has been walking since he was a baby. Why does he have to learn how to walk now?

---

16. **Protestant soup:** soup provided by the hated English.

WORDS
TO
KNOW

privilege (prĭv′və-lĭj) *n.* a special benefit or advantage
clamoring (klăm′ər-ĭng) *adj.* making loud demands;
crying out **clamor** *v.*

Then her finger moved in the moonlight,
Her musket shattered the moonlight,
Shattered her breast in the moonlight and warned him—
with her death.

He hears the shot and escapes but when he learns at dawn
how Bess died he goes into a rage and returns for revenge
only to be shot down by the redcoats.

Blood-red were his spurs in the golden noon; wine-red was
his velvet coat,
When they shot him down on the highway,
Down like a dog on the highway,
And he lay in his blood on the highway, with a bunch of
lace at his throat.

Seamus wipes his sleeve across his face and sniffles. He
says, There was no call at all to shift you up here away from
Patricia when you didn't even know what happened to the
highwayman and Bess. 'Tis a very sad story and when I said it
to my wife she wouldn't stop crying the whole night till we
went to bed. She said there was no call for them redcoats to
shoot that highwayman, they are responsible for half the
troubles of the world and they never had any pity on the Irish,
either. Now if you want to know any more poems, Frankie,
tell me and I'll get them from the pub and bring 'em back in
my head.

Pause & Reflect

Pause & Reflect

1. How does Frank find out the ending of the poem? **(Clarify)**

_____

_____

_____

_____

2. What happens to Bess and the highwayman in the poem? **(Clarify)**

_____

_____

_____

3. Seamus cries after reciting the poem and says there was "no call at all" to separate Frank from Patricia. Why is Seamus still so upset by this incident? **(Draw Conclusions)**

_____

_____

_____

_____

CHALLENGE

Based on this selection, what do you think life was like in Ireland in the 1940s? Circle passages that support your opinions. **(Evaluate)**

Active Reading SkillBuilder

Making Inferences

Every time people use bits of evidence to figure something out, they are **making inferences.** They are combining facts with what they already know from personal experience. Making inferences is an important skill in reading nonfiction as well as fiction. It allows readers to learn more about people, places, or events that they encounter in their reading. As you read this excerpt from *Angela's Ashes,* record the facts you learn from your reading and any inferences you make. Also record other clues that help you make the inferences.

What I Know as Fact	What I Can Infer	Other Clues That Led to Inference
Frank's father kissed him for the first time in the hospital.	Frank's father is not demonstrative but he still loves Frank.	

Literary Analysis SkillBuilder

Memoir

In a **memoir,** a writer usually describes important events from his or her own life. Most memoirs share the following characteristics:

• They use the first-person point of view.

• They are true accounts of actual events.

• Although basically personal, they may also deal with historical events or social issues.

• They often include the writer's feelings and opinions about historical or social issues.

On the chart below, list instances from the excerpt from *Angela's Ashes* where the author refers to historical or social issues. Also, describe any opinions about these issues that are expressed either by the author or by someone else in the selection.

from Angela's Ashes	
References to Historical or Social Issues	Opinions Expressed
The war	Good for jobs

Follow Up: What does the evidence in your chart tell you about Ireland and the Irish people during the time in which this memoir was written?

Words to Know SkillBuilder

Words to Know

clamoring	induced	perfidy	privilege	relapse
exception	pagan	potent	recite	torrent

A. Complete each analogy with one of the words above. In an analogy, the last two words must be related in the same way that the first two are related.

1. SLOW : RAPID : : weak : _____

2. GOODNESS : EVIL : : honesty : _____

3. AFFECTED : CAUSED : : influenced : _____

4. HEALTH : ILLNESS : : recovery : _____

5. BELIEF : FAITH : : heathen : _____

6. SNOWSTORM : BLIZZARD : : flood : _____

7. EAR : LISTEN : : mouth : _____

8. LAW : EXEMPTION : : rule : _____

B. Circle the word in each group that is closest in meaning to the boldfaced word.

1. **perfidy**	doubt	treachery	alarm	confusion
2. **pagan**	worker	leader	promoter	heathen
3. **privilege**	advantage	reward	idleness	mystery
4. **potent**	disturbing	weak	powerful	wicked
5. **induced**	forced	influenced	prevented	accomplished
6. **clamoring**	speaking	objecting	listening	demanding
7. **relapse**	worsening	restriction	interruption	surprise

C. Write several interview questions for a magazine interview with Frank McCourt. Use at least **four** of the Words to Know.

A Christmas Memory

Truman Capote

Before You Read

Connect to Your Life

What special family holiday traditions do you observe each year?
Write your responses in the chart below.

HOLIDAY	TRADITION

Key to the Story

WHAT YOU NEED TO KNOW "A Christmas Memory" is based on real
people from Truman Capote's childhood. In 1928, when Capote was five
years old, he went to live with his mother's cousins. The oldest cousin,
Jenny Faulk, ran a hat shop in Monroeville, Alabama. She took several
young relatives into her home out of a sense of family duty, but she
showed the children little affection. Jenny's sister, Sook Faulk, also lived
in the house. In this selection, Capote remembers Miss Sook as his best
and wisest friend.

A Christmas Memory

Truman Capote

PREVIEW   This short story is set in an old house in rural Alabama in the 1930s. The narrator, Buddy, recalls the last Christmas season he shared with his "best friend," an elderly female cousin. Buddy was seven years old at the time.

SHORT STORY

Reading Tips

"A Christmas Memory" is a work of **autobiographical fiction**. It is drawn from the writer's memories of a real person from his past and of the actual experiences they shared.

- Read the first few paragraphs slowly to get a feel for the **setting** and **main character**.

- Some of Capote's descriptions are complicated and difficult to understand. Don't get caught up in phrases you don't understand. Mark the passages that confuse you and move on. Focus on the main ideas of the story and come back to untangle the difficult passages after you have finished reading.

FOCUS

The narrator begins by setting the scene and describing his best friend.

MARK IT UP   As you read, circle the words and phrases that help you to picture the friend and to understand her. Examples are highlighted.

Imagine a morning in late November. A coming of winter morning more than twenty years ago.

Consider the kitchen of a spreading old house in a country town. A great black stove is its main feature; but there is also a big round table and a fireplace with two rocking chairs placed in front of it. Just today the fireplace commenced its seasonal roar.

A woman with shorn white hair is standing at the kitchen window. She is wearing tennis shoes and a shapeless gray sweater over a summery calico dress. She is small and sprightly, like a bantam hen; but, due to a long youthful illness, her shoulders are pitifully hunched. Her face is remarkable—not unlike Lincoln's, craggy like that, and tinted by sun and wind; but it is delicate too, finely boned, and her eyes are sherry-colored and timid. "Oh my," she exclaims, her breath smoking the windowpane, "it's fruitcake weather!"

As the story begins...

- The narrator recalls events that happened at Christmas when he lived with his cousins in Alabama.

- He describes his best friend.

English Learner Support

CULTURE

Traditions A *fruitcake* is a cake made with spices, nuts, and candied or dried fruits. Fruitcake is a traditional food served at Christmastime.

Pause & Reflect

1. Review the details you marked. Circle any phrases below that describe the narrator's friend. **(Clarify)**

   weathered skin and
     short white hair

   small, lively, and tough

   fashionable

   simple and sensitive

![pencil] **MARK IT UP**   2. Reread the boxed passage on this page. Underline the words and phrases that show the relationship between the two main characters. **(Clarify)**

As the story continues...

- Buddy and his friend gather pecans.

- They count the money in their Fruitcake Fund.

What Does It Mean?

Paraphernalia means "items used for a particular activity." Here, the narrator refers to items needed for a picnic, such as sandwiches, fruit, napkins, and cups.

20   The person to whom she is speaking is myself. I am seven; she is sixty-something. We are cousins, very distant ones, and we have lived together—well, as long as I can remember. Other people inhabit the house, relatives; and though they have power over us, and frequently make us cry, we are not, on the whole, too much aware of them. We are each other's best friend. She calls me Buddy, in memory of a boy who was formerly her best friend. The other Buddy died in the 1880's, when she was still a child. She is still a child.

"I knew it before I got out of bed," she says, turning away 30 from the window with a purposeful excitement in her eyes. "The courthouse bell sounded so cold and clear. And there were no birds singing; they've gone to warmer country, yes indeed. Oh, Buddy, stop stuffing biscuit and fetch our buggy. Help me find my hat. We've thirty cakes to bake."

Pause & Reflect

FOCUS

Every year, Buddy and his friend make Christmas fruitcakes to give as gifts. Read to find out how they get the ingredients they need.

40 ![pencil] **MARK IT UP** As you read, note in the margins how they get money for their supplies.

It's always the same: a morning arrives in November, and my friend, as though officially <u>inaugurating</u> the Christmas time of year that <u>exhilarates</u> her imagination and fuels the blaze of her heart, announces: "It's fruitcake weather! Fetch our buggy. Help me find my hat."

The hat is found, a straw cartwheel corsaged with velvet roses out-of-doors has faded: it once belonged to a more fashionable relative. Together, we guide our buggy, a dilapidated baby carriage, out to the garden and into a grove of pecan trees. The buggy is mine; that is, it was bought for me when I was born. It is made of wicker, rather unraveled, 50 and the wheels wobble like a drunkard's legs. But it is a faithful object; springtimes, we take it to the woods and fill it with flowers, herbs, wild fern for our porch pots; in the summer, we pile it with picnic paraphernalia and sugar-cane fishing poles and roll it down to the edge of a creek; it has its

WORDS
TO
KNOW

inaugurate (ĭn-ô′gyə-rāt′) *v.* to make a formal beginning of

exhilarate (ig-zĭl′ə-rāt′) *v.* to make merry or lively

winter uses, too: as a truck for hauling firewood from the yard to the kitchen, as a warm bed for Queenie, our tough little orange and white rat terrier who has survived distemper[1] and two rattlesnake bites. Queenie is trotting beside it now.

Three hours later we are back in the kitchen hulling a
60 heaping buggyload of windfall pecans. Our backs hurt from gathering them: how hard they were to find (the main crop having been shaken off the trees and sold by the orchard's owners, who are not us) among the concealing leaves, the frosted, deceiving grass. Caarackle! A cheery crunch, scraps of miniature thunder sound as the shells collapse and the golden mound of sweet oily ivory meat mounts in the milk-glass bowl. Queenie begs to taste, and now and again my friend sneaks her a mite, though insisting we deprive ourselves. "We mustn't, Buddy. If we start, we won't stop. And there's
70 scarcely enough as there is. For thirty cakes." The kitchen is growing dark. Dusk turns the window into a mirror: our reflections mingle with the rising moon as we work by the fireside in the firelight. At last, when the moon is quite high, we toss the final hull into the fire and, with joined sighs, watch it catch flame. The buggy is empty, the bowl is brimful.

We eat our supper (cold biscuits, bacon, blackberry jam) and discuss tomorrow. Tomorrow the kind of work I like best begins: buying. Cherries and citron, ginger and vanilla and canned Hawaiian pineapple, rinds and raisins and walnuts and
80 whiskey and oh, so much flour, butter, so many eggs, spices, flavorings: why, we'll need a pony to pull the buggy home.

But before these purchases can be made, there is the question of money. Neither of us has any. Except for skinflint sums persons in the house occasionally provide (a dime is considered very big money); or what we earn ourselves from various activities: holding rummage sales, selling buckets of hand-picked blackberries, jars of homemade jam and apple jelly and peach preserves, rounding up flowers for funerals and weddings. Once we won seventy-ninth prize, five dollars,
90 in a national football contest. Not that we know a fool thing about football. It's just that we enter any contest we hear about: at the moment our hopes are centered on the fifty-thousand-dollar Grand Prize being offered to name a new brand of coffee (we suggested "A.M."; and, after some hesitation, for my friend thought it perhaps sacrilegious, the

---

1. **distemper:** an infectious viral disease of dogs.

✏ MARK IT UP WORD POWER

Mark words that you'd like to add to your **Personal Word List**. After reading, you can record the words and their meanings beginning on page 402.

What Does It Mean?
Concealing means "hiding something." In this case, the leaves were covering, or hiding, the pecans.

What Does It Mean?
Citron is a fruit that is too bitter to eat. Its thick peel is often boiled in sugar syrup and used in baked goods.

What Does It Mean?
A *skinflint* is a selfish person who is unwilling to spend money. *Skinflint sums* means "the small amount of money a selfish person shares."

What Does It Mean?
Sacrilegious means "disrespectful toward sacred things."

slogan "A.M.! Amen!"). To tell the truth, our only *really* profitable enterprise was the Fun and Freak Museum we conducted in a back-yard woodshed two summers ago. The Fun was a stereopticon[2] with slide views of Washington and New York lent us by a relative who had been to those places (she was furious when she discovered why we'd borrowed it); the Freak was a three-legged biddy chicken hatched by one of our own hens. Everybody hereabouts wanted to see that biddy: we charged grownups a nickel, kids two cents. And took in a good twenty dollars before the museum shut down due to the decease of the main attraction.

But one way and another we do each year accumulate Christmas savings, a Fruitcake Fund. These moneys we keep hidden in an ancient bead purse under a loose board under the floor under a chamber pot under my friend's bed. The purse is seldom removed from this safe location except to make a deposit or, as happens every Saturday, a withdrawal; for on Saturdays I am allowed ten cents to go to the picture show. My friend has never been to a picture show, nor does she intend to: "I'd rather hear you tell the story, Buddy. That way I can imagine it more. Besides, a person my age shouldn't squander their eyes. When the Lord comes, let me see him clear." In addition to never having seen a movie, she has never: eaten in a restaurant, traveled more than five miles from home, received or sent a telegram, read anything except funny papers and the Bible, worn cosmetics, cursed, wished someone harm, told a lie on purpose, let a hungry dog go hungry. Here are a few things she has done, does do: killed with a hoe the biggest rattle-snake ever seen in this county (sixteen rattles), dip snuff[3] (secretly), tame hummingbirds (just try it) till they balance on her finger, tell ghost stories (we both believe in ghosts) so tingling they chill you in July, talk to herself, take walks in the rain, grow the prettiest japonicas[4] in town, know the recipe for every sort of old-time Indian cure, including a magical wart remover.

2. **stereopticon** (stĕr′ē-ŏp′tĭ-kŏn): an early slide projector that could merge two images of the same scene on a screen, resulting in a 3-D effect.

3. **dip snuff**: to rub (dip) a finely ground tobacco (snuff) on one's teeth and gums.

4. **japonica** (jə-pŏn′ĭ-kə): an ornamental bush with red flowers.

English Learner Support

CULTURE

Films *Picture show* is an old-fashioned term for "movie."

☑ **Reading Check**

What do you learn about Buddy's friend from the list of things that she has done and never done?

WORDS TO KNOW

squander (skwŏn′dər) *v.* to spend or use wastefully

Now, with supper finished, we retire to the room in a faraway part of the house where my friend sleeps in a scrap-quilt-covered iron bed painted rose pink, her favorite color. Silently, wallowing in the pleasures of <u>conspiracy</u>, we take the bead purse from its secret place and spill its contents on the scrap quilt. Dollar bills, tightly rolled and green as May buds. Somber fifty-cent pieces, heavy enough to weight a dead man's eyes.[5] Lovely dimes, the liveliest coin, the one that really jingles. Nickels and quarters, worn smooth as creek pebbles. But mostly a hateful heap of bitter-odored pennies. Last summer others in the house contracted to pay us a penny for every twenty-five flies we killed. Oh, the carnage of August: the flies that flew to heaven! Yet it was not work in which we took pride. And, as we sit counting pennies, it is as though we were back tabulating dead flies. Neither of us has a head for figures; we count slowly, lose track, start again. According to her calculations, we have $12.73. According to mine, exactly $13. "I do hope you're wrong, Buddy. We can't mess around with thirteen. The cakes will fall. Or put somebody in the cemetery. Why, I wouldn't dream of getting out of bed on the thirteenth." This is true: she always spends thirteenths in bed. So, to be on the safe side, we subtract a penny and toss it out the window.

Pause & **Reflect**

FOCUS
Read to find out how Buddy and his friend obtain whiskey for their fruitcakes and who will receive them.

Of the ingredients that go into our fruitcakes, whiskey is the most expensive, as well as the hardest to obtain: State laws forbid its sale. But everybody knows you can buy a bottle from Mr. Haha Jones. And the next day, having completed our more <u>prosaic</u> shopping, we set out for Mr. Haha's business address, a "sinful" (to quote public opinion) fish-fry and dancing café down by the river. We've been there before, and on the same errand; but in previous

---

5. **heavy enough to weight a dead man's eyes:** from the custom of putting coins on the closed eyes of corpses to keep the eyelids from opening.

WORDS
TO
KNOW

conspiracy (kən-spîr′ə-sē) *n.* a joining or acting together in a secret way, often with wrongful motives
prosaic (prō-zā′ĭk) *adj.* dull; commonplace

Superstitions Some people believe that the number thirteen is bad luck. The highlighted sentence means that Buddy's friend is superstitious and worries that if they have exactly thirteen dollars, something bad will happen.

Pause & **Reflect**

Review the notes you made as you read. Then complete the sentence that follows:

To me, the *funniest/most unusual* thing the two friends do to get money for their Fruitcake Fund is_____

_____

_____

_____.

(Evaluate)

As the story continues . . .

• The friends get the last of their ingredients and make the fruitcakes.

years our dealings have been with Haha's wife, an iodine-dark Indian woman with brassy peroxided hair and a dead-tired disposition. Actually, we've never laid eyes on her husband, though we've heard that he's an Indian too. A giant with razor scars across his cheeks. They call him Haha because he's so gloomy, a man who never laughs. As we approach his café (a large log cabin festooned inside and out with chains of garish-gay naked light bulbs and standing by the river's muddy edge under the shade of river trees where moss drifts through the branches like gray mist) our steps slow down. Even Queenie stops prancing and sticks close by. People have been murdered in Haha's café. Cut to pieces. Hit on the head. There's a case coming up in court next month.

Naturally these goings-on happen at night when the colored lights cast crazy patterns and the Victrola[6] wails. In the daytime Haha's is shabby and deserted. I knock at the door, Queenie barks, my friend calls: "Mrs. Haha, ma'am? Anyone to home?"

Footsteps. The door opens. Our hearts overturn. It's Mr. Haha Jones himself! And he is a giant; he *does* have scars; he *doesn't* smile. No, he glowers at us through Satan-tilted eyes and demands to know: "What you want with Haha?"

For a moment we are too paralyzed to tell. Presently my friend half-finds her voice, a whispery voice at best: "If you please, Mr. Haha, we'd like a quart of your finest whiskey."

His eyes tilt more. Would you believe it? Haha is smiling! Laughing, too. "Which one of you is a drinkin' man?"

"It's for making fruitcakes, Mr. Haha. Cooking."

This sobers him. He frowns. "That's no way to waste good whiskey." Nevertheless, he retreats into the shadowed café and seconds later appears carrying a bottle of daisy-yellow unlabeled liquor. He demonstrates its sparkle in the sunlight and says: "Two dollars."

We pay him with nickels and dimes and pennies. Suddenly, as he jangles the coins in his hand like a fistful of dice, his face softens. "Tell you what," he proposes, pouring the money back into our bead purse, "just send me one of them fruitcakes instead."

"Well," my friend remarks on our way home, "there's a

---

6. **Victrola:** a trademark for a brand of old record player that would play grooved black discs with a needle.

The InterActive Reader PLUS
126 For English Learners

WORDS
TO
KNOW

garish (gâr´ĭsh) *adj.* too bright or gaudy

What Does It Mean?

Paralyzed means "powerless" or "unable to move." Here, it means that they are so frightened, they feel as though they cannot even move.

READ ALOUD Lines 180–199

As you read aloud, use your voice to express the humor of this scene.

✔ Reading Check

Why are Buddy and his friend afraid of Haha before they meet him?

lovely man. We'll put an extra cup of raisins in *his* cake."

The black stove, stoked with coal and firewood, glows like a lighted pumpkin. Eggbeaters whirl, spoons spin round in bowls of butter and sugar, vanilla sweetens the air, ginger spices it; melting, nose-tingling odors saturate the kitchen, suffuse the house, drift out to the world on puffs of chimney smoke. In four days our work is done. Thirty-one cakes, dampened with whiskey, bask on windowsills and shelves.

Who are they for?

210 Friends. Not necessarily neighbor friends: indeed, the larger share is intended for persons we've met maybe once, perhaps not at all. People who've struck our fancy. Like President Roosevelt. Like the Reverend and Mrs. J. C. Lucey, Baptist missionaries to Borneo who lectured here last winter. Or the little knife grinder who comes through town twice a year. Or Abner Packer, the driver of the six o'clock bus from Mobile, who exchanges waves with us every day as he passes in a dust-cloud whoosh. Or the young Wistons, a California couple whose car one afternoon broke down outside the

220 house and who spent a pleasant hour chatting with us on the porch (young Mr. Wiston snapped our picture, the only one we've ever had taken). Is it because my friend is shy with everyone *except* strangers that these strangers, and merest acquaintances, seem to us our truest friends? I think yes. Also, the scrapbooks we keep of thank-you's on White House stationery, time-to-time communications from California and Borneo, the knife grinder's penny post cards, make us feel connected to eventful worlds beyond the kitchen with its view of a sky that stops.

Pause & Reflect

230 **FOCUS**

The fruitcakes are done. Read to find out what happens when the two friends celebrate the completion of their task.

Now a nude December fig branch grates against the window. The kitchen is empty, the cakes are gone; yesterday we carted the last of them to the post office, where the cost of stamps turned our purse inside out. We're broke. That rather depresses me, but my friend insists on celebrating—with two inches

English Learner Support
VOCABULARY

Idiom *Struck our fancy* describes people that Buddy and his cousin like for no particular reason.

Pause & Reflect

✎ **MARK IT UP** 1. Circle the words and phrases in the story that describe Mr. Haha Jones. **(Clarify)**

2. How does Buddy's friend act during her meeting with Mr. Haha? Circle the words below that describe her. **(Evaluate)**

shy   bold

polite   scared

courageous   disrespectful

3. Review the boxed passage on page 126. Why do you think Mr. Haha gives back the money the two friends offer him? **(Infer)**

_____

_____

_____

As the story continues . . .

• The friends celebrate.

• Their relatives disapprove of their celebration.

✔ Reading Check

How do Buddy and his friend celebrate the completion of their baking?

What Does It Mean?

Some people believe that alcohol is the *road to ruination* because it can ruin a person's life. In this passage, Buddy's relatives are remembering other relatives (Cousin Kate, Uncle Charlie, and Uncle Charlie's brother-in-law) who have been "ruined" by drinking alcohol.

✔ Reading Check

Buddy's friend says that she is "old and funny," but Buddy says she is "fun." Explain how she is different from most people her age.

of whiskey left in Haha's bottle. Queenie has a spoonful in a bowl of coffee (she likes her coffee chicory-flavored and
240 strong). The rest we divide between a pair of jelly glasses. We're both quite awed at the prospect of drinking straight whiskey; the taste of it brings screwed-up expressions and sour shudders. But by and by we begin to sing, the two of us singing different songs simultaneously. I don't know the words to mine, just: *Come on along, come on along, to the dark-town strutters' ball*. But I can dance: that's what I mean to be, a tap dancer in the movies. My dancing shadow rollicks on the walls; our voices rock the chinaware; we giggle: as if unseen hands were tickling us. Queenie rolls on her back, her
250 paws plow the air, something like a grin stretches her black lips. Inside myself, I feel warm and sparky as those crumbling logs, carefree as the wind in the chimney. My friend waltzes round the stove, the hem of her poor calico skirt pinched between her fingers as though it were a party dress: *Show me the way to go home*, she sings, her tennis shoes squeaking on the floor. *Show me the way to go home.*

Enter: two relatives. Very angry. Potent with eyes that scold, tongues that scald. Listen to what they have to say, the words tumbling together into a wrathful tune: "A child of
260 seven! whiskey on his breath! are you out of your mind? feeding a child of seven! must be loony! road to ruination! remember Cousin Kate? Uncle Charlie? Uncle Charlie's brother-in-law? shame! scandal! humiliation! kneel, pray, beg the Lord!"

Queenie sneaks under the stove. My friend gazes at her shoes, her chin quivers, she lifts her skirt and blows her nose and runs to her room.

Long after the town has gone to sleep and the house is silent except for the chimings of clocks and the sputter of
270 fading fires, she is weeping into a pillow already as wet as a widow's handkerchief.

"Don't cry," I say, sitting at the bottom of her bed and shivering despite my flannel nightgown that smells of last winter's cough syrup, "don't cry," I beg, teasing her toes, tickling her feet, "you're too old for that."

"It's because," she hiccups, "I am too old. Old and funny."

"Not funny. Fun. More fun than anybody. Listen. If you don't stop crying you'll be so tired tomorrow we can't go cut a tree."

She straightens up. Queenie jumps on the bed (where Queenie is not allowed) to lick her cheeks. "I know where we'll find real pretty trees, Buddy. And holly, too. With berries big as your eyes. It's way off in the woods. Farther than we've ever been. Papa used to bring us Christmas trees from there: carry them on his shoulder. That's fifty years ago. Well, now: I can't wait for morning."

Pause & Reflect

Morning. Frozen rime[7] lusters the grass; the sun, round as an orange and orange as hot-weather moons, balances on the horizon, burnishes the silvered winter woods. A wild turkey calls. A renegade hog grunts in the undergrowth. Soon, by the edge of knee-deep, rapid-running water, we have to abandon the buggy. Queenie wades the stream first, paddles across barking complaints at the swiftness of the current, the pneumonia-making coldness of it. We follow, holding our shoes and equipment (a hatchet, a burlap sack) above our heads. A mile more: of chastising thorns, burrs and briers that catch at our clothes; of rusty pine needles brilliant with gaudy fungus and molted feathers. Here, there, a flash, a flutter, an ecstasy of shrillings remind us that not all the birds have flown south. Always, the path unwinds through lemony sun pools and pitch-black vine tunnels. Another creek to cross: a disturbed armada of speckled trout froths the water round us, and frogs the size of plates practice belly flops; beaver workmen are building a dam. On the farther shore, Queenie shakes herself and trembles. My friend shivers, too: not with cold but enthusiasm. One of her hat's ragged roses sheds a petal as she lifts her head and inhales the pine-heavy air. "We're almost there; can you smell it, Buddy?" she says, as though we were approaching an ocean.

And, indeed, it is a kind of ocean. Scented acres of holiday trees, prickly-leafed holly. Red berries shiny as Chinese bells:

---

7. **rime:** a white frost.

Lugging it like a kill means dragging the tree behind them, as hunters might drag a deer they have killed.

English Learner Support

LANGUAGE

Dialect When the mill owner's wife says "giveya," she combines several words—"I will give you"—into one. She offers to give Buddy and his cousin a quarter for the Christmas tree that they have dragged from the woods into town.

More About...

(FIVE-AND-DIMES) F. W. Woolworth created a chain of department stores that sold a variety of inexpensive goods such as decorations, household items, and toys. Because many items were sold for five or ten cents, such stores were called *five-and-dimes* or *dime stores*.

black crows swoop upon them screaming. Having stuffed our burlap sacks with enough greenery and crimson to garland a dozen windows, we set about choosing a tree. "It should be," muses my friend, "twice as tall as a boy. So a boy can't steal the star." The one we pick is twice as tall as me. A brave handsome 320 brute that survives thirty hatchet strokes before it keels with a creaking rending cry. Lugging it like a kill, we commence the long trek out. Every few yards we abandon the struggle, sit down and pant. But we have the strength of triumphant huntsmen; that and the tree's virile, icy perfume revive us, goad us on. Many compliments accompany our sunset return along the red clay road to town; but my friend is sly and noncommittal when passers-by praise the treasure perched in our buggy: what a fine tree, and where did it come from? "Yonderways," she murmurs vaguely. Once a car stops, and the 330 rich mill owner's lazy wife leans out and whines: "Giveya two-bits[8] cash for that ol tree." Ordinarily my friend is afraid of saying no; but on this occasion she promptly shakes her head: "We wouldn't take a dollar." The mill owner's wife persists. "A dollar, my foot! Fifty cents. That's my last offer. Goodness, woman, you can get another one." In answer, my friend gently reflects: "I doubt it. There's never two of anything."

Home: Queenie slumps by the fire and sleeps till tomorrow, snoring loud as a human.

A trunk in the attic contains: a shoebox of ermine[9] tails (off 340 the opera cape of a curious lady who once rented a room in the house), coils of frazzled tinsel gone gold with age, one silver star, a brief rope of dilapidated, undoubtedly dangerous candylike light bulbs. Excellent decorations, as far as they go, which isn't far enough: my friend wants our tree to blaze "like a Baptist window," droop with weighty snows of ornament. But we can't afford the made-in-Japan splendors at the (five-and-dime.) So we do what we've always done: sit for days at the kitchen table with scissors and crayons and stacks of colored paper. I make sketches and my friend cuts them out: 350 lots of cats, fish too (because they're easy to draw), some apples, some watermelons, a few winged angels devised from

---

8. **two-bits:** twenty-five cents

9. **ermine** (ûr′mĭn): the soft, white fur of a weasel of northern regions.

WORDS
TO
KNOW

goad (gōd) *v.* to urge

noncommittal (nŏn′kə-mĭt′l) *adj.* not revealing one's opinion or purpose

saved-up sheets of Hershey-bar tin foil. We use safety pins to attach these creations to the tree; as a final touch, we sprinkle the branches with shredded cotton (picked in August for this purpose). My friend, surveying the effect, clasps her hands together. "Now honest, Buddy. Doesn't it look good enough to eat?" Queenie tries to eat an angel.

After weaving and ribboning holly wreaths for all the front windows, our next project is the fashioning of family gifts. Tie-dye scarves for the ladies, for the men a home-brewed lemon and licorice and aspirin syrup to be taken "at the first Symptoms of a Cold and after Hunting." But when it comes time for making each other's gift, my friend and I separate to work secretly. I would like to buy her a pearl-handled knife, a radio, a whole pound of chocolate-covered cherries (we tasted some once, and she always swears: "I could live on them, Buddy, Lord yes I could—and that's not taking his name in vain"). Instead, I am building her a kite. She would like to give me a bicycle (she's said so on several million occasions: "If only I could, Buddy. It's bad enough in life to do without something *you* want; but confound it, what gets my goat is not being able to give somebody something you want *them* to have. Only one of these days I will, Buddy. Locate you a bike. Don't ask how. Steal it, maybe"). Instead, I'm fairly certain that she is building me a kite—the same as last year and the year before: the year before that we exchanged slingshots. All of which is fine by me. For we are champion kite fliers who study the wind like sailors; my friend, more accomplished than I, can get a kite aloft when there isn't enough breeze to carry clouds.

Pause & Reflect

380

FOCUS

Read to find out how the two friends spend their Christmas.

MARK IT UP Underline passages that reveal the old woman's feelings about Buddy.

Christmas Eve afternoon we scrape together a nickel and go to the butcher's to buy Queenie's traditional gift, a good gnawable beef bone. The bone, wrapped in funny paper, is placed high in the tree near the silver star. Queenie knows it's there. She squats at the foot of the tree staring up in a trance of greed: when bedtime arrives she refuses

---

✔ **Reading Check**

What presents would the narrator and his friend like to give each other? What do they give instead?

English Learner Support
VOCABULARY

Idiom *Gets my goat* means "makes me angry or annoyed."

Pause & Reflect

1. Review the passages you marked. Why do you think the old woman refuses to sell the tree to the mill owner's wife, even for a dollar? **(Infer)**

_____

_____

_____

_____

2. At this point in the story, what is your opinion of Buddy and his friend? **(Make Judgments)**

_____

_____

_____

_____

As the story ends...
• The friends buy Queenie a gift.
• They celebrate Christmas together.

to budge. Her excitement is equaled by my own. I kick the covers and turn my pillow as though it were a scorching summer's night. Somewhere a rooster crows: falsely, for the sun is still on the other side of the world.

"Buddy, are you awake?" It is my friend, calling from her room, which is next to mine; and an instant later she is sitting on my bed holding a candle. "Well, I can't sleep a hoot," she declares. "My mind's jumping like a jack rabbit. Buddy, do you think Mrs. Roosevelt will serve our cake at dinner?" We huddle in the bed, and she squeezes my hand I-love-you. "Seems like your hand used to be so much smaller. I guess I hate to see you grow up. When you're grown up, will we still be friends?" I say always. "But I feel so bad, Buddy. I wanted so bad to give you a bike. I tried to sell my cameo Papa gave me. Buddy"—she hesitates, as though embarrassed—"I made you another kite." Then I confess that I made her one, too; and we laugh. The candle burns too short to hold. Out it goes, exposing the starlight, the stars spinning at the window like a visible caroling that slowly, slowly daybreak silences. Possibly we doze; but the beginnings of dawn splash us like cold water: we're up, wide-eyed and wandering while we wait for others to waken. Quite deliberately my friend drops a kettle on the kitchen floor. I tap dance in front of closed doors. One by one the household emerges, looking as though they'd like to kill us both; but it's Christmas, so they can't. First, a gorgeous breakfast: just everything you can imagine—from flapjacks[10] and fried squirrel to hominy grits and honey-in-the-comb. Which puts everyone in a good humor except my friend and me. Frankly, we're so impatient to get at the presents we can't eat a mouthful.

Well, I'm disappointed. Who wouldn't be? With socks, a Sunday school shirt, some handkerchiefs, a hand-me-down sweater, and a year's subscription to a religious magazine for children. *The Little Shepherd*. It makes me boil. It really does.

My friend has a better haul. A sack of satsumas,[11] that's her best present. She is proudest, however, of a white wool shawl knitted by her married sister. But she says her favorite gift is the kite I built her. And it is very beautiful; though not as beautiful as the one she made me, which is blue and

---

10. **flapjacks:** pancakes.

11. **satsumas** (săt-sōō′məz): fruit similar to tangerines.

⁴³⁰ scattered with gold and green Good Conduct stars;¹² moreover, my name is painted on it, "Buddy."

"Buddy, the wind is blowing."

The wind is blowing, and nothing will do till we've run to a pasture below the house where Queenie has scooted to bury her bone (and where, a winter hence, Queenie will be buried, too). There, plunging through the healthy waist-high grass, we unreel our kites, feel them twitching at the string like sky fish as they swim into the wind. Satisfied, sun-warmed, we sprawl in the grass and peel satsumas and watch our kites <u>cavort</u>.

⁴⁴⁰ Soon I forget the socks and hand-me-down sweater. I'm as happy as if we'd already won the fifty-thousand-dollar Grand Prize in that coffee-naming contest.

"My, how foolish I am!" my friend cries, suddenly alert, like a woman remembering too late she has biscuits in the oven. "You know what I've always thought?" she asks in a tone of discovery and not smiling at me but a point beyond. "I've always thought a body would have to be sick and dying before they saw the Lord. And I imagined that when he came it would be like looking at the Baptist window: pretty as ⁴⁵⁰ colored glass with the sun pouring through, such a shine you don't know it's getting dark. And it's been a comfort: to think of that shine taking away all the spooky feeling. But I'll wager it never happens. I'll wager at the very end a body realizes the Lord has already shown himself. That things as they are"— her hand circles in a gesture that gathers clouds and kites and grass and Queenie pawing earth over her bone—"just what they've always seen, was seeing him. As for me, I could leave the world with today in my eyes."

This is our last Christmas together.

⁴⁶⁰ Life separates us. Those who Know Best decide that I belong in a (military school.) And so follows a miserable succession of bugle-blowing prisons, grim reveille-ridden¹³ summer camps. I have a new home too. But it doesn't count. Home is where my friend is, and there I never go.

---

12. **Good Conduct stars:** small, shiny, glued paper stars often awarded to children for good behavior or perfect attendance.

13. **reveille-ridden** (rĕv′ə-lē): dominated by an early-morning signal, as on a bugle, to wake soldiers or campers.

WORDS
TO   **cavort** (kə-vôrt′) *v.* to leap or romp about
KNOW

Reading Check
Who are "Those who Know Best"? How do you think the narrator feels about them?

More About . . .
(MILITARY SCHOOL) Military academies are boarding schools known for their strict discipline. Many are for boys only. Students live at the school and are called *cadets.* They follow a structured schedule that includes studies, sports, and military training.

1. Review the passages you marked. How would you describe the old woman's feelings about Buddy? **(Evaluate)**

_____

_____

_____

2. Reread the boxed passage on page 133. Which of the following sentences below does *not* express the old woman's attitudes? Cross it out. **(Draw Conclusions)**

People can see the Lord in their everyday lives.

Death is a terrible thing.

MARK IT UP **3.** Buddy is sent away to military school. What happens to his friend? Underline the clues on this page that helped you to figure out your answer. **(Infer)**

_____

_____

CHALLENGE

Review the selection and star passages that strike you as memorable. What do you like about the passages you marked? How does Capote's writing **style** help make the passages particularly memorable?

And there she remains, puttering around the kitchen. Alone with Queenie. Then alone. ("Buddy dear," she writes in her wild hard-to-read script, "yesterday Jim Macy's horse kicked Queenie bad. Be thankful she didn't feel much. I wrapped her in a Fine Linen sheet and rode her in the buggy down to
470 Simpson's pasture where she can be with all her Bones. . . ."). For a few Novembers she continues to bake her fruitcakes single-handed; not as many, but some: and, of course, she always sends me "the best of the batch." Also, in every letter she encloses a dime wadded in toilet paper: "See a picture show and write me the story." But gradually in her letters she tends to confuse me with her other friend, the Buddy who died in the 1880's; more and more, thirteenths are not the only days she stays in bed: a morning arrives in November, a leafless birdless coming of winter morning, when she cannot
480 rouse herself to exclaim: "Oh my, it's fruitcake weather!"

And when that happens, I know it. A message saying so merely confirms a piece of news some secret vein had already received, <u>severing</u> from me an irreplaceable part of myself, letting it loose like a kite on a broken string. That is why, walking across a school campus on this particular December morning, I keep searching the sky. As if I expected to see, rather like hearts, a lost pair of kites hurrying toward heaven.

WORDS
TO   **sever** (sĕv′ər) *v.* to cut off
KNOW

Active Reading SkillBuilder

Noting Sensory Details

Good descriptive writing is usually rich in **imagery**—words and phrases that appeal to the various senses. Capote gives readers a vivid, lasting impression of his holiday memory by creating descriptions that appeal to one or more of the five senses. While reading "A Christmas Memory," use the chart to note phrases or details that seem especially striking. For each description, check off the sense or senses it appeals to.

Description	Sight	Smell	Hearing	Taste	Touch
Cracking open the pecans	✔		✔	✔	

Literary Analysis SkillBuilder

Autobiographical Fiction

Autobiography is the story of a person's life written by that person. **Fiction** is
a narrative that springs from the imagination of the writer, though it may be based
on actual events and people. "A Christmas Memory" combines both of these forms.
Use the chart below to identify the elements of fiction—characters, plot, setting, and
theme—in Capote's story.

Characters

Main: _____

Minor: _Mr. Haha Jones_____

Plot

Rising Action: _The two friends gather pecans,_____

_____

Climax: _____

Falling Action: _____

Setting

Place: _____ Time: _____

Importance of Setting: _____

Theme:

_____

_____

Words to Know SkillBuilder

Words to Know

cavort	exhilarate	goad	noncommittal	sever
conspiracy	garish	inaugurate	prosaic	squander

A. Fill in each set of blanks with the correct word from the word list. (One word will be used twice.) Then use the boxed letters to complete the sentence below the puzzle.

1. People who are part of a plot or scheme are involved in this.

   ___ ___ ___ ___ □ ___ □ ___ ___ ___

2. Workers who accidentally do this to a power line will cause a blackout.

   ___ □ ___ ___ ___

3. This describes anything that is boring or unoriginal.

   ___ ___ ___ □ ___ □ ___

4. It's easy to do this with time, especially when you have homework to do.

   ___ ___ ___ ___ ___ □ □ ___

5. In the United States, we do this to a presidency every four years.

   ___ □ ___ ___ ___ ___ ___ ___ □ ___

6. You might do this when you're feeling really happy—or really goofy.

   ___ ___ ___ ___ □ ___

7. This is what you do when you strongly encourage someone to do something.

   ___ □ ___ ___

8. If your answer is "Maybe, maybe not," this describes you.

   ___ ___ ___ ___ □ ___ ___ ___ ___ ___ ___ ___

9. This might well describe the costumes of clowns and circus performers.

   ___ ___ ___ ___ □ ___

10. People do this to a relationship if they decide never to see one another again.

    ___ □ □ ___ ___

11. If something does this to you, you want to sing and dance and laugh.

    □ ___ ___ ___ □ ___ ___ ___ □ ___

Complete the following sentence with the words that the boxed letters spell out.

Buddy and his friend send a Christmas fruitcake to _____.

B. Write a paragraph or two telling the story of a "picture show" as Buddy might tell it in a letter to his friend. You can describe a real movie you have seen or a made-up one. Use at least **four** of the Words to Know in your work.

Song
OF THE
OPEN ROAD

WALT WHITMAN

THE ROAD
NOT TAKEN

ROBERT FROST

Before You Read

Connect to Your Life

What images come to mind when you think of an open road? Write your
answers in the web below.

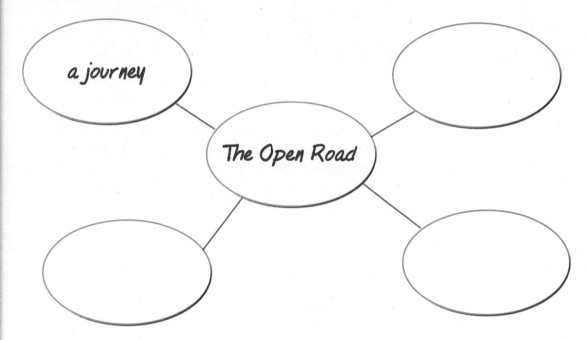

a journey

The Open Road

Key to the Poems

WHAT'S THE BIG IDEA? Both of the poems in this selection are about
making choices. What do you do when you have an important choice to
make? Jot down your ideas on the lines below.

_____

_____

_____

_____

_____

_____

Song
OF THE
OPEN ROAD

WALT WHITMAN

PREVIEW Life is often called a journey. All of us have been "on the road" in one way or another. Here are two popular American poems that treat this idea in slightly different ways.

As the poem begins . . .

- The speaker sets off on a journey.
- He has no final destination in mind.
- He looks forward to the adventure.

What Does It Mean?

Afoot means "walking" or "on foot."

English Learner Support
VOCABULARY

Idiom *Light-hearted* means "happy and carefree."

Pause & Reflect

1. Look back at the words you underlined. You might say that the **mood** of this person is _____

_____.

(Infer)

MARK IT UP 2. Circle three words or phrases in the poem that describe the speaker's previous life. (Clarify)

FOCUS

As you read, imagine that you are meeting the speaker of Whitman's poem.
MARK IT UP Underline any words that tell you the mood of this person.

Afoot and light-hearted I take to the open road,
Healthy, free, the world before me,
The long brown path before me leading wherever I choose.
Henceforth[1] I ask not good fortune, I myself am good fortune,
5 Henceforth I whimper no more, postpone no more, need nothing,
Done with indoor complaints,[2] libraries, querulous[3] criticisms,
Strong and content I travel the open road.

Pause & Reflect

---

1. **henceforth:** from this time forward.
2. **indoor complaints:** illnesses caused by a lack of fresh air and outdoor exercise.
3. **querulous** (kwĕr′ə-ləs): complaining; grumbling.

THE ROAD NOT TAKEN

ROBERT FROST

More About . . .

MAKING CHOICES This poem is a metaphor for making choices. It compares making an important life decision to choosing which road to take.

FOCUS
The speaker of this poem is recalling a choice he made some time in the past. Read to find out how the speaker feels about that choice.

As the poem begins . . .

• A traveler stands at a fork in the road.

• He chooses which road to take.

• He thinks about the effects of that decision.

Two roads diverged[1] in a yellow wood,
And sorry I could not travel both
And be one traveler, long I stood
And looked down one as far as I could
5 To where it bent in the undergrowth;

Then took the other, as just as fair,
And having perhaps the better claim,
Because it was grassy and wanted wear;
Though as for that the passing there
10 Had worn them really about the same,

And both that morning equally lay
In leaves no step had trodden[2] black.
Oh, I kept the first for another day!
Yet knowing how way leads on to way,
15 I doubted if I should ever come back.

I shall be telling this with a sigh
Somewhere ages and ages hence:
Two roads diverged in a wood, and I—
I took the one less traveled by,
20 And that has made all the difference.

English Learner Support
VOCABULARY

Usage *Wanted wear* means "hadn't been walked on."

✔ **Reading Check**
Explain the last two lines of the poem in your own words.

Pause **&** *Reflect*

MARK IT UP What is the difference between the two roads? Circle any lines and phrases that tell you.

CHALLENGE
One poem is free verse and one has rhyme and a rhythm pattern. How do these different forms help each speaker convey his message? **(Evaluate)**

Pause **&** *Reflect*

---

1. **diverged** (dĭ-vûrjd′): branched out; went in different directions.
2. **trodden** (trŏd′n): walked or trampled.

Active Reading SkillBuilder

Paraphrasing

Paraphrasing is simply putting things in one's own words. It is often useful in helping a reader to better understand a poem. Paraphrasing often uses simpler forms or words, but it is not necessarily shorter, since it is not a summary but a reshaping of information. To be able to paraphrase, a reader must find the main idea, notice important details, and think of a simpler or more familiar way of saying what the writer has written. While reading "Song of the Open Road" and "The Road Not Taken," use the chart to write down the main idea of each poem in your own words. Then write a paraphrase of each poem.

"Song of the Open Road"

Main Idea:
Paraphrase:

"The Road Not Taken"

Main Idea:
Paraphrase:

Literary Analysis SkillBuilder

Rhyme Scheme/Free Verse

Most rhyming poems have a distinctive **rhyme scheme.** A rhyme scheme is charted by using a letter of the alphabet to represent the sound at the end of each line. Lines that rhyme are given the same letter. Whenever a new sound is introduced at the end of a line, it gets a new letter. Read "The Road Not Taken" aloud, and chart the poem's rhyme scheme below.

Stanza 1	Stanza 2	Stanza 3	Stanza 4
1. *a*	1.	1.	1.
2. *b*	2.	2.	2.
3. *a*	3.	3.	3.
4.	4.	4.	4.
5.	5.	5.	5.

Poetry with no regular pattern of rhyme or rhythm is called **free verse.** Free verse often uses other sound devices, such as repetition, that help hold the poem together. Reread "Song of the Open Road," and write down words or phrases that are repeated. Then describe the effects of the repetition.

Words and Phrases That Repeat	Effects of Repetition

Follow Up: Explain how the form of each poem fits the spirit or thought of the poem.

I Have a Dream
Dr. Martin Luther King, Jr.

Glory & Hope
NELSON MANDELA

Before You Read

Connect to Your Life

What does the word *justice* mean to you? Write your ideas in the word web.

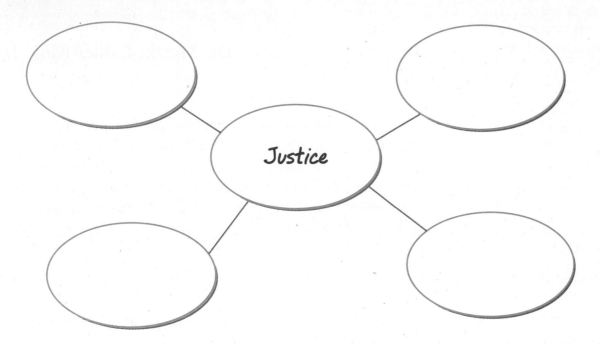

Key to the Speeches

WHAT YOU NEED TO KNOW Martin Luther King, Jr., and Nelson Mandela are heroes of the struggle for civil rights. Both grew up in societies that were segregated, or separated by race. During the 1950s and 1960s, Dr. King led nonviolent protests against racial injustice in America. He delivered his famous "I Have a Dream" speech from the steps of the Lincoln Memorial during the 1963 March on Washington for Jobs and Freedom. In South Africa, Nelson Mandela worked to overthrow the policy of *apartheid,* or strict separation of the races. Mandela organized protests against South Africa's all-white government. In 1964, he was sentenced to life in prison. He was released, however, in 1990, and he negotiated an end to apartheid. In 1994, he became president of South Africa after the country's first free elections. "Glory and Hope" was President Mandela's inaugural address.

Reading Tips

A **speech** is the oral presentation of a speaker's ideas and beliefs. It is writing that is meant to be heard.

• Watch for words and phrases that express strong emotion. These words and phrases were chosen to stir the emotions of the **audience**.

I Have A Dream

Dr. Martin Luther King, Jr.

PREVIEW "I Have a Dream," by Dr. Martin Luther King, Jr., has been called one of the great speeches of the 20th century. The speech was delivered before 200,000 people who took part in the 1963 March on Washington, D.C. Here, King calls for racial equality and freedom. He speaks on behalf of all African Americans, protesting injustice and sharing his dreams for the future.

As the speech begins . . .

• King remembers Abraham Lincoln.

• He says Lincoln gave hope to the slaves.

• King points out that African Americans still aren't free.

FOCUS

King begins by recalling the history of African Americans since the Civil War. **MARK IT UP** As you read, underline problems that African Americans still face in 1963. An example is highlighted.

I am happy to join with you today in what will go down in history as the greatest demonstration for freedom in the history of our nation.

Five score[1] years ago, a great American, in whose symbolic shadow we stand today, signed the Emancipation Proclamation.[2] This momentous decree came as a great beacon light of hope to millions of Negro slaves who had been seared in the flames of withering injustice. It came as a joyous daybreak to end the long night of their captivity.

But one hundred years later, the Negro still is not free; one

English Learner Support

CULTURE

Language Throughout this speech, King uses the term *Negro* to refer to African Americans.

---

1. **five score:** 100. (The phrasing recalls the beginning of Abraham Lincoln's Gettysburg Address: "Four score and seven years ago...")

2. **Emancipation Proclamation** (ĭ-măn′sə-pā′shen prŏk′lə-mā′shən): a document issued by President Abraham Lincoln during the Civil War, declaring that all slaves in states still at war with the union were free.

hundred years later, the life of the Negro is still sadly crippled by the manacles of segregation and the chains of discrimination; one hundred years later, the Negro lives on a lonely island of poverty in the midst of a vast ocean of material prosperity; one hundred years later, the Negro is still languishing in the corners of American society and finds himself in exile in his own land.

Pause & Reflect

What Does It Mean?
Manacles are handcuffs or restraints. King describes segregation as a restraint that cripples African Americans' sense of dignity and pride.

Pause & Reflect
MARK IT UP Summarize the main point King is making.

_____

_____

_____

FOCUS
King says that the Constitution and the Declaration of Independence promise freedom. He compares these promises to a check, or promissory note, that needs to be cashed.
MARK IT UP As you read, underline the reasons for the march.

So we've come here today to dramatize a shameful condition. In a sense we've come to our nation's capital to cash a check. When the architects of our republic wrote the magnificent words of the Constitution and the Declaration of Independence, they were signing a promissory note[3] to which every American was to fall heir. This note was the promise that all men, yes, black men as well as white men, would be guaranteed the unalienable rights of life, liberty, and the pursuit of happiness.

It is obvious today that America has <u>defaulted</u> on this promissory note insofar as her citizens of color are concerned. Instead of honoring this sacred obligation, America has given the Negro people a bad check, a check which has come back marked "insufficient funds." But we refuse to believe that the bank of justice is bankrupt. We refuse to believe that there are insufficient funds in the great vaults of opportunity of this nation. And so we've come to cash this check, a check that will give us upon demand the riches of freedom and the security of justice.

As the speech continues . . .
• King explains the reasons for the march.
• He says that black Americans have been denied their rights.

More About . . .
CASHING A CHECK King uses this check as an extended metaphor to explain that the government of the United States made a promise that it didn't keep.

What Does It Mean?
To *fall heir* means "to inherit."

---

3. **promissory** (prŏm′ĭ-sôr′ē) **note**: a written promise to repay a loan.

WORDS TO KNOW   **default** (dĭ-fôlt′) *v.* to fail to keep a promise, especially a promise to repay a loan

We have also come to this hallowed spot to remind America of the fierce urgency of now. This is no time to engage in the luxury of cooling off or to take the tranquilizing drug of gradualism.[4] Now is the time to make real the promises of democracy; now is the time to rise from the dark and desolate valley of segregation to the sunlit path of racial justice; now is the time to lift our nation from the quicksands of racial injustice to the solid rock of brotherhood; now is the time to make justice a reality for all of God's children. It would be fatal for the nation to overlook the urgency of the moment. This sweltering summer of the Negro's <u>legitimate</u> discontent will not pass until there is an invigorating autumn of freedom and equality.

Pause & Reflect

Pause & Reflect

MARK IT UP Reread the boxed passage on this page, and circle the phrase that is repeated. What does King want people to do? (**Main Idea**)

As the speech continues . . .

- King calls for justice.
- He explains his nonviolent principles.

English Learner Support

LANGUAGE

Metaphor The highlighted phrase is a metaphor that compares the way African Americans are waiting for their rights to one who stands on a threshold, or doorway, before entering a building.

FOCUS

Now King presents two warnings—one to the nation and one to his people. Read to find out what he warns each of these groups against.

Nineteen sixty-three is not an end, but a beginning. And those who hope that the Negro needed to blow off steam and will now be content will have a rude awakening if the nation returns to business as usual. There will be neither rest nor tranquility in America until the Negro is granted his citizenship rights. The whirlwinds of revolt will continue to shake the foundations of our nation until the bright day of justice emerges.

But there is something that I must say to my people, who stand on the worn threshold which leads into the palace of justice. In the process of gaining our rightful place, we must not be guilty of wrongful deeds. Let us not seek to satisfy our thirst for freedom by drinking from the cup of bitterness and hatred. We must forever conduct our struggle on the high plain of dignity and discipline. We must not allow our creative protests to degenerate[5] into physical violence. Again and again we must rise to the majestic heights of meeting physical force with soul

---

4. **gradualism:** a policy of seeking to reach a goal slowly, in gradual stages.

5. **degenerate** (dĭ-jĕn'ə-rāt´): descend; decline.

WORDS
TO
KNOW

legitimate (lə-jĭt'ə-mĭt) *adj.* justifiable; reasonable

force. The marvelous new militancy,[6] which has engulfed the Negro community, must not lead us to a distrust of all white people. For many of our white brothers, as evidenced by their presence here today, have come to realize that their destiny is tied up with our destiny. And they have come to realize that their freedom is <u>inextricably</u> bound to our freedom. We cannot walk alone. And as we walk, we must make the pledge that we shall always march ahead. We cannot turn back.

There are those who are asking the devotees[7] of civil rights, "When will you be satisfied?" We can never be satisfied as long as the Negro is the victim of the unspeakable horrors of police brutality; we can never be satisfied as long as our bodies, heavy with the fatigue of travel, cannot gain lodging in the motels of the highways and the hotels of the cities; we cannot be satisfied as long as the Negro's basic <u>mobility</u> is from a smaller ghetto to a larger one; we can never be satisfied as long as our children are stripped of their selfhood and robbed of their dignity by signs stating For Whites Only; we cannot be satisfied as long as the Negro in Mississippi cannot vote and a Negro in New York believes he has nothing for which to vote. No! No, we are not satisfied, and we will not be satisfied until "justice rolls down like waters and righteousness like a mighty stream."

Pause **&** **Reflect**

FOCUS
King concludes on a positive note. Read to find out what hopes King has for the future.
▸ MARK IT UP Underline the words that tell what he dreams.

I am not unmindful that some of you have come here out of great trials and tribulations. Some of you have come fresh from narrow jail cells. Some of you have come from areas where your quest for freedom left you battered by the storms of persecution and staggered by the winds of police brutality. You have been the

---

6. **militancy:** aggressiveness in pursuing a goal.

7. **devotees:** people devoted to something.

| WORDS TO KNOW | **inextricably** (ĭn-ĕk′strĭ-kə-blē) *adv.* in a way impossible to untangle |
| | **mobility** (mō-bĭl′ĭ-tē) *n.* an ability to move (as from one social class to another) |

More About . . .

JUSTICE Dr. King, a Baptist minister, makes several *allusions,* or references, to the Bible in his speech. The quotation in these lines is from the Book of Amos in the Bible (Amos 5:24). Amos was a prophet who challenged the rich to act justly toward the poor.

Pause **&** **Reflect**

▸ MARK IT UP **1.** Review lines 68–84. Circle four actions King warns his people against. **(Clarify)**

2. In lines 85–99, King explains why people must continue to struggle for civil rights. In the list below, star the reasons he gives. **(Cause and Effect)**

police brutality

poor health care

forced separation of the races

voting restrictions

unemployment

As the speech ends . . .

• King recalls how his listeners have suffered.

• He shares his dream of a just future.

More About . . .

JAIL CELLS During the 1960s, civil rights workers organized protests to end segregation and gain the right to vote. Although the protests were peaceful, those who participated were often jailed.

veterans of creative suffering. Continue to work with the faith
that unearned suffering is redemptive.[8] Go back to
110 Mississippi. Go back to Alabama. Go back to South Carolina.
Go back to Georgia. Go back to Louisiana. Go back to the
slums and ghettos of our Northern cities, knowing that
somehow this situation can and will be changed. Let us not
wallow in the valley of despair.

I say to you today, my friends, even though we face the
difficulties of today and tomorrow, I still have a dream. It is a
dream deeply rooted in the American dream. I have a dream
that one day this nation will rise up and live out the true
meaning of its creed, "We hold these truths to be self-evident;
120 that all men are created equal." I have a dream that one day
on the red hills of Georgia, sons of former slaves and the sons
of former slave owners will be able to sit down together at the
table of brotherhood. I have a dream that one day even the
state of Mississippi, a state sweltering with the heat of
injustice, sweltering with the heat of oppression, will be
transformed into an oasis of freedom and justice. I have a
dream that my four little children will one day live in a nation
where they will not be judged by the color of their skin, but
by the content of their character.

130 I have a dream today!

I have a dream that one day down in Alabama—with its
vicious racists, with its Governor having his lips dripping with
the words of interposition and nullification[9]—one day right
there in Alabama, little black boys and black girls will be able
to join hands with little white boys and white girls as sisters
and brothers.

I have a dream today!

I have a dream that one day every valley shall be exalted,[10]
and every hill and mountain shall be made low. The rough
140 places will be plain and the crooked places will be made
straight, "and the glory of the Lord shall be revealed, and all
flesh shall see it together."

READ ALOUD Lines 116–129

Read aloud the boxed passage
on this page. Note how King
repeats /s/ sounds and /k/
sounds at the beginnings of
words. This technique is called
alliteration. What effect does
such repetition have?

More About . . .

EXALTED According to the
Biblical prophet Isaiah, the
valleys would be raised and the
mountains lowered to prepare
for God's coming. People would
then live in peace. The quotation is from Isaiah 40:5.

✔ **Reading Check**

What major change in society
does King dream about?
Summarize King's dream in
your own words.

---

8. **is redemptive:** is a way of earning freedom or salvation.

9. **Governor...interposition** (ĭn´tər-pə-zĭsh´ən) **and nullification:** When ordered by
the federal government to allow the integration of the University of Alabama,
Governor George Wallace claimed that the principle of nullification (a state's
alleged right to refuse to accept a federal law) allowed him to resist the
government's "interposition," or interference in state affairs.

10. **exalted:** raised up.

This is our hope. This is the faith that I go back to the South with. With this faith we will be able to hew[11] out of the mountain of despair a stone of hope. With this faith we will be able to transform the jangling <u>discords</u> of our nation into a beautiful symphony of brotherhood. With this faith we will be able to work together, to pray together, to struggle together, to go to jail together, to stand up for freedom together, knowing
150 that we will be free one day. And this will be the day. This will be the day when all of God's children will be able to sing with new meaning, "My country 'tis of thee, sweet land of liberty, of thee I sing. Land where my fathers died, land of the pilgrims' pride, from every mountainside, let freedom ring." And if America is to be a great nation, this must become true.

So let freedom ring from the prodigious[12] hilltops of New Hampshire; let freedom ring from the mighty mountains of New York; let freedom ring from the heightening Alleghenies of Pennsylvania; let freedom ring from the snowcapped
160 Rockies of Colorado; let freedom ring from the curvaceous slopes of California. But not only that. Let freedom ring from Stone Mountain of Georgia; let freedom ring from Lookout Mountain of Tennessee; let freedom ring from every hill and molehill of Mississippi. "From every mountainside, let freedom ring."

And when this happens, and when we allow freedom to ring, when we let it ring from every village and every hamlet, from every state and every city, we will be able to speed up that day when all of God's children—black men and white
170 men, Jews and Gentiles, Protestants and Catholics—will be able to join hands and sing in the words of the old Negro spiritual, "Free at last. Free at last. Thank God Almighty, we are free at last."

Pause & Reflect

---

11. **hew:** hack.
12. **prodigious** (prə-dĭj′əs): magnificent.

WORDS
TO   **discord** (dĭs′kôrd′) *n.* a harsh mixture of sounds; conflict
KNOW

English Learner Support
CULTURE

Songs The highlighted words are lines from a popular patriotic hymn called "America." The lyrics were written by Samuel F. Smith in 1832.

More About...

(SPIRITUALS) A *spiritual* is a religious folk song of African American origin. Many spirituals celebrate being free after escaping from slavery. This quotation is from the song "Free at Last."

Pause & Reflect

1. How do you feel about the dream that King describes? (Connect)

_____

_____

_____

_____

2. King waited until the end of his speech to describe his dream. Circle any of the following statements that help to explain why. (Text Structure)

saved most important point for last

wanted to end on positive note

felt people would not understand his dream

Glory & Hope

BY NELSON MANDELA

PREVIEW In 1994, South Africa held its first election in which all races could vote. Nelson Mandela was elected president. "Glory & Hope" is the speech Mandela gave to celebrate the first free election and the new policy of majority rule. In this speech, President Mandela thanks those who supported the free election, and he presents his hopes for the future of South Africa.

As the speech begins . . .

- Mandela has just become the first black president of South Africa.

- He welcomes guests from other nations.

MARK IT UP KEEP TRACK

Remember to use these marks to keep track of your understanding.

✔ ..... I understand.

? ..... I don't understand this.

! ..... Interesting or surprising idea

FOCUS

In the years before Mandela's election, South Africa was bitterly divided. In the opening part of his speech, Mandela appeals to all the different people in his country. He wants the nation to be based on justice and liberty for all.

MARK IT UP As you read, circle the words and phrases that describe Mandela's goals for South Africa's future. An example is highlighted.

Your majesties, your royal highnesses, distinguished guests, comrades and friends: Today, all of us do, by our presence here, and by our celebrations in other parts of our country and the world, confer glory and hope to newborn liberty.

Out of the experience of an extraordinary human disaster[1] that lasted too long must be born a society of which all humanity will be proud.

Our daily deeds as ordinary South Africans must produce an actual South African reality that will reinforce humanity's belief in justice, strengthen its confidence in the nobility of the human soul and <u>sustain</u> all our hopes for a glorious life for all.

---

1. **an extraordinary human disaster:** apartheid—the official policy of racial segregation formerly practiced in South Africa.

WORDS TO KNOW

sustain (sə-stān´) v. to keep alive; support

All this we owe both to ourselves and to the peoples of the world who are so well represented here today.

To my compatriots, I have no hesitation in saying that each one of us is as intimately attached to the soil of this beautiful country as are the famous jacaranda trees of Pretoria[2] and the mimosa trees of the bushveld.[3]

Each time one of us touches the soil of this land, we feel a sense of personal renewal. The national mood changes as the seasons change.

We are moved by a sense of joy and exhilaration when the grass turns green and the flowers bloom.

That spiritual and physical oneness we all share with this common homeland explains the depth of the pain we all carried in our hearts as we saw our country tear itself apart in terrible conflict, and as we saw it spurned, outlawed and isolated by the peoples of the world, precisely because it has become the universal base of the pernicious ideology and practice of racism and racial oppression.

We, the people of South Africa, feel fulfilled that humanity has taken us back into its bosom, that we, who were outlaws not so long ago, have today been given the rare privilege to be host to the nations of the world on our own soil.

We thank all our distinguished international guests for having come to take possession with the people of our country of what is, after all, a common victory for justice, for peace, for human dignity.

We trust that you will continue to stand by us as we tackle the challenges of building peace, prosperity, nonsexism, nonracialism and democracy.

We deeply appreciate the role that the masses of our people and their democratic, religious, women, youth, business, traditional and other leaders have played to bring about this conclusion. Not least among them is my Second Deputy President, the Honorable F. W. de Klerk.[4]

WORDS
TO
KNOW

intimately (ĭn′tə-mĭt-lē) *adv.* closely
pernicious (pər-nĭsh′əs) *adj.* deadly; harmful

What Does It Mean?
Compatriots means "people from the same country."

What Does It Mean?
Exhilaration means "great joy."

More About . . .
SANCTIONS AGAINST SOUTH AFRICA Other nations protested South Africa's treatment of its nonwhite population. In 1963, South Africa was suspended from the United Nations. In 1986, the U.S. Congress passed trade restrictions against South Africa. These restrictions were lifted when apartheid ended.

Reading Check
What does Mandela ask the nations of the world to do for South Africa?

Pause & *Reflect*

Review the words and phrases you circled as you read. What are Mandela's goals for South Africa? **(Clarify)**

_____

_____

_____

We would also like to pay tribute to our security forces, in all their ranks, for the distinguished role they have played in securing our first democratic elections and the transition to democracy, from bloodthirsty forces which still refuse to see the light.

Pause & *Reflect*

As the speech ends . . .

- Mandela expresses his vision of the future.
- He promises to work for peace.
- He hopes South Africa will be a "rainbow nation."

What Does It Mean?

Political emancipation means that the people of South Africa have the freedom to elect the politicians they choose, regardless of race. It also means that they are free from a government that will discriminate against nonwhites.

English Learner Support
LANGUAGE

Figure of Speech *Walk tall* means "be proud."

FOCUS

Mandela now provides a more detailed description of his hopes for the future.
MARK IT UP As you read, underline the phrases that tell what Mandela hopes for the people of South Africa.

60

The time for the healing of the wounds has come.

The moment to bridge the chasms that divide us has come.

The time to build is upon us.

We have, at last, achieved our political emancipation. We pledge ourselves to liberate all our people from the continuing bondage of poverty, deprivation,[5] suffering, gender and other discrimination.

We succeeded to take our last steps to freedom in conditions of relative peace. We commit ourselves to the construction of a complete, just and lasting peace.

70 We have triumphed in the effort to implant hope in the breasts of the millions of our people. We enter into a covenant[6] that we shall build the society in which all South Africans, both black and white, will be able to walk tall, without any fear in their hearts, assured of their inalienable right to human dignity—a rainbow nation at peace with itself and the world.

As a token of its commitment to the renewal of our country, the new Interim[7] Government of National Unity will, as a matter of urgency, address the issue of amnesty for

---

5. **deprivation** (dĕp′rə-vā′shən): a lack of the necessities or comforts of life.

6. **covenant** (kŭv′ə-nənt): solemn agreement.

7. **interim:** temporary.

WORDS
TO
KNOW

amnesty (ăm′nĭ-stē) *n.* a general pardon, especially one granted by a government to people who have committed political offenses

80 various categories of our people who are currently serving terms of imprisonment.

We dedicate this day to all the heroes and heroines in this country and the rest of the world who sacrificed in many ways and surrendered their lives so that we could be free.

Their dreams have become reality. Freedom is their reward.

We are both humbled and elevated by the honor and privilege that you, the people of South Africa, have bestowed on us, as the first President of a united, democratic, nonracial and nonsexist South Africa, to lead our country out of the **90** valley of darkness.

We understand it still that there is no easy road to freedom.

We know it well that none of us acting alone can achieve success.

We must therefore act together as a united people, for national <u>reconciliation</u>, for nation building, for the birth of a new world.

> Let there be justice for all.
> Let there be peace for all.
> Let there be work, bread, water and salt for all.
> **100** Let each know that for each the body, the mind and the soul have been freed to fulfill themselves.
> Never, never and never again shall it be that this beautiful land will again experience the oppression of one by another and suffer the indignity of being the skunk of the world.
> The sun shall never set on so glorious a human achievement!
> Let freedom reign. God bless Africa!

Pause & Reflect

WORDS
TO
KNOW

reconciliation (rĕk′ən-sĭl′ē-ā′shən) *n.* a return to a state of friendship or harmony

---

English Learner Support
LANGUAGE

Metaphor Both Martin Luther King, Jr., and Nelson Mandela use a similar metaphor in speaking about the movement of their people toward greater freedom and justice. In "I Have a Dream" (see pages 146–151), King refers to the "valley of despair" that African Americans must leave. Here, Mandela writes of the "valley of darkness" out of which he will lead South Africans.

Pause & Reflect

READ ALOUD Read aloud the boxed passage at the end of the speech in a manner that conveys Mandela's emotion. Do you think the conclusion is an effective one? *Yes/No*, because

_____

_____

_____.

(Text Structure)

CHALLENGE

Both King and Mandela use **repetition** to emphasize key ideas in their speeches. Highlight repeated words or phrases in each speech. Then decide why the speakers chose to repeat those particular words or phrases. **(Text Structure)**

Active Reading SkillBuilder

Analyzing Text Structure

Good readers analyze **text structure** when they evaluate a selection based on the way it is put together. Structure includes the following elements:

- **order** of the ideas in the text
- **supporting elements** that draw attention to the main idea
- **transitions**—the way ideas connect to or build on each other

Use the chart to record elements of structure for "I Have a Dream." Continue the chart on separate paper if you need to.

King's Speech

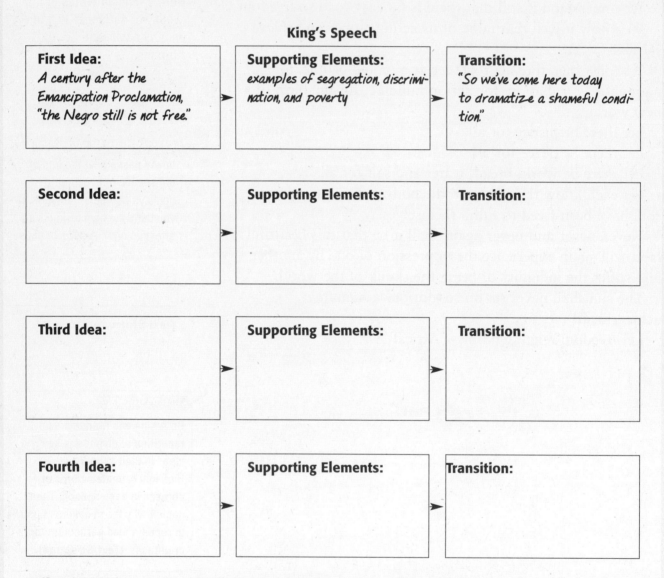

First Idea:	Supporting Elements:	Transition:
A century after the Emancipation Proclamation, "the Negro still is not free."	examples of segregation, discrimination, and poverty	"So we've come here today to dramatize a shameful condition."

Second Idea:	Supporting Elements:	Transition:

Third Idea:	Supporting Elements:	Transition:

Fourth Idea:	Supporting Elements:	Transition:

Follow Up: Make a similar chart for Nelson Mandela's speech, "Glory and Hope."

Literary Analysis SkillBuilder

Speech

A **speech** is meant to be heard. The oral presentation of a speech allows the listener to hear the speaker's emotions, as well as his or her opinions and proposals. Speakers must consider the following points when preparing to deliver a speech:

- their purpose for giving the speech
- the main idea they want to emphasize
- the words and phrases to stress
- the emotions they wish to convey

Imagine you are King or Mandela. In the chart, identify the purpose and main idea of your speech. Then note words or phrases that you would emphasize. Last, record the emotions you wish to convey.

Title of Speech:	
Purpose of Speech:	
Main Idea:	
Words or Phrases to Emphasize:	
Emotions to Convey:	

Follow Up: Read your speech aloud to a classmate. Be ready to give reasons for your method of delivery.

Words to Know SkillBuilder

Words to Know

amnesty	discord	intimately	mobility	reconciliation
default	inextricably	legitimate	pernicious	sustain

A. Think about the meaning of each underlined word. Then fill in the blank with the letter of the correct definition.

1. Is it possible to avoid <u>discord</u> when opposing views clash? _____

2. The <u>pernicious</u> practice of racism can result in violence. _____

3. To some individuals, violence seems like a <u>legitimate</u> tool. _____

4. Without the <u>mobility</u> to improve their lives, people often feel helpless. _____

5. When governments <u>default</u> on commitments, people can become bitterly disappointed. _____

6. Racial justice is not <u>inextricably</u> linked with violence. _____

7. Some feel that justice is more <u>intimately</u> linked to nonviolence. _____

8. King and Mandela have promoted peace and <u>reconciliation</u>. _____

9. These ideals could lead to <u>amnesty</u>, freeing people from prison. _____

10. Positive ideals can help prevent violence and <u>sustain</u> harmony. _____

Definitions

A. in a way impossible to change
B. a return to a state of friendship or harmony
C. to fail to keep a promise
D. a harsh mixture of sounds; conflict
E. a general pardon, especially one granted by a government
F. an ability to move (as from one social class to another)
G. justifiable; reasonable
H. to keep alive; support
I. closely
J. deadly; harmful

B. Write an announcement for a rally to celebrate equality. Use at least **three** Words to Know.

from

I KNOW WHY THE CAGED BIRD SINGS

MAYA ANGELOU

Before You Read

Connect to Your Life

In this selection, Maya Angelou describes how a friend, Mrs. Flowers, taught her an important lesson. Has there been a friend or a teacher in your life who helped you learn an important lesson? Fill in the chart below.

PERSON	WHAT I LEARNED
My grandfather	I have to work hard to achieve my goals.

Key to the Autobiography

WHAT YOU NEED TO KNOW Maya Angelou overcame many difficult obstacles in her childhood. Her parents divorced when she was three years old, and she and her brother moved back and forth between the homes of their mother and grandmother. At the age of eight, Angelou stopped speaking for a while. After five years of silence, she overcame her fear of speaking with the help of family members and friends. This selection shows how Mrs. Flowers, a family friend, taught Maya Angelou that language and speech are important.

from

I KNOW WHY THE CAGED BIRD SINGS

MAYA ANGELOU

PREVIEW In this excerpt from her **autobiography** Angelou writes about her childhood in the 1930s. Her name was Marguerite Johnson then. She lived with her grandmother, called Momma, and her brother Bailey. Her grandmother owned a general store in their small, segregated Arkansas town.

AUTOBIOGRAPHY

Before You Read
If you are using *The Language of Literature* . . .

- Use the information on page 480 to prepare for reading.

- Look at the art on pages 482 and 485. What impressions do the pictures give of the people and **setting?**

Reading Tips
- Angelou wrote her **autobiography** as an adult. However, she tells her story from the **point of view** of herself as a young girl.

- As you read, look for details that explain young Marguerite's feelings.

As the autobiography begins . . .
- The narrator is Marguerite Johnson, the young Maya Angelou.

- The setting is a small town in Arkansas.

- Marguerite talks about Mrs. Flowers, an important person in her life.

MARK IT UP **KEEP TRACK**

As you read, you can use these marks to keep track of your understanding.

✔..... I understand.

?..... I don't understand this.

!..... Interesting or surprising idea

FOCUS
In this section Marguerite introduces Mrs. Flowers. Marguerite also explains why she is embarrassed by her own grandmother.

MARK IT UP As you read, underline details that show why Marguerite is embarrassed. One example is highlighted.

For nearly a year, I sopped around the house, the Store, the school and the church, like an old biscuit, dirty and inedible. Then I met, or rather got to know, the lady who threw me my first life line.

Mrs. Bertha Flowers was the <u>aristocrat</u> of Black Stamps. She had the grace of control to appear warm in the coldest weather, and on the Arkansas summer days it seemed she had a private breeze which swirled around, cooling her. She was thin without the taut look of wiry people, and her printed voile dresses and flowered hats were as right for her as denim overalls for a farmer. She was our side's answer to the richest white woman in town.

WORDS
TO
KNOW
aristocrat (ə-rĭs′tə-krăt′) *n.* a person held in high standing for superior tastes and manners

Her skin was a rich black that would have peeled like a plum if snagged, but then no one would have thought of getting close enough to Mrs. Flowers to ruffle her dress, let alone snag her skin. She didn't encourage familiarity. She wore gloves too.

I don't think I ever saw Mrs. Flowers laugh, but she smiled often. A slow widening of her thin black lips to show even, small white teeth, then the slow, effortless closing. When she chose to smile on me, I always wanted to thank her. The action was so graceful and inclusively benign.[1]

She was one of the few gentlewomen I have ever known, and has remained throughout my life the measure of what a human being can be.

Momma had a strange relationship with her. Most often when she passed on the road in front of the Store, she spoke to Momma in that soft yet carrying voice, "Good day, Mrs. Henderson." Momma responded with "How you, Sister Flowers?"

Mrs. Flowers didn't belong to our church, nor was she Momma's familiar.[2] Why on earth did she insist on calling her Sister Flowers? Shame made me want to hide my face. Mrs. Flowers deserved better than to be called Sister. Then, Momma left out the verb. Why not ask, "How *are* you, Mrs. Flowers?" With the unbalanced passion of the young, I hated her for showing her ignorance to Mrs. Flowers. It didn't occur to me for many years that they were as alike as sisters, separated only by formal education.

Although I was upset, neither of the women was in the least shaken by what I thought an unceremonious greeting. Mrs. Flowers would continue her easy gait up the hill to her little bungalow,[3] and Momma kept on shelling peas or doing whatever had brought her to the front porch.

Occasionally, though, Mrs. Flowers would drift off the road and down to the Store and Momma would say to me, "Sister,

---

1. **inclusively benign** (bĭ-nīn′): good-natured and kindly in a way that takes others in.

2. **familiar:** a close friend or associate.

3. **bungalow** (bŭng′gə-lō): a small, one-story house or cottage.

WORDS TO KNOW

familiarity (fə-mĭl′yăr′ĭ-tē) *n.* behavior that implies a close friendship

you go on and play." As I left I would hear the beginning of an intimate conversation. Momma persistently using the wrong verb, or none at all.

"Brother and Sister Wilcox is sho'ly the meanest—" "Is," Momma? "Is"? Oh, please, not "is," Momma, for two or more. But they talked, and from the side of the building where I waited for the ground to open up and swallow me, I heard the soft-voiced Mrs. Flowers and the textured voice of my grandmother merging and melting. They were interrupted from time to time by giggles that must have come from Mrs. Flowers (Momma never giggled in her life). Then she was gone.

She appealed to me because she was like people I had never met personally. Like women in English novels who walked the moors[4] (whatever they were) with their loyal dogs racing at a respectful distance. Like the women who sat in front of roaring fireplaces, drinking tea incessantly from silver trays full of scones and crumpets.[5] Women who walked over the "heath"[6] and read morocco-bound[7] books and had two last names divided by a hyphen. It would be safe to say that she made me proud to be Negro, just by being herself.

She acted just as refined as whitefolks in the movies and books and she was more beautiful, for none of them could have come near that warm color without looking gray by comparison.

It was fortunate that I never saw her in the company of powhitefolks. For since they tend to think of their whiteness as an evenizer, I'm certain that I would have had to hear her spoken to commonly as Bertha, and my image of her would have been shattered like the unmendable Humpty-Dumpty. One summer afternoon, sweet-milk fresh in my memory, she stopped at the Store to buy provisions. Another Negro woman of her health and age would have been expected to

---

4. **moors:** broad areas of open land with patches of low shrubs and marshes.
5. **scones** (skōnz)**and crumpets** (krŭm′pĭts): Scones are small, sweet biscuits; crumpets are rolls similar to English muffins.
6. **heath** (hēth): a moor.
7. **morocco-bound** (mə-rŏk′ō): bound, or covered, in soft leather.

WORDS
TO
KNOW
incessantly (ĭn-sĕs′ənt-lē) *adv.* continuously; nonstop

English Learner Support
LANGUAGE

Dialect When Momma says, "Brother and Sister Wilcox is sho'ly the meanest—," she is speaking in dialect. *Dialect* is a way people in a particular region of a country speak. Momma means, "Brother and Sister Wilcox are surely the meanest."

What Does It Mean?
Powhitefolks is a combination of three words: poor white folks.

English Learner Support
CULTURE

Nursery Rhymes In the well-known children's nursery rhyme, Humpty-Dumpty breaks because he's an egg. Here's the rhyme: "Humpty-Dumpty sat on a wall, / Humpty-Dumpty had a great fall. / All the king's horses, / And all the king's men, / Couldn't put Humpty together again."

What Does It Mean?
The highlighted phrase explains that this particular summer afternoon is still fresh in the author's memory.

✔ **Reading Check**
What are the qualities that Marguerite admires in Mrs. Flowers?

Pause & Reflect

1. Look back at the details you underlined as you read. Why is Marguerite sometimes ashamed of her grandmother? **(Clarify)**

_____

_____

_____

_____

2. Why do you think Mrs. Flowers wants to talk with Marguerite? **(Predict)**

_____

_____

_____

_____

As the autobiography continues . . .

- Momma embarrasses Marguerite in front of Mrs. Flowers.

- Mrs. Flowers talks to Marguerite about her behavior in school.

carry the paper sacks home in one hand, but Momma said, "Sister Flowers, I'll send Bailey up to your house with these things."

She smiled that slow dragging smile, "Thank you, Mrs. Henderson. I'd prefer Marguerite, though." My name was beautiful when she said it. "I've been meaning to talk to her, anyway." They gave each other age-group looks.

Momma said, "Well, that's all right then. Sister, go and change your dress. You going to Sister Flowers's."

Pause & Reflect

FOCUS

Getting ready to visit Mrs. Flowers is no easy job. Read to find out what happens to Marguerite.

The chifforobe[8] was a maze. What on earth did one put on to go to Mrs. Flowers's house? I knew I shouldn't put on a Sunday dress. It might be sacrilegious. Certainly not a house dress, since I was already wearing a fresh one. I chose a school dress, naturally. It was formal without suggesting that going to Mrs. Flowers's house was equivalent to attending church.

I trusted myself back into the Store.

"Now, don't you look nice." I had chosen the right thing, for once.

"Mrs. Henderson, you make most of the children's clothes, don't you?"

"Yes, ma'am. Sure do. Store-bought clothes ain't hardly worth the thread it take to stitch them."

"I'll say you do a lovely job, though, so neat. That dress looks professional."

Momma was enjoying the seldom-received compliments. Since everyone we knew (except Mrs. Flowers, of course) could sew competently, praise was rarely handed out for the commonly practiced craft.

---

8. **chifforobe** (shĭf'ə-rōb'): a chest of drawers combined with a small closet for storing clothes.

WORDS TO KNOW

sacreligious (săk'rə-lĭj'əs) *adj.* disrespectful toward a sacred person, place or thing

"I try, with the help of the Lord, Sister Flowers, to finish the inside just like I does the outside. Come here, Sister."

I had buttoned up the collar and tied the belt, apronlike, in back. Momma told me to turn around. With one hand she pulled the strings and the belt fell free at both sides of my waist. Then her large hands were at my neck, opening the button loops. I was terrified. What was happening?

"Take it off, Sister." She had her hands on the hem of the dress.

"I don't need to see the inside, Mrs. Henderson, I can tell . . ." But the dress was over my head and my arms were stuck in the sleeves. Momma said, "That'll do. See here, Sister Flowers, I French-seams around the armholes." Through the cloth film, I saw the shadow approach. "That makes it last longer. Children these days would bust out of sheet-metal clothes. They so rough."

"That is a very good job, Mrs. Henderson. You should be proud. You can put your dress back on, Marguerite."

"No ma'am. Pride is a sin. And 'cording to the Good Book, it goeth before a fall."

What Does It Mean?
Goeth before a fall means "leads to destruction."

"That's right. So the Bible says. It's a good thing to keep in mind."

I wouldn't look at either of them. Momma hadn't thought that taking off my dress in front of Mrs. Flowers would kill me stone dead. If I had refused, she would have thought I was trying to be "womanish." Mrs. Flowers had known that I would be embarrassed and that was even worse. I picked up the groceries and went out to wait in the hot sunshine. It would be fitting if I got a sunstroke and died before they came outside. Just dropped dead on the slanting porch.

There was a little path beside the rocky road, and Mrs. Flowers walked in front swinging her arms and picking her way over the stones.

She said, without turning her head, to me, "I hear you're doing very good school work, Marguerite, but that it's all written. The teachers report that they have trouble getting you to talk in class." We passed the triangular farm on our left, and the path widened to allow us to walk together. I hung back in the separate unasked and unanswerable questions.

✔ **Reading Check**
What problem does Marguerite have, both in and out of school?

"Come and walk along with me, Marguerite." I couldn't have refused even if I wanted to. She pronounced my name so nicely. Or more correctly, she spoke each word with such

English Learner Support
VOCABULARY

Prefixes The words *unasked* and *unanswerable* in this sentence have the prefix *un-*, which means *not*.
un + asked = not asked
un + answerable = not answerable

MARK IT UP Mrs. Henderson makes Marguerite take off her dress in order to show Mrs. Flowers the quality of the sewing. Circle words on page 165 that describe Marguerite's reaction. **(Cause and Effect)**

As the autobiography ends . . .

• Mrs. Flowers gives Marguerite some important advice and lends her a book.

• Marguerite ends her visit with the feeling that she is special to someone.

✔ **Reading Check**

What does Mrs. Flowers tell Marguerite she must do with the book she lends her?

clarity that I was certain a foreigner who didn't understand English could have understood her.

"Now no one is going to make you talk—possibly no one can. But bear in mind, language is man's way of communicating with his fellow man, and it is language alone which separates him from the lower animals." That was a totally new idea to me, and I would need time to think about it.

Pause & Reflect

FOCUS
Now Mrs. Flowers will begin to teach Marguerite some "lessons in living."
MARK IT UP Underline the passages that explain what Mrs. Flowers wants Marguerite to do in order to overcome her problem.

"Your grandmother says you read a lot. Every chance you get. That's good, but not good enough. Words mean more than what is set down on paper. It takes the human voice to infuse them with the shades of deeper meaning."

I memorized the part about the human voice infusing words. It seemed so valid and poetic.

She said she was going to give me some books and that I not only must read them, I must read them aloud. She suggested that I try to make a sentence sound in as many different ways as possible.

"I'll accept no excuse if you return a book to me that has been badly handled." My imagination boggled at the punishment I would deserve if in fact I did abuse a book of Mrs. Flowers's. Death would be too kind and brief.

The odors in the house surprised me. Somehow I had never connected Mrs. Flowers with food or eating or any other common experience of common people. There must have been an outhouse, too, but my mind never recorded it.

The sweet scent of vanilla had met us as she opened the door.

"I made tea cookies this morning. You see, I had planned to invite you for cookies and lemonade so we could have this

WORDS
TO   **infuse** (ĭn-fyōōz´) v. to inject, add to
KNOW

190 little chat. The lemonade is in the (icebox)"

It followed that Mrs. Flowers would have ice on an ordinary day, when most families in our town bought ice late on Saturdays only a few times during the summer to be used in the wooden ice-cream freezers.

She took the bags from me and disappeared through the kitchen door. I looked around the room that I had never in my wildest fantasies imagined I would see. Browned photographs leered or threatened from the walls, and the white, freshly done curtains pushed against themselves and
200 against the wind. I wanted to gobble up the room entire and take it to Bailey, who would help me analyze and enjoy it.

"Have a seat, Marguerite. Over there by the table." She carried a platter covered with a tea towel. Although she warned that she hadn't tried her hand at baking sweets for some time, I was certain that like everything else about her the cookies would be perfect.

They were flat, round wafers, slightly browned on the edges and butter-yellow in the center. With the cold lemonade they were sufficient for childhood's lifelong diet. Remembering my
210 manners, I took nice little lady-like bites off the edges. She said she had made them expressly for me and that she had a few in the kitchen that I could take home to my brother. So I jammed one whole cake in my mouth, and the rough crumbs scratched the insides of my jaws, and if I hadn't had to swallow, it would have been a dream come true.

As I ate she began the first of what we later called "my lessons in living." She said that I must always be intolerant of ignorance but understanding of illiteracy. That some people, unable to go to school, were more educated and even more
220 intelligent than college professors. She encouraged me to listen carefully to what country people called (mother wit) That in those homely sayings was couched the collective wisdom of generations.

When I finished the cookies she brushed off the table and brought a thick, small book from the bookcase. I had read *A Tale of Two Cities* and found it up to my standards as a romantic novel. She opened the first page and I heard poetry for the first time in my life.

More About . . .

(ICEBOXES) During the time of Maya Angelou's childhood (the 1940s), many people in rural areas did not have refrigerators. Instead, people purchased ice and stored it in iceboxes along with any food that might spoil. In Marguerite's town, many people only buy ice for their iceboxes a few times a year. The fact that Mrs. Flowers has ice on an ordinary weekday lets you know that she has more money than many of the people who live in the town.

✔ Reading Check
What does Mrs. Flowers serve Marguerite?

More About . . .

(MOTHER WIT) is a term that means "natural intelligence," or "common sense." Mrs. Flowers's "lessons in living" teach Marguerite that even though some people haven't had the opportunity to go to school, they can still be smart and give good advice.

WORDS
TO
KNOW

illiteracy (ĭ-lĭt'ər-ə-sē) *n.* a lack of the ability to read and write

from **Caged Bird** **167**

"It was the best of times and the worst of times . . ."[9] Her voice slid in and curved down through and over the words. She was nearly singing. I wanted to look at the pages. Were they the same that I had read? Or were there notes, music, lined on the pages, as in a hymn book? Her sounds began <u>cascading</u> gently. I knew from listening to a thousand preachers that she was nearing the end of her reading, and I hadn't really heard, heard to understand, a single word.

"How do you like that?"

It occurred to me that she expected a response. The sweet vanilla flavor was still on my tongue, and her reading was a wonder in my ears. I had to speak.

I said, "Yes, ma'am." It was the least I could do, but it was the most also.

"There's one more thing. Take this book of poems and memorize one for me. Next time you pay me a visit, I want you to recite."

I have tried often to search behind the <u>sophistication</u> of years for the enchantment I so easily found in those gifts. The <u>essence</u> escapes but its <u>aura</u> remains. To be allowed, no, invited, into the private lives of strangers, and to share their joys and fears, was a chance to exchange the Southern bitter wormwood for a cup of mead with Beowulf or a hot cup of tea and milk with Oliver Twist.[10] When I said aloud, "It is a far, far better thing that I do, than I have ever done . . ."[11] tears of love filled my eyes at my selflessness.

On that first day, I ran down the hill and into the road (few

---

9. **"It was . . . worst of times . . .":** This opening sentence of Charles Dickens' novel *A Tale of Two Cities* is famous for its apparent contradictions. The novel is set in Paris and London during the French Revolution (1789-1799).

10. **"a chance to exchange . . . with Oliver Twist:** Angelou here compares her existence as a black child in the bigoted South to wormwood, a bitter herb. She hopes to escape this bitterness by turning instead to mead, a sweet drink, or tea with milk, common beverages to such characters as Beowulf and Oliver twist from English literature.

11. **"It is a far . . . have ever done . . .":** a quotation from the very end of *A Tale of Two Cities*. It is spoken by a man who nobly sacrifices his own life to save that of another.

WORDS TO KNOW

cascading (kă-skā′dĭng) *v.* falling or flowing, like a waterfall
sophistication (sə-fĭs′tĭ-kā′shən) *n.* the state of being experienced; maturity
essence (ĕs′əns) *n.* the basic or most important quality
aura (ôr′ə) *n.* the unique but undefinable atmosphere that surrounds a person, an object, or an event

---

MARK IT UP WORD POWER

Remember to mark words that you'd like to add to your **Personal Word List**. Later, you can record the words and their meanings beginning on page 402.

✔ **Reading Check**

How does Marguerite react when Mrs. Flowers reads aloud?

cars ever came along it) and had the good sense to stop
running before I reached the Store.

I was liked, and what a difference it made. I was respected
not as Mrs. Henderson's grand-child or Bailey's sister but for
just being Marguerite Johnson.

Childhood's logic never asks to be proved (all conclusions
are absolute). I didn't question why Mrs. Flowers had singled
me out for attention, nor did it occur to me that Momma
might have asked her to give me a little talking to. All I cared
about was that she had made tea cookies for *me* and read to
me from her favorite book. It was enough to prove that she
liked me.

Pause & Reflect

Pause & Reflect

1. Review the passages that you
   underlined. What does Mrs.
   Flowers want Marguerite to do?
   (Clarify)

   _____
   _____
   _____
   _____

2. How does Mrs. Flowers view
   the illiterate, or those that can't
   read? **(Draw Conclusions)**

   _____
   _____
   _____

3. Reread the boxed passage on
   page 168. Angelou says she was
   "invited into the private lives of
   strangers." What is she referring to here? **(Infer)**

   _____
   _____
   _____
   _____

CHALLENGE

Review the dialogue spoken
by Mrs. Flowers and Mrs.
Henderson (Momma). Highlight
each woman's speech in a different color. Compare and contrast the ways that each woman
uses language. **(Compare and
Contrast)**

Active Reading SkillBuilder

Understanding Point of View

Most autobiographies are written from the first-person **point of view,** which means
that the narrator tells everything in his or her own words. However, autobiographies
often reflect the viewpoints of two people—the writer as he or she experienced
events, and the writer writing about the event years later. As you read this excerpt
from Angelou's autobiography, use the chart to record Angelou's observations about
Mrs. Flowers from both her child and adult viewpoints.

Observations About Mrs. Flowers	
Child's Viewpoint	**Adult's Viewpoint**
Why on earth did she insist on calling her Sister Flowers? Shame made me want to hide my face.	*She was one of the few gentlewomen I have ever known, and has remained throughout my life the measure of what a human being can be.*

Literary Analysis SkillBuilder

Autobiography

An **autobiography** is the story of a person's life written by that person. Autobiographies are based on the writer's memories and sometimes on diaries and letters. An autobiography is generally more subjective than a biography, or an account of a person's life written by someone else. Biographies are based on research and interviews. Reread the selection and look for details that might have been omitted if it were written by someone other than Angelou. What information might a biographer have included that Angelou did not? Use the chart to record your ideas.

Maya Angelou's Autobiography	
Details a Biographer Might Omit	**Information a Biographer Might Include**
"When she chose to smile on me I always wanted to thank her."	Annie Henderson ran the only African-American-owned general store in town.

Words to Know SkillBuilder

Words to Know

aristocrat	cascading	familiarity	incessantly	sacrilegious
aura	essence	illiteracy	infuse	sophistication

A. For each phrase in the first column, find the phrase in the second column that is closest in meaning. Write the letter of that phrase in the blank.

1. a sacrilegious objection   A. a floral aura

_____ 2. constantly discouraging   B. crumbling and tumbling

_____ 3. the nature of youth   C. incessantly depressing

_____ 4. a flowery atmosphere   D. a high-class lass

_____ 5. collapsing and cascading   E. the essence of adolescence

_____ 6. a young female aristocrat   F. infuse the cruise with the blues

_____ 7. add sadness to the voyage   G. a profane complaint

B. On each blank line, write the word from the word list that the poem describes.

We start escaping this when we
Sing "A-B-C-D-E-F-G."
That song is not enough, and yet
The first step *is* the alphabet!

_____
(1)

Those who possess this are rarely afraid
To go out and to deal with society.
If you lack it, then dinners with too many forks
Can fill you with fear and anxiety.

_____
(2)

You might behave with this by giving somebody a hug.
You might address a gentleman as "Pop."
Now if you're truly friendly with the folks you treat with this,
That's great. If not, I'd recommend you stop.

_____
(3)

C. Imagine that, as an adult, Marguerite wrote a letter to thank Mrs. Flowers for her kindness and interest. Write a paragraph or two that could be in that letter. Use at least **four** of the Words to Know in your work.

Jack London

To Build a Fire

Before You Read

Connect to Your Life

What words or phrases come to mind when you hear the word *cold?*
Write them in this word web.

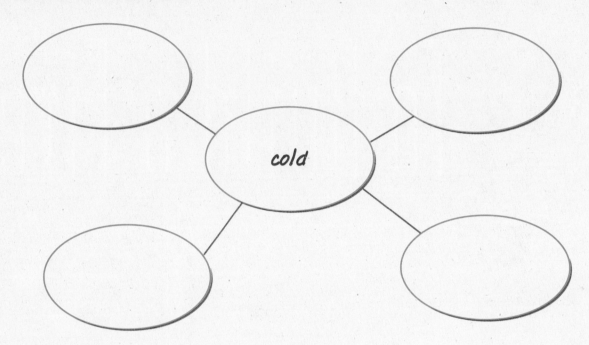

cold

Key to the Story

WHAT'S THE BIG IDEA? This story builds suspense slowly as a man struggles
to survive in extreme cold. Think of a suspenseful or scary movie or TV show
you have seen recently. What happened in that show to build suspense? List
the show and tell what happened.

Name of show: _____

What happened: _____

_____

_____

_____

Jack London To Build a Fire

PREVIEW The coldest temperature ever recorded in North America was 81.4° below zero F. This temperature was recorded in 1947 in the Yukon, a region of northern Canada—and the **setting** of this **short story**. The writer describes a man's journey through this region in the dead of winter. With a dog at his heels, the man faces a life-or-death struggle against the cold.

Reading Tips

This story is an adventure tale, filled with exciting events. However, it is a long story and has many difficult words. To keep your reading on track, try this strategy.

- Remember that you don't have to understand every word to follow the **plot**. Keep reading at a comfortable pace. Let the **suspense** carry you along.

FOCUS

A man walks through the snow in the Yukon wilderness. Read to find out about him and the arctic world in which he travels.

MARK IT UP As you read, underline the details that help you form an impression of the arctic world. An example is highlighted.

🔟

Day had broken cold and gray, exceedingly cold and gray, when the man turned aside from the main Yukon trail and climbed the high earth-bank, where a dim and little-travelled trail led eastward through the fat spruce timberland. It was a steep bank, and he paused for breath at the top, excusing the act to himself by looking at his watch. It was nine o'clock. There was no sun nor hint of sun, though there was not a cloud in the sky. It was a clear day, and yet there seemed an <u>intangible</u> pall over the face of things, a subtle gloom that made the day dark, and that was due to the absence of sun. This fact did not worry the man. He was used to the lack of sun. It had been days since he had seen the sun, and he knew that a few more days must pass before that cheerful orb,[1] due south, would just peep above the sky line and dip immediately from view.

As the story begins . . .

- A man is hiking in the Yukon.
- The man's trail is solid snow and ice as far as the eye can see.

English Learner Support
VOCABULARY

Idiom *Day had broken* means that the day had just begun.

More About . . .
THE YUKON The Yukon is a region of Canada near the North Pole. It is so far north that there is very little sun there in the winter.

---

1. **orb:** globe.

WORDS
TO
KNOW

intangible (ĭn-tăn′jə-bəl) *adj.* difficult to perceive; vague

Nature A *spruce* tree is a kind of evergreen tree. It stays green all year round, and it never drops its needle-like leaves. Spruce trees are often used as Christmas trees.

Pause **&** *Reflect*

1. Review the details you marked. What is your impression of the arctic world? **(Visualize)**

_____

_____

_____

_____

2. Which phrase below describes the man in the story? Circle or check it. **(Infer)**

lacks imagination

hates the gloomy sky

fears the cold

is used to winters in the Yukon

3. Reread the boxed lines on this page. Check the sentence below that states a true con- clusion about the man. **(Draw Conclusions)**

He knows that he can brave the cold.

He does not realize the dangers of the cold.

20   The man flung a look back along the way he had come. The Yukon lay a mile wide and hidden under three feet of ice. On top of this ice were as many feet of snow. It was all pure white, rolling in gentle <u>undulations</u> where the ice jams of the freeze-up had formed. North and south, as far as his eye could see, it was unbroken white, save for a dark hairline that curved and twisted from around the spruce-covered island to the south, and that curved and twisted away into the north, where it disappeared behind another spruce-covered island. This dark hairline was the trail—the main trail—that led

30 south five hundred miles to the Chilcoot Pass, Dyea, and salt water; and that led north seventy miles to Dawson, and still on to the north a thousand miles to Nulato, and finally to St. Michael, on Bering Sea, a thousand miles and half a thousand more.

  But all this—this mysterious, far-reaching hairline trail, the absence of sun from the sky, the tremendous cold, and the strangeness and weirdness of it all—made no impression on the man. It was not because he was long used to it. He was a newcomer in the land, a *chechaquo*, and this was his first

40 winter. The trouble with him was that he was without imagination. He was quick and alert in the things of life, but only in the things, and not in the significances. Fifty degrees below zero meant eighty-odd degrees of frost. Such fact impressed him as being cold and uncomfortable, and that was all. It did not lead him to meditate upon his frailty as a creature of temperature, and upon man's frailty in general, able only to live within certain narrow limits of heat and cold; and from there on it did not lead him to the conjectural[2] field of immortality and man's place in the universe. Fifty degrees

50 below zero stood for a bite of frost that hurt and that must be guarded against by the use of mittens, ear flaps, warm moccasins, and thick socks. Fifty degrees below zero was to him just precisely fifty degrees below zero. That there should be anything more to it than that was a thought that never entered his head.

Pause **&** *Reflect*

---

  2. **conjectural** (kən-jĕk′chə-rəl): involving guesswork.

WORDS
TO   **undulation** (ŭn′jə-′lā′shən) *n.* a wavelike shape
KNOW

FOCUS

The man continues his journey to Henderson Creek. Read to find out how the cold affects him and his dog.

As he turned to go, he spat speculatively.[3] There was a sharp, explosive crackle that startled him. He spat again. And again, in the air, before it could fall to the snow, the spittle crackled. He knew that at fifty below spittle crackled on the snow, but this spittle had crackled in the air. Undoubtedly it was colder than fifty below—how much colder he did not know. But the temperature did not matter. He was bound for the old claim[4] on the left fork of Henderson Creek, where the boys were already. They had come over across the divide from the Indian Creek country, while he had come the roundabout way to take a look at the possibilities of getting out logs in the spring from the islands in the Yukon. He would be in to camp by six o'clock; a bit after dark, it was true, but the boys would be there, a fire would be going, and a hot supper would be ready. As for lunch, he pressed his hand against the protruding bundle under his jacket. It was also under his shirt, wrapped up in a handkerchief and lying against the naked skin. It was the only way to keep the biscuits from freezing. He smiled agreeably to himself as he thought of those biscuits, each cut open and sopped in bacon grease, and each enclosing a generous slice of fried bacon.

He plunged in among the big spruce trees. The trail was faint. A foot of snow had fallen since the last sled had passed over, and he was glad he was without a sled, travelling light. In fact, he carried nothing but the lunch wrapped in the handkerchief. He was surprised, however, at the cold. It certainly was cold, he concluded, as he rubbed his numb nose and cheekbones with his mittened hand. He was a warm-whiskered man, but the hair on his face did not protect the high cheek-bones and the eager nose that thrust itself aggressively into the frosty air.

At the man's heels trotted a dog, a big native husky, the proper wolf dog, gray-coated and without any visible or temperamental[5] difference from its brother, the wild wolf. The animal was depressed by the tremendous cold. It knew that it was no time for travelling. Its instinct told it a truer tale than was told to the man by the man's judgment. In reality, it was

As the story continues . . .

• The man realizes that it is much colder than he had thought.

• A dog is walking with the man.

More About . . .

CLAIMS The Yukon was a wilderness until gold was discovered there in 1896. Then the population grew. Men, hoping to find gold, would claim land by driving a stake into the ground. Then they recorded the claim at the nearest government office.

MARK IT UP WORD POWER

Mark words that you'd like to add to your **Personal Word List**. After reading, you can record the words and their meanings beginning on page 402.

What Does It Mean?

Instinct is a way of behaving that a person or animal is born with. It is usually a response to something that happens in the person's or animal's environment.

---

3. **speculatively** (spĕk′yə-lə-tĭv-le): out of curiosity.

4. **claim**: a tract of public land claimed by a miner.

5. **temperamental**: involving a characteristic way of behaving.

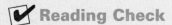

What do we learn about the
temperature from the dog's
instinct?

not merely colder than fifty below zero; it was colder than
sixty below, than seventy below. It was seventy-five below
zero. Since the freezing point is thirty-two above zero, it
meant that one hundred and seven degrees of frost obtained.[6]
The dog did not know anything about thermometers. Possibly
100 in its brain there was no sharp consciousness of a condition of
very cold such as was in the man's brain. But the brute had its
instinct. It experienced a vague but menacing apprehension
that subdued it and made it slink along at the man's heels, and
that made it question eagerly every unwonted[7] movement of
the man as if expecting him to go into camp or to seek shelter
somewhere and build a fire. The dog had learned fire, and it
wanted fire, or else to burrow under the snow and cuddle its
warmth away from the air.

The frozen moisture of its breathing had settled on its fur in
110 a fine powder of frost, and especially were its jowls, muzzle
and eyelashes whitened by its crystalled breath. The man's red
beard and mustache were likewise frosted, but more solidly,
the deposit taking the form of ice and increasing with every
warm, moist breath he exhaled. Also, the man was chewing
tobacco, and the muzzle of ice held his lips so rigidly that he
was unable to clear his chin when he expelled the juice. The
result was that a crystal beard of the color and solidity of
amber[8] was increasing its length on his chin. If he fell down it
would shatter itself, like glass, into brittle fragments. But he
120 did not mind the <u>appendage</u>.

It was the penalty all tobacco chewers paid in that country,
and he had been out before in two cold snaps. They had not
been so cold as this, but by the spirit thermometer[9] at Sixty
Mile he knew that they had been registered at fifty below and
at fifty-five.

Pause **&** **Reflect**

What Does It Mean?

The word *muzzle* can mean a
piece of leather or wire that is
put over an animal's snout to
prevent it from biting and eating.
The ice that has collected
around the man's mouth is
acting as a muzzle.

Pause **&** **Reflect**

1. How does the man know that
the temperature is colder than
50 degrees below zero? **(Cause
and Effect)**

_____

_____

_____

_____

2. Reread the boxed lines on this
page. Describe how the cold has
affected the appearance of both
man and dog. **(Visualize)**

_____

_____

_____

_____

---

6. **obtained:** existed.

7. **unwonted:** unusual.

8. **amber:** a clear yellow gemstone consisting of fossilized tree sap.

9. **spirit thermometer:** a thermometer in which temperature is indicated by the
height of a column of colored alcohol.

WORDS
TO
KNOW

appendage (ə-pĕn′dĭj) *n.* something attached to a
larger object

As the man continues his journey, he must watch out for traps, or places where underground springs flow.

130 ✎ MARK IT UP As you read, underline details that tell you about these traps and their dangers.

He held on through the level stretch of woods for several miles, crossed a wide flat . . . and dropped down a bank to the frozen bed of a small stream. This was Henderson Creek, and he knew he was ten miles from the forks. He looked at his watch. It was ten o'clock. He was making four miles an hour, and he calculated that he would arrive at the forks at half-past twelve. He decided to celebrate that event by eating his lunch there.

The dog dropped in again at his heels, with a tail drooping discouragement, as the man swung along the creek bed. The furrow of the old sled trail was plainly visible, but a dozen
140 inches of snow covered the marks of the last runners. In a month no man had come up or down that silent creek. The man held steadily on. He was not much given to thinking, and just then particularly he had nothing to think about save that he would eat lunch at the forks and that at six o'clock he would be in camp with the boys. There was nobody to talk to; and, had there been, speech would have been impossible because of the ice muzzle on his mouth. So he continued monotonously to chew tobacco and to increase the length of his amber beard.

150 Once in a while the thought reiterated[10] itself that it was very cold and that he had never experienced such cold. As he walked along he rubbed his cheekbones and nose with the back of his mittened hand. He did this automatically, now and again changing hands. But, rub as he would, the instant he stopped his cheekbones went numb, and the following instant the end of his nose went numb. He was sure to frost his cheeks; he knew that, and experienced a pang of regret that he had not devised a nose strap of the sort Bud wore in cold snaps. Such a strap passed across the cheeks, as well, and saved
160 them. But it didn't matter much, after all. What were frosted cheeks? A bit painful, that was all; they were never serious.

Empty as the man's mind was of thoughts, he was keenly observant, and he noticed the changes in the creek, the curves and bends and timber jams,[11] and always he sharply noted

- The man thinks about eating lunch and when he will reach the camp.
- The man notices a dangerous change in the trail.
- He makes the dog walk ahead of him on the trail.

English Learner Support
LANGUAGE

Usage The highlighted phrase means the man does not usually spend much time thinking.

What Does It Mean?
He was sure to frost his cheeks means that the man knows he will get frostbite on his cheeks.

More About . . .
FROSTBITE AND BLOOD CIRCULATION Frostbite is the injury or destruction of skin and the tissue beneath the skin. It is caused by prolonged contact to freezing or subfreezing temperatures. In cold temperatures, it is very important to keep moving so that blood continues to circulate throughout the body. Blood circulation is what keeps body parts warm. If the man stands still for too long in the cold, the fluids in his body will begin to freeze. Usually, the body parts that are the farthest away from the heart —nose, ears, fingers, toes—are the first to lose circulation.

What Does It Mean?
A *cold snap* is a brief time of very cold weather.

---

10. **reiterated** (rē-ĭt′ə-rā′tĭd): repeated.
11. **timber jams**: piled-up masses of floating logs and branches.

where he placed his feet. Once, coming around a bend he shied abruptly, like a startled horse, curved away from the place where he had been walking, and retreated several paces back along the trail. The creek he knew was frozen clear to the bottom—no creek could contain water in that arctic winter—but he knew also that there were springs that bubbled out from the hillsides and ran along under the snow and on top the ice of the creek. He knew that the coldest snaps never froze these springs, and he knew likewise their danger. They were traps. They hid pools of water under the snow that might be three inches deep, or three feet. Sometimes a skin of ice half an inch thick covered them, and in turn was covered by the snow. Sometimes there were alternate layers of water and ice skin, so that when one broke through he kept on breaking through for a while, sometimes wetting himself to the waist.

That was why he had shied in such panic. He had felt the give under his feet and heard the crackle of a snow-hidden ice skin. And to get his feet wet in such a temperature meant trouble and danger. At the very least it meant delay, for he would be forced to stop and build a fire, and under its protection to bare his feet while he dried his socks and moccasins. He stood and studied the creek bed and its banks, and decided that the flow of water came from his right. He reflected awhile, rubbing his nose and cheeks, then skirted to the left, stepping gingerly and testing the footing for each step. Once clear of the danger, he took a fresh chew of tobacco and swung along at his four-mile gait.[12]

In the course of the next two hours he came upon several similar traps. Usually the snow above the hidden pools had a sunken, candied appearance that advertised the danger. Once again, however, he had a close call; and once, suspecting danger, he compelled the dog to go on in front. The dog did not want to go. It hung back until the man shoved it forward, and then it went quickly across the white, unbroken surface. Suddenly it broke through, floundered to one side, and got away to firmer footing. It had wet its forefeet and legs, and almost immediately the water that clung to it turned to ice. It made quick efforts to lick the ice off its legs, then dropped down in the snow and began to bite out the ice that had

12. **four-mile gait:** walking pace of four miles per hour.

What Does It Mean?

The highlighted sentence means that it is dangerous if the man gets his feet wet because once they are wet, they will freeze very quickly. If his feet are frozen, he can't walk, so he can't get himself to safety.

What Does It Mean?

The man is rubbing his nose and cheeks to keep them warm and to avoid getting frostbite.

formed between the toes. This was a matter of instinct. To permit the ice to remain would mean sore feet. It did not know this. **It merely obeyed the mysterious prompting that arose from the deep crypts[13] of its being.** But the man knew, having achieved a judgment on the subject, and he removed the mitten from his right hand and helped tear out the ice particles. He did not expose his fingers more than a minute, and was astonished at the swift numbness that <u>smote</u> them. It certainly was cold. He pulled on the mitten hastily, and beat the hand savagely across his chest.

Pause **&** *Reflect*

What Does It Mean?
The highlighted sentence means that the dog obeyed his instinct.

Pause **&** *Reflect*

MARK IT UP 1. What should the man have done to protect his nose and cheeks? Circle the phrase on page 179 that tells the answer. **(Clarify)**

2. What happens to the dog after the man pushes it onto a trap in the snow? **(Cause and Effect)**

_____

_____

_____

_____

FOCUS
The man and the dog arrive at the forks of Henderson Creek. Read to find out more about their relationship.

At twelve o'clock the day was at its brightest. Yet the sun was too far south on its winter journey to clear the horizon. The bulge of the earth intervened between it and Henderson Creek, where the man walked under a clear sky at noon and cast no shadow. At half-past twelve, to the minute, he arrived at the forks of the creek. He was pleased at the speed he had made. If he kept it up, he would certainly be with the boys by six. He unbuttoned his jacket and shirt and drew forth his lunch. The action consumed no more than a quarter of a minute, yet in that brief moment the numbness laid hold of the exposed fingers. He did not put the mitten on, but, instead, struck the fingers a dozen sharp smashes against his leg. Then he sat down on a snow-covered log to eat. The sting that followed upon the striking of his fingers against his leg ceased so quickly that he was startled. He had had no chance to take a bite of biscuit. He struck the fingers repeatedly and returned them to the mitten, baring the

As the story continues . . .

• The man stops to eat lunch. He builds a fire to thaw out the ice on his face.

• The dog does not want to leave the warm fire, but the man whistles and calls angrily. They continue walking.

13. **crypts:** underground chambers; hidden places.

WORDS
TO
KNOW

smite (smīt) *v.* to strike; *past tense*—**smote** (smōt)

At this point

- the man takes off his mittens so he can eat lunch
- the ice on his face makes eating impossible
- his fingers are becoming numb

What does he need to do?

What Does It Mean?

The man is moving around, stomping his feet and swinging his arms to stay warm and keep his blood circulating.

What Does It Mean?

The highlighted words mean that for a brief time, the man has found a way to warm himself outdoors.

other hand for the purpose of eating. He tried to take a mouthful, but the ice muzzle prevented. He had forgotten to build a fire and thaw out. He chuckled at his foolishness, and as he chuckled he noted the numbness creeping into the exposed fingers. Also, he noted that the stinging which had first come to his toes when he sat down was already passing 240 away. He wondered whether the toes were warm or numb. He moved them inside the moccasins and decided that they were numb.

He pulled the mitten on hurriedly and stood up. He was a bit frightened. He stamped up and down until the stinging returned into the feet. It certainly was cold, was his thought. That man from Sulphur Creek had spoken the truth when telling how cold it sometimes got in the country. And he had laughed at him at the time! That showed one must not be too sure of things. There was no mistake about it, it *was* cold. He 250 strode up and down, stamping his feet and threshing his arms, until reassured by the returning warmth. Then he got out matches and proceeded to make a fire. From the undergrowth, where high water of the previous spring had lodged a supply of seasoned twigs, he got his firewood. Working carefully from a small beginning, he soon had a roaring fire, over which he thawed the ice from his face and in the protection of which he ate his biscuits. For the moment the cold of space was outwitted. The dog took satisfaction in the fire, stretching out close enough for warmth and far enough 260 away to escape being singed.

When the man had finished, he filled his pipe and took his comfortable time over a smoke, then he pulled on his mittens, settled the ear flaps of his cap firmly about his ears, and took the creek trail up the left fork. The dog was disappointed and yearned back towards the fire. This man did not know cold. Possibly all the generations of his ancestry had been ignorant of cold, of real cold, of cold one hundred and seven degrees below freezing point. But the dog knew; all its ancestry knew, and it had inherited 270 the knowledge. And it knew that it was not good to walk abroad in such fearful cold. It was the time to lie snug in a hole in the snow and wait for a curtain of cloud to be drawn across the face of outer space whence this cold came. On the other hand, there was no keen intimacy between the

dog and the man. The one was the toil slave[14] of the other, and the only caresses it had ever received were the caresses of the whip lash and of harsh and menacing throat sounds that threatened the whip lash. So the dog made no effort to communicate its apprehension to the man. It was not
280 concerned in the welfare of the man; it was for its own sake that it yearned back toward the fire. But the man whistled, and spoke to it with the sound of whip lashes, and the dog swung in at the man's heels and followed after.

Pause **&** *Reflect*

> **FOCUS**
> Read to find out what happens to endanger the man's life and what he does as a result.

The man took a chew of tobacco and proceeded to start a new amber beard. Also, his moist breath quickly powdered with white his mustache, eyebrows, and lashes. There did not seem to be so many springs on the left fork of the
290 Henderson, and for half an hour the man saw no signs of any. And then it happened. At a place where there were no signs, where the soft, unbroken snow seemed to advertise solidity beneath, the man broke through. It was not deep. He wet himself halfway to the knees before he floundered out to the firm crust. He was angry, and cursed his luck aloud. He had hoped to get into camp with the boys at six o'clock, and this would delay him an hour, for he would have to build a fire and dry out his footgear. This was imperative[15] at that low temperature—he knew that
300 much; and he turned aside to the bank, which he climbed. On top, tangled in the underbrush about the trunks of several small spruce trees, was a high-water deposit[16] of dry firewood—sticks and twigs, principally, but also larger portions of seasoned branches and fine, dry, last year's

---

14. **toil slave:** slave who performs hard labor.
15. **imperative** (ĭm-pĕr′ə-tĭv): urgently necessary.
16. **high-water deposit:** debris left on the bank of a stream as the water recedes from its highest level.

Pause **&** *Reflect*

📖 **READ ALOUD** **1.** Read aloud the boxed sentences on page 182. What does the dog know that the man does not? **(Compare and Contrast)**

_____
_____
_____
_____

2. Do you think the man will be able to reach camp safely? *Yes/No*, because _____

_____
_____
_____

(Predict)

As the story continues . . .

• The man falls through the ice.

• He makes another fire to dry his shoes and feet before they freeze.

grasses. He threw down several large pieces on top of the snow. This served for a foundation and prevented the young flame from drowning itself in the snow it otherwise would melt. The flame he got by touching a match to a small shred of birch bark that he took from his pocket. This burned even more readily than paper. Placing it on the foundation, he fed the young flame with wisps of dry grass and with the tiniest dry twigs.

He worked slowly and carefully, keenly aware of his danger. Gradually, as the flame grew stronger, he increased the size of the twigs with which he fed it. He squatted in the snow, pulling the twigs out from their entanglement in the brush and feeding directly to the flame. He knew there must be no failure. When it is seventy-five below zero, a man must not fail in his first attempt to build a fire—that is, if his feet are wet. If his feet are dry, and he fails, he can run along the trail for half a mile and restore his circulation. But the circulation of wet and freezing feet cannot be restored by running when it is seventy-five below. No matter how fast he runs, the wet feet will freeze the harder.

All this the man knew. The old-timer on Sulphur Creek had told him about it the previous fall, and now he was appreciating the advice. Already all sensation had gone out of his feet. To build the fire he had been forced to remove his mittens, and the fingers had quickly gone numb. His pace of four miles an hour had kept his heart pumping blood to the surface of his body and to all the <u>extremities</u>. But the instant he stopped, the action of the pump eased down. The cold of space smote the unprotected tip of the planet, and he, being on that unprotected tip, received the full force of the blow. The blood of his body recoiled before it. The blood was alive, like the dog, and like the dog it wanted to hide away and cover itself up from the fearful cold. So long as he walked four miles an hour, he pumped the blood, willy-nilly,[17] to the surface; but now it ebbed away and sank down into the recesses of his body. The extremities were the first to feel its absence. His wet feet froze the faster,

What Does It Mean?

Smote is the past tense of *smite*. In the highlighted part of the sentence, the author is creating a visual image in which outer space "hits" the top of Earth—the North Pole.

---

17. **willy-nilly:** unavoidably.

WORDS
TO
KNOW

extremity (ĭk-strĕm′ĭ-tē) *n.* a hand or a foot

and his exposed fingers numbed the faster, though they had not yet begun to freeze. Nose and cheeks were already freezing, while the skin of all his body chilled as it lost its blood.

But he was safe. Toes and nose and cheeks would be only touched by the frost, for the fire was beginning to burn with strength. He was feeding it with twigs the size of his finger. In another minute he would be able to feed it with branches the size of his wrist, and then he could remove his wet footgear, and, while it dried, he could keep his naked feet warm by the fire, rubbing them at first, of course, with snow. The fire was a success. He was safe. He remembered the advice of the old-timer on Sulphur Creek, and smiled. The old-timer had been very serious in laying down the law that no man must travel alone in (the Klondike) after fifty below. Well, here he was; he had had the accident; he was alone; and he had saved himself. Those old-timers were rather womanish, some of them, he thought. All a man had to do was to keep his head, and he was all right. Any man who was a man could travel alone. But it was surprising, the rapidity with which his cheeks and nose were freezing. And he had not thought his fingers could go lifeless in so short a time. Lifeless they were, for he could scarcely make them move together to grip a twig, and they seemed remote from his body and from him. When he touched a twig, he had to look and see whether or not he had hold of it. The wires were pretty well down between him and his finger ends.

All of which counted for little. There was the fire, snapping and crackling and promising life with every dancing flame. He started to untie his moccasins. They were coated with ice; the thick German socks were like sheaths of iron halfway to the knees; and the moccasin strings were like rods of steel all twisted and knotted as by some conflagration.[18] For a moment he tugged with his numb fingers, then, realizing the folly of it, he drew his sheath knife.

But before he could cut the strings, it happened. It was his own fault or, rather, his mistake. He should not have built the fire under the spruce tree. He should have built it in the open. But it had been easier to pull the twigs

✔ **Reading Check**
What forces the man to stop his journey? What does he do as a result?

More About . . .

THE KLONDIKE *The Klondike is a region of the Yukon Territory in Canada, just east of Alaska. In 1896, gold was discovered there, leading to the gold rush of 1897–1898.*

English Learner Support
VOCABULARY

Idiom The highlighted words mean that the man has lost all feeling in his fingertips. The nerves to his fingertips have become numb.

English Learner Support
LANGUAGE

Pronouns The pronoun *it* refers to the attempt or effort the man is making to untie the string.

---

18. **conflagration** (kŏn′flə-grā′shən): large, destructive fire.

Pause & Reflect

✏ **MARK IT UP** **1.** The man recalls the law of the wild that the old-timer on Sulphur Creek told him. Underline the sentence on page 185 that tells this law. **(Clarify)**

2. Reread the boxed sentences on this page. **Visualize,** or picture in your mind, the events that cause the fire to go out. Then write a sentence to **summarize** them.

_____

_____

_____

_____

As the story continues . . .

• The man tries to build another fire, but his fingers are frozen and numb.

from the brush and drop them directly on the fire. Now the tree under which he had done this carried a weight of snow on its boughs. No wind had blown for weeks, and each bough was full freighted. Each time he had pulled a twig he had communicated a slight agitation[19] to the tree—an imperceptible agitation, so far as he was concerned, but an agitation sufficient to bring about the disaster. High up in the tree one bough capsized[20] its load of snow. This fell on the boughs beneath, capsizing them. This process continued, spreading out and involving the whole tree. It grew like an avalanche, and it descended upon the man and the fire, and the fire was blotted out! Where it had burned was a mantle of fresh and disordered snow.

Pause & Reflect

FOCUS

Read to find out the steps the man takes to try to rebuild the fire.

✏ **MARK IT UP** As you read, list his actions in the margins.

The man was shocked. It was as though he had just heard his own sentence of death. For a moment he sat and stared at the spot where the fire had been. Then he grew very calm. Perhaps the old-timer on Sulphur Creek was right. If he had only had a trail mate he would have been in no danger now. The trail mate could have built the fire. Well, it was up to him to build the fire over again, and this second time there must be no failure. Even if he succeeded, he would most likely lose some toes. His feet must be badly frozen by now, and there would be some time before the second fire was ready.

Such were his thoughts, but he did not sit and think them. He was busy all the time they were passing through his mind. He made a new foundation for a fire, this time in the open, where no treacherous tree could blot it out. Next he gathered dry grasses and tiny twigs from the high-water flotsam.[21] He could not bring his fingers together to pull them out, but he was able to gather them by the handful. In this way he got

---

19. **agitation:** disturbance.

20. **capsized:** overturned.

21. **flotsam** (flŏt′səm): debris.

many rotten twigs and bits of green moss that were undesirable, but it was the best he could do. He worked methodically, even collecting an armful of the larger branches to be used later when the fire gathered strength. And all the while the dog sat and watched him, a certain wistfulness in its eyes, for it looked upon him as the fire provider, and the fire was slow in coming.

When all was ready, the man reached in his pocket for a second piece of birch bark. He knew the bark was there, and though he could not feel it with his fingers, he could hear its crisp rustling as he fumbled for it. Try as he would, he could not clutch hold of it. And all the time, in his consciousness, was the knowledge that each instant his feet were freezing. This thought tended to put him in a panic, but he fought against it and kept calm. He pulled on his mittens with his teeth, and threshed his arms back and forth, beating his hands with all his might against his sides. He did this sitting down, and he stood up to do it; and all the while the dog sat in the snow, its wolf brush of a tail curled around warmly over its forefeet, its sharp wolf ears pricked forward intently as it watched the man. And the man, as he beat and threshed with his arms and hands, felt a great surge of envy as he regarded the creature that was warm and secure in its natural covering.

After a time he was aware of the first faraway signals of sensations in his beaten fingers. The faint tingling grew stronger till it evolved into a stinging ache that was excruciating, but which the man hailed with satisfaction. He stripped the mitten from his right hand and fetched forth the birch bark. The exposed fingers were quickly going numb again. Next he brought out his bunch of sulphur matches. But the tremendous cold had already driven the life out of his fingers. In his effort to separate one match from the others, the whole bunch fell into the snow. He tried to pick it out of the snow, but failed. The dead fingers could neither clutch nor touch. He was very careful. He drove the thought of his freezing feet, and nose, and cheeks, out of his mind, devoting his whole soul to the matches. He watched, using the sense of vision in place of that of touch, and when he saw his fingers on each side the bunch, he closed them—that is, he willed to close them, for the wires were down, and the fingers did not obey. He pulled the mitten on the right hand,

Reading Tip

Fill in the last two boxes of the flowchart with the events that are happening in the story.

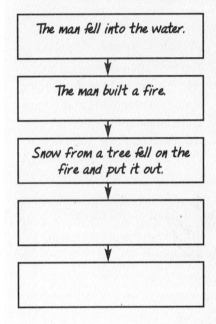

The man fell into the water.

↓

The man built a fire.

↓

Snow from a tree fell on the fire and put it out.

↓

↓

✔ Reading Check

Why does the man have trouble grabbing the matches?

and beat it fiercely against his knee. Then, with both mittened hands, he scooped the bunch of matches, along with much snow, into his lap. Yet he was no better off.

460 After some manipulation he managed to get the bunch between the heels of his mittened hands. In this fashion he carried it to his mouth. The ice crackled and snapped when by a violent effort he opened his mouth. He drew the lower jaw in, curled the upper lip out of the way and scraped the bunch with his upper teeth in order to separate a match. He succeeded in getting one, which he dropped on his lap. He was no better off. He could not pick it up. Then he devised a way. He picked it up in his teeth and scratched it on his leg. Twenty times he scratched before he succeeded in lighting it.

470 As it flamed he held it with his teeth to the birch bark. But the burning brimstone[22] went up his nostrils and into his lungs, causing him to cough spasmodically. The match fell into the snow and went out.

The old-timer on Sulphur Creek was right, he thought in the moment of controlled despair that <u>ensued</u>: after fifty below, a man should travel with a partner. He beat his hands, but failed in exciting any sensation. Suddenly he bared both hands, removing the mittens with his teeth. He caught the whole bunch between the heels of his hands. His arm muscles

480 not being frozen enabled him to press the hand heels tightly against the matches. Then he scratched the bunch along his leg. It flared into flame, seventy sulphur matches at once! There was no wind to blow them out. He kept his head to one side to escape the strangling fumes, and held the blazing bunch to the birch bark. As he so held it, he became aware of sensation in his hand. His flesh was burning. He could smell it. Deep down below the surface he could feel it. The sensation developed into pain that grew acute. And still he endured it, holding the flame of the matches clumsily to the

490 bark that would not light readily because his own burning hands were in the way, absorbing most of the flame.

At last, when he could endure no more, he jerked his hands apart. The blazing matches fell sizzling into the snow, but the birch bark was alight. He began laying dry grasses and the

---

22. **brimstone**: sulfur—a chemical used in match heads.

WORDS
TO
KNOW

ensue (ĕn-soo') *v.* to occur as a reult; follow

tiniest twigs on the flame. He could not pick and choose, for he had to lift the fuel between the heels of his hands. Small pieces of rotten wood and green moss clung to the twigs, and he bit them off as well as he could with his teeth. He cherished[23] the flame carefully and awkwardly. It meant life, and it must not perish. The withdrawal of blood from the surface of his body now made him begin to shiver, and he grew more awkward. A large piece of green moss fell squarely on the little fire. He tried to poke it out with his fingers, but his shivering frame made him poke too far, and he disrupted the nucleus of the little fire, the burning grasses and the tiny twigs separating and scattering. He tried to poke them together again, but in spite of the tenseness of the effort, his shivering got away with him, and the twigs were hopelessly scattered. Each twig gushed a puff of smoke and went out. The fire provider had failed. As he looked <u>apathetically</u> about him, his eyes chanced on the dog, sitting across the ruins of the fire from him, in the snow, making restless, hunching movements, slightly lifting one forefoot and then the other, shifting its weight back and forth on them with wistful eagerness.

Pause & Reflect

FOCUS

Read to find out about the man's wild idea to save his life.

The sight of the dog put a wild idea into his head. He remembered the tale of the man, caught in a blizzard, who killed a steer and crawled inside the carcass, and so was saved. He would kill the dog and bury his hands in the warm body until the numbness went out of them. Then he could build another fire. He spoke to the dog, calling it to him; but in his voice was a strange note of fear that frightened the animal, who had never known the man to speak in such a way before. Something was the matter, and its suspicious nature sensed danger—it knew not what

23. **cherished:** tended; guarded.

WORDS TO KNOW

apathetically (ăp´ə-thĕt´ĭ-klē) *adv.* with little interest or emotion

1. Review the list you made of the man's actions to rebuild the fire. What is the most difficult step in rebuilding the fire? Why is that step so difficult? **(Evaluate)**

_____
_____
_____
_____

2. Why does the man allow his hands to burn? **(Infer)**

_____
_____
_____
_____

MARK IT UP 3. Circle the sentence on this page that explains what falls on the flame, eventually putting it out.

As the story continues . . .

- The man turns to the dog for warmth, but the dog will not come close.
- The man tries to get feeling back into his body.

What Does It Mean?

The highlighted phrase means that because the man's feet are frozen, he can't feel the ground beneath them.

READ ALOUD **Lines 543–549**

The man can no longer use his hands. Vary the tone and volume of your voice to express his surprise and despair.

English Learner Support
VOCABULARY

Draw Here, *draw* means "to pull the knife from its sheath."

---

danger, but somewhere, somehow, in its brain arose an apprehension of the man. It flattened its ears down at the sound of the man's voice, and its restless, hunching
530 movements and the liftings and shiftings of its forefeet became more pronounced; but it would not come to the man. He got on his hands and knees and crawled toward the dog. This unusual posture again excited suspicion, and the animal sidled mincingly²⁴ away.

The man sat up in the snow for a moment and struggled for calmness. Then he pulled on his mittens, by means of his teeth, and got upon his feet. He glanced down at first in order to assure himself that he was really standing up, for the absence of sensation in his feet left him unrelated to the earth.
540 His erect position in itself started to drive the webs of suspicion from the dog's mind; and when he spoke peremptorily, with the sound of whip lashes in his voice, the dog rendered its customary allegiance and came to him. As it came within reaching distance, the man lost his control. His arms flashed out to the dog, and he experienced genuine surprise when he discovered that his hands could not clutch, that there was neither bend nor feeling in his fingers. He had forgotten for the moment that they were frozen and that they were freezing more and more. All this happened quickly, and
550 before the animal could get away, he encircled its body with his arms. He sat down in the snow, and in this fashion held the dog, while it snarled and whined and struggled.

But it was all he could do, hold its body encircled in his arms and sit there. He realized that he could not kill the dog. There was no way to do it. With his helpless hands he could neither draw nor hold his sheath knife nor throttle the animal. He released it, and it plunged wildly away, with tail between its legs, and still snarling. It halted forty feet away and surveyed him curiously, with ears sharply pricked forward.
560 The man looked down at his hands in order to locate them, and found them hanging on the ends of his arms. It struck him as curious that one should have to use his eyes in order to find out where his hands were. He began threshing his arms back

---

24. **sidled** (sīd'ld) **mincingly:** moved sideways with small steps.

WORDS
TO
KNOW

peremptorily (pə-rĕmp'tə-rĭ-lē) *adv.* in a commanding manner

and forth, beating the mittened hands against his sides. He did this for five minutes, violently, and his heart pumped enough blood up to the surface to put a stop to his shivering. But no sensation was aroused in the hands. He had an impression that they hung like weights on the ends of his arms, but when he tried to run the impression down, he could not find it.

570   A certain fear of death, dull and oppressive, came to him. This fear quickly became poignant[25] as he realized that it was no longer a mere matter of freezing his fingers and toes, or of losing his hands and feet, but that it was a matter of life and death with the chances against him. This threw him into a panic, and he turned and ran along the old, dim trail. The dog joined in behind and kept up with him. He ran blindly, without intention, in fear such as he had never known in his life. Slowly, as he plowed and floundered through the snow, he began to see things again—the banks of the creek, the old
580 timber jams, the leafless aspens, and the sky. The running made him feel better. He did not shiver. Maybe, if he ran on, his feet would thaw out; and, anyway, if he ran far enough, he would reach camp and the boys. Without doubt he would lose some fingers and toes and some of his face; but the boys would take care of him, and save the rest of him when he got there. And at the same time there was another thought in his mind that said he would never get to the camp and the boys; that he would soon be stiff and dead. This thought he kept in the background and refused to consider. Sometimes it pushed
590 itself forward and demanded to be heard, but he thrust it back and strove[26] to think of other things.

Pause & Reflect

FOCUS
Read to find out what happens to the man and the dog.

It struck him as curious that he could run at all on feet so frozen that he could not feel them when they struck the earth and took the weight of his body. He seemed to himself to skim along above the surface, and to have no connection with the earth.

---

25. **poignant** (poin'yənt): painful; distressing.
26. **strove**: tried hard; struggled.

Pause & Reflect

1. What is the man's wild idea to save his life? (Clarify)

_____

_____

_____

_____

2. Why does the wild idea fail? (Cause and Effect)

_____

_____

_____

_____

3. The fear of death throws the man into a panic. Circle the phrase below that tells how he acts. (Clarify)

curses the old-timer

runs wildly

stabs the dog

sets himself on fire

As the story ends . . .

- The man continues to run, but he cannot feel anything.
- Soon he begins to walk slowly.

Somewhere he had once seen a winged Mercury,[27] and he wondered if Mercury felt as he felt when skimming over the earth.

His theory of running until he reached camp and the boys had one flaw in it: he lacked the endurance. Several times he stumbled, and finally he tottered, crumpled up, and fell. When he tried to rise, he failed. He must sit and rest, he decided, and next time he would merely walk and keep on going. As he sat and regained his breath, he noted that he was feeling quite warm and comfortable. He was not shivering, and it even seemed that a warm glow had come to his chest and trunk. And yet, when he touched his nose or cheeks, there was no sensation. Running would not thaw them out. Nor would it thaw out his hands and feet. Then the thought came to him that the frozen portions of his body must be extending. He tried to keep this thought down, to forget it, to think of something else; he was aware of the panicky feeling that it caused, and he was afraid of the panic. But the thought asserted itself, and persisted, until it produced a vision of his body totally frozen. This was too much, and he made another wild run along the trail. Once he slowed down to a walk, but the thought of the freezing extending itself made him run again.

And all the time the dog ran with him, at his heels. When he fell down a second time, it curled its tail over its forefeet and sat in front of him, facing him, curiously eager and intent. The warmth and security of the animal angered him, and he cursed it till it flattened down its ears appeasingly. This time the shivering came more quickly upon the man. He was losing in his battle with the frost. It was creeping into his body from all sides. The thought of it drove him on, but he ran no more than a hundred feet, when he staggered and pitched headlong. It was his last panic. When he had recovered his breath and control, he sat up and entertained in his mind the conception of meeting death with dignity. However, the conception did not come to him in such terms. His idea of it was that he had been making a fool of himself, running around like a chicken

---

27. **Mercury:** the messenger of the gods in Roman mythology, who flew about by means of wings on his helmet and sandals.

WORDS
TO
KNOW
appeasingly (ə-pē′zĭng-lē) *adv.* in a way intended to soothe angry feelings

with its head cut off—such was the simile that occurred to him. Well, he was bound to freeze anyway, and he might as well take it decently. With this newfound peace of mind came the first glimmerings of drowsiness. A good idea, he thought, to sleep off to death. It was like taking an <u>anesthetic</u>. Freezing was not so bad as people thought. There were lots worse ways to die.

640 He pictured the boys finding his body the next day. Suddenly he found himself with them, coming along the trail and looking for himself. And, still with them, he came around a turn in the trail and found himself lying in the snow. He did not belong with himself any more, for even then he was out of himself, standing with the boys and looking at himself in the snow. It certainly was cold, was his thought. When he got back to the States he could tell the folks what real cold was. He drifted on from this to a vision of the old-timer on Sulphur Creek. He could see him quite clearly, warm and

650 comfortable, and smoking a pipe.

"You were right, old hoss;[28] you were right," the man mumbled to the old-timer of Sulphur Creek.

Then the man drowsed off into what seemed to him the most comfortable and satisfying sleep he had ever known. The dog sat facing him and waiting. The brief day drew to a close in a long, slow twilight. There were no signs of a fire to be made, and, besides, never in the dog's experience had it known a man to sit like that in the snow and make no fire. As the twilight drew on, its eager yearning for the fire mastered

660 it, and with a great lifting and shifting of forefeet, it whined softly, then flattened its ears down in anticipation of being chidden[29] by the man. But the man remained silent. Later the dog whined loudly. And still later it crept close to the man and caught the scent of death. This made the animal bristle and back away. A little longer it delayed, howling under the stars that leaped and danced and shone brightly in the cold sky. Then it turned and trotted up the trail in the direction of the camp it knew, where there were other food providers and fire providers.

Pause **&** *Reflect*

---

28. **old hoss:** old horse—here used as an affectionate term of address.
29. **chidden:** scolded.

WORDS TO KNOW   **anesthetic** (ăn′ĭs-thĕt′ĭk) *n.* a drug used to kill pain or to make a patient unconscious during surgery

Pause **&** **Reflect**

1. What prevents the man from running all the way to camp? **(Clarify)**

_____

_____

_____

✏ **MARK IT UP** **2.** Describe the man's attitude as he finally faces death. Circle details on this page that help you understand his attitude. **(Infer)**

_____

_____

_____

3. Check the phrase below that tells what the man's final thoughts are about. **(Infer)**

his friends   his dog

the old-timer   his feet

✏ **CHALLENGE**

At the end of the story, the dog trots off in search of fire and food. Mark other passages in the story that tell about the dog or his actions. How are the dog and the man different? How do you think the story would be different without the dog? Why do you think the author chose to include the dog in this story? **(Author's Purpose)**

Active Reading SkillBuilder

Visualizing

Many examples of imagery are visual—that is, they appeal to a reader's sense of sight. The process of forming a mental picture from a written description is called **visualizing.** As you read "To Build a Fire," practice your visualizing skills. In the diagram below, write or sketch descriptions from the story that help you to picture the setting, characters, or action. An example is shown.

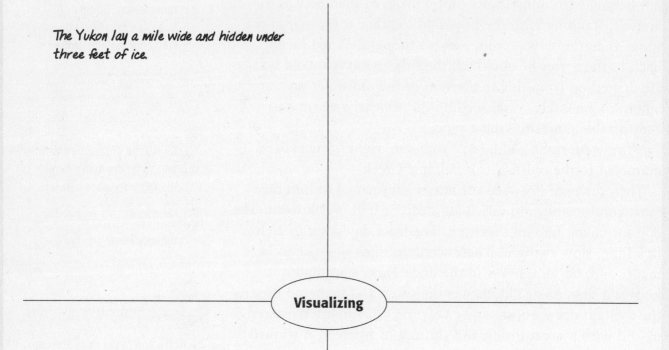

The Yukon lay a mile wide and hidden under three feet of ice.

Visualizing

Literary Analysis SkillBuilder

Imagery

Writers use **imagery** to create a picture in the reader's mind or to remind the reader of a familiar sensation. Imagery is language that appeals to one or more of the five senses—sight, smell, hearing, taste, and touch. Go back through the story and look for words and phrases that appeal to each of the five senses. In the chart, list as many different kinds of images as you can find. An example is shown.

Imagery in "To Build a Fire"	
Sight	"a subtle gloom that made the day dark"
Smell	
Hearing	
Taste	
Touch	

Words to Know SkillBuilder

Words to Know

| anesthetic | appeasingly | ensue | intangible | smite |
| apathetically | appendage | extremity | peremptorily | undulation |

A. Fill in each set of blanks with the correct word from the word list.

1. This describes something that is vague and hard to figure out.
   _ _ _ _ _ _ ☐ _ _ _

2. This word is used when something happens as a result of something else.
   _ ☐ ☐ _ _ _

3. This is the manner in which you take command of a situation.
   _ _ _ _ _ _ ☐ _ _ ☐ _ _ _

4. You probably would want this if you were having surgery.
   _ ☐ _ _ _ _ _ _ _ ☐ _

5. You have one of these at the end of each arm and leg.
   _ _ ☐ _ _ _ _ _

Complete the following sentence with the word the boxed letters spell out.

In "To Build a Fire," the dog's _____ is truer than the man's judgment.

B. Fill in each blank with the correct word from the word list.

1. The _____ of the sand looked almost like the ocean waves.

2. In the strong gust of wind, the man felt the sand _____ him in the face.

3. He was not interested in the sand, however; he _____ brushed the grains from his face.

4. He focused on the leash he held so tightly, it was like an _____ to his arm.

5. The man spoke _____ to the dog straining at the leash; he feared the tense animal would break loose and run into the crashing waves.

C. Write a brief, personal response to "To Build a Fire." Use at least **three** Words to Know.

The Scarlet Ibis

James Hurst

Before You Read

Connect to Your Life

In this story, the narrator is often cruel to his younger brother, even though he loves him. Have you ever been cruel to someone you love? Why or why not? Write your responses in the space below.

_____

_____

_____

_____

Key to the Story

WHAT'S THE BIG IDEA? Expectations are ideas about what a person is able to do or become. The narrator has high expectations of his younger brother. Think of the people who have expectations of you. Who are they? What do they expect from you? Fill in the word web below with your responses.

Expectations

My parents expect me to . . .

do my chores _____

_____

_____

_____

_____

_____

The Scarlet Ibis

James Hurst

SHORT STORY

Reading Tips

"The Scarlet Ibis" is about the relationship between the **narrator** and his brother, Doodle. The story includes many long sentences with vivid details about the **setting.** As you read, try not to get bogged down in the sentences. Keep moving and stay focused on the two brothers. The following questions can help:

- Is the narrator a good big brother to Doodle?
- How does the narrator now feel about his childhood actions?

MARK IT UP **KEEP TRACK**

As you read, you can use these marks to keep track of your understanding.

✔ ..... I understand.

? ..... I don't understand this.

! ..... Interesting or surprising idea

As the story begins . . .

- A first-person narrator is telling a story from his childhood.

PREVIEW "The Scarlet Ibis" is set in the South around the time of World War I (1914–1918). In this story, the narrator remembers his physically-challenged brother, Doodle, who was born tiny and weak. Although Doodle is not expected to live, he does. When the narrator tries to turn Doodle into the brother he always wanted, the results are not what either boy expects.

FOCUS

The story begins with memories of a day from the narrator's childhood.

MARK IT UP As you read, underline details that help you to **infer,** or guess, when and where the story takes place. Examples are highlighted.

It was in the clove[1] of seasons, summer was dead but autumn had not yet been born, that the ibis lit in the bleeding tree. The flower garden was stained with rotting brown magnolia petals and ironweeds grew rank[2] amid the purple phlox. The five o'clocks by the chimney still marked time, but the oriole nest in the elm was untenanted and rocked back and forth like an empty cradle. The last graveyard flowers were blooming, and their smell drifted across the cotton field and through every room of our house, speaking softly the names of our dead. It's strange that

1. **clove:** a separation or split.
2. **rank:** growing wildly and vigorously.

Review the details you marked.
When and where does the story
take place? **(Infer)**

When? _____

_____

Where? _____

_____

Reading Tip

The narrator begins by explaining that the ibis came during the time between summer and fall. After he sets the scene in this section, the narrator's story goes back even further in time in the next section of reading.

As the story continues . . .

• The narrator's brother is born with serious physical challenges.

• As the brother grows, he surprises the family by trying to do things they never expected him to do.

English Learner Support

CULTURE

Folklore The highlighted phrase means that people who were born with cauls were treated with awe and respect.

✔ **Reading Check**

Why do Doodle's parents wait three months to name him?

all this is still so clear to me, now that that summer has long since fled and time has had its way. A grindstone stands where the bleeding tree stood, just outside the kitchen door, and now if an oriole sings in the elm, its song seems to die up in the leaves, a silvery dust. The flower garden is prim, the house a gleaming white, and the pale fence across the yard stands straight and spruce. But sometimes (like right now), as I sit in the cool, green-draped parlor, the grindstone begins to turn, and time with all its changes is ground away—and I remember Doodle.

Pause **&** Reflect

FOCUS
Now the narrator tells about his younger brother, Doodle.
MARK IT UP As you read, circle statements that reveal the narrator's feelings and attitudes toward his younger brother.

Doodle was just about the craziest brother a boy ever had. Of course, he wasn't a crazy crazy like old Miss Leedie, who was in love with President Wilson and wrote him a letter every day, but was a nice crazy, like someone you meet in your dreams. He was born when I was six and was, from the outset, a disappointment. He seemed all head, with a tiny body which was red and shriveled like an old man's. Everybody thought he was going to die—everybody except Aunt Nicey, who had delivered him. She said he would live because he was born in a caul,[3] and cauls were made from Jesus' nightgown. Daddy had Mr. Heath, the carpenter, build a little mahogany coffin for him. But he didn't die, and when he was three months old, Mama and Daddy decided they might as well name him. They named him William Armstrong, which was like tying a big tail on a small kite. Such a name sounds good only on a tombstone.

I thought myself pretty smart at many things, like holding my breath, running, jumping, or climbing the vines in Old Woman Swamp, and I wanted more than anything else someone to race to Horsehead Landing, someone to box with,

---

3. **caul** (kôl): a thin membrane that covers the head of some babies at birth.

and someone to perch with in the top fork of the great pine behind the barn, where across the fields and swamps you could see the sea. I wanted a brother. But Mama, crying, told me that even if William Armstrong lived, he would never do these things with me. He might not, she sobbed, even be "all there." He might, as long as he lived, lie on the rubber sheet in the center of the bed in the front bedroom where the white marquisette curtains billowed out in the afternoon sea breeze, rustling like palmetto fronds.[4]

It was bad enough having an <u>invalid</u> brother, but having one who possibly was not all there was unbearable, so I began to make plans to kill him by smothering him with a pillow. However, one afternoon as I watched him, my head poked between the iron posts of the foot of the bed, he looked straight at me and grinned. I skipped through the rooms, down the echoing halls, shouting, "Mama, he smiled. He's all there! He's all there!" and he was.

When he was two, if you laid him on his stomach, he began to move himself, straining terribly. The doctor said that with his weak heart this strain would probably kill him, but it didn't. Trembling, he'd push himself up, turning first red, then a soft purple, and finally collapse back onto the bed like an old worn-out doll. I can still see Mama watching him, her hand pressed tight across her mouth, her eyes wide and unblinking. But he learned to crawl (it was his third winter), and we brought him out of the front bedroom, putting him on the rug before the fireplace. For the first time he became one of us.

As long as he lay all the time in bed, we called him William Armstrong, even though it was formal and sounded as if we were referring to one of our ancestors, but with his creeping around on the deerskin rug and beginning to talk, something had to be done about his name. It was I who renamed him. When he crawled, he crawled backward, as if he were in reverse and couldn't change gears. If you called him, he'd turn around as if he were going in the other direction, then he'd back right up to you to be picked up. Crawling backward

 Reading Check

Why does the narrator want a brother?

English Learner Support
VOCABULARY

Idiom A person who is *not all there* has limited mental abilities.

MARK IT UP **WORD POWER**

Mark words that you'd like to add to your **Personal Word List**. After reading, you can record the words and their meanings beginning on page 402.

---

4. **palmetto fronds:** the fanlike leaves of a kind of palm tree.

WORDS
TO   **invalid** (ĭn′və-lĭd) *n.* too ill to live a normal life
KNOW

1. Reread the statements you circled about the narrator's feelings. **Summarize** his feelings toward Doodle at this point in the story.

_____

_____

_____

_____

2. What special challenges does Doodle face? Underline details on pages 200–202 that describe Doodle and the problems he faces. **(Locate Details)**

3. As a child, how would you have felt about having a brother like Doodle? **(Connect)**

_____

_____

_____

_____

As the story continues . . .

• The narrator pulls Doodle around in a go-cart their father builds.

• The narrator takes Doodle to the narrator's favorite place.

• Doodle is afraid when the narrator makes him touch the coffin in the barn loft.

made him look like a doodlebug, so I began to call him Doodle, and in time even Mama and Daddy thought it was a better name than William Armstrong. Only Aunt Nicey disagreed. She said caul babies should be treated with special respect since they might turn out to be saints. Renaming my
90 brother was perhaps the kindest thing I ever did for him, because nobody expects much from someone called Doodle.

Although Doodle learned to crawl, he showed no signs of walking, but he wasn't idle. He talked so much that we all quit listening to what he said. It was about this time that Daddy built him a go-cart and I had to pull him around. At first I just paraded him up and down the piazza,[5] but then he started crying to be taken out into the yard, and it ended up by my having to lug him wherever I went. If I so much as picked up my cap, he'd start crying to go with me, and
100 Mama would call from wherever she was, "Take Doodle with you."

FOCUS

As the narrator becomes more responsible for Doodle, their relationship changes. Read to find out about those changes.

He was a burden in many ways. The doctor had said that he mustn't get too excited, too hot, too cold, or too tired and that he must always be treated gently. A long list of don'ts went with him, all of which I ignored once we got out of the house. To discourage his coming with me, I'd run with him across the ends of the
110 cotton rows and <u>careen</u> him around corners on two wheels. Sometimes I accidentally turned him over, but he never told Mama. His skin was very sensitive, and he had to wear a big straw hat whenever he went out. When the going got rough and he had to cling to the sides of the go-cart, the hat slipped

---

5. **piazza** (pē-ăz′ə): a large covered porch.

WORDS
TO
KNOW   **careen** (kə-rēn′) v. to rush carelessly

all the way down over his ears. He was a sight. Finally, I could see I was licked. Doodle was my brother and he was going to cling to me forever, no matter what I did, so I dragged him across the burning cotton field to share with him the only beauty I knew, Old Woman Swamp. I pulled the go-cart through the sawtooth fern, down into the green dimness where the palmetto fronds whispered by the stream. I lifted him out and set him down in the soft rubber grass beside a tall pine. His eyes were round with wonder as he gazed about him, and his little hands began to stroke the rubber grass. Then he began to cry.

"For heaven's sake, what's the matter?" I asked, annoyed.

"It's so pretty," he said. "So pretty, pretty, pretty."

After that day Doodle and I often went down into Old Woman Swamp. I would gather wildflowers, wild violets, honeysuckle, yellow jasmine, snakeflowers, and water lilies, and with wire grass we'd weave them into necklaces and crowns. We'd bedeck ourselves with our handiwork and loll about thus beautified, beyond the touch of the everyday world. Then when the slanted rays of the sun burned orange in the tops of the pines, we'd drop our jewels into the stream and watch them float away toward the sea.

There is within me (and with sadness I have watched it in others) a knot of cruelty borne by the stream of love, much as our blood sometimes bears the seed of our destruction, and at times I was mean to Doodle. One day I took him up to the barn loft and showed him his casket, telling him how we all had believed he would die. It was covered with a film of Paris green[6] sprinkled to kill the rats, and screech owls had built a nest inside it.

Doodle studied the mahogany box for a long time, then said, "It's not mine."

"It is," I said. "And before I'll help you down from the loft, you're going to have to touch it."

"I won't touch it," he said sullenly.

"Then I'll leave you here by yourself," I threatened, and made as if I were going down.

Doodle was frightened of being left. "Don't go leave me, Brother," he cried, and he leaned toward the coffin. His hand, trembling, reached out, and when he touched the casket he

What Does It Mean?
To *bedeck* is to cover something with decorations.

What Does It Mean?
When the narrator says there is "a knot of cruelty borne by the stream of love," he means that even though he loves Doodle, he is sometimes mean, or cruel, to him.

---

6. **Paris green:** a poisonous green powder used to kill pests.

Pause  Reflect

MARK IT UP Reread the boxed passage on page 203. Circle the lines that tell why the narrator decides to take Doodle to Old Woman Swamp. **(Cause and Effect)**

As the story continues . . .

• The narrator begins to teach Doodle to walk.

• Finally, Doodle is able to stand on his own for a few seconds.

• The narrator discovers that he is becoming proud of Doodle.

English Learner Support

LANGUAGE

Metaphor In the highlighted passage, the author is comparing pride to a seed. The passage foreshadows both the good and bad effects of the narrator's pride in his brother's achievements.

screamed. A screech owl flapped out of the box into our faces, scaring us and covering us with Paris green. Doodle was paralyzed, so I put him on my shoulder and carried him down the ladder, and even when we were outside in the bright sunshine, he clung to me, crying, "Don't leave me. Don't
160 leave me."

Pause  Reflect

FOCUS

Now the narrator decides to teach Doodle to walk. Read to find out what motivates him to do so.

When Doodle was five years old, I was embarrassed at having a brother of that age who couldn't walk, so I set out to teach him. We were down in Old Woman Swamp and it was spring and the sick-sweet smell of bay flowers hung everywhere like a mournful song. "I'm going to teach you to walk, Doodle," I said.

He was sitting comfortably on the soft grass, leaning back
170 against the pine. "Why?" he asked.

I hadn't expected such an answer. "So I won't have to haul you around all the time."

"I can't walk, Brother," he said.

"Who says so?" I demanded.

"Mama, the doctor—everybody."

"Oh, you can walk," I said, and I took him by the arms and stood him up. He collapsed onto the grass like a half-empty flour sack. It was as if he had no bones in his little legs.

"Don't hurt me, Brother," he warned.

180 "Shut up. I'm not going to hurt you. I'm going to teach you to walk." I heaved him up again, and again he collapsed.

This time he did not lift his face up out of the rubber grass. "I just can't do it. Let's make honeysuckle wreaths."

"Oh yes you can, Doodle," I said. "All you got to do is try. Now come on," and I hauled him up once more.

It seemed so hopeless from the beginning that it's a miracle I didn't give up. But all of us must have something or someone to be proud of, and Doodle had become mine. I did not know then that pride is a wonderful, terrible thing, a seed that
190 bears two vines, life and death. Every day that summer we

went to the pine beside the stream of Old Woman Swamp, and I put him on his feet at least a hundred times each afternoon. Occasionally I too became discouraged because it didn't seem as if he was trying, and I would say, "Doodle, don't you *want* to learn to walk?"

He'd nod his head, and I'd say, "Well, if you don't keep trying, you'll never learn." Then I'd paint for him a picture of us as old men, white-haired, him with a long white beard and me still pulling him around in the go-cart. This never failed to make him try again.

Finally one day, after many weeks of practicing, he stood alone for a few seconds. When he fell, I grabbed him in my arms and hugged him, our laughter pealing through the swamp like a ringing bell. Now we knew it could be done. Hope no longer hid in the dark palmetto thicket but perched like a cardinal in the lacy toothbrush tree, brilliantly visible.

"Yes, yes," I cried, and he cried it too, and the grass beneath us was soft and the smell of the swamp was sweet.

Pause & Reflect

FOCUS

Read to discover how the narrator feels when others learn that Doodle can walk.

MARK IT UP Circle words and phrases that help you to understand the narrator's feelings.

With success so <u>imminent</u>, we decided not to tell anyone until he could actually walk. Each day, barring rain, we sneaked into Old Woman Swamp, and by cotton-picking time Doodle was ready to show what he could do. He still wasn't able to walk far, but we could wait no longer. Keeping a nice secret is very hard to do, like holding your breath. We chose to reveal all on October eighth, Doodle's sixth birthday, and for weeks ahead we mooned around the house, promising everybody a most spectacular surprise. Aunt Nicey said that, after so much talk, if we produced

WORDS
TO
KNOW

imminent (ĭm′ə-nənt) *adj.* about to occur

READ ALOUD Read aloud the boxed passage on page 204. Which of the words listed below tells why the narrator taught Doodle to walk? Circle one. **(Evaluate)**

generosity

pride

jealousy

English Learner Support
LANGUAGE

Pronouns Pronouns are words that refer to people, places, or things. In the paragraph that begins with *Finally one day,* highlight in one color all of the pronouns that refer to Doodle. Use another color to highlight the pronouns that refer to the narrator. Circle the pronouns that refer to both of them.

As the story continues . . .

• Soon, Doodle is able to walk a short distance on his own.

• The rest of the family is surprised to see that Doodle can walk.

• Doodle and the narrator pass the time by making up stories.

anything less tremendous than the Resurrection,[7] she was going to be disappointed.

At breakfast on our chosen day, when Mama, Daddy, and Aunt Nicey were in the dining room, I brought Doodle to the door in the go-cart just as usual and had them turn their backs, making them cross their hearts and hope to die if they peeked. I helped Doodle up, and when he was standing alone
230 I let them look. There wasn't a sound as Doodle walked slowly across the room and sat down at his place at the table. Then Mama began to cry and ran over to him, hugging him and kissing him. Daddy hugged him too, so I went to Aunt Nicey, who was thanks praying in the doorway, and began to waltz her around. We danced together quite well until she came down on my big toe with her brogans,[8] hurting me so badly I thought I was crippled for life.

Doodle told them it was I who had taught him to walk, so everyone wanted to hug me, and I began to cry.
240 "What are you crying for?" asked Daddy, but I couldn't answer. They did not know that I did it for myself; that pride, whose slave I was, spoke to me louder than all their voices, and that Doodle walked only because I was ashamed of having a crippled brother.

Within a few months Doodle had learned to walk well and his go-cart was put up in the barn loft (it's still there) beside his little mahogany coffin. Now, when we roamed off together, resting often, we never turned back until our destination had been reached, and to help pass the time,
250 we took up lying.[9] From the beginning Doodle was a terrible liar and he got me in the habit. Had anyone stopped to listen to us, we would have been sent off to Dix Hill.

My lies were scary, involved, and usually pointless, but Doodle's were twice as crazy. People in his stories all had wings and flew wherever they wanted to go. His favorite lie was about a boy named Peter who had a pet peacock with a ten-foot tail. Peter wore a golden robe that glittered so brightly that when he walked through the sunflowers
260 they turned away from the sun to face him. When Peter

READ ALOUD Lines 225–244

As you read aloud, try to express the narrator's different feelings about Doodle's accomplishment.

English Learner Support
LANGUAGE

Usage In the highlighted phrase, the narrator says that he was a slave to pride. He means that he felt he had to help Doodle learn to walk so he wouldn't be ashamed of him.

 Reading Check

Why does the narrator teach Doodle to walk?

---

7. **the Resurrection:** the rising of Jesus Christ from the dead after his burial.

8. **brogans** (brō′gənz): heavy, ankle-high work shoes.

9. **lying:** here used to refer to the telling of tall tales, not untruths intended to deceive.

was ready to go to sleep, the peacock spread his magnificent tail, enfolding the boy gently like a closing go-to-sleep flower, burying him in the gloriously <u>iridescent</u>, rustling vortex.[10] Yes, I must admit it. Doodle could beat me lying.

Doodle and I spent lots of time thinking about our future. We decided that when we were grown we'd live in Old Woman Swamp and pick dog-tongue for a living. Beside the stream, he planned, we'd build us a house of whispering leaves and the swamp birds would be our chickens. All day
270   long (when we weren't gathering dog-tongue) we'd swing through the cypresses on the rope vines, and if it rained we'd huddle beneath an umbrella tree and play stickfrog. Mama and Daddy could come and live with us if they wanted to. He even came up with the idea that he could marry Mama and I could marry Daddy. Of course, I was old enough to know this wouldn't work out, but the picture he painted was so beautiful and serene that all I could do was whisper Yes, yes.

Pause & Reflect

FOCUS

The narrator continues to push Doodle to develop his skills.
280   **MARK IT UP** As you read, underline the different activities in Doodle's "development program."

Once I had succeeded in teaching Doodle to walk, I began to believe in my own <u>infallibility</u>, and I prepared a terrific development program for him, unknown to Mama and Daddy, of course. I would teach him to run, to swim, to climb trees, and to fight. He, too, now believed in my infallibility, so we set the deadline for these accomplishments less than a year away, when, it had been decided, Doodle could start to school.

That winter we didn't make much progress, for I was in
290   school and Doodle suffered from one bad cold after another. But when spring came, rich and warm, we raised our sights

---

10. **vortex:** a whirlpool or whirlwind; here, a reference to the funnel-shaped covering of feathers.

WORDS TO KNOW	**iridescent** (ĭr'ĭ-dĕs'ənt) *adj.* shining with shifting rainbow colors
	infallibility (ĭn-făl'ə-bĭl'ĭ-tē) *n.* an inability to make errors

Pause & Reflect

1. Review the words and phrases you marked. How does the narrator feel after he shows his parents that Doodle can walk? **(Cause and Effect)**

_____

_____

_____

_____

2. How would you describe each boy's feelings for his brother now? **(Evaluate)**

Narrator: _____

_____

Doodle: _____

_____

As the story continues . . .

• The narrator begins teaching Doodle to run, climb, swim, and row.

• The summer of 1918 brings hardship for the family.

• The narrator quickens the pace in training Doodle to become more athletic.

☑ **Reading Check**

During the summer of 1918,

- the crops died because there was no rain

- a hurricane came and tipped over trees and ruined both the cotton crop and the corn crop

- a war began, and a local family lost a son in it

How do these events affect the narrator and Doodle?

English Learner Support

LANGUAGE

Simile In the highlighted text, the author is comparing the way the hurricane ripped trees from the earth to the way a hawk might rip off pieces of chicken to eat.

again. Success lay at the end of summer like a pot of gold, and our campaign got off to a good start. On hot days, Doodle and I went down to Horsehead Landing, and I gave him swimming lessons or showed him how to row a boat. Sometimes we descended into the cool greenness of Old Woman Swamp and climbed the rope vines or boxed scientifically beneath the pine where he had learned to walk. Promise hung about us like the leaves, and wherever we 300 looked, ferns unfurled and birds broke into song.

That summer, the summer of 1918, was blighted. In May and June there was no rain and the crops withered, curled up, then died under the thirsty sun. One morning in July a hurricane came out of the east, tipping over the oaks in the yard and splitting the limbs of the elm trees. That afternoon it roared back out of the west, blew the fallen oaks around, snapping their roots and tearing them out of the earth like a hawk at the entrails[11] of a chicken. Cotton bolls were wrenched from the stalks and lay like green walnuts in the 310 valleys between the rows, while the cornfield leaned over uniformly so that the tassels touched the ground. Doodle and I followed Daddy out into the cotton field, where he stood, shoulders sagging, surveying the ruin. When his chin sank down onto his chest, we were frightened, and Doodle slipped his hand into mine. Suddenly Daddy straightened his shoulders, raised a giant knuckly fist, and with a voice that seemed to rumble out of the earth itself began cursing heaven, hell, the weather, and the Republican Party.[12] Doodle and I, prodding each other and giggling, went back to the house, 320 knowing that everything would be all right.

And during that summer, strange names were heard through the house: Château-Thierry, Amiens, Soissons, and in her blessing at the supper table, Mama once said, "And bless the Pearsons, whose boy Joe was lost at Belleau Wood."[13]

So we came to that clove of seasons. School was only a few weeks away, and Doodle was far behind schedule. He could barely clear the ground when climbing up the rope vines, and his swimming was certainly not passable. We decided to

---

11. **entrails**: internal organs.

12. **Republican Party**: in 1918, most Southerners were democrats.

13. **Château-Thierry** (shä-tō-tyĕ-rē′), **Amiens** (ä-myăN′), **Soissons** (swä-sôN′)... **Belleau** (bĕ-lō′) **Wood**: places in France where famous battles were fought near the end of World War I.

double our efforts, to make that last drive and reach our pot
330 of gold. I made him swim until he turned blue and row until
he couldn't lift an oar. Wherever we went, I purposely walked
fast, and although he kept up, his face turned red and his eyes
became glazed. Once, he could go no further, so he collapsed
on the ground and began to cry.

"Aw, come on, Doodle," I urged. "You can do it. Do you
want to be different from everybody else when you start
school?"

"Does it make any difference?"

"It certainly does," I said. "Now, come on," and I helped
340 him up.

Pause & Reflect

FOCUS

One day, the brothers discover an unusual bird, the scarlet ibis.

✎ MARK IT UP As you read, mark a **D** next to passages that show Doodle's feelings about the bird.

As we slipped through dog days,[14] Doodle began to look feverish, and Mama felt his forehead, asking him if he felt ill. At night he didn't sleep well, and sometimes he had nightmares, crying out until I touched him and said, "Wake up, Doodle. Wake up."

It was Saturday noon, just a few days before school was to start. I should have already admitted
350 defeat, but my pride wouldn't let me. The excitement of our program had now been gone for weeks, but still we kept on with a tired <u>doggedness</u>. It was too late to turn back, for we had both wandered too far into a net of expectations and had left no crumbs behind.

Daddy, Mama, Doodle, and I were seated at the dining-room table having lunch. It was a hot day, with all the windows and doors open in case a breeze should come. In the kitchen Aunt Nicey was humming softly. After a long silence,

---

14. **dog days:** the hot, uncomfortable days between early July and early September (named after the Dog Star, Sirius, which rises and sets with the sun at that time).

WORDS
TO   **doggedness** (dô′gĭd-nĭs) *n.* persistence; stubbornness
KNOW

Pause & Reflect

1. How successful is Doodle in his training program? (**Evaluate**)

_____

_____

2. Review the activities you underlined. Do you think the narrator is realistic about Doodle's abilities? Rate the narrator's judgment on a scale of one to five. Then give a reason for your rating. (**Make Judgments**)

1	2	3	4	5
very unrealistic				very realistic

_____

_____

_____

As the story continues . . .

• A strange bird appears in a tree outside the family house and then falls dead.

• Doodle buries the bird and sings sadly.

• Doodle and the narrator continue Doodle's training.

What Does It Mean?

In the highlighted text, the narrator means that he and Doodle had such high expectations of Doodle's progress that they couldn't admit failure. Success had become too important to them, and they *had left no crumbs behind,* or they had no way of turning back from their program.

Daddy spoke. "It's so calm, I wouldn't be surprised if we had
360 a storm this afternoon."

"I haven't heard a rain frog," said Mama, who believed in
signs, as she served the bread around the table.

"I did," declared Doodle. "Down in the swamp."

"He didn't," I said contrarily.

"You did, eh?" said Daddy, ignoring my denial.

"I certainly did," Doodle <u>reiterated</u>, scowling at me over
the top of his iced-tea glass, and we were quiet again.

Suddenly, from out in the yard, came a strange croaking
noise. Doodle stopped eating, with a piece of bread poised
370 ready for his mouth, his eyes popped round like two blue
buttons. "What's that?" he whispered.

I jumped up, knocking over my chair, and had reached the
door when Mama called, "Pick up the chair, sit down again,
and say excuse me."

By the time I had done this, Doodle had excused himself
and had slipped out into the yard. He was looking up into the
bleeding tree. "It's a great big red bird!" he called.

The bird croaked loudly again, and Mama and Daddy came
out into the yard. We shaded our eyes with our hands against
380 the hazy glare of the sun and peered up through the still
leaves. On the topmost branch a bird the size of a chicken,
with scarlet feathers and long legs, was perched <u>precariously</u>.
Its wings hung down loosely, and as we watched, a feather
dropped away and floated slowly down through the green
leaves.

"It's not even frightened of us," Mama said.

"It looks tired," Daddy added. "Or maybe sick."

Doodle's hands were clasped at his throat, and I had never
seen him stand still so long. "What is it?" he asked.

390 Daddy shook his head. "I don't know, maybe it's—"

At that moment the bird began to flutter, but the wings
were uncoordinated, and amid much flapping and a spray of
flying feathers, it tumbled down, bumping through the limbs
of the bleeding tree and landing at our feet with a thud. Its
long, graceful neck jerked twice into an S, then straightened
out, and the bird was still. A white veil came over the eyes

WORDS
TO
KNOW

reiterate (rē-ĭt′ə-rāt) *v.* to repeat
precariously (prĭ-kâr′ē-əs-lē) *adv.* insecurely; in a
dangerous way

and the long white beak unhinged. Its legs were crossed and its clawlike feet were delicately curved at rest. Even death did not mar its grace, for it lay on the earth like a broken vase of red flowers, and we stood around it, awed by its <u>exotic</u> beauty.

"It's dead," Mama said.

"What is it?" Doodle repeated.

"Go bring me the bird book," said Daddy.

I ran into the house and brought back the bird book. As we watched, Daddy thumbed through its pages. "It's a scarlet ibis," he said, pointing to a picture. "It lives in the tropics—South America to Florida. A storm must have brought it here."

Sadly, we all looked back at the bird. A scarlet ibis! How many miles it had traveled to die like this, in *our* yard, beneath the bleeding tree.

"Let's finish lunch," Mama said, nudging us back toward the dining room.

"I'm not hungry," said Doodle, and he knelt down beside the ibis.

"We've got peach cobbler for dessert," Mama tempted from the doorway.

Doodle remained kneeling. "I'm going to bury him."

"Don't you dare touch him," Mama warned. "There's no telling what disease he might have had."

"All right," said Doodle. "I won't."

Daddy, Mama, and I went back to the dining-room table, but we watched Doodle through the open door. He took out a piece of string from his pocket and, without touching the ibis, looped one end around its neck. Slowly, while singing softly "Shall We Gather at the River," he carried the bird around to the front yard and dug a hole in the flower garden, next to the petunia bed. Now we were watching him through the front window, but he didn't know it. His awkwardness at digging the hole with a shovel whose handle was twice as long as he was made us laugh, and we covered our mouths with our hands so he wouldn't hear.

More About...

BIRD SYMBOLISM Birds are often used as symbols. For example, the dove is a symbol of peace, and the eagle is a symbol of the United States. In this selection, the scarlet ibis—an exotic visitor— becomes a symbol for Doodle. Both are sick, weak, fragile, and awkward, but they are also both beautiful. An owl, a symbol of both death and wisdom, flies out of Doodle's coffin (on pages 203–204).

✔ **Reading Check**

What is the rest of the family doing while Doodle is burying the dead ibis?

WORDS
TO
KNOW

exotic (ĭg-zŏt′ĭk) *adj.* excitingly strange

1. How did the scarlet ibis end up
in the family's backyard and
what happened to it there?
(Cause and Effect)

_____

_____

_____

_____

2. How does each boy respond to
the scarlet ibis? (Compare and
Contrast)

_____

_____

_____

_____

3. Review the passages you
marked with a **D** as you read.
Why do you think Doodle is so
moved by the scarlet ibis?
(Infer)

_____

_____

_____

_____

_____

As the story ends . . .

• A thunderstorm begins while
Doodle and the narrator are
outside.

• The narrator runs ahead,
leaving Doodle behind.

When Doodle came into the dining room, he found us
seriously eating our cobbler. He was pale and lingered just
inside the screen door. "Did you get the scarlet ibis buried?"
asked Daddy.

Doodle didn't speak but nodded his head.

"Go wash your hands, and then you can have some peach
440 cobbler," said Mama.

"I'm not hungry," he said.

"Dead birds is bad luck," said Aunt Nicey, poking her head
from the kitchen door. "Specially *red* dead birds!"

As soon as I had finished eating, Doodle and I hurried off
to Horsehead Landing. Time was short, and Doodle still had a
long way to go if he was going to keep up with the other boys
when he started school. The sun, gilded with the yellow cast
of autumn, still burned fiercely, but the dark green woods
through which we passed were shady and cool. When we
450 reached the landing, Doodle said he was too tired to swim, so
we got into a skiff and floated down the creek with the tide.
Far off in the marsh a rail was scolding, and over on the
beach locusts were singing in the myrtle trees. Doodle did not
speak and kept his head turned away, letting one hand trail
limply in the water.

FOCUS
Read the rest of the
story to find out what
happens when a
storm arises.

After we had drifted a long way, I put the
oars in place and made Doodle row
back against the tide. Black clouds
began to gather in the southwest, and
he kept watching them, trying to pull
460 the oars a little faster. When we reached Horsehead Landing,
lightning was playing across half the sky and thunder roared
out, hiding even the sound of the sea. The sun disappeared
and darkness descended, almost like night. Flocks of marsh
crows flew by, heading inland to their roosting trees; and two
egrets, squawking, arose from the oyster-rock shallows and
careened away.

Doodle was both tired and frightened, and when he stepped from the skiff he collapsed onto the mud, sending an armada of fiddler crabs rustling off into the marsh grass. I helped him up, and as he wiped the mud off his trousers, he smiled at me ashamedly. He had failed and we both knew it, so we started back home, racing the storm. We never spoke (What are the words that can solder[15] cracked pride?), but I knew he was watching me, watching for a sign of mercy. The lightning was near now, and from fear he walked so close behind me he kept stepping on my heels. The faster I walked, the faster he walked, so I began to run. The rain was coming, roaring through the pines, and then, like a bursting Roman candle, a gum tree ahead of us was shattered by a bolt of lightning. When the deafening peal of thunder had died, and in the moment before the rain arrived, I heard Doodle, who had fallen behind, cry out, "Brother, Brother, don't leave me! Don't leave me!"

The knowledge that Doodle's and my plans had come to naught[16] was bitter, and that streak of cruelty within me awakened. I ran as fast as I could, leaving him far behind with a wall of rain dividing us. The drops stung my face like nettles,[17] and the wind flared the wet glistening leaves of the bordering trees. Soon I could hear his voice no more.

I hadn't run too far before I became tired, and the flood of childish spite evanesced[18] as well. I stopped and waited for Doodle. The sound of rain was everywhere, but the wind had died and it fell straight down in parallel paths like ropes hanging from the sky. As I waited, I peered through the downpour, but no one came. Finally I went back and found him huddled beneath a red nightshade bush beside the road. He was sitting on the ground, his face buried in his arms, which were resting on his drawn-up knees. "Let's go, Doodle," I said.

He didn't answer, so I placed my hand on his forehead and lifted his head. Limply, he fell backward onto the earth. He

470

480

490

500

What Does It Mean?
A *Roman candle* is a kind of firework.

**Reading Check**
Why did the narrator run ahead of Doodle and leave him behind?

Reading Tip
The relationship between the narrator and his brother is very important. Review what you've read. Then, fill in the last three boxes of this flowchart to show how the narrator's feelings toward his brother change.

> When Doodle was born, the narrator was disappointed with him.

> When the narrator learned that his brother might not be "all there," he wanted to kill him.

---

15. **solder** (sŏd′ər): to join or bond together.

16. **naught**: nothing.

17. **nettles**: weeds covered with stinging hairs.

18. **evanesced** (ĕv′ə-nĕst′): disappeared; vanished.

_____

_____

_____

_____

_____

_____

_____

_____

_____

_____

CHALLENGE

Foreshadowing is a writer's use of hints or clues to show what will happen later in the story. Look back through the story and mark passages that foreshadow what eventually happens. Why do you think Hurst chose to use foreshadowing?

had been bleeding from the mouth, and his neck and the front of his shirt were stained a brilliant red.

"Doodle! Doodle!" I cried, shaking him, but there was no answer but the ropy rain. He lay very awkwardly, with his head thrown far back, making his vermilion[19] neck appear unusually long and slim. His little legs, bent sharply at the knees, had never before seemed so fragile, so thin.

I began to weep, and the tear-blurred vision in red before me looked very familiar. "Doodle!" I screamed above the pounding storm and threw my body to the earth above his. For a long long time, it seemed forever, I lay there crying, sheltering my fallen scarlet ibis from the <u>heresy</u> of rain.

Pause & Reflect

---

19. **vermilion** (vər-mĭl′yən): bright red or scarlet.

WORDS
TO
KNOW

heresy (hĕr′ĭ-sē) *n.* an action or opinion contrary to what is generally thought of as right

Active Reading SkillBuilder

Drawing Conclusions About the Narrator

To make an inference, readers look at details and make logical guesses about what they mean. To **draw a conclusion,** readers combine these inferences with what they already know. An active reader of fiction is constantly making inferences and drawing conclusions about what the characters are doing or thinking and what motivates them. As you read this selection, use the chart to record three passages from which you can infer something about the narrator. Using these inferences, draw a conclusion about him.

Passage	Inference
"It was bad enough having an invalid brother, but having one who possibly was not all there was unbearable."	The narrator is insensitive to others and is thinking only of himself.

Conclusion

Literary Analysis SkillBuilder

Theme

A **theme** is the central idea or message in a work of fiction. It is a perception about life or human nature that the writer shares with the reader. Ways to look for a theme in a story include:

- reviewing what happens to the main character. (Does the character change during the story? What does the character learn about life?)
- skimming key phrases and sentences that say something about life or people in general.
- thinking about the story's title. (Does it have a meaning that could lead to a major theme?)
- remembering that a story may have more than one theme.

Go back through the story and list statements that go under the headings in the chart below.

What Narrator Learns	Key Passages	Importance of Title
Lines 116-117: Doodle was my brother and he was going to cling to me no matter what I did...		

Follow Up: Write the themes you find in complete sentences. Compare your themes with those of classmates.

Words to Know SkillBuilder

Words to Know

careen	exotic	imminent	invalid	precariously
doggedness	heresy	infallibility	iridescent	reiterate

A. Decide which word from the word list belongs in each numbered blank. Then write the word on the blank line on the right.

No, "Misisipi" isn't how to spell the state. To be
Correct you must (1) both s's and the p.

_____
(1)

That vase is priceless! Children, stop!
Do not (2) about the shop!

_____
(2)

When I begin to fidget, you can tell
My boredom means my (3) farewell.

_____
(3)

To anyone who knows geography,
"The world is flat" is simply (4)!

_____
(4)

Spilled oil isn't lovely, but when it reflects the light,
It makes an odd and interesting, (5) sight.

_____
(5)

My parents said no when I asked for a pup.
I kept pleading as days and weeks passed.
At last they gave in when I didn't give up,
So, my (6) paid off at last!

_____
(6)

B. Fill in each blank with the correct word from the word list.

1. If you spell _____ wrong, it's a trait you don't have!

2. The Korean dish kim-chee is as _____ to a Canadian as Canadian bacon is to a Korean.

3. We moved in with my _____ grandparents to take care of them when their health failed.

4. A straw hat would sit on your head _____ during a windstorm.

C. Imagine that ten years have passed since Doodle's death. What advice do you think the narrator would give a child who was in a situation that was similar to the one the narrator had been in while Doodle was alive? Write down that advice, using at least **three** of the Words to Know.

from

BLACK
boy

Richard Wright

Before You Read

Connect to Your Life

What are your hopes and dreams? What do you hope to become? In the chart below, list some of the dreams and goals you hope to achieve.

MY DREAMS AND GOALS	WHAT I MIGHT DO TO ACHIEVE THEM

Key to the Autobiography

WHAT YOU NEED TO KNOW Richard Wright grew up in the South during the early 1900s. At that time, discrimination against African Americans was legal through what were called the Jim Crow laws. These laws required separate public facilities, such as schools and buses, for blacks and whites. Blacks received less schooling than whites or were given only vocational education. Blacks who fought such discrimination were often beaten or killed. Because these laws were in place, the hopes, dreams, and goals of many blacks were restricted.

Richard Wright's dreams of becoming a writer were challenged when he published his first newspaper article. Surprisingly, the challenges came from within his own community.

Reading Tips

As you read, keep in mind that the author was only 15 years old during the events described. In this era, young people were taught to please and obey their elders.

- Look for details that help you understand the author's rebellious personality.

- Pay close attention to the **dialogue** and what it reveals about the personalities of the speakers.

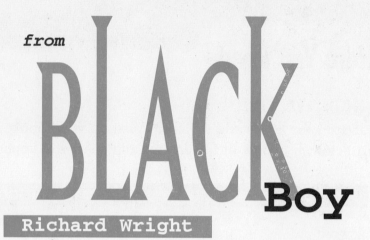

from **BLACK Boy**

Richard Wright

PREVIEW Today, Richard Wright is remembered as an important American author, but he began with very few advantages. At the time described in this excerpt from his **autobiography,** Wright lived in Jackson, Mississippi. Like other African Americans who lived in the South in the early 1900s, Wright faced many forms of discrimination. In this part of his autobiography, he tells about his early beginnings as a writer.

As the autobiography begins . . .

- Richard Wright is an an eighth grader living in the South in the early 1900s.

- He writes a story and brings it to the local African American newspaper editor, who agrees to publish it.

MARK IT UP **KEEP TRACK**

As you read, you can use these marks to keep track of your understanding.

✔ ..... I understand.

? ..... I don't understand this.

! ..... Interesting or surprising idea

FOCUS

One afternoon, Wright was bored in his eighth-grade classroom. Then an idea struck him. Read to find out how that idea changed his life.

MARK IT UP As you read, jot down notes in the margins to describe your impressions of the author.

The eighth grade days flowed in their hungry path, and I grew more conscious of myself; I sat in classes, bored, wondering, dreaming. One long dry afternoon I took out my composition book and told myself that I would write a story; it was sheer idleness that led me to it. What would the story be about? It resolved itself into a plot about a villain who wanted a widow's home, and I called it *The Voodoo of Hell's Half-Acre.*

It was crudely atmospheric, emotional, <u>intuitively</u> psychological, and stemmed from pure feeling. I finished it in three days and then wondered what to do with it.

The local Negro newspaper! That's it . . . I sailed into the office and shoved my ragged composition book under the nose of the man who called himself the editor.

WORDS TO KNOW

intuitively (ĭn-tōō′ĭ-tĭv-lē) *adv.* in a way that involves knowing something without having consciously learned it

"What's that?" he asked.

"A story," I said.

20 "A news story?"

"No, fiction."

"All right. I'll read it," he said.

He pushed my composition book back on his desk and looked at me curiously, sucking at his pipe.

"But I want you to read it *now*," I said.

He blinked. I had no idea how newspapers were run. I thought that one took a story to an editor, and he sat down then and there and read it and said yes or no.

"I'll read this and let you know about it tomorrow,"he said.

30 I was disappointed; I had taken time to write it, and he seemed distant and uninterested.

"Give me the story," I said, reaching for it.

He turned from me, took up the book, and read ten pages or more.

"Won't you come in tomorrow?" he asked. "I'll have it finished then."

I honestly relented.

"All right," I said. "I'll stop in tomorrow."

I left with the conviction that he would not read it. Now, where
40 else could I take it after he had turned it down? The next after-noon, en route to my job, I stepped into the newspaper office.

"Where's my story?" I asked.

"It's in galleys," he said.

"What's that?" I asked; I did not know what galleys were.

"It's set up in type," he said. "We're publishing it."

"How much money will I get?" I asked, excited.

"We can't pay for manuscript," he said.

"But you sell your papers for money," I said with logic.

"Yes, but we're young in business," he explained.

50 "But you're asking me to *give* you my story, but you don't *give* your papers away," I said.

He laughed.

"Look, you're just starting. This story will put your name before our readers. Now, that's something," he said.

"But if the story is good enough to sell to your readers, then you ought to give me some of the money you get from it," I insisted.

READ ALOUD Lines 47–57

As you read aloud the dialogue, notice how determined the young author is.

English Learner Support
VOCABULARY

Conviction *Conviction* means "strong belief."

More About . . .

GALLEYS A *galley* is a printed draft of a newspaper story that is read for errors before the final draft is printed in the paper.

What Does It Mean?

When the editor uses the term *young in business,* he means that the newspaper hasn't been in business very long and doesn't make a lot of money yet.

Reading Check

Why doesn't the editor pay Wright for the story?

WORDS
TO
KNOW **relent** (rǐ-lěnt') *v.* to become less harsh, strict, or stubborn

from **Black Boy** **221**

What Does It Mean?

Here, the word *installments* means "portions of a literary work."

Pause & Reflect

Look back at the notes you wrote in the margins. What are your impressions of Richard Wright? **(Evaluate)**

_____

_____

_____

_____

As the autobiography continues . . .

- Wright is criticized by his friends and family for writing the story.

- Wright wonders if he has done something wrong.

He laughed again, and I sensed that I was amusing him.

60 "I'm going to offer you something more valuable than money," he said. "I'll give you a chance to learn to write."

I was pleased, but I still thought he was taking advantage of me.

"When will you publish my story?"

"I'm dividing it into three installments," he said. "The first installment appears this week. But the main thing is this: Will you get news for me on a space rate basis?"[1]

"I work mornings and evenings for three dollars a week," I said.

"Oh," he said. "Then you better keep that. But what are 70 you doing this summer?"

"Nothing."

"Then come to see me before you take another job," he said. "And write some more stories."

Pause & Reflect

FOCUS

As this autobiography continues, the people in the town have now read Wright's story in the paper.

MARK IT UP As you read, circle key words or sentences that show how different people react to his story.

A few days later my classmates came to me with baffled eyes, holding copies of the *Southern Register* in their hands.

"Did you really write that story?" they asked me.

"Yes."

"Why?"

"Because I wanted to."

"Where did you get it from?"

"I made it up."

"You didn't. You copied it out of a book."

"If I had, no one would publish it."

"But what are they publishing it for?"

"So people can read it."

"Who told you to do that?"

"Nobody."

90 "Then why did you do it?"

"Because I wanted to," I said again.

They were convinced that I had not told them the truth. We had never had any instruction in literary matters at school; the

1. **space rate basis:** a system of payment based on the length of the articles.

literature of the nation or the Negro had never been mentioned. My schoolmates could not understand why anyone would want to write a story; and, above all, they could not understand why I had called it *The Voodoo of Hell's Half-Acre*. The mood out of which a story was written was the most <u>alien</u> thing conceivable to them. They looked at me with
100 new eyes, and a distance, a suspiciousness, came between us. If I had thought anything in writing the story, I had thought that perhaps it would make me more acceptable to them, and now it was cutting me off from them more completely than ever.

At home the effects were no less disturbing. Granny came into my room early one morning and sat on the edge of my bed.

"Richard, what is this you're putting in the papers?" she asked.

"A story," I said.
110 "About what?"

"It's just a story, Granny."

"But they tell me it's been in three times."

"It's the same story. It's in three parts."

"But what is it about?" she insisted.

I <u>hedged</u>, fearful of getting into a religious argument.

"It's just a story I made up," I said.

"Then it's a lie," she said.

"Granny, please . . . I'm sorry," I pleaded. "But it's hard to tell you about the story. You see, Granny, everybody knows
120 that the story isn't true, but . . ."

"Then why write it?" she asked.

"Because people might want to read it."

"That's the Devil's work," she said and left.

My mother also was worried.

"Son, you ought to be more serious," she said. "You're growing up now, and you won't be able to get jobs if you let people think that you're weak-minded. Suppose the superintendent of schools would ask you to teach here in Jackson, and he found out that you had been writing stories?"
130 I could not answer her.

"I'll be all right, Mama," I said.

Uncle Tom, though surprised, was highly critical and contemptuous. The story had no point, he said. And whoever

WORDS
TO
KNOW

alien (āʹlē-ən) *adj.* foreign; strange; unfamiliar
hedge (hĕj) *v.* to avoid giving a direct answer

 **Reading Check**
Why don't Richard's classmates understand what he has done?

English Learner Support
VOCABULARY

Idiom *It was cutting me off from them* means that the author feels more separated from his family because he has written this story.

What Does It Mean?
Highly critical and contemptuous means that Uncle Tom criticized Wright and his story.

English Learner Support
LANGUAGE

Metaphor The highlighted phrase is a metaphor. Wright is comparing his story writing to trying to swim or row a boat against the river's current.

Pause & **Reflect**

Wright's own emotional response to people's reactions was one of _____

_____

because _____

_____.

(Infer)

As the autobiography ends . . .

• Wright dreams of going north and becoming a writer someday.

• He knows that these dreams are not meant for African Americans, but he continues to believe in them.

What Does It Mean?

Symbolized means "represented." In this passage, Wright explains that, to him, the North represented a place that offered him everything he didn't have and couldn't experience in the South.

heard of a story by the title of *The Voodoo of Hell's Half-Acre?* Aunt Addie said that it was a sin for anyone to use the word "hell" and that what was wrong with me was that I had nobody to guide me. She blamed the whole thing upon my upbringing.

In the end I was so angry that I refused to talk about the story. From no quarter,[2] with the exception of the Negro newspaper editor, had there come a single encouraging word. It was rumored that the principal wanted to know why I had used the word "hell." I felt that I had committed a crime. Had I been conscious of the full extent to which I was pushing against the current of my environment, I would have been frightened altogether out of my attempts at writing. But my reactions were limited to the attitude of the people about me, and I did not speculate or generalize.

Pause & **Reflect**

FOCUS
Wright now describes his dream of becoming a writer. As you read, look for details about that dream and the obstacles in the way.

I dreamed of going north and writing books, novels. The North symbolized to me all that I had not felt and seen; it had no relation whatever to what actually existed. Yet, by imagining a place where everything was possible, I kept hope alive in me. But where had I got this notion of doing something in the future, of going away from home and accomplishing something that would be recognized by others? I had, of course, read my Horatio Alger stories, my pulp stories, and I knew my Get-Rich-Quick Wallingford series[3] from cover to cover, though I had sense enough not to hope to get rich; even to my naive imagination that possibility was too remote. I knew that I lived in a

_____

2. **quarter**: direction.

3. **Horatio Alger stories . . . Wallingford series**: works of popular fiction about achieving wealth through hard work or cleverness.

| WORDS TO KNOW | **speculate** (spĕk′yə-lāt′) *v.* to guess |
| | **naive** (nä-ēv′) *adj.* simple in a natural and perhaps foolish way; unsophisticated |

country in which the aspirations of black people were limited, marked off. Yet I felt that I had to go somewhere and do something to redeem my being alive.

I was building up in me a dream which the entire educational system of the South had been rigged to <u>stifle</u>. I was feeling the very thing that the state of Mississippi had spent millions of dollars to make sure that I would never feel; I was becoming aware of the thing that the Jim Crow laws had been drafted and passed to keep out of my consciousness; I was acting on impulses that southern senators in the nation's capital had striven to keep out of Negro life; I was beginning to dream the dreams that the state had said were wrong, that the schools had said were taboo.[4]

Had I been <u>articulate</u> about my ultimate aspirations, no doubt someone would have told me what I was bargaining for; but nobody seemed to know, and least of all did I. My classmates felt that I was doing something that was vaguely wrong, but they did not know how to express it. As the outside world grew more meaningful, I became more concerned, tense; and my classmates and my teachers would say: "Why do you ask so many questions?" Or: "Keep quiet."

I was in my fifteenth year; in terms of schooling I was far behind the average youth of the nation, but I did not know that. In me was shaping a yearning for a kind of consciousness, a <u>mode</u> of being that the way of life about me had said could not be, must not be, and upon which the penalty of death had been placed. Somewhere in the dead of the southern night my life had switched onto the wrong track, and, without my knowing it, the locomotive of my heart was rushing down a dangerously steep slope, heading for a collision, <u>heedless</u> of the warning red lights that blinked all about me, the sirens and the bells and the screams that filled the air.

Pause & Reflect

---

4. **taboo:** forbidden.

WORDS
TO
KNOW

stifle (stī′fəl) *v.* to smother; hold back
articulate (är-tĭk′yə-lĭt) *adj.* clear and effective in speech
mode (mōd) *n.* a manner or way
heedless (hēd′lĭs) *adj.* unmindful; careless; unaware

English Learner Support
LANGUAGE

Diction *In me was shaping a yearning* could be restated as "a yearning was forming in me."

Pause & Reflect

1. Wright wants to move to the North and become a writer. What do you think are the main obstacles that Wright has to overcome? **(Evaluate)**

_____

_____

_____

_____

MARK IT UP 2. Why do you think Wright believed he could realize his dream in the North? Circle passages on pages 224–225 that support your opinion. **(Infer)**

_____

_____

_____

_____

CHALLENGE

In the boxed passage, Wright compares his life to a locomotive, or a train. Because he decided to try for a better life, he believes he has put his future in danger. If his life is a locomotive, then what in his life is the steep slope? What might the collision be? What are the warning lights?

from **Black Boy** 225

Active Reading SkillBuilder

Making Inferences

Richard Wright, the author of *Black Boy,* does not directly state his opinion about the people he describes. Instead, he communicates indirectly through the choices he makes—choices about which events to recount, what methods of characterization to use, and how to structure the story. In order to understand the author's perspective toward these people, the reader must **make inferences** based on what is stated in the text and on common sense. As you read, complete the chart below by identifying three examples of dialogue and what they reveal about the person speaking. Then make an inference about the author's perspective on each person. One example is given.

Character: Young Richard

What He/She Says	What This Reveals About Him/Her	Author's Perspective
"But I want you to read it *now.* . . ."	Young Richard is impatient and demanding.	The author might be amused by his youthful impatience.

Character: _____

What He/She Says	What This Reveals About Him/Her	Author's Perspective

Character: _____

What He/She Says	What This Reveals About Him/Her	Author's Perspective

Literary Analysis SkillBuilder

Dialogue

Conversation between two or more characters in a work of literature is called
dialogue. Well-written dialogue not only moves a story forward but helps the writer
with characterization by revealing the personalities of the speakers. Reread one
of the three primary dialogues in the excerpt from *Black Boy*—either one of the
two conversations Richard has with the editor or the one he has with Granny.
On the chart below, identify three or four passages from the dialogue and tell
what each passage conveys about the character speaking. An example is given.

Passage from Dialogue	Character Speaking	What It Conveys About the Character
"But you're asking me to give you my story, but you don't give your papers away...."	Richard	He is not afraid to stand to stand up for his rights.

Follow Up: Share your chart with other students. Discuss why readers might
interpret the same passage of dialogue in different ways.

Words to Know SkillBuilder

Words to Know

alien	hedge	intuitively	naive	speculate
articulate	heedless	mode	relent	stifle

A. Fill in each set of blanks with the correct word from the word list. The boxed letters will spell out what the editor offered in exchange for Wright's short story.

1. A good lecturer or master of ceremonies is this (and a *really* good one can tell jokes, too).

2. If you don't really want to say yes but you don't really want to say no, you may do this.

3. Something doesn't have to be from outer space to be this; it just has to be unfamiliar to you.

4. Even with all their barometers and satellite photos, weather forecasters basically do this.

5. If you feel something in your bones or know something you haven't been taught, this is how you know it.

6. This can be a system, a procedure, a manner, a method, a process, a way, or a style.

7. If this describes how you take care of your horse, you may find yourself steedless as well.

8. You try to do this to your coughs if you're at a play and to your yawns if you're pretending to be interested.

9. The phrase "a babe in the woods" describes a person who is this, since young children naturally are.

10. You might beg, flatter, or plead in an attempt to get a stern person to do this.

B. Write a short letter in which Granny or Aunt Addie expresses her worries about the narrator's writing activities. Use at least **four** of the Words to Know.

A VOICE

Pat Mora

THE JOURNEY

Mary Oliver

Before You Read

Connect to Your Life

What good advice have you been given in your life? Did this advice come from family or friends? Did it come from people who are older than you or from people your own age?

WHO GAVE THE ADVICE?	WHAT ADVICE DID HE OR SHE GIVE?

Key to the Poems

WHAT'S THE BIG IDEA? The poems in this selection both deal with finding one's voice. Complete the word web by writing words that come to mind when you think of the word *voice*.

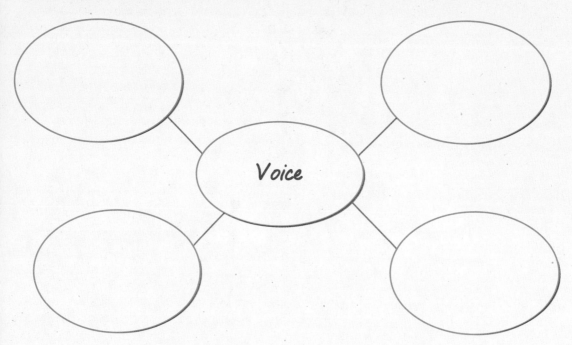

A Voice

Pat Mora

POETRY

PREVIEW In "A Voice," the speaker describes the struggles of her mother's youth. Her mother was born in Mexico and moved with her family to the United States. Though the mother's family did not allow her to speak English at home, she mastered the language. She even traveled to the state capitol to deliver a speech that she had written. Now her daughter looks back on that experience and draws her own lessons from her mother's example.

> **FOCUS**
> The poem begins with a glimpse into the past of the speaker's mother.
> **MARK IT UP** As you read, underline details that show you what the mother's home life and family were like.

Even the lights on the stage unrelenting
as the desert sun couldn't hide the other
students, their eyes also unrelenting,
students who spoke English every night

5 as they ate their meat, potatoes, gravy.
Not you. In your house that smelled like
rose powder, you spoke Spanish formal
as your father, the judge without a courtroom

Reading Tips

As you read each poem, try to imagine the **speaker** and the person being spoken to.

- In the first poem, the **speaker** is talking to her mother—the "you" in the poem. Look for clues that tell how the speaker feels about her mother's way of dealing with life's challenges.

- The second poem is about a turning point in a person's life. Look for clues about what the "you" in the poem is turning away from.

As the poem begins . . .

- The speaker lists the things her mother accomplished when she was young.

- The speaker's mother enjoyed using words and learned to speak English.

English Learner Support
LANGUAGE

Simile The poet compares the lights on the stage to the desert sun, which shines constantly and without relief.

Slang *Spunky* means "full of high spirits."

Reading Tip

The author uses figurative language to make her writing more vivid. The simile *slow as a hot river* compares the way the father walks to a river with a very slow current. Slow rivers have more time to absorb the sun's heat. *Spunky as a peacock* is a simile that compares the speaker's mother's voice to a proud, colorful peacock.

Pause & Reflect

Review the details you underlined. How would you describe the home life of the speaker's mother? **(Infer)**

_____

_____

_____

_____

As the poem ends . . .

- The daughter tells about the time her mother tried to give a speech.

- The speaker explains the lesson her mother has taught her.

✔ Reading Check

Why did the mother want to hide?

10
in the country he floated to in the dark
on a flatbed truck. He walked slow
as a hot river down the narrow hall
of your house. You never dared to race past him,

to say, "Please move," in the language
you learned effortlessly, as you learned to run,
15
the language forbidden at home, though your mother
said you learned it to fight with the neighbors.

You liked winning with words. You liked
writing speeches about patriotism and democracy.
You liked all the faces looking at you, all those eyes.
20
"How did I do it?" you ask me now. "How did I do it

when my parents didn't understand?"
The family story says your voice is the voice
of an aunt in Mexico, spunky as a peacock.
Family stories sing of what lives in the blood.

Pause & Reflect

FOCUS

The speaker now turns her attention to the scene at the state capitol, where the mother, then a girl, was expected to make a speech. Read to find out what happened that day and what she later accomplished.

✏ MARK IT UP Underline details that describe where the speech took place and what made it difficult.

25
You told me only once about the time you went
to the state capitol, your family proud as if
you'd been named governor. But when you looked
around, the only Mexican in the auditorium,
you wanted to hide from those strange faces.

30 Their eyes were pinpricks, and you faked
hoarseness. You, who are never at a loss
for words, felt your breath stick in your throat

like an ice-cube. "I can't," you whispered.
"I can't." Yet you did. Not that day but years later.
35 You taught the four of us to speak up.
This is America, Mom. The undo-able is done

in the next generation. Your breath moves
through the family like the wind
moves through the trees.

Pause & *Reflect*

English Learner Support
LANGUAGE

Simile Here, the writer compares her mother's fear of speaking to the physical sensation of an ice cube caught in the throat.

✔ **Reading Check**
In what way did the mother fail? How did she succeed?

Pause & *Reflect*

1. Review the details you marked as you read. In one sentence, **summarize** what made it so hard for the girl to deliver her **speech**.

_____

_____

_____

_____

READ ALOUD 2. Read aloud lines 35–37 as if you were the speaker. What do you think the speaker means by saying, "The undo-able is done in the next generation"? **(Infer)**

_____

_____

_____

_____

THE JOURNEY

Mary Oliver

Reading Tip

Read the poem aloud with a partner one sentence at a time. Use your own words to paraphrase each sentence.

As the poem begins . . .

- A woman makes a decision to leave her family against their wishes.

- She believes that her decision is the right one, but she still feels upset by their response.

What Does It Mean?

This cry for help is from the people who depend on the character who is leaving. They want her to fix their lives.

✔ Reading Check

What is the decision that the "you" in the poem makes?

PREVIEW "The Journey" describes the decision of a woman to leave her home, despite the advice of others who try to keep her there. The speaker tells how the woman left the pleading voices behind. Then, as the woman entered her new life, she began to hear her own voice.

> **FOCUS**
> The "you" in this poem was facing a crisis at home, so she began a kind of "journey." **MARK IT UP** Underline details that describe what made her life difficult at home.

One day you finally knew
what you had to do, and began,
though the voices around you
kept shouting
5 their bad advice—
though the whole house
began to tremble
and you felt the old tug
at your ankles.
10 "Mend my life!"
each voice cried.
But you didn't stop.
You knew what you had to do,
though the wind pried
15 with its stiff fingers
at the very foundations,
though their melancholy[1]
was terrible.

Pause **&** *Reflect*

1. **melancholy** (mĕl′ən-kŏl′ē): great sadness; depression.

FOCUS
Read to find out about the new voice that
the woman discovers on her journey.

It was already late
20 enough, and a wild night,
and the road full of fallen
branches and stones.
But little by little,
as you left their voices behind,
25 the stars began to burn
through the sheets of clouds,
and there was a new voice
which you slowly
recognized as your own,
30 that kept you company
as you strode deeper and deeper
into the world,
determined to do
the only thing you could do—
35 determined to save
the only life you could save.

Pause **&** *Reflect*

As the poem ends . . .

- The speaker compares the woman's decision to leave to a walk on a road full of stones and branches.

- She begins to realize that her decision to leave was the right one.

✔ **Reading Check**

What is the new voice that the speaker hears on her journey?

English Learner Support
LANGUAGE

Repetition Note the many repeated words on the second page of the poem. Repetition is a strategy for emphasizing words and ideas.

Pause **&** *Reflect*

What seems to be the goal of the journey? **(Infer)**

_____

_____

_____

CHALLENGE

Both poems indirectly reveal something about the speakers. Mark the lines or passages that reveal something about the speakers. Compare and contrast the speakers in the two poems. What do you learn about them and what they value? **(Evaluate)**

Active Reading SkillBuilder

Understanding Diction

To gain a better understanding of a writer's use of **diction,** notice any words or phrases that strike you as vivid, unusual, or surprising, or that have strong associations with particular experiences, situations, or feelings you've encountered in your own life. As you read "A Voice," fill in the word webs below. Write an interesting word from the poem in the center of each web. Use the other circles in the web to explore the word's meanings and associations. One web has been partially completed.

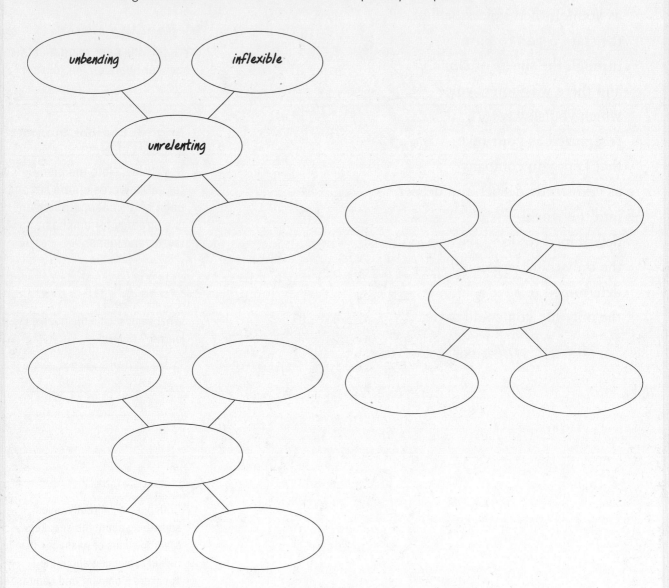

Follow Up: On a separate paper, make three more webs to fill in while reading "The Journey."

Literary Analysis SkillBuilder

Author's Perspective and Diction

An **author's perspective** is the viewpoint he or she expresses in a piece of literature. In poetry, this perspective is often disclosed, in part, through **diction.** Diction is a writer's specific choice of words and the way those words are arranged in a sentence. Reread "A Voice" and "The Journey," and select a word from each poem that seems to be particularly effective. Using the webs below, record the word, its definition or definitions, other words the poet could have chosen, and the associations (or connotations) that the word has for you.

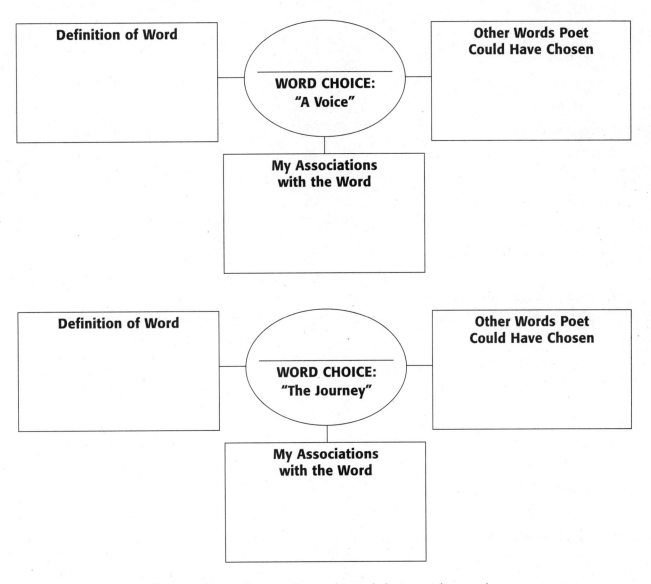

Definition of Word

WORD CHOICE:
"A Voice"

Other Words Poet Could Have Chosen

My Associations with the Word

Definition of Word

WORD CHOICE:
"The Journey"

Other Words Poet Could Have Chosen

My Associations with the Word

Follow Up: With a group of students, discuss what each word choice might reveal about the author's perspective.

Building Vocabulary SkillBuilder

Look at the words in each pair below. Think about the difference between the connotations of the words. Then write two sentences, each using one of the words. Be sure that the sentences reflect the connotations of the words.

1. aroma/smell _____

_____

2. particular/picky _____

_____

3. chat/chatter _____

_____

4. train/educate _____

_____

5. eternal/endless _____

_____

6. imitate/mimic _____

_____

7. childlike/childish _____

_____

8. argument/debate _____

_____

9. old-fashioned/outdated _____

_____

10. leave/abandon _____

_____

11. ashamed/embarrassed _____

_____

12. control/dominate _____

_____

13. excuse/forgive _____

_____

14. unusual/peculiar _____

_____

15. abundant/extravagant _____

_____

On Writing

The House On

MANGO ST

Sandra Cisneros

Before You Read

Connect to Your Life

Think about a time you discovered you were somehow different from your friends, your family, or people in your community. Jot down words and phrases that help define who you are.

artistic

_____

_____

_____

_____

_____

_____

_____

Key to the Essay

WHAT YOU NEED TO KNOW In this essay, Sandra Cisneros explains how she came to write *The House on Mango Street*. She also explores influences that helped her become a writer. In *The House on Mango Street*, Cisneros breaks from traditional writing, and she challenges what was considered "normal" and "American."

On Writing

The House on Mango Street

Sandra Cisneros

PREVIEW In 1984 Sandra Cisneros published *The House on Mango Street,* a book of fiction based on her childhood memories. Its narrator is a girl named Esperanza. Years later, Cisneros remembered how she felt as she was writing that book—when she was still trying to discover her own identity. The following selection is the introduction that appeared in the 10th anniversary edition of her novel.

Reading Tips

The author wrote this introduction to her novel to explain what inspired her work and how she views herself as a writer.

- As you read, look for any sentences that express a **main idea.** Often, such sentences appear at the beginnings of paragraphs.

- Pay close attention to details about the author's life, which will help you to understand her development as a writer.

FOCUS

In this first section Cisneros tells what she learned about herself when she studied writing at the University of Iowa.

✏️ **MARK IT UP** As you read, underline sentences that express the main idea in each paragraph. Examples are highlighted.

It's been ten years since *The House on Mango Street* was first published. I began writing it in graduate school, the spring of 1977, in Iowa City. I was twenty-two years old.

I'm thirty-eight now, far from that time and place, but the questions from readers remain, Are these stories true? Are you Esperanza?

When I began *The House on Mango Street,* I thought I was writing a memoir. By the time I finished it, my memoir was no longer memoir, no longer autobiographical. It had <u>evolved</u> into a collective story peopled with several lives from my past and

As the essay begins . . .

- Sandra Cisneros began her writing career in graduate school in Iowa City.

- Cisneros grew up in Chicago, a city of many cultures.

- She tells that she decided her writing would be different than her classmates' writing.

WORDS TO KNOW   **evolve** (ĭ-vŏlv') *v.* to develop gradually

present, placed in one fictional time and neighborhood—Mango Street.

A story is like a Giacometti[1] sculpture. The farther away it is from you, the clearer you can see it. In Iowa City, I was undergoing several changes of identity. For the first time I was

20 living alone, in a community very different in class and culture from the one where I was raised. This caused so much unrest I could barely speak, let alone write about it. The story I was living at twenty-two would have to wait, but I could take the story of an earlier place, an earlier (voice,) and record that on paper.

The voice of *Mango Street* and all my work was born at one moment, when I realized I was different. This sounds absurd and simple, but until Iowa City, I assumed the world was like Chicago, made up of people of many cultures all

30 living together—albeit[2] not happily at times but still coexisting. In Iowa, I was suddenly aware of feeling odd when I spoke, as if I were a foreigner. But this was my land too. This is not to say I hadn't felt this "otherness" before in Chicago, but I hadn't felt it quite as keenly as I did in graduate school. I couldn't articulate what it was that was happening, except I knew I felt ashamed when I spoke in class, so I chose not to speak.

I can say my political consciousness[3] began the moment I recognized my otherness. I was in a graduate seminar on

40 memory and the imagination. The books required were Vladimir Nabokov's *Speak Memory*, Isak Dinesen's *Out of Africa*, and Gaston Bachelard's *Poetics of Space*.[4] I had enjoyed the first two, but as usual I said nothing, just listened to the dialogue around me, too afraid to speak. The third book, though, left me baffled. I assumed I just didn't get it because I wasn't as smart as everyone else, and if I didn't say

---

1. **Giacometti** (jä-kə-mĕt′ē): Alberto Giacometti, a Swiss sculptor of the 1900s known for his extremely thin, stalklike sculptures.
2. **albeit** (ôl-bē′ĭt): although.
3. **political consciousness:** awareness of the relationships among groups within a society.
4. **Vladimir . . . Space:** Vladimir Nabokov (nə-bô′kəf): Russian-born U.S. novelist who describes his youth in the autobiographical work *Speak, Memory;* Isak Dinesen (dē′nĭ-sən): Danish writer who lived for 17 years in Kenya, a country in eastern Africa, and wrote about that period of her life in her memoir *Out of Africa;* Gaston Bachelard (bäsh-lär′): French writer and philosopher whose *Poetics of Space* deals with his theory that daydreaming and fantasizing are the highest functions of the mind, and that the human experience is revealed most fully through the imagination.

anything, maybe no one would notice.

The conversation, I remember, was about the house of memory—the attic, the stairwells, the cellar. Attic? My family lived in third-floor (flats) for the most part, because noise traveled down. Stairwells reeked of Pine Sol from the Saturday scrubbing. We shared them with the people downstairs; they were public zones no one except us thought to clean. We mopped them all right, but not without resentment for cleaning up some other people's trash. And as for cellars, we had a basement, but who'd want to hide in there? Basements were filled with urban fauna.[5] Everyone was scared to go in there including the meter reader and the landlord. What was this guy Bachelard talking about when he mentioned the familiar and comforting house of memory? It was obvious he never had to clean one or pay the landlord rent for one like ours.

Then it occurred to me that none of the books in this class or in any of my classes, in all the years of my education, had ever discussed a house like mine. Not in books or magazines or films. My classmates had come from real houses, real neighborhoods, ones they could point to, but what did I know?

When I went home that evening and realized my education had been a lie—had made <u>presumptions</u> about what was "normal," what was American, what was valuable—I wanted to quit school right then and there, but I didn't. Instead, I got angry, and anger when it is used to act, when it is used nonviolently, has power. I asked myself what I could write about that my classmates could not. I didn't know what I wanted exactly, but I did have enough sense to know what I *didn't* want. I didn't want to sound like my classmates; I didn't want to keep imitating the writers I had been reading. Their voices were right for *them* but not for *me*.

Pause & Reflect

---

5. **fauna** (fô′nə): animals.

WORDS
TO
KNOW

presumption (prĭ-zŭmp′shən) *n.* the act of assuming something is true

A *flat* is an apartment that has all of its rooms on the same floor. A flat would not have an attic, stairs, or a cellar.

✔ **Reading Check**

What are some key facts you have learned about Cisneros's family and home?

Pause **&** *Reflect*

1. Cisneros felt that her education had been "a lie." Circle two statements below that explain why she felt that way. **(Analyze)**

   She did not like to learn.

   Her education did not reflect her life or background.

   She had been made to feel like an outsider.

   Teachers were mean to her.

   _____

   _____

   _____

   _____

✎ MARK IT UP **2.** Review the sentences that you underlined as you read. Star one that you think states the **main idea** of the essay. **(Evaluate)**

3. Life in Iowa City felt strange and different to Cisneros. How did this actually help her? **(Cause and Effect)**

   _____

   _____

   _____

   _____

- Cisneros decided to use the language and events of her own life in her writing.
- She explains how she wrote a collection of stories that became a novel.

What Does It Mean?

A *monologue* is a long speech.

English Learner Support
LANGUAGE

Prefixes The prefix *anti-* means "against" or "opposing." Something that is *academic* is related to formal education. *Antiacademic* means "against academics." *anti* + *academic* = against academics

Reading Tip

The long highlighted sentence is made up of clauses that begin with the word *when*. Mark each clause in a different color pen or pencil. Be sure you understand one clause before you move on to the next one.

---

80 **FOCUS**
Now Cisneros tells how she discovered her own voice as a writer.

Instead, I searched for the "ugliest" subjects I could find, the most un-"poetic"—slang, monologues in which waitresses or kids talked their own lives. I was trying as best I could to write the kind of book I had *never* seen in a library or in a school, the kind of book not even my professors could write. Each week I <u>ingested</u> the class readings and then went off and did the opposite. It was a quiet revolution, perhaps a reaction taken to extremes, but it was out of this negative experience that I found something positive: my own voice.

90 The language in *Mango Street* is based on speech. It's very much an antiacademic voice—a child's voice, a girl's voice, a poor girl's voice, a spoken voice, the voice of an American-Mexican. It's in this rebellious realm of antipoetics[6] that I tried to create a poetic text with the most unofficial language I could find. I did it neither ingenuously[7] nor naturally. It was as clear to me as if I were tossing a Molotov.[8]

At one time or another, we all have felt other. When I teach writing, I tell the story of the moment of discovering **100** and naming my otherness. It is not enough simply to sense it; it has to be named, and then written about from there. Once I could name it, I ceased being ashamed and silent. I could speak up and celebrate my otherness as a woman, as a working-class person, as an American of Mexican descent. When I recognized the places where I departed from my neighbors, my classmates, my family, my town, my brothers, when I discovered what I knew that no one else in the room knew, and then spoke it in a voice that was my voice, the voice I used when I was sitting in the kitchen, dressed in my **110** pajamas, talking over a table littered with cups and dishes, when I could give myself permission to speak from that intimate space, then I could talk and sound like myself, not like me trying to sound like someone I wasn't. Then I could speak, shout, laugh from a place that was uniquely mine, that

---

6. **antipoetics** (ăn′tĭ-pō-ĕt′ĭks): poetry that rejects traditional poetic techniques.

7. **ingenuously** (ĭn-jĕn′yo͞o-əs-lē): in a naive or straightforward way.

8. **Molotov** (mŏl′ə-tôf′): Molotov cocktail; a handmade bomb that is set on fire and thrown. It was named for the Soviet politician Vyacheslav Molotov, who ordered the production of such bombs during World War II.

WORDS
TO
KNOW

ingest (ĭn-jĕst′) *v.* to take in, like food

was no one else's in the history of the universe, that would never be anyone else's, ever.

I wrote these stories that way, guided by my heart and by my ear. I was writing a novel and didn't know I was writing a novel; if I had, I probably couldn't have done it. I knew I
120 wanted to tell a story made up of a series of stories that would make sense if read alone, or that could be read all together to tell one big story, each story contributing to the whole—like beads in a necklace. I hadn't seen a book like this before. After finishing my book, I would discover these novels later: Gwendolyn Brooks' *Maud Martha,* Nellie Campobello's *Cartucho,* Ermilo Abreu Gómez's *Canek,* and Tomás Rivera's *Y no se lo tragó la tierra.*[9]

When I was writing *Mango Street,* I remember reading Nicanor Parra's[10] *Antipoems* and delighting in their
130 irreverence to "Poetry," just as I had been delighted by Carl Sandburg's[11] wise-guy, working-class voice and Gwendolyn Brooks' *Bronzeville* poems.[12] I remember I was trying to write something that was a cross between fiction and poetry—like Jorge Luis Borges'[13] *Dream Tigers,* a book whose stories read like fables, but with the lyricism and succinctness of poetry.

Pause & Reflect

---

9. **Gwendolyn . . . tierra:** Gwendolyn Brooks: American poet and novelist whose novel *Maud Martha* depicts an African-American girl growing up in Chicago; Nellie Campobello: Mexican writer whose work *Cartucho: Relatos de la lucha en el norte de México* (Tales of the Struggle in Northern Mexico) depicts the period of the Mexican Revolution, which she lived through as a child; Ermilo Abreu Gómez: Mexican writer whose work *Canek* is one of three sections of a larger work, *Mayan Heroes,* and depicts an event in Mayan history; Tomás Rivera: American writer who wrote *Y no se lo tragó la tierra* (ē nō sĕ lō trä-gō' lä tyĕ'rä) (And the Earth Did Not Devour Him), a bilingual collection of short stories.

10. **Nicanor Parra** (pä'rä): Chilean poet who in his Poems and Antipoems attempts to reach ordinary people by using simple, direct language and by writing about everyday problems, often from a humorous or ironic point of view.

11. **Carl Sandburg:** popular Midwestern U.S. poet and writer, whose best-known works include the poems "Chicago" and "Fog," and a six-volume biography of Abraham Lincoln that was awarded the Pulitzer Prize in 1939.

12. *Bronzeville* **poems:** *A Street in Bronzeville,* Brooks's first published collection of poetry, in which she reveals the extraordinary in the everyday lives of her neighbors.

13. **Jorge Luis Borges** (bôr'hĕs): Argentine poet and short story writer whose work helped bring Latin American literature to the attention of readers throughout the Western world.

What Does It Mean?
Succinctness means "expressing something clearly in just a few words."

Pause & Reflect

1. Cisneros says that she searched for the "ugliest subjects." What does she mean by that? **(Infer)**

_____

_____

_____

_____

READ ALOUD **2.** Read aloud the boxed passage on page 244. It describes the language used in *The House on Mango Street.* Why do you think Cisneros chose to use the voice of a little girl to narrate her book? **(Make Judgments)**

_____

_____

_____

_____

As the essay ends . . .

- Cisneros says that she wanted to help the people in her community, but she also wanted to write.

- In the end, she feels she has contributed to her community with her writing.

READ ALOUD Lines 144–151

Use your voice to express the feelings of the writer at work, "molding" her collection of stories into a unified book.

Reading Tip

Make a list of some of the ways Cisneros put together her novel.

What Does It Mean?

In the highlighted sentence, Cisneros explains that she was always taught how to write, but she was never taught what she should write about.

English Learner Support
VOCABULARY

Idiom To *roll up one's sleeves* means "to get ready for hard work."

FOCUS

Read to find out how Cisneros finished her book and learned to bring together the "two halves" of her life.

I finished writing my book in November 1982, miles from the Iowa cornfields. I had traveled a great distance both physically and mentally from the book's inception. And in the meantime, lots of things happened to me. I taught Latino high-school dropouts and counseled Latina students. Because I often felt helpless as a teacher and counselor to alter their lives, their stories began to surface in my "memoir"; then *Mango Street* ceased to be my story. I arranged and diminished events on Mango Street to speak a message, to take from different parts of other people's lives and create a story like a collage. I merged characters from my twenties with characters from my teens and childhood. I edited, changed, shifted the past to fit the present. I asked questions I didn't know to ask when I was an adolescent. But best of all, writing in a younger voice allowed me to name that thing without a name, that shame of being poor, of being female, of being not quite good enough, and examine where it had come from and why, so I could exchange shame for celebration.

I had never been trained to think of poems or stories as something that could change someone's life. I had been trained to think about where a line ended or how best to work a metaphor. It was always the "how" and not the "what" we talked about in class. Even while I was teaching in the Chicago community, the two halves of my life were at odds with each other—the half that wanted to roll up my sleeves and do something for the community, and the half that wanted to retreat to my kitchen and write. I still believed my writing couldn't save anyone's life but my own.

In the ten years since *Mango Street* has been published those two halves of my life have met and merged. I believe this because I've witnessed families buying my book for themselves and for family members, families for whom

WORDS
TO
KNOW

inception (ĭn-sĕp′shən) *n.* the beginning

spending money on a book can be a sacrifice. Often they bring a mother, father, sibling, or cousin along to my readings, or I am introduced to someone who says their son or daughter read my book in a class and brought it home for them. And there are the letters from readers of all ages and colors who write to say I have written their story. The raggedy state of my books that some readers and educators hand me to sign is the best compliment of all. These are my <u>affirmations</u> and blessings.

₁₈₀

Pause **&** *Reflect*

English Learner Support
VOCABULARY

Raggedy State Cisneros is pleased that her books are in a *raggedy state* because this means that they are worn out from having been read and reread many times.

Pause **&** *Reflect*

Cisneros's aim was to find a voice that was her own and nobody else's. Yet she also wanted her writing to reach out to other people. How was she able to "merge" her two halves? **(Infer)**

_____

_____

_____

_____

CHALLENGE

Cisneros describes different works of literature that delighted her, including the poetry of Carl Sandburg and Gwendolyn Brooks. Read a few poems by one these authors and discuss them with a classmate.

WORDS
TO
KNOW

affirmation (ăf′ər-mā′shən) *n.* something that supports the validity or truth of something else

Active Reading SkillBuilder

Main Idea and Summarizing

The **main idea** of a work of nonfiction is the writer's most important, or central, idea. Sometimes the main idea is stated directly in a topic sentence, or it may be implied, or suggested, by the details the writer gives. To understand an implied main idea, the reader must make an inference based on the details.

A **summary** is a short restatement or retelling of written or spoken material. It includes only the main idea and the most important points and details. As you read "On Writing *The House on Mango Street,*" use the chart to list important details that relate to the topic of the essay. Then write the main idea of the essay in your own words, based on the details you have listed.

Topic: On Writing *The House on Mango Street*

Important Details
"In Iowa, I was suddenly aware of feeling odd when I spoke, as if I were a foreigner." (p. 242)

Main Idea

Literary Analysis SkillBuilder

Voice

A writer's unique way of using language to convey his or her personality through writing is referred to as the writer's **voice.** Among the elements that work together to create voice are sentence structure, word choice, and tone. For example, some writers use short simple sentences, while others use long complicated ones. Certain writers use concrete words; other prefer abstract terms. A writer's tone, or attitude toward the subject, might be sarcastic, passionate, or humorous. Choose a passage from "On Writing *The House on Mango Street*" and analyze the sentence length, word choice, and tone. On the chart, quote examples from the passage that demonstrate these elements of voice and help to convey the personal, informal, and conversational voice that Cisneros uses.

Cisneros's Voice

Sentence Length	Word Choice	Tone

Words to Know SkillBuilder

Words to Know

affirmation   evolve   inception   ingest   presumption

A. Fill in each set of blanks with the correct word from the word list. The boxed letters will spell out the writer's way of using language to convey her personality in her writing.

1. This is what an idea can do: gradually develop into a full-blown story.

   __ ☐ __ __ __ __ __

2. Authors want this when they hope they have written a good story.

   __ __ __ __ __ __ __ __ __ ☐ __

3. Writers do this with books, as well as with lunch!

   ☐ __ __ __ __ __ __

4. This is the starting point for a story, poem, play, or biography.

   __ __ ☐ __ __ __ __ __ __

5. Writers make this when they assume that others will love their work!

   __ __ ☐ __ __ __ __ __ __ __ __

Complete the following sentence with the word that the boxed letters spell out.

Sandra Cisneros uses a _____ that is informal and personal in "On Writing *The House on Mango Street.*"

B. Think about each definition below. Then fill in the blank with the correct word from the word list.

1. _____ : the act of assuming something is true

2. _____ : to develop gradually

3. _____ : something that supports the validity or truth of something else

4. _____ : to take in, like food

5. _____ : the beginning

C. Imagine that you are forming a Writer's Club. Write a list of guidelines for members to follow. Use at least **two** Words to Know in your guidelines.

TRIFLES

Susan Glaspell

Before You Read

Connect to Your Life

Have you ever felt lonely, even though you were around other people?
Why do you think you felt that way? Write your response in the space
below.

_____

_____

_____

_____

_____

_____

_____

_____

Key to the Story

WHAT YOU NEED TO KNOW This play is set on a Midwestern farm
in the early 1900s. Farm life at that time was very different from what it is
today. Few farmers owned cars or tractors. Some farmers had telephones,
but most did not. Neither television nor radio had been invented yet. In
fact, some farmhouses didn't even have electricity. These conditions often
created a sense of isolation, especially among farm women.

TRIFLES

Susan Glaspell

PREVIEW *Trifles* is a one-act play about an investigation into the murder of a farmer named John Wright. As the play opens, the County Attorney, the Sheriff, his wife, and two neighbors arrive at the Wright farmhouse. The men are searching for evidence of a motive for the murder. Meanwhile, the women uncover the trifles—the seemingly unimportant details—that could determine the fate of the prime suspect, the dead man's wife.

Reading Tips

As the title *Trifles* suggests, important information can be found in the details of this **drama**.

- The diagram on the left can help you to visualize the **setting**, as described in the **stage directions** on page 254. As you read *Trifles*, pay close attention to the stage directions. They provide key information about the characters and their actions.

- Notice what the **dialogue** reveals about the characters.

- Look for clues that reveal a **motive** for the murder of John Wright.

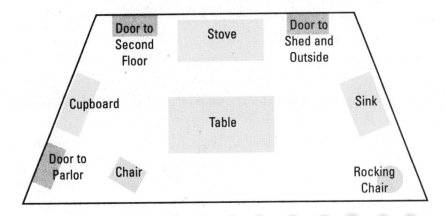

Door to Second Floor · Stove · Door to Shed and Outside · Cupboard · Table · Sink · Door to Parlor · Chair · Rocking Chair

MARK IT UP **KEEP TRACK**

As you read, you can use these marks to keep track of your understanding.

✔ ..... I understand.

? ..... I don't understand this.

! ..... Interesting or surprising idea

Cast of Characters

George Henderson, **County Attorney**
Henry Peters, **Sheriff**
Lewis **Hale,** a neighboring farmer
Mrs. Peters
Mrs. Hale

- The setting and the characters are introduced.

More About . . .

In a murder investigation, the (Sheriff) makes an arrest, and the (County Attorney) prosecutes the case in court. Here, the fact that the County Attorney accompanies the Sheriff shows the unusual nature of the crime.

Pause & Reflect

1. Review the boxed passage on this page. Jot down one or two details about each of the following characters. **(Clarify)**

County Attorney Henderson:

_____

_____

The Sheriff: _____

_____

Mrs. Peters (the Sheriff's wife):

_____

_____

Mr. Hale: _____

_____

Mrs. Hale: _____

_____

MARK IT UP 2. How do you know that something unusual happened at the house? Circle details that give clues. **(Infer)**

FOCUS

MARK IT UP As you read the opening **stage directions,** underline the words and phrases that help you to picture the setting and the characters. Examples are highlighted. Also make use of the diagram provided on the previous page.

SCENE: *The kitchen in the now abandoned farmhouse of John Wright, a gloomy kitchen, and left without having been put in order—the walls covered with a faded wallpaper. Downstage right is a door leading to the parlor. On the right wall above this door is a built-in kitchen cupboard with shelves in the upper portion and drawers below. In the rear wall at right, up two steps, is a door opening onto stairs leading to the second floor. In the rear wall at left is a door to the shed and from there to the outside. Between these two*
10 *doors is an old-fashioned black iron stove. Running along the left wall from the shed door is an old iron sink and sink shelf, in which is set a hand pump. Downstage of the sink is an uncurtained window. Near the window is an old wooden rocker. Center stage is an unpainted wooden kitchen table with straight chairs on either side. There is a small chair downstage right. Unwashed pans under the sink, a loaf of bread outside the breadbox, a dish towel on the table—other signs of incompleted work. At the rear the shed door opens and the* (Sheriff) *comes in followed by the* (County Attorney) *and*
20 *Hale. The* Sheriff *and* Hale *are men in middle life, the* County Attorney *is a young man; all are much bundled up and go at once to the stove. They are followed by the two women—the* Sheriff's *wife, Mrs. Peters, first; she is a slight wiry woman, a thin nervous face. Mrs. Hale is larger and would ordinarily be called more comfortable-looking, but she is disturbed now and looks fearfully about as she enters. The women have come in slowly, and stand close together near the door.*

Pause & Reflect

FOCUS

The visitors to the Wright farmhouse discuss the strange events of the day before. John Wright was found murdered.

MARK IT UP As you read on, underline the words and phrases that reveal the kind of man John Wright was. Circle the passage that tells how he died.

County Attorney *(at stove rubbing his hands)*. This feels good. Come up to the fire, ladies.

30 **Mrs. Peters** *(after taking a step forward)*. I'm not—cold.

Sheriff *(unbuttoning his overcoat and stepping away from the stove to right of table as if to mark the beginning of official business)*. Now, Mr. Hale, before we move things about, you explain to Mr. Henderson just what you saw when you came here yesterday morning.

County Attorney *(crossing down to left of the table)*. By the way, has anything been moved? Are things just as you left them yesterday?

Sheriff *(looking about)*. It's just the same. When it dropped
40 below zero last night, I thought I'd better send Frank out this morning to make a fire for us—*(sits right of center table)* no use getting pneumonia with a big case on, but I told him not to touch anything except the stove—and you know Frank.

County Attorney. Somebody should have been left here yesterday.

Sheriff. Oh—yesterday. When I had to send Frank to Morris Center for that man who went crazy—I want you to know I had my hands full yesterday. I knew you could get back from Omaha by today and as long as I went over every-
50 thing here myself—

County Attorney. Well, Mr. Hale, tell just what happened when you came here yesterday morning.

Hale *(crossing down to above table)*. Harry and I had started to town with a load of potatoes. We came along the road from my place and as I got here I said, "I'm going to see if I can't get John Wright to go in with me on a party tele- phone."[1] I spoke to Wright about it once before and he

---

1. **party telephone:** A form of telephone circuit in which the telephone users— referred to as parties by the telephone company—within a particular community had to share the same phone line.

As the play continues . . .

- All five characters are in a farmhouse kitchen.

- The County Attorney listens as Mr. Hale describes the events of the day before.

Reading Tip

The words in italics after a character's name tell readers what the character is doing on stage. The County Attorney rubs his hands at the stove and says, "This feels good. Come up to the fire, ladies." As you read, imagine the characters moving around on a stage, as if you were watching a show.

English Learner Support
LANGUAGE

Idiom When the Sheriff says "I had my hands full," he means that he was busy.

MARK IT UP WORD POWER

Mark words that you'd like to add to your **Personal Word List.** After reading, you can record the words and their meanings begin- ning on page 402.

Reading Check

Why did Mr. Hale stop by the Wrights' house?

put me off, saying folks talked too much anyway, and all he asked was peace and quiet—I guess you know about how much he talked himself; but I thought maybe if I went to the house and talked about it before his wife, though I said to Harry that I didn't know as what his wife wanted made much difference to John—

County Attorney. Let's talk about that later, Mr. Hale. I do want to talk about that, but tell now just what happened when you got to the house.

Hale. I didn't hear or see anything; I knocked at the door, and still it was all quiet inside. I knew they must be up, it was past eight o'clock. So I knocked again, and I thought I heard somebody say, "Come in." I wasn't sure, I'm not sure yet, but I opened the door—this door *(indicating the door by which the two women are still standing)* and there in that rocker—*(pointing to it)* sat Mrs. Wright. *(They all look at the rocker downstage left.)*

County Attorney. What—was she doing?

Hale. She was rockin' back and forth. She had her apron in her hand and was kind of—pleating it.

County Attorney. And how did she—look?

Hale. Well, she looked queer.

County Attorney. How do you mean—queer?

Hale. Well, as if she didn't know what she was going to do next. And kind of done up.

County Attorney *(takes out notebook and pencil and sits left of center table).* How did she seem to feel about your coming?

Hale. Why, I don't think she minded—one way or other. She didn't pay much attention. I said, "How do, Mrs. Wright, it's cold, ain't it?" And she said, "Is it?"—and went on kind of pleating at her apron. Well, I was surprised; she didn't ask me to come up to the stove, or to set down, but just sat there, not even looking at me, so I said, "I want to see John." And then she—laughed. I guess you would call it a laugh. I thought of Harry and the team outside, so I said a little sharp: "Can't I see John?" "No," she says, kind o' dull like. "Ain't he home?" says I. "Yes," says she, "he's home." "Then why can't I see him?" I asked her, out

Reading Tip
Retell the story Mr. Hale tells the Sheriff in your own words.

✔ **Reading Check**
What was Mrs. Wright doing when Mr. Hale entered the house?

English Learner Support
LANGUAGE

Idiom The words *done up* mean "exhausted."

of patience. "'Cause he's dead," says she. *"Dead?"* says I. She just nodded her head, not getting a bit excited, but rockin' back and forth. "Why—where is he?" says I, not knowing what to say. She just pointed upstairs—like that *(himself pointing to the room above)*. I started for the stairs, with the idea of going up there. I walked from there to here—then I says, "Why, what did he die of?" "He died of a rope round his neck," says she, and just went on pleatin' at her apron. Well, I went out and called Harry. I thought I might—need help. We went upstairs and there he was lyin'—

County Attorney. I think I'd rather have you go into that upstairs, where you can point it all out. Just go on now with the rest of the story.

Hale. Well, my first thought was to get that rope off. It looked . . . *(Stops. His face twitches.)* . . . but Harry, he went up to him, and he said, "No, he's dead all right, and we'd better not touch anything." So we went back downstairs. She was still sitting that same way. "Has anybody been notified?" I asked. "No," says she, unconcerned. "Who did this, Mrs. Wright?" said Harry. He said it businesslike—and she stopped pleatin' of her apron. "I don't know," she says. "You don't *know?*" says Harry. "No," says she. "Weren't you sleepin' in the bed with him?" says Harry. "Yes," says she, "but I was on the inside." "Somebody slipped a rope round his neck and strangled him and you didn't wake up?" says Harry. "I didn't wake up," she said after him. We must 'a' looked as if we didn't see how that could be, for after a minute she said, "I sleep sound." Harry was going to ask her more questions but I said maybe we ought to let her tell her story first to the coroner, or the sheriff, so Harry went fast as he could to Rivers' place, where there's a telephone.

County Attorney. And what did Mrs. Wright do when she knew that you had gone for the coroner?

Hale. She moved from the rocker to that chair over there *(pointing to a small chair in the downstage right corner)* and just sat there with her hands held together and looking down. I got a feeling that I ought to make some

READ ALOUD Lines 113–123

As you read these lines aloud, try to picture this scene. What is unusual about Mrs. Wright's explanation?

English Learner Support

LANGUAGE

Dialect *We must 'a' looked* is written in dialect and could be rewritten as "We must have looked."

English Learner Support

VOCABULARY

Idiom When Mrs. Wright says "I sleep sound," she means that when she is sleeping, it is hard to wake her up.

Pause **&** *Reflect*

From the details you underlined, what can you **infer** about the sort of man John Wright was? Circle any words below that describe him.

shy	negative
quiet	generous
talkative	unfriendly

As the play continues . . .

- The County Attorney notices that the kitchen is not clean.
- Mrs. Hale and Mrs. Peters stay and tidy up the kitchen.
- The men go upstairs where the body was found.

What Does It Mean?

Preserves are fruit that has been cooked with sugar and sealed in glass jars to make it last longer.

conversation, so I said I had come in to see if John wanted to put in a telephone, and at that she started to laugh, and then she stopped and looked at me—scared. (*The* County Attorney, *who has had his notebook out, makes a note.*) I
140 dunno, maybe it wasn't scared. I wouldn't like to say it was. Soon Harry got back, and then Dr. Lloyd came, and you, Mr. Peters, and so I guess that's all I know that you don't.

Pause **&** *Reflect*

FOCUS

The men continue to hunt for clues. The County Attorney comments on the messiness of the kitchen.

MARK IT UP As you read, underline the words and actions that reveal the men's attitudes towards women. These attitudes will influence later events.

County Attorney (*rising and looking around*). I guess we'll go upstairs first—and then out to the barn and around there. (*To the* Sheriff) You're convinced that there was nothing important here—nothing that would point to any motive?

Sheriff. Nothing here but kitchen things. (*The* County Attorney, *after again looking around the kitchen, opens the door of a cupboard closet in right wall. He brings a small chair from right—gets up on it and looks on a shelf.*
150 *Pulls his hand away, sticky.*)

County Attorney. Here's a nice mess. (*The women draw nearer upstage center.*)

Mrs. Peters (*to the other woman*). Oh, her fruit; it did freeze. (*To the Lawyer*) She worried about that when it turned so cold. She said the fire'd go out and her jars would break.

Sheriff (*rises*). Well, can you beat the women! Held for murder and worryin' about her preserves.

County Attorney (*getting down from chair*). I guess before we're through she may have something more serious than
160 preserves to worry about. (*crosses down right center*)

Hale. Well, women are used to worrying over (trifles.) *(The two women move a little closer together.)*

County Attorney *(with the gallantry of a young politician).* And yet, for all their worries, what would we do without the ladies? *(The women do not unbend. He goes below the center table to the sink, takes a* (dipperful) *of water from the pail and, pouring it into a basin, washes his hands. While he is doing this, the* Sheriff *and* Hale *cross to cupboard, which they inspect. The* County Attorney *starts to wipe his hands on the roller towel, turns it for a cleaner place.)* Dirty towels! *(Kicks his foot against the pans under the sink.)* Not much of a housekeeper, would you say, ladies?

Mrs. Hale *(stiffly).* There's a great deal of work to be done on a farm.

County Attorney. To be sure. And yet *(with a little bow to her)* I know there are some Dickson County farmhouses which do not have such roller towels. *(He gives it a pull to expose its full length again.)*

Mrs. Hale. Those towels get dirty awful quick. Men's hands aren't always as clean as they might be.

County Attorney. Ah, loyal to your sex, I see. But you and Mrs. Wright were neighbors. I suppose you were friends, too.

Mrs. Hale *(shaking her head).* I've not seen much of her of late years. I've not been in this house—it's more than a year.

County Attorney *(crossing to women upstage center).* And why was that? You didn't like her?

Mrs. Hale. I liked her all well enough. Farmers' wives have their hands full, Mr. Henderson. And then—

County Attorney. Yes—?

Mrs. Hale *(looking about).* It never seemed a very cheerful place.

County Attorney. No—it's not cheerful. I shouldn't say she had the homemaking instinct.

Mrs. Hale. Well, I don't know as Wright had, either.

County Attorney. You mean that they didn't get on very well?

170
180
190

More About . . .
Remember that (Trifles) is the title of the play. It means "things that are of little importance or value." Think about why the writer might have chosen this word for the title of the play.

More About . . .
There is no running water on the farm. Water is brought in from a well (a hole dug in the earth to reach water) and is kept in a pail in the kitchen. A cup or small pan is (dipped) into the pail to get water when it is needed.

English Learner Support
LANGUAGE

Dialect The highlighted sentence could be rewritten as, "I haven't seen very much of her lately."

What Does It Mean?
An *instinct* is an urge or impulse to do things in a certain way.

Pause & Reflect

1. From the details you marked, what can you **infer** about the men's attitudes toward women?

_____

_____

_____

_____

MARK IT UP 2. How does Mrs. Hale seem to feel about Minnie Wright? Circle passages on page 259 that support your opinion. **(Draw Conclusions)**

_____

_____

_____

As the play continues . . .

- As the women collect clothes for Mrs. Wright, they talk about her hard life.

- The women discuss the idea that Mrs. Wright might have killed her husband.

READ ALOUD Lines 210–221

As you read aloud these lines, try to express the differences between Mrs. Hale's attitude towards the men and the attitude of Mrs. Peters. With whom would you side?

English Learner Support

LANGUAGE

Idiom When Mrs. Hale says that the deputy sheriff *might have got a little of this on,* she means that he may be responsible for some of the mess in the kitchen.

Mrs. Hale. No, I don't mean anything. But I don't think a place'd be any cheerfuller for John Wright's being in it.

County Attorney. I'd like to talk more of that a little later. I want to get the lay of things upstairs now. *(He goes past the women to upstage right where steps lead to a stair door.)*

Sheriff. I suppose anything Mrs. Peters does'll be all right. She was to take in some clothes for her, you know, and a few little things. We left in such a hurry yesterday.

County Attorney. Yes, but I would like to see what you take, Mrs. Peters, and keep an eye out for anything that might be of use to us.

Mrs. Peters. Yes, Mr. Henderson. *(The men leave by upstage right door to stairs. The women listen to the men's steps on the stairs, then look about the kitchen.)*

Pause & Reflect

FOCUS

The mood in the kitchen becomes calmer and more thoughtful after the women are left alone.

MARK IT UP As you read, underline details that help you get to know Minnie Wright and the life she led.

Mrs. Hale *(crossing left to sink)*. I'd hate to have men coming into my kitchen, snooping around and criticizing. *(She arranges the pans under sink which the lawyer had shoved out of place.)*

Mrs. Peters. Of course it's no more than their duty. *(crosses to cupboard upstage right)*

Mrs. Hale. Duty's all right, but I guess that deputy sheriff that came out to make the fire might have got a little of this on. *(Gives the roller towel a pull.)* Wish I'd thought of that sooner. Seems mean to talk about her for not having things slicked up when she had to come away in such a hurry. *(Crosses right to Mrs. Peters at cupboard.)*

Mrs. Peters *(who has been looking through cupboard, lifts one end of a towel that covers a pan).* She had bread set. *(Stands still.)*

Mrs. Hale *(eyes fixed on a loaf of bread beside the breadbox, which is on a low shelf of the cupboard).* She was going to put this in there. *(Picks up loaf, then abruptly drops it. In a manner of returning to familiar things.)* It's a shame about her fruit. I wonder if it's all gone. *(Gets up on the chair and looks.)* I think there's some here that's all right, Mrs. Peters. Yes—here; *(holding it toward the window)* this is cherries, too. *(looking again)* I declare I believe that's the only one. *(Gets down, jar in her hand. Goes to the sink and wipes it off on the outside.)* She'll feel awful bad after all her hard work in the hot weather. I remember the afternoon I put up my cherries last summer. *(She puts the jar on the big kitchen table, center of the room. With a sigh, is about to sit down in the rocking chair. Before she is seated realizes what chair it is; with a slow look at it, steps back. The chair which she has touched rocks back and forth. Mrs. Peters moves to center table and they both watch the chair rock for a moment or two.)*

Mrs. Peters *(shaking off the mood which the empty rocking chair has evoked; now in a businesslike manner she speaks).* Well, I must get those things from the front room closet. *(She goes to the door at the right, but, after looking into the other room, steps back).* You coming with me, Mrs. Hale? You could help me carry them. *(They go in the other room; reappear, Mrs. Peters carrying a dress, petticoat and skirt, Mrs. Hale following with a pair of shoes.)* My, it's cold in there. *(She puts the clothes on the big table, and hurries to the stove.)*

Mrs. Hale. Wright was close.² I think maybe that's why she kept so much to herself. She didn't even belong to the Ladies' Aid. I suppose she felt she couldn't do her part, and then you don't enjoy things when you feel shabby. I heard she used to wear pretty clothes and be lively, when she was Minnie Foster, one of the town girls singing in the choir. But that—oh, that was thirty years ago. This all you was to take in?

---

2. **close:** secretive; not open or friendly.

What Does It Mean?
Mrs. Wright had been making bread. The highlighted sentence means that she had put the dough out to rise.

✔ **Reading Check**
What do Mrs. Hale's actions tell you about what she is thinking?

English Learner Support
GRAMMAR

Prefix The prefix *re-* in *reappear* makes the word *appear* mean "appear again." *re + appear = appear again*

More About . . .
LADIES' AID The Ladies' Aid was a local church organization that sponsored social events. These types of organizations provided some relief from the isolation and loneliness of farm life.

What Does It Mean?
Minnie Foster is the same woman as Mrs. Wright. *Foster* was her maiden name, or her last name before she married John Wright.

Reading Tip

What was Mrs. Wright's life like before and after her marriage to John Wright? Fill in the following chart.

Before	After

What Does It Mean?

Sarcastic means "mocking or making fun of in a sharp way." Mrs. Peters is worried that Mr. Henderson will make fun of Mrs. Wright at her trial.

English Learner Support

Dialect The phrase *they was slipping* can be rewritten in standard English as "they were slipping."

What Does It Mean?

A *motive* is a reason for a person to act in a certain way.

✔ Reading Check

Why doesn't Mrs. Hale believe that Mrs. Wright killed her husband?

Mrs. Peters. She said she wanted an apron. Funny thing to want, for there isn't much to get you dirty in jail, goodness knows. But I suppose just to make her feel more natural. *(crosses to cupboard.)* She said they was in the top drawer in this cupboard. Yes, here. And then her little shawl that always hung behind the door. *(Opens stair door and looks.)* Yes, here it is. *(Quickly shuts door leading upstairs.)*

Mrs. Hale *(abruptly moving toward her).* Mrs. Peters?

270 **Mrs. Peters.** Yes, Mrs. Hale? *(At upstage right door.)*

Mrs. Hale. Do you think she did it?

Mrs. Peters *(in a frightened voice).* Oh, I don't know.

Mrs. Hale. Well, I don't think she did. Asking for an apron and her little shawl. Worrying about her fruit.

Mrs. Peters *(Starts to speak, glances up, where footsteps are heard in the room above. In a low voice).* Mr. Peters says it looks bad for her. Mr. Henderson is awful sarcastic in a speech and he'll make fun of her sayin' she didn't wake up.

280 **Mrs. Hale.** Well, I guess John Wright didn't wake when they was slipping that rope under his neck.

Mrs. Peters *(crossing slowly to table and placing shawl and apron on table with other clothing).* No, it's strange. It must have been done awful crafty and still. They say it was such a—funny way to kill a man, rigging it all up like that.

Mrs. Hale *(crossing to left of* Mrs. Peters *at table).* That's just what Mr. Hale said. There was a gun in the house. He says that's what he can't understand.

290 **Mrs. Peters.** Mr. Henderson said coming out that what was needed for the case was a motive; something to show anger, or—sudden feeling.

Mrs. Hale *(who is standing by the table).* Well, I don't see any signs of anger around here. *(She puts her hand on the dishtowel which lies on the table, stands looking down at table, one-half of which is clean, the other half messy.)* It's wiped to here. *(Makes a move as if to finish work, then turns and looks at loaf of bread outside the breadbox.*

Drops towel. In that voice of coming back to familiar
300 *things.)* Wonder how they are finding things upstairs.
(Crossing below table to downstage right) I hope she had
it a little more readied-up[3] up there. You know, it seems
kind of sneaking. Locking her up in town and then coming out here and trying to get her own house to turn
against her!

Mrs. Peters. But, Mrs. Hale, the law is the law.

Mrs. Hale. I s'pose 'tis. *(unbuttoning her coat)* Better loosen
up your things, Mrs. Peters. You won't feel them when
you go out. *(Mrs. Peters takes off her fur tippet,[4] goes to*
310 *hang it on chair back left of table, stands looking at the*
work basket on floor near downstage left window.)

Mrs. Peters. She was piecing a quilt. *(She brings the large*
sewing basket to the center table and they look at the
bright pieces, Mrs. Hale *above the table and* Mrs. Peters
left of it.)

Mrs. Hale. It's a log cabin pattern.[5] Pretty, isn't it? I wonder if
she was goin' to quilt it or just knot it?[6] *(Footsteps have*
been heard coming down the stairs. The Sheriff *enters*
followed by Hale *and the* County Attorney.)

320 Sheriff. They wonder if she was going to quilt it or just knot
it! *(The men laugh, the women look <u>abashed</u>.)*

County Attorney *(rubbing his hands over the stove).* Frank's
fire didn't do much up there, did it? Well, let's go out to
the barn and get that cleared up. *(The men go outside by*
upstage left door.)

Pause & Reflect

---

3. **readied-up:** *dialect,* made ready; straightened up.
4. **tippet:** a scarflike or shawllike garment.
5. **log cabin pattern:** a common pattern for a quilt.
6. **quilt it or just knot it:** the bottom and top layers of a quilt are either
   quilted—sewn together—or knotted—held together with yarn tied into
   knots. Knotting is a much simpler and faster method.

WORDS
TO   **abashed** (ə-băshd´) *adj.* embarrassed or ashamed **abash** *v.*
KNOW

English Learner Support
LANGUAGE

Contractions The sentence *I
s'pose 'tis* could be rewritten
as "I suppose it is."

Pause & *Reflect*

1. Review the details you underlined about Minnie Wright on
pages 261–263. Then **summarize**
what you learned about her.

_____

_____

_____

_____

READ ALOUD   2. Read aloud
the boxed passage on page 262.
What did Mr. Henderson say
was needed for the case against
Minnie Wright? **(Clarify)**

_____

_____

_____

3. A loaf of bread outside the
breadbox, a half-wiped table—
such details provide clues. What
do you think happened to upset
Minnie Wright's daily routine?
(Infer)

_____

_____

_____

_____

As the play continues . . .

- Mrs. Hale and Mrs. Peters notice that Mrs. Wright's sewing is knotted and tangled.

- Mrs. Hale begins to fix the sewing.

- They find an empty birdcage.

- The women open Mrs. Wright's sewing box and make another discovery.

More About . . .

EVIDENCE can be objects that are found or words that were written or spoken that will help to prove a crime. The men in this story are mostly offstage looking for evidence that will prove Mrs. Wright killed her husband.

English Learner Support
LANGUAGE

Idiom The highlighted sentence means that the stitches were very messy.

READ ALOUD Lines 342–350

As you read this dialogue, use your voice to express the difference between the calm Mrs. Hale and the nervous Mrs. Peters.

FOCUS

The two women continue to talk about the investigation and Minnie Wright. As they talk, they look at various items in her kitchen. **MARK IT UP** Read to uncover three clues about what happened on the night of the murder. Circle each clue you find.

Mrs. Hale *(resentfully)*. I don't know as there's anything so strange, our takin' up our time with little things while we're waiting for them to get the evidence. *(She sits in chair right of table smoothing out a block with decision.)* I don't see as it's anything to laugh about.

Mrs. Peters *(apologetically)*. Of course they've got awful important things on their minds. *(Pulls up a chair and joins Mrs. Hale at the left of the table.)*

Mrs. Hale *(examining another block)*. Mrs. Peters, look at this one. Here, this is the one she was working on, and look at the sewing! All the rest of it has been so nice and even. And look at this! It's all over the place! Why, it looks as if she didn't know what she was about! *(After she has said this they look at each other, then start to glance back at the door. After an instant Mrs. Hale has pulled at a knot and ripped the sewing.)*

Mrs. Peters. Oh, what are you doing, Mrs. Hale?

Mrs. Hale *(mildly)*. Just pulling out a stitch or two that's not sewed very good. *(threading a needle)* Bad sewing always made me fidgety.

Mrs. Peters *(with a glance at door, nervously)*. I don't think we ought to touch things.

Mrs. Hale. I'll just finish up this end. *(suddenly stopping and leaning forward)* Mrs. Peters?

Mrs. Peters. Yes, Mrs. Hale?

Mrs. Hale. What do you suppose she was so nervous about?

Mrs. Peters. Oh—I don't know, I don't know as she was nervous. I sometimes sew awful queer when I'm just tired. *(Mrs. Hale starts to say something, looks at Mrs. Peters, then goes on sewing.)* Well, I must get these things wrapped up. They may be through sooner than we think. *(Putting apron and other things together)* I wonder where I can find a piece of paper, and string. *(Rises.)*

Mrs. Hale. In that cupboard, maybe.

360 **Mrs. Peters** *(crosses right looking in cupboard)*. Why, here's a birdcage. *(Holds it up.)* Did she have a bird, Mrs. Hale?

Mrs. Hale. Why, I don't know whether she did or not—I've not been here for so long. There was a man around last year selling canaries cheap, but I don't know as she took one; maybe she did. She used to sing real pretty herself.

Mrs. Peters *(glancing around)*. Seems funny to think of a bird here. But she must have had one, or why would she have a cage? I wonder what happened to it?

Mrs. Hale. I s'pose maybe the cat got it.

370 **Mrs. Peters.** No, she didn't have a cat. She's got that feeling some people have about cats—being afraid of them. My cat got in her room and she was real upset and asked me to take it out.

Mrs. Hale. My sister Bessie was like that. Queer, ain't it?

Mrs. Peters *(examining the cage)*. Why, look at this door. It's broke. One hinge is pulled apart. *(Takes a step down to Mrs. Hale's right.)*

Mrs. Hale *(looking too)*. Looks as if someone must have been rough with it.

380 **Mrs. Peters.** Why, yes. *(She brings the cage forward and puts it on the table.)*

Mrs. Hale *(glancing toward upstage left door)*. I wish if they're going to find any evidence they'd be about it. I don't like this place.

Mrs. Peters. But I'm awful glad you came with me, Mrs. Hale. It would be lonesome for me sitting here alone.

Mrs. Hale. It would, wouldn't it? *(dropping her sewing)* But I tell you what I do wish, Mrs. Peters. I wish I had come over sometimes when she was here. I—*(looking around the room)*—wish I had.

390 **Mrs. Peters.** But of course you were awful busy, Mrs. Hale— your house and your children.

Reading Tip

Make a list of the pieces of evidence the women find in the kitchen.

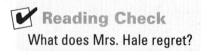

Reading Check

What does Mrs. Hale regret?

Mrs. Hale *(rises and crosses left).* I could've come. I stayed away because it weren't cheerful—and that's why I ought to have come. I—*(looking out left window)*—I've never liked this place. Maybe because it's down in a hollow and you don't see the road. I dunno what it is, but it's a lonesome place and always was. I wish I had come over to see Minnie Foster sometimes. I can see now—*(shakes her head)*

400

Mrs. Peters *(left of table and above it).* Well, you mustn't reproach yourself, Mrs. Hale. Somehow we just don't see how it is with other folks until—something turns up.

Mrs. Hale. Not having children makes less work—but it makes a quiet house, and Wright out to work all day, and no company when he did come in. *(turning from window)* Did you know John Wright, Mrs. Peters?

Mrs. Peters. Not to know him; I've seen him in town. They say he was a good man.

410

Mrs. Hale. Yes—good; he didn't drink, and kept his word as well as most, I guess, and paid his debts. But he was a hard man, Mrs. Peters. Just to pass the time of day with him—*(shivers)* Like a raw wind that gets to the bone. *(pauses, her eye falling on the cage)* I should think she would 'a' wanted a bird. But what do you suppose went with it?

Mrs. Peters. I don't know, unless it got sick and died. *(She reaches over and swings the broken door, swings it again, both women watch it.)*

420

Mrs. Hale. You weren't raised round here, were you? *(Mrs. Peters shakes her head.)* You didn't know—her?

Mrs. Peters. Not till they brought her yesterday.

Mrs. Hale. She—come to think of it, she was kind of like a bird herself—real sweet and pretty, but kind of timid and—fluttery. How—she—did—change. *(Silence; then as if struck by a happy thought and relieved to get back to everyday things, crosses right above* Mrs. Peters *to cupboard, replaces small chair used to stand on to its original place downstage right.)* Tell you what, Mrs. Peters, why don't you take the quilt in with you? It might take up her mind.

430

What Does It Mean?

Reproach means "blame."

English Learner Support

LANGUAGE

Simile The words *like a raw wind* compare Mr. Wright to a very cold wind. Mrs. Hale means that Mr. Wright was unfriendly and made people uneasy.

English Learner Support

LANGUAGE

Dialect The highlighted sentence means "What do you think happened to it?"

READ ALOUD **Lines 423–431**

Mrs. Hale has a sudden insight about Minnie Wright. As you read, try to express how Mrs. Hale now feels about her.

Mrs. Peters. Why, I think that's a real nice idea, Mrs. Hale. There couldn't possibly be any objection to it, could there? Now, just what would I take? I wonder if her patches are in here—and her things. *(They look in the sewing basket.)*

Mrs. Hale *(crosses to right of table).* Here's some red. I expect this has got sewing things in it. *(Brings out a fancy box.)* What a pretty box. Looks like something somebody would give you. Maybe her scissors are in here. *(Opens box. Suddenly puts her hand to her nose.)* Why— *(Mrs. Peters bends nearer, then turns her face away.)* There's something wrapped up in this piece of silk.

Mrs. Peters. Why, this isn't her scissors.

Mrs. Hale *(lifting the silk).* Oh, Mrs. Peters—it's—*(Mrs. Peters bends closer.)*

Mrs. Peters. It's the bird.

Mrs. Hale. But, Mrs. Peters—look at it! Its neck! Look at its neck! It's all—other side to.[7]

Mrs. Peters. Somebody—wrung—its—neck. *(Their eyes meet. A look of growing <u>comprehension</u>, of horror. Steps are heard outside, Mrs. Hale slips box under quilt pieces, and sinks into her chair. Enter Sheriff and County Attorney. Mrs. Peters steps downstage left and stands looking out of window.)*

County Attorney *(as one turning from serious things to little pleasantries).* Well, ladies, have you decided whether she was going to quilt it or knot it? *(Crosses to center above table.)*

Pause **&** *Reflect*

---

7. **other side to:** back side forward. The bird's head was facing the wrong way.

WORDS
TO
KNOW

comprehension (kŏm′prē-hĕn′shən) *n.* awareness and understanding

---

What do Mrs. Hale and Mrs. Peters think happened to the bird?

What Does It Mean?

To *quilt it or knot it* refers to two different ways to finish sewing a quilt. As the story progresses, the term *knot it* takes on another meaning as well. It refers to the way that John Wright was killed, with a rope knotted around his neck.

Pause **&** *Reflect*

1. Complete the sentence that follows: Mrs. Hale rips out and restitches Mrs. Wright's last quilting stitches because_____

_____

_____.

(Cause and Effect)

2. The women now think they know what happened on the night of the murder. What do you **predict** will happen next?

_____

_____

_____

_____

- The County Attorney notices the birdcage.
- Mrs. Hale remembers that Mrs. Wright was once pretty and cheerful.
- The men cannot find a motive or reason for the crime.

✔ Reading Check

Why does Mrs. Hale say they think the cat ate the canary?

MARK IT UP WORD POWER

Remember to mark words that you'd like to add to your **Personal Word List**. Later, you can record the words and their meanings beginning on page 402.

English Learner Support
LANGUAGE

Dashes There are many dashes in these lines. Each dash represents a pause in the speech. Because Mrs. Peters is recalling an emotional story, she has a hard time getting her words out smoothly.

FOCUS

The women have discovered an important piece of evidence—a dead canary.

MARK IT UP Read to find out what the women decide to do with their evidence.

Mrs. Peters. We think she was going to—knot it. *(Sheriff crosses to right of stove, lifts stove lid and glances at fire, then stands warming hands at stove.)*

County Attorney. Well, that's interesting, I'm sure. *(Seeing the birdcage.)* Has the bird flown?

Mrs. Hale *(putting more quilt pieces over the box)*. We think the—cat got it.

County Attorney *(preoccupied)*. Is there a cat? *(Mrs. Hale glances in a quick covert way at Mrs. Peters.)*

Mrs. Peters *(turning from window takes a step in)*. Well, not now. They're superstitious, you know. They leave.

County Attorney *(to Sheriff Peters, continuing an interrupted conversation)*. No sign at all of anyone having come from the outside. Their own rope. Now let's go up again and go over it piece by piece. *(They start upstairs.)* It would have to have been someone who knew just the— *(Mrs. Peters sits down left of table. The two women sit there not looking at one another, but as if peering into something and at the same time holding back. When they talk now it is in the manner of feeling their way over strange ground, as if afraid of what they are saying, but as if they cannot help saying it.)*

Mrs. Hale *(hesitantly and in hushed voice)*. She liked the bird. She was going to bury it in that pretty box.

Mrs. Peters *(in a whisper)*. When I was a girl—my kitten—there was a boy took a hatchet, and before my eyes—and before I could get there— *(covers her face an instant)* If they hadn't held me back I would have—*(catches herself, looks upstairs where steps are heard, falters weakly)*—hurt him.

Mrs. Hale *(with a slow look around her)*. I wonder how it would seem never to have had any children around. *(pause)* No, Wright wouldn't like the bird—a thing that sang. She used to sing. He killed that, too.

WORDS
TO
KNOW
preoccupied (prē-ŏk′yə-pīd′) *adj.* absorbed in other thoughts
covert (kō′vərt) *adj.* concealed; secretive

Mrs. Peters *(moving uneasily)*. We don't know who killed the bird.

Mrs. Hale. I knew John Wright.

Mrs. Peters. It was an awful thing was done in this house that night, Mrs. Hale. Killing a man while he slept, slipping a rope around his neck that choked the life out of him.

Mrs. Hale. His neck. Choked the life out of him. *(Her hand goes out and rests on the birdcage.)*

⑤⓪⓪ Mrs. Peters *(with rising voice)*. We don't know who killed him. We don't *know*.

Mrs. Hale *(her own feeling not interrupted)*. If there'd been years and years of nothing, then a bird to sing to you, it would be awful—still, after the bird was still.

Mrs. Peters *(something within her speaking)*. I know what stillness is. When we homesteaded[8] in Dakota, and my first baby died—after he was two years old, and me with no other then—

Mrs. Hale *(moving)*. How soon do you suppose they'll be ⑤①⓪ through looking for the evidence?

Mrs. Peters. I know what stillness is. *(pulling herself back)* The law has got to punish crime, Mrs. Hale.

Mrs. Hale *(not as if answering that)*. I wish you'd seen Minnie Foster when she wore a white dress with blue ribbons and stood up there in the choir and sang. *(a look around the room)* Oh, I *wish* I'd come over here once in a while! That was a crime! That was a crime! Who's going to punish that?

Mrs. Peters *(looking upstairs)*. We mustn't—take on.

⑤②⓪ Mrs. Hale. I might have known she needed help! I know how things can be—for women. I tell you, it's queer, Mrs. Peters. We live close together and we live far apart. We all go through the same things—it's all just a different kind of the same thing. *(Brushes her eyes. Noticing the jar of fruit, reaches out for it.)* If I was you I wouldn't tell her her fruit was gone. Tell her it *ain't*. Tell her it's all right. Take this in to prove it to her. She—she may never know whether it was broke or not.

Reading Check

What does Mrs. Peters mean when she says "I know what stillness is"?

Reading Check

Mrs. Hale says that *she* committed a crime because she never came to visit Mrs. Wright. Why do you think she says this?

READ ALOUD Lines 520–528

Try to express the different feelings Mrs. Hale is experiencing. What has she come to realize?

---

8. **homesteaded**: settled and farmed on land that was given to settlers by the U.S. government following the 1862 Homestead Act; ownership was granted after the settler had lived on the land for five years.

Mrs. Peters *(takes the jar, looks about for something to wrap it*
530 *in; takes petticoat from the clothes brought from the other*
room, very nervously begins winding this around the jar; in
a false voice). My, it's a good thing the men couldn't hear
us. Wouldn't they just laugh! Getting all stirred up over a
little thing like a—dead canary. As if that could have anything to do with—with—wouldn't they *laugh! (The men*
are heard coming downstairs.)

Mrs. Hale *(under her breath).* Maybe they would—maybe
they wouldn't.

County Attorney. No, Peters, it's all perfectly clear except a
540 reason for doing it. But you know juries when it comes to
women. If there was some definite thing. *(Crosses slowly*
to above table. Sheriff crosses downstage right. Mrs. Hale
and Mrs. Peters remain seated at either side of table.)
Something to show—something to make a story about—a
thing that would connect up with this strange way of
doing it—*(The women's* eyes meet *for an instant. Enter*
Hale *from outer door.)*

Hale *(remaining upstage left by door).* Well, I've got the team
around. Pretty cold out there.

550 **County Attorney.** I'm going to stay awhile by myself. *(To the*
Sheriff) You can send Frank out for me, can't you? I want
to go over everything. I'm not satisfied that we can't do
better.

Sheriff. Do you want to see what Mrs. Peters is going to take
in? *(The* Lawyer *picks up the apron, laughs.)*

County Attorney. Oh, I guess they're not very dangerous things
the ladies have picked out. *(Moves a few things about, dis-*
turbing the quilt pieces which cover the box. Steps back.)
No, Mrs. Peters doesn't need supervising. For that matter a
560 sheriff's wife is married to the law. Ever think of it that
way, Mrs. Peters?

Mrs. Peters. Not—just that way.

Sheriff *(chuckling).* Married to the law. *(Moves to downstage*
right door to the other room.) I just want you to come in
here a minute, George. We ought to take a look at these
windows.

County Attorney (*scoffingly*). Oh, windows!

Sheriff. We'll be right out, Mr. Hale. (Hale *goes outside. The* Sheriff *follows the* County Attorney *into the other room.* Then Mrs. Hale rises, *hands tight together, looking intensely at* Mrs. Peters, *whose eyes make a slow turn, finally meeting* Mrs. Hale's. *A moment* Mrs. Hale *holds her, then her own eyes point the way to where the box is concealed. Suddenly* Mrs. Peters *throws back quilt pieces and tries to put the box in the bag she is carrying. It is too big. She opens box, starts to take bird out, cannot touch it, goes to pieces, stands there helpless. Sound of a knob turning in the other room,* Mrs. Hale *snatches the box and puts it in the pocket of her big coat. Enter* County Attorney *and* Sheriff, *who remains downstage right.*)

County Attorney (*crosses to upstage left door* <u>facetiously</u>). Well, Henry, at least we found out that she was not going to quilt it. She was going to—what is it you call it, ladies?

Mrs. Hale (*standing center below table facing front, her hand against her pocket*). We call it—knot it, Mr. Henderson.

Curtain

Pause & Reflect

Reading Check

What do the two women do with the evidence they find?

Pause & Reflect

MARK IT UP **1.** What do the women decide to do with their evidence? Underline details in the play that help you know this. **(Infer)**

_____

_____

_____

_____

2. What would you have done if you were in Mrs. Hale's or Mrs. Peters's position? **(Connect)**

_____

_____

_____

_____

3. In your opinion, who killed John Wright and why? **(Evaluate)**

_____

_____

_____

_____

CHALLENGE

One important **symbol** in this play is the dead canary. Explain why this symbol is so important. What does it suggest about Mrs. Wright's situation? **(Evaluate)**

WORDS TO KNOW   **facetiously** (fə-sē′shəs-lē) *adv.* in a manner not to be taken seriously; humorously

Trifles **271**

Active Reading SkillBuilder

Making Inferences

Inferences are logical guesses based on facts. Readers often need to draw inferences to make sense of what they read or see. In *Trifles,* characters notice clues that allow them to make inferences. These clues are often isolated and seemingly unimportant. When put together, however, they form the basis for inferences about the murder. As you read *Trifles,* use the chart to record details that might turn out to be clues to the murderer. Also record any inferences you can make from those details.

Clues to the Murderer in *Trifles*	Page Number	Inferences
1. *a half-wiped table*	*228*	*Mrs. Wright was in a hurry or was interrupted.*
2.		
3.		
4.		
5.		
6.		
7.		
8.		

Literary Analysis SkillBuilder

Dramatic Irony

Dramatic irony occurs when the reader or viewer of a story or play is aware of information but a character is not aware of it. In *Trifles*, the reader is aware of certain clues that the women have uncovered, but the men do not notice this evidence. Go back through the play and find several pieces of evidence that the women know about but the men do not. On the chart, record the evidence as well as the inference that might be drawn from each clue.

What the women know	What they infer
Careless sewing	Mrs. Wright was nervous or tired.

Follow Up: How does this dramatic irony help you interpret Mrs. Hale's final statement about knots?

Words to Know SkillBuilder

Words to Know

abashed   comprehension   covert   facetiously   preoccupied

A. For each phrase in the first column, find the phrase in the second column that is closest in meaning. Write the letter of that phrase in the blank.

_____	1. shamed by the collision	A. jestingly testing
_____	2. a distracted advisor	B. a covert Rover
_____	3. a covert conversation	C. secretive speaking
_____	4. abashed by Snow White	D. a preoccupied guide
_____	5. an undercover police dog	E. abashed by the crash
_____	6. facetiously quizzing	F. concentrating on ratings
_____	7. preoccupied by grades	G. embarrassed by the fairest
_____	8. an understanding of stress	H. a comprehension of tension

B. Fill in each blank with the correct word from the word list.

I had the idea that the teacher was talking about the American Revolution, but

I didn't hear a word. I was _____ with reading a novel

hidden inside my history textbook. This _____ activity

held my attention throughout the class. The next day we had a quiz to test our

_____ of the previous day's lesson, and I was quite

_____ to realize that I couldn't even answer the question,

"What was a main idea in yesterday's lecture?" So instead of giving a serious answer, I

_____ wrote, "You said the colonists were revolting."

Needless to say, I didn't get a passing grade.

C. Imagine that you are directing a production of *Trifles*. Write a short speech that you might give on the first day of rehearsal in which you give your overall vision of what should occur on-stage. Use at least **three** of the Words to Know.

Saki

The
Open
Window

Before You Read

Connect to Your Life

Why do you think people play pranks on one another? What possible responses are they looking for? Record your thoughts in the space below.

_____

_____

_____

_____

_____

_____

_____

Key to the Story

WHAT YOU NEED TO KNOW Saki, a pen name for Hector Hugh Munro, was a member of the upper class, and often made fun of upper-class traditions. One of these traditions was to follow a set of "proper" manners. These included presenting formal letters of introduction when visiting strangers. Another custom was the "nerve cure," or a trip to a rural place to treat nervousness and irritability. Only wealthy people were able to afford this treatment.

The Open Window

SAKI

Reading Tips
To appreciate this story, you will need to pay careful attention to each of the **main characters.** Keep in mind that appearances can be deceiving.

- Notice what the different characters are thinking about, especially Mr. Nuttel. Look for **details** that describe his thoughts or worries.

- Try to imagine the characters as they speak. Notice how each person sees the situation from a different angle.

- This story is written using a formal language that can be very confusing. First, try reading the story aloud and stopping after every few paragraphs to summarize what you just read. Then reread confusing passages, using a dictionary to help with any words you don't know.

PREVIEW "The Open Window" is about upper-class people in England in the early 1900s. As the story opens, a young man named Framton Nuttel is paying a visit to a family living in the country. He doesn't know them, but he has a letter from his sister introducing him to the lady of the house. As the story opens, he is talking to the lady's niece.

FOCUS
As you read, look for what is going on in Mr. Nuttel's mind.
MARK IT UP Underline any **details** that show why he's supposed to be making this visit. An example is highlighted.

"My aunt will be down presently, Mr. Nuttel," said a very self-possessed young lady of fifteen; "in the mean-time you must try and put up with me."

Framton Nuttel endeavored to say the correct something that should duly flatter the niece of the moment without unduly discounting the aunt that was to come. Privately he doubted more than ever whether these formal visits on a succession of total strangers would do much toward helping the nerve cure[1] which he was supposed to be undergoing.

As the story begins . . .

- Framton Nuttel has come to the country to cure his nerves.

- He chats with a young woman while waiting for her aunt to join them.

- The young woman tells Nuttel that her aunt has suffered a tragedy.

What Does It Mean?
Endeavored means "tried hard."

---

1. **nerve cure:** treatment for nervousness or anxiety.

English Learner Support

LANGUAGE

Formal Language When the author says, "that would be since your sister's time," he means "that would have been after your sister was here."

Pause **&** *Reflect*

1. Review the details you marked. This visit to the country is supposed to be good for Mr. Nuttel because _____

_____

_____.

(Clarify)

2. In this conversation, the girl seems to be more _____

_____

than Mr. Nuttel. **(Evaluate)**

As the story continues . . .

- The niece tells the story of the tragedy.

- The aunt, Mrs. Sappleton, joins Framton and the niece.

"I know how it will be," his sister had said when he was preparing to migrate to this rural retreat; "you will bury yourself down there and not speak to a living soul, and your nerves will be worse than ever from moping. I shall just give you letters of introduction to all the people I know there. Some of them, as far as I can remember, were quite nice."

20 Framton wondered whether Mrs. Sappleton, the lady to whom he was presenting one of the letters of introduction, came into the nice division.

"Do you know many of the people round here?" asked the niece, when she judged that they had had sufficient silent communion.

"Hardly a soul," said Framton. "My sister was staying here, at the rectory,[2] you know, some four years ago, and she gave me letters of introduction to some of the people here."

He made the last statement in a tone of distinct regret.

"Then you know practically nothing about my aunt?" 30 pursued the self-possessed young lady.

"Only her name and address," admitted the caller. He was wondering whether Mrs. Sappleton was in the married or widowed state. An undefinable something about the room seemed to suggest masculine habitation.[3]

"Her great tragedy happened just three years ago," said the child; "that would be since your sister's time."

"Her tragedy?" asked Framton; somehow in this restful country spot tragedies seemed out of place.

Pause **&** *Reflect*

FOCUS

40 Read to find about Mrs. Sappleton's tragedy and how the characters feel about it.

MARK IT UP Circle words and phrases that tell you about how Mr. Nuttel reacts.

"**You may wonder** why we keep that window wide open on an October afternoon," said the niece, indicating a large French window[4] that opened on to a lawn.

"It is quite warm for the time of the year," said Framton; "but has that window got anything to do with the tragedy?"

---

2. **the rectory** (rĕk′tə-rē): the parish priest's house.

3. **masculine habitation** (măs′kyə-lĭn hăb-ĭ-tā′shən): that men lived there.

4. **French window**: a pair of windows that extend to the floor and open like doors.

"Out through that window, three years ago to a day, her husband and her two young brothers went off for their day's shooting. They never came back. In crossing the moor to their favorite snipe[5]-shooting ground they were all three engulfed by a treacherous piece of bog. It had been that dreadful wet summer, you know, and places that were safe in other years gave way suddenly without warning. Their bodies were never recovered. That was the dreadful part of it." Here the child's voice lost its self-possessed note and became falteringly human. "Poor aunt always thinks that they will come back some day, they and the little brown spaniel that was lost with them, and walk in that window just as they used to do. That is why the window is kept open every evening till it is quite dusk. Poor dear aunt, she has often told me how they went out, her husband with his white waterproof coat over his arm, and Ronnie, her youngest brother, singing 'Bertie, why do you bound?' as he always did to tease her, because she said it got on her nerves. Do you know, sometimes on still, quiet evenings like this, I almost get a creepy feeling that they will all walk in through that window—"

She broke off with a little shudder. It was a relief to Framton when the aunt bustled into the room with a whirl of apologies for being late in making her appearance.

"I hope Vera has been amusing you?" she said.

"She has been very interesting," said Framton.

"I hope you don't mind the open window," said Mrs. Sappleton briskly; "my husband and brothers will be home directly from shooting, and they always come in this way. They've been out for snipe in the marshes today, so they'll make a fine mess over my poor carpets. So like you menfolk, isn't it?"

She rattled on cheerfully about the shooting and the scarcity of birds, and the prospects[6] for duck in the winter. To Framton it was all purely horrible. He made a desperate but only partially successful effort to turn the talk on to a less ghastly topic; he was conscious that his hostess was giving him only a fragment of her attention, and her eyes were constantly straying past him to the open window and the lawn beyond. It was certainly an unfortunate coincidence that he should have paid his visit on this tragic anniversary.

---

5. **snipe:** a long-billed bird found in marshy areas.

6. **prospects:** expectations.

English Learner Support
LANGUAGE

Diction *For their day's shooting* could be rewritten as "to spend the day shooting." The men in this story hunt birds to shoot.

What Does It Mean?
A *moor* is a piece of open, rolling land. A *bog* is a swamp.

Reading Tip
In your own words, summarize the tragedy that occurred.

MARK IT UP WORD POWER

Mark words that you'd like to add to your **Personal Word List.** After reading, you can record the words and their meanings beginning on page 402.

What Does It Mean?
Here, *scarcity* means that there are very few birds.

Reading Check
How would you describe Mrs. Sappleton?

More About...

MEDICINE IN THE 1900s Many British doctors in the 1900s believed that most mental illnesses could be cured with (complete rest.)

What Does It Mean?

Ailments and infirmities are illnesses and weaknesses.

Pause & **Reflect**

Look over the words and phrases you circled that describe Mr. Nuttel's reaction. In one sentence, **summarize** Mr. Nuttel's state of mind at this time.

_____

_____

_____

As the story ends . . .

• The husband and sons are seen through the open window.

• Mr. Nuttel is shocked.

English Learner Support

VOCABULARY

Figure of Speech *Bolted out* means "left quickly."

"The doctors agree in ordering me (complete rest,) an absence of mental excitement, and avoidance of anything in the nature of violent physical exercise," announced Framton, who labored under the tolerably widespread delusion that total strangers and chance acquaintances are hungry for the least detail of one's ailments and infirmities, their cause and cure. "On the matter of diet they are not so much in agreement," he continued.

"No?" said Mrs. Sappleton, in a voice which only replaced a yawn at the last moment. Then she suddenly brightened into alert attention—but not to what Framton was saying.

"Here they are at last!" she cried. "Just in time for tea, and don't they look as if they were muddy up to the eyes!"

Framton shivered slightly, and turned toward the niece with a look intended to convey sympathetic comprehension. The child was staring out through the open window with dazed horror in her eyes. In a chill shock of nameless fear Framton swung round in his seat and looked in the same direction.

Pause & **Reflect**

FOCUS

Everybody turns to look out the window. Read to find out what happens next.

In the deepening twilight three figures were walking across the lawn toward the window; they all carried guns under their arms, and one of them was additionally burdened with a white coat hung over his shoulders. A tired brown spaniel kept close at their heels. Noiselessly they neared the house, and then a hoarse young voice chanted out of the dusk:

"I said, Bertie, why do you bound?"

Framton grabbed wildly at his stick and hat; the hall door, the gravel drive, and the front gate were dimly noted stages in his headlong retreat. A cyclist coming along the road had to run into the hedge to avoid imminent[7] collision.

"Here we are, my dear," said the bearer of the white mackintosh, coming in through the window; "fairly muddy, but most of it's dry. Who was that who bolted out as we came up?"

_____

7. **imminent** (ĭm′ə-nənt): about to occur.

"A most extraordinary man, a Mr. Nuttel," said Mrs. Sappleton; "could only talk about his illnesses, and dashed off without a word of goodbye or apology when you arrived. One would think he had seen a ghost."

"I expect it was the spaniel," said the niece calmly; "he told me he had a horror of dogs. He was once hunted into a cemetery somewhere on the banks of the Ganges[8] by a pack of pariah dogs[9], and had to spend the night in a newly dug grave with the creatures snarling and grinning and foaming just above him. Enough to make anyone lose his nerve."

Romance[10] at short notice was her specialty.

Pause & Reflect

Pause & Reflect

MARK IT UP   **1.** Reread the boxed passage on page 280, and circle words that show how Mr. Nuttel responds to the sight of the three males and their spaniel. **(Locate Specific Details)**

2. Mr. Nuttel leaves in a hurry because _____

_____

_____.

(Infer)

READ ALOUD   **3.** Read aloud the last two paragraphs in a manner that conveys Vera's imagination and personality. Would you like to have Vera as a friend? Explain. **(Connect)**

_____

_____

_____

_____

CHALLENGE

Now that you know how the story ends, look back and star any clues that might suggest that Vera is making up her tale—or that show how cleverly she fools Mr. Nuttel. **(Analyze)**

8. **Ganges** (găn'jēz): a large river in northern India.

9. **pariah** (pə-rī'ə) **dogs:** dogs that have escaped from their owners and become wild.

10. **romance:** highly imaginative fiction.

Active Reading SkillBuilder

Making Judgments

When readers evaluate a character, an event, a topic, an author, or a selection, they are using the skill of **making judgments.** They can give reasons for why they like or dislike something, agree or disagree with a statement or issue, or place a value on an action or outcome. The key to doing a good job in making judgments is to develop a set of criteria, or rules against which something is evaluated. As you read "The Open Window," pay attention to Vera's behavior. On the chart below, write down your thoughts about the kind of person she is.

Vera's Behavior	Judgment
She welcomes Framton into the house.	She has good manners.

Literary Analysis SkillBuilder

Point of View

Point of view refers to the perspective from which events in a story are told. The two main types of point of view are first-person and third-person. The **third-person omniscient point of view** allows the story to be told by an all-knowing narrator, who can comment on the thoughts, feelings, and actions of all the characters. In the chart below, list details from the story about each of the characters. Then circle any of the details that a reader couldn't know about that character if the narrator had been one of the other characters instead of being omniscient.

What the Narrator Tells Us	
About Nuttel	*He is not sure this visit is a good idea.*
About Vera	*She is self-possessed.*
About Vera's Aunt	

Follow Up: Rewrite part of "The Open Window" in the first-person, with either Vera, Nuttel, or Mrs. Sappleton as the narrator. Remember that your narrator will be limited in what he or she knows.

THE WANDERINGS

OF ODYSSEUS

from

THE ODYSSEY

HOMER

Translated by Robert Fitzgerald

Before You Read

Connect to Your Life

Use the word web to record what you think of when you hear the word "hero."

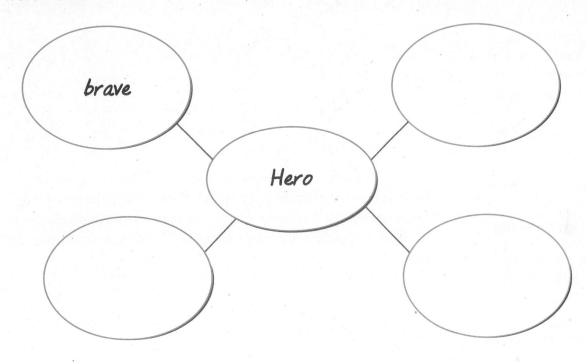

brave

Hero

Key to the Epic

WHAT DO YOU THINK? To Homer's audience, the *Odyssey*—with all of its gods and goddesses, monsters, and strange lands—seemed full of mystery and danger. Today, fantasy and science fiction books and movies tell stories of mystery and adventure as well. What is your favorite fantasy or science fiction story? What makes that story exciting?

Story: _____

What makes it exciting or mysterious: _____

_____

_____

_____

Reading Tips

The *Odyssey* (ŏd′ĭ-sē) is an **epic poem,** or a long poem that tells a story about a hero. Many people find it difficult to read this type of story, especially at first. The following strategies can help.

- Focus on the action. When you come across a long sentence, look for the main subject and verb.

- Read the information printed in italics within the selection. This information has been provided by the editors. It summarizes what happens between the excerpts of the *Odyssey* that are included here.

- Use the Guide for Reading on the right-hand pages. This information will help you follow the story and explain difficult vocabulary.

- To read actively, answer the questions and complete the activities in the sidebars.

THE WANDERINGS OF ODYSSEUS

from

THE ODYSSEY
HOMER

Translated by Robert Fitzgerald

PREVIEW Homer introduces his hero in the opening lines of this **epic.** Odysseus (ō-dĭs′yōos), king of Ithaca (ĭth′ə-kə), has taken part in a fierce war against Troy. Since then he has spent years trying to get back home again. The *Odyssey* is the story of his adventures on that homeward journey.

FOCUS

In these opening lines from the *Odyssey*, the poet asks a goddess for inspiration. He describes Odysseus' character and gives a brief summary of his wanderings.

MARK IT UP As you read, underline words and phrases that help you to understand Odysseus. Examples are highlighted.

BOOK ONE INVOCATION

Sing in me, Muse, and through me tell the story
of that man skilled in all ways of contending,
the wanderer, harried for years on end,
after he plundered the stronghold
5 on the proud height of Troy.

Use this guide for help with unfamiliar words
and difficult passages.

Reading Tip

As you read, think of the *Odyssey* as an
adventure story. Odysseus will be meeting
enemies and facing dangers in the same
way as some of your favorite movie heroes.

✎ MARK IT UP | WORD POWER

Mark words that you'd like to add to your
Personal Word List. After reading, you
can record the words and their meanings
beginning on page 402.

Reading Tip

Don't worry that this epic is written in verse.
Read the selection as though it were a
regular story. The more you read, the more
you will get used to the language and form.

As the epic begins . . .

• Homer asks a goddess to help him tell the
  story of Odysseus' adventures.

• Homer will tell how Odysseus struggled
  to save his own life and bring his shipmates home.

English Learner Support
CULTURE

Muses In Greek mythology, there are
nine *Muses.* Each one governs a different
art or science and provides inspiration
for artists.

More About . . .

Troy was an ancient city, located in the
country now known as Turkey. It was the
legendary site of the Trojan War and was
captured by Greek forces in 1200 B.C.

---

1 **Muse:** goddess of poetry and a daughter of
Zeus.
2 **contending:** fighting.
3 **harried:** attacked; harrassed.

He saw the townlands
and learned the minds of many distant men,
and weathered many bitter nights and days
in his deep heart at sea, while he fought only
10 to save his life, to bring his shipmates home.
But not by will nor valor could he save them,
for their own recklessness destroyed them all—
children and fools, they killed and feasted on
the cattle of Lord Helios, the Sun,
15 and he who moves all day through heaven
took from their eyes the dawn of their return.
Of these adventures, Muse, daughter of Zeus,
tell us in our time, lift the great song again.

Pause & Reflect

  *The poet goes on to describe some of Odysseus' adventures
during his ten years on the Mediterranean Sea as he tries to
get home. For seven of those years he is held captive by the
goddess Calypso (kə-lĭp'sō). With the help of the goddess
Athena (ə-thē'nə), Odysseus finally persuades Calypso to let
him go, and she helps him build a raft to leave her island.
After Odysseus sails away, his raft is destroyed by storms.*
  *Alone and exhausted, Odysseus is washed up on the land
of the Phaeacians (fē-ā'shənz), where Alcinous(ăl-sĭn'ō-əs) is
king. Alcinous gives a banquet in honor of Odysseus and
asks him to reveal who he is and where he came from.
Odysseus relates to the king his adventures up to that time.
His account makes up Books 9-12 of the* Odyssey.

11 **valor:** courage and boldness.

12–16 Odysseus' men killed cattle belonging to the sun-god Helios. As punishment, Zeus destroyed the ship and its crew. Odysseus was the only survivor.

Reading Tip
Working in pairs, read ten lines of the epic, stop, and have one partner summarize what has taken place. Continue to read the epic this way.

More About . . .
(Zeus) is the father of all the Greek gods and is the most powerful god of the ancient Greeks. His home is on Mount Olympus.

Pause & Reflect

1. After the war, what did Odysseus want to do? **(Clarify)**

_____

_____

_____

2. Review the words and phrases that you underlined as you read. How would you describe Odysseus? **(Infer)**

_____

_____

_____

_____

MARK IT UP 3. Circle the phrase in the opening passage that explains why Odysseus' shipmates were killed. **(Clarify)**

NEW COASTS AND POSEIDON'S SON

PREVIEW In Book Nine Odysseus tells the story of his adventures with the Cicones (sĭ-kō′nēz) and the Lotus Eaters. Next, he describes his travels to the land of the Cyclopes (sī-klō′pēz), a race of giant, one-eyed monsters. Odysseus and his men are trapped in a cave by the Cyclops (sī′-klŏps) Polyphemus (pŏl′ə-fē′məs), who eats two men at every meal. As you will see, Odysseus can only escape by outsmarting the Cyclops.

FOCUS
Odysseus starts off the tale of his adventures by telling about his background.
MARK IT UP As you read, underline any words or phrases that describe his feelings about home.

> "What shall I
> say first? What shall I keep until the end?
> The gods have tried me in a thousand ways.
> But first my name: let that be known to you,
> 5 and if I pull away from pitiless death,
> friendship will bind us, though my land lies far.
>
> I am Laertes' son, Odysseus.
> Men hold me
> formidable for guile in peace and war:
> this fame has gone abroad to the sky's rim.
> 10 My home is on the peaked sea-mark of Ithaca
> under Mount Neion's wind-blown robe of leaves,
> in sight of other islands—Dulichium,
> Same, wooded Zacynthus—Ithaca
> being most lofty in that coastal sea,
> 15 and northwest, while the rest lie east and south.
> A rocky isle, but good for a boy's training;
> I shall not see on earth a place more dear,

WORDS TO KNOW **formidable** (fôr′mĭ-də-bəl) *adj.* inspiring admiration, awe, or fear
guile (gīl) *n.* skillful slyness; craftiness

As the epic continues . . .

- Odysseus tells of his reputation for being skillful in war and in peace.

- Odysseus describes how he was held for years on an island by the goddess Calypso and how he was tempted by the enchantress Circe.

3 **tried:** tested.

More About . . .

EPIC HEROES represent the ideals of a nation or race. They often go on long, dangerous adventures that require courage and superhuman strength. They also have human faults, such as arrogance.

7 **Laertes** (lā-ûr′tēz); **hold:** regard.

 **Reading Check**

Where is Odysseus' home? How does he feel about it?

11–13 **Mount Neion's** (nē′ŏnz′) . . . **Dulichium** (dōō-lĭk′ē-əm) . . . **Same** (sā′mē) . . . **Zacynthus** (zə-sĭn′thəs).

though I have been detained long by Calypso,
loveliest among goddesses, who held me
20   in her smooth caves, to be her heart's delight,
as Circe of Aeaea, the enchantress,
desired me, and detained me in her hall.
But in my heart I never gave consent.
Where shall a man find sweetness to surpass
25   his own home and his parents? In far lands
he shall not, though he find a house of gold.

What of my sailing, then, from Troy?

                           What of those years
of rough adventure, weathered under Zeus?"

Pause & Reflect

FOCUS

On their way home from the war, Odysseus and his
men fight more battles and then face a new kind of
threat from the Lotus Eaters.

MARK IT UP As you read, circle the lines that
describe what happens to those who eat the
Lotus plant.

---

*Soon after leaving Troy, Odysseus and his crew land near
Ismarus, the city of the Cicones. The Cicones are allies of the
Trojans and therefore enemies of Odysseus. Odysseus and his
crew raid the Cicones, robbing and killing people, until the
Ciconian army kills 72 of Odysseus' men and drives the rest
out to sea. Delayed by a storm for two days, Odysseus and
his remaining companions continue their journey.*

"I might have made it safely home, that time,
30   but as I came round Malea the current
took me out to sea, and from the north
a fresh gale drove me on, past Cythera.
Nine days I drifted on the teeming sea
before dangerous high winds. Upon the tenth
35   we came to the coastline of the Lotus Eaters,
who live upon that flower. We landed there
to take on water. All ships' companies

18–22 Odysseus refers to two beautiful goddesses, Calypso (kə-lĭp′sō) and Circe (sûr′sē), who have delayed him on their islands. (Details about Circe appear in Book 10.) Notice, however, that Odysseus seems homesick for his own family and homeland. At this point in the story, Odysseus has been away from home for more than 18 years—10 of them spent in the war at Troy.

28 weathered: survived.

33 teeming: abundant; full.

Pause & Reflect

1. Review what you underlined. How would you **summarize** Odysseus' feelings about Ithaca, his home?

_____

_____

_____

2. Review the boxed passage on page 290. How might Odysseus' guile, or craftiness, help him deal with an enemy who is stronger than he is? **(Infer)**

_____

_____

_____

_____

As the epic continues . . .

- Odysseus tells about a storm at sea that blew his ships off the path toward home.

- He describes arriving at the land of the Lotus Eaters and what happened there.

Reading Tip

As you read, jot down the events that occur in the land of the Lotus Eaters.

English Learner Support

LANGUAGE

Expression *Live upon* means that the Lotus Eaters eat the flower; it is their main source of food.

mustered alongside for the mid-day meal.
Then I sent out two picked men and a runner

40 to learn what race of men that land sustained.
They fell in, soon enough, with Lotus Eaters,
who showed no will to do us harm, only
offering the sweet Lotus to our friends—
but those who ate this honeyed plant, the Lotus,

45 never cared to report, nor to return:
they longed to stay forever, browsing on
that native bloom, forgetful of their homeland.
I drove them, all three wailing, to the ships,
tied them down under their rowing benches,

50 called the rest: 'All hands aboard;
come, clear the beach and no one taste
the Lotus, or you lose your hope of home.'
Filing in to their places by the rowlocks
my oarsmen dipped their long oars in the surf,

55 and we moved out again on our sea faring.

Pause & *Reflect*

FOCUS

Odysseus and his crew now head for the land of the
Cyclopes.
MARK IT UP As you read, circle any passages that
suggest this might be a dangerous place to go.

In the next land we found were Cyclopes,
giants, louts, without a law to bless them.
In ignorance leaving the fruitage of the earth in mystery
to the immortal gods, they neither plow

60 nor sow by hand, nor till the ground, though grain—
wild wheat and barley—grows untended, and
wine-grapes, in clusters, ripen in heaven's rain.
Cyclopes have no muster and no meeting,
no consultation or old tribal ways,

65 but each one dwells in his own mountain cave
dealing out rough justice to wife and child,
<u>indifferent</u> to what the others do."

WORDS
TO
KNOW

indifferent (ĭn-dĭf′ər-ənt) *adj.* having no interest in or concern for

38 **mustered:** assembled; gathered.

57 **louts:** clumsy, stupid people.

63 **muster:** a gathering or assembly. The Cyclopes do not meet or cooperate; they have no sense of community.

English Learner Support
VOCABULARY

Idiom To *fall in with* means "to meet or join with someone."

Pause Reflect

1. Look back at the lines you circled. What happens to those who eat the Lotus? **(Clarify)**

_____

_____

_____

2. Odysseus forces his men to return to their ships. Why does he have to tie them down? **(Infer)**

_____

_____

_____

_____

As the epic continues . . .

• The crew's next adventure is in the land of the Cyclopes, mean giants who live in caves.

• Odysseus rows ashore with twelve men.

English Learner Support
LANGUAGE

Sentence Structure The highlighted sentence means "There were Cyclopes in the next land we found."

✔ **Reading Check**
What are some of Odysseus' criticisms of the Cyclopes?

Across the bay from the land of the Cyclopes is a lush,
deserted island. Odysseus and his crew land on the island in a
dense fog and spend several days feasting on wine and wild
goats and observing the mainland, where the Cyclopes live.
On the third day, Odysseus and his company of men set out
to learn if the Cyclopes are friends or foes.

"When the young Dawn with fingertips of rose
came in the east, I called my men together
70   and made a speech to them:

                              'Old shipmates, friends,
the rest of you stand by; I'll make the crossing
in my own ship, with my own company,
and find out what the mainland natives are—
for they may be wild savages, and lawless,
75   or hospitable and god-fearing men.'
At this I went aboard, and gave the word
to cast off by the stern. My oarsmen followed,
filing in to their benches by the rowlocks,
and all in line dipped oars in the gray sea.

80   As we rowed on, and nearer to the mainland,
at one end of the bay, we saw a cavern
yawning above the water, screened with laurel,
and many rams and goats about the place
inside a sheepfold—made from slabs of stone
85   earthfast between tall trunks of pine and rugged
towering oak trees.

                              A prodigious man
slept in this cave alone, and took his flocks
to graze afield—remote from all companions,
knowing none but savage ways, a brute
90   so huge, he seemed no man at all of those
who eat good wheaten bread; but he seemed rather
a shaggy mountain reared in solitude.
We beached there, and I told the crew
to stand by and keep watch over the ship;
95   as for myself I took my twelve best fighters
and went ahead. I had a goatskin full
of that sweet liquor that Euanthes' son,
Maron, had given me. He kept Apollo's

68 This use of "with fingertips of rose" to describe the personified Dawn is a famous epithet—a descriptive phrase that presents a trait of a person or thing. Watch for other uses of this epithet in the poem. Be on the lookout for other epithets.

77 stern: the rear end of a ship.

82 screened with laurel: partially hidden by laurel trees.
84 sheepfold: a pen for sheep.

86 prodigious (prə-dǐj'əs)**:** enormous, huge.

97–98 Euanthes' (yōo-ăn'thēz) **. . . Maron** (mâr'ŏn').

Reading Tip
Use the following word web to describe the Cyclops.

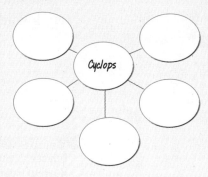

Cyclops

English Learner Support
LANGUAGE

Metaphor Odysseus compares the Cyclops to a *shaggy mountain*. This means that the Cyclops is hairy and extremely large.

What Does It Mean?
Reared means "raised" or "brought up."

✔ Reading Check
What does Odysseus take with him when he goes to see the Cyclops?

holy grove at Ismarus; for kindness
100 we showed him there, and showed his wife and child,
he gave me seven shining golden talents
perfectly formed, a solid silver winebowl,
and then this liquor—twelve two-handled jars
of brandy, pure and fiery. Not a slave
105 in Maron's household knew this drink; only
he, his wife and the storeroom mistress knew;
and they would put one cupful—ruby-colored,
honey-smooth—in twenty more of water,
but still the sweet scent hovered like a fume
110 over the winebowl. No man turned away
when cups of this came round.

                                        A wineskin full
I brought along, and victuals in a bag,
for in my bones I knew some towering brute
would be upon us soon—all outward power,
115 a wild man, ignorant of civility.

Pause & Reflect

FOCUS

Odysseus and 12 men enter the cave of a Cyclops.
Read to find out how the Cyclops reacts to strangers.

We climbed, then, briskly to the cave. But Cyclops
had gone afield, to pasture his fat sheep,
so we looked round at everything inside:
a drying rack that sagged with cheeses, pens
120 crowded with lambs and kids, each in its class:
firstlings apart from middlings, and the 'dewdrops,'
or newborn lambkins, penned apart from both.
And vessels full of whey were brimming there—
bowls of earthenware and pails for milking.
125 My men came pressing round me, pleading:

                                        'Why not
Take these cheeses, get them stowed, come back,
throw open all the pens, and make a run for it?
We'll drive the kids and lambs aboard. We say
put out again on good salt water!'

101 talents: bars of gold or silver of a specified weight, used as money in ancient Greece.

112 victuals (vĭt'lz)**:** food.

115 civility: polite behavior.

120 kids: young goats.

121–122 The Cyclops has separated his lambs into three age groups.

123 whey: the watery part of milk, which separates from the curds, or solid part, during the making of cheese.

129 good salt water: the open sea. (The men want to rob the Cyclops and quickly sail away.)

Pause **& Reflect**

1. Review the passages you underlined. Why should Odysseus be extra cautious in dealing with the Cyclopes? **(Making Judgments)**

_____

_____

_____

_____

2. If you were part of Odysseus' crew, how would you feel about your captain at this point? **(Connect)**

_____

_____

_____

_____

As the epic continues . . .

- Odysseus and his men enter the cave of the Cyclops.
- Odysseus asks the Cyclops for his help.
- The Cyclops ignores his request and eats two of the men.

Reading Check

What do Odysseus' men want to do when they arrive at the cave?

Ah,

130 how sound that was! Yet I refused. I wished
to see the caveman, what he had to offer—
no pretty sight, it turned out, for my friends.

We lit a fire, burnt an offering,
and took some cheese to eat; then sat in silence
135 around the embers, waiting. When he came
he had a load of dry boughs on his shoulder
to stoke his fire at suppertime. He dumped it
with a great crash into that hollow cave,
and we all scattered fast to the far wall.
140 Then over the broad cavern floor he ushered
the ewes he meant to milk. He left his rams
and he-goats in the yard outside, and swung
high overhead a slab of solid rock
to close the cave. Two dozen four-wheeled wagons,
145 with heaving wagon teams, could not have stirred
the tonnage of that rock from where he wedged it
over the doorsill. Next he took his seat
and milked his bleating ewes. A practiced job
he made of it, giving each ewe her suckling;
150 thickened his milk, then, into curds and whey,
sieved out the curds to drip in withy baskets,
and poured the whey to stand in bowls
cooling until he drank it for his supper.
When all these chores were done, he poked the fire,
155 heaping on brushwood. In the glare he saw us.

'Strangers,' he said, 'who are you? And where from?
What brings you here by sea ways—a fair traffic?
Or are you wandering rogues, who cast your lives
like dice, and ravage other folk by sea?'

160 We felt a pressure on our hearts, in dread
of that deep rumble and that mighty man.
But all the same I spoke up in reply:

'We are from Troy, Achaeans, blown off course
by shifting gales on the Great South Sea;
165 homeward bound, but taking routes and ways
uncommon; so the will of Zeus would have it.
We served under Agamemnon, son of Atreus—
the whole world knows what city

133 burnt an offering: burned a portion of the food as an offering to secure the gods' goodwill. (Such offerings were frequently performed by Greek sailors during difficult journeys.)

137 stoke: build up; feed.

141 ewes: female sheep.

144–147 Notice the size of the rock that closes the entrance of the Cyclops' cave.

157–159 The Cyclops asks whether the seafaring men are here for honest trading ("fair traffic") or are dishonest people ("rogues") who steal from ("ravage") those they meet.

163 Achaeans (ə-kē'ənz): Greeks.

167 Agamemnon (ăg'ə-měm'nŏn'): the Greek king (Menelaus' brother) who led the war against the Trojans; **Atreus** (ā'trē-əs).

✏️ **▶ JOT IT DOWN | Reread Lines 129–132**

Odysseus waits for the Cyclops instead of doing what his men ask. What does this suggest about Odysseus' nature? **(Evaluate)**

_____

_____

What Does It Mean?

When Homer writes that the Cyclops *ushered the ewes,* he means that the Cyclops led or guided the ewes (female sheep) into the cave.

English Learner Support
VOCABULARY

Stirred Here, the word *stirred* means "moved" rather than "mixed."

Reading Tip

Use the following flow chart to keep track of the things that the Cyclops does in this section.

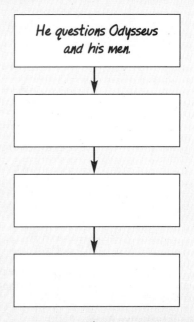

He questions Odysseus and his men.

he laid waste, what armies he destroyed.

170 It was our luck to come here; here we stand,
beholden for your help, or any gifts
you give—as custom is to honor strangers.
We would <u>entreat</u> you, great Sir, have a care
for the gods' courtesy; Zeus will <u>avenge</u>
175 the unoffending guest.'

He answered this
from his brute chest, unmoved:

'You are a ninny,
or else you come from the other end of nowhere,
telling me, mind the gods! We Cyclopes
care not a whistle for your thundering Zeus
180 or all the gods in bliss; we have more force by far.
I would not let you go for fear of Zeus—
you or your friends—unless I had a <u>whim</u> to.

Tell me, where was it, now, you left your ship—
around the point, or down the shore, I wonder?'

185 He thought he'd find out, but I saw through this,
and answered with a ready lie:

'My ship?
Poseidon Lord, who sets the earth a-tremble,
broke it up on the rocks at your land's end.
A wind from seaward served him, drove us there.
190 We are survivors, these good men and I.'

Neither reply nor pity came from him,
but in one stride he clutched at my companions
and caught two in his hands like squirming puppies
to beat their brains out, spattering the floor.
195 Then he dismembered them and made his meal,
gaping and crunching like a mountain lion—
everything: innards, flesh, and marrow bones.
We cried aloud, lifting our hands to Zeus,
powerless, looking on at this, <u>appalled</u>;

WORDS
TO
KNOW

entreat (ĕn-trēt′) v. to ask earnestly; beg
avenge (ə-vĕnj′) v. to take revenge on behalf of
whim (hwĭm) n. a sudden impulse or notion; fancy
appalled (ə-pôld′) adj. filled with dismay; horrified **appall** v.

171 beholden: indebted.

172–175 It was a sacred Greek custom to honor strangers with food and gifts. Odysseus is warning the Cyclops that Zeus will punish anyone who mistreats a guest.

176 ninny: fool.

187 Poseidon Lord: Poseidon (pō-sīd'n), the god of the sea and of earthquakes, who also happens to be the Cyclops' father.

193–196 The two similes in this passage emphasize the helplessness of the men ("like squirming puppies") and the savagery of the Cyclops ("gaping and crunching like a mountain lion").

READ ALOUD Lines 176–182

Listen to the speech the giant makes "from his brute chest." What kind of hospitality is the fellow likely to offer? **(Predict)**

English Learner Support
VOCABULARY

Idiom *I saw through this* means that Odysseus knew that the Cyclops was trying to trick him.

☑ Reading Check

Why does Odysseus lie and tell the Cyclops that all of his other men died in a shipwreck?

200 but Cyclops went on filling up his belly
     with manflesh and great gulps of whey,
     then lay down like a mast among his sheep.
     My heart beat high now at the chance of action,
     and drawing the sharp sword from my hip I went
205 along his flank to stab him where the midriff
     holds the liver. I had touched the spot
     when sudden fear stayed me: if I killed him
     we perished there as well, for we could never
     move his <u>ponderous</u> doorway slab aside.
210 So we were left to groan and wait for morning.

Pause & Reflect

FOCUS

Odysseus must now try to outwit the Cyclops. Read
to find out what strategies he comes up with.
MARK IT UP As you read, make notes in the margin
to describe what Odysseus does.

     When the young Dawn with fingertips of rose
     lit up the world, the Cyclops built a fire
     and milked his handsome ewes, all in due order,
     putting the sucklings to the mothers. Then,
215 his chores being all dispatched, he caught
     another brace of men to make his breakfast,
     and whisked away his great door slab
     to let his sheep go through—but he, behind,
     reset the stone as one would cap a quiver.
220 There was a din of whistling as the Cyclops
     rounded his flock to higher ground, then stillness.
     And now I pondered how to hurt him worst,
     if but Athena granted what I prayed for.
     Here are the means I thought would serve my turn:
225 a club, or staff, lay there along the fold—
     an olive tree, felled green and left to season
     for Cyclops' hand. And it was like a mast
     a lugger of twenty oars, broad in the beam—

WORDS
TO
KNOW
     ponderous (pŏn′dər-əs) *adj.* heavy in a clumsy way; bulky

1. According to Greek custom, strangers were supposed to be treated with kindness. How does the Cyclops treat his guests? **(Infer)**

_____

_____

_____

4. Why doesn't Odysseus kill the giant in his sleep? Underline the sentence on pages 302–304 that tells you. **(Cause and Effect)**

_____

_____

_____

As the epic continues . . .

•The Cyclops wakes up and eats two more of the men.

•Odysseus plans a way to escape.

215 dispatched: completed.
216 brace: pair.
218–219 The Cyclops reseals the cave with the massive rock as easily as an ordinary human places the cap on a container of arrows.
220 din: noise.

223 Odysseus calls on his protector, the goddess Athena, for help as he forms a plan.
225 fold: a pen for sheep.

228 lugger: a small, wide sailing ship.

What Does It Mean?

When Odysseus says *serve my turn,* he means that the large piece of wood is just what he needs. It is perfect for his purpose.

a deep-sea-going craft—might carry:
230 so long, so big around, it seemed. Now I
chopped out a six-foot section of this pole
and set it down before my men, who scraped it;
and when they had it smooth, I hewed again
to make a stake with pointed end. I held this
235 in the fire's heart and turned it, toughening it,
then hid it, well back in the cavern, under
one of the dung piles in profusion there.

Now came the time to toss for it: who ventured
along with me? whose hand could bear to thrust
240 and grind that spike in Cyclops' eye, when mild
sleep had mastered him? As luck would have it,
the men I would have chosen won the toss—
four strong men, and I made five as captain.

At evening came the shepherd with his flock,
245 his woolly flock. The rams as well, this time,
entered the cave: by some sheep-herding whim—
or a god's bidding—none were left outside.
He hefted his great boulder into place
and sat him down to milk the bleating ewes
250 in proper order, put the lambs to suck,
and swiftly ran through all his evening chores.
Then he caught two more men and feasted on them.
My moment was at hand, and I went forward
holding an ivy bowl of my dark drink,
255 looking up, saying:

                              'Cyclops, try some wine.
Here's liquor to wash down your scraps of men.
Taste it, and see the kind of drink we carried
under our planks. I meant it for an offering
if you would help us home. But you are mad,
260 unbearable, a bloody monster! After this,
will any other traveler come to see you?'

He seized and drained the bowl, and it went down
so fiery and smooth he called for more:
'Give me another, thank you kindly. Tell me,
265 how are you called? I'll make a gift will please you.
Even Cyclopes know the wine-grapes grow
out of grassland and loam in heaven's rain,

233 hewed: chopped.

237 profusion: abundance.

JOT IT DOWN   **Reread Lines 238–243**

What does Odysseus plan to do to the Cyclops? **(Clarify)**

_____

_____

☑ **Reading Check**

Why does Odysseus give wine to the Cyclops?

English Learner Support

VOCABULARY

Idiom _Under our planks_ means "under the deck of our ship."

but here's a bit of nectar and ambrosia!'

Three bowls I brought him, and he poured them down.
270 I saw the fuddle and flush come over him,
then I sang out in cordial tones:

                                   'Cyclops,
you ask my honorable name? Remember
the gift you promised me, and I shall tell you.
My name is Nohbdy: mother, father, and friends,
275 everyone calls me Nohbdy.'

                                   And he said:
'Nohbdy's my meat, then, after I eat his friends.
Others come first. There's a noble gift, now.'

Even as he spoke, he reeled and tumbled backward,
his great head lolling to one side: and sleep
280 took him like any creature. Drunk, hiccupping,
he dribbled streams of liquor and bits of men.

Now, by the gods, I drove my big hand spike
deep in the embers, charring it again,
and cheered my men along with battle talk
285 to keep their courage up: no quitting now.
The pike of olive, green though it had been,
reddened and glowed as if about to catch.
I drew it from the coals and my four fellows
gave me a hand, lugging it near the Cyclops
290 as more than natural force nerved them; straight
forward they sprinted, lifted it, and rammed it
deep in his crater eye, and I leaned on it
turning it as a shipwright turns a drill
in planking, having men below to swing
295 the two-handled strap that spins it in the groove.
So with our brand we bored that great eye socket
while blood ran out around the red hot bar.
Eyelid and lash were seared; the pierced ball
hissed broiling, and the roots popped.
                                   In a smithy
300 one sees a white-hot axehead or an adze
plunged and wrung in a cold tub, screeching steam—
the way they make soft iron hale and hard—:

268 nectar (nĕk′tər) **and ambrosia**
(ăm-brō′zhə)**:** the drink and food of
the gods.

270 fuddle and flush: the state of
confusion and redness of the face caused by
drinking alcohol.

READ ALOUD Lines 274–275

Say the name *Nohbdy* out loud and listen to
what it sounds like. What might Odysseus
be planning?

☑ **Reading Check**

What happens to the Cyclops after he
drinks the wine?

286 the pike: the pointed stake.

What Does It Mean?

Here, *catch* means "catch fire."

290 as more. . .nerved them: with a courage
and strength far beyond the ordinary.

292–295 Odysseus compares the way he
stabs the Cyclops in the eye to the way a ship-
builder drills a hole in a board.

READ ALOUD Lines 296–299

Notice how the poet uses vivid imagery to
describe the blinding of the Cyclops. Which
words sound like what they are describing?
(Evaluate)

299 smithy: blacksmith's shop.

300 adze (ădz)**:** an axlike tool with a curved
blade.

just so that eyeball hissed around the spike.
The Cyclops bellowed and the rock roared round him,
305 and we fell back in fear. Clawing his face
he tugged the bloody spike out of his eye,
threw it away, and his wild hands went groping;
then he set up a howl for Cyclopes
who lived in caves on windy peaks nearby.
310 Some heard him; and they came by divers ways
to clump around outside and call:

                       'What ails you,
Polyphemus? Why do you cry so sore
in the starry night? You will not let us sleep.
Sure no man's driving off your flock? No man
315 has tricked you, ruined you?'

                              Out of the cave
the mammoth Polyphemus roared in answer:

'Nohbdy, Nohbdy's tricked me, Nohbdy's ruined me!'

To this rough shout they made a sage reply:

'Ah well, if nobody has played you foul
320 there in your lonely bed, we are no use in pain
given by great Zeus. Let it be your father,
Poseidon Lord, to whom you pray.'

                            So saying
they trailed away. And I was filled with laughter
to see how like a charm the name deceived them.

Pause & Reflect

310 **divers:** various.

318 **sage:** wise.

Pause & Reflect

1. Review the notes that you made as you read. Briefly **summarize** how Odysseus is able to blind the Cyclops.

_____

_____

_____

_____

✎ MARK IT UP 2. Why don't the other Cyclopes come to Polyphemus' aid? Circle the passage in lines 319–322 that tells the answer. **(Clarify)**

3. The men are still trapped in the cave. How do you think the men will try to escape? **(Predict)**

_____

_____

_____

_____

✎ CHALLENGE

Homer often uses comparisons known as **similes** to make his descriptions vivid. Review the similes in lines 219, 227–229, 292–295, and 299–303. Then write your own simile to describe some aspect of the Cyclops.

_____

_____

_____

_____

FOCUS

With the Cyclops angry and no clear escape in view,
Odysseus must come up quickly with a plan.

MARK IT UP As you read, underline details that
describe the escape attempt.

325 Now Cyclops, wheezing as the pain came on him,
fumbled to wrench away the great doorstone
and squatted in the breach with arms thrown wide
for any silly beast or man who bolted—
hoping somehow I might be such a fool.
330 But I kept thinking how to win the game:
death sat there huge; how could we slip away?
I drew on all my wits, and ran through tactics,
reasoning as a man will for dear life,
until a trick came—and it pleased me well.
335 The Cyclops' rams were handsome, fat, with heavy
fleeces, a dark violet.

                                    Three abreast
I tied them silently together, twining
cords of willow from the ogre's bed;
then slung a man under each middle one
340 to ride there safely, shielded left and right.
So three sheep could convey each man. I took
the woolliest ram, the choicest of the flock,
and hung myself under his kinky belly,
pulled up tight, with fingers twisted deep
345 in sheepskin ringlets for an iron grip.
So, breathing hard, we waited until morning.

When Dawn spread out her fingertips of rose
the rams began to stir, moving for pasture,
and peals of bleating echoed round the pens
350 where dams with udders full called for a milking.
Blinded, and sick with pain from his head wound,
the master stroked each ram, then let it pass,
but my men riding on the pectoral fleece
the giant's blind hands blundering never found.
355 Last of them all my ram, the leader, came,
weighted by wool and me with my meditations.
The Cyclops patted him, and then he said:

327 breach: opening.

330–334 Notice Odysseus' great mental struggle and, as you read on, the clever plan he has managed to come up with on the spot.

336–341 Odysseus ties three sheep together side by side, with a man hanging under the middle one.

338 ogre: giant or monster.

353 pectoral fleece: the wool covering a sheep's chest.

As the epic continues . . .

- The Cyclops sits in the cave doorway, blocking the exit.
- Odysseus thinks of a way to escape.

Reading Tip

Reread lines 336–354. State these lines, which explain how Odysseus escapes from the cave, in your own words.

'Sweet cousin ram, why lag behind the rest
in the night cave? You never linger so,
360 but graze before them all, and go afar
to crop sweet grass, and take your stately way
leading along the streams, until at evening
you run to be the first one in the fold.
Why, now, so far behind? Can you be grieving
365 over your Master's eye? That carrion rogue
and his accurst companions burnt it out
when he had conquered all my wits with wine.
Nohbdy will not get out alive, I swear.
Oh, had you brain and voice to tell
370 where he may be now, dodging all my fury!
Bashed by this hand and bashed on this rock wall
his brains would strew the floor, and I should have
rest from the outrage Nohbdy worked upon me.'
He sent us into the open, then. Close by,
375 I dropped and rolled clear of the ram's belly,
going this way and that to untie the men.
With many glances back, we rounded up
his fat, stiff-legged sheep to take aboard,
and drove them down to where the good ship lay.
380 We saw, as we came near, our fellows' faces
shining; then we saw them turn to grief
tallying those who had not fled from death.
I hushed them, jerking head and eyebrows up,
and in a low voice told them: 'Load this herd;
385 move fast, and put the ship's head toward the breakers.'
They all pitched in at loading, then embarked
and struck their oars into the sea. Far out,
as far off shore as shouted words would carry,
I sent a few back to the adversary:

390 'O Cyclops! Would you feast on my companions?
Puny, am I, in a Caveman's hands?
How do you like the beating that we gave you,
you damned cannibal? Eater of guests
under your roof! Zeus and the gods have paid you!'

Pause & *Reflect*

WORDS
TO
KNOW

adversary (ăd'vər-sĕr'ē) *n.* an opponent; enemy

365 carrion rogue: The Cyclops is insulting Odysseus by calling him this. *Carrion* means "Feeding on dead things."

385 put . . . the breakers: turn the ship around so that it is heading toward the open sea.

390–394 Notice that Odysseus assumes that the gods are on his side.

English Learner Support
VOCABULARY

Accurst *Accurst* means "cursed."

JOT IT DOWN   **Reread Lines 380–382**

The faces of the waiting sailors turn from happiness to grief as they watch Odysseus and his men returning. Why? **(Draw Conclusions)**

_____

_____

English Learner Support
VOCABULARY

Idiom *Pitched in* means "helped."

Pause **&** Reflect

1. Review the details that you underlined as you read. How do the men manage to get safely out of the cave? **(Summarize)**

_____

_____

_____

2. The Cyclops checks the rams as they leave the cave. Why can't he find the men? **(Infer)**

_____

_____

_____

3. Odysseus insults the Cyclops as the ship is sailing away. If you were traveling with Odysseus, what would you think of such an action? **(Connect)**

_____

_____

_____

FOCUS

Odysseus and his sailors are on their way to
escaping. Read to find out if anything can still
go wrong.

395   The
blind thing in his doubled fury broke
        a hilltop in his hands and heaved it after us.

Ahead of our black prow it struck and sank
whelmed in a spuming geyser, a giant wave
that washed the ship stern foremost back to shore.
400   I got the longest boathook out and stood
fending us off, with furious nods to all
to put their backs into a racing stroke—
row, row, or perish. So the long oars bent
kicking the foam sternward, making head
405   until we drew away, and twice as far.

Now when I cupped my hands I heard the crew
in low voices protesting:

                            'Godsake, Captain!
Why bait the beast again? Let him alone!'

'That tidal wave he made on the first throw
410   all but beached us.'

                            'All but stove us in!'

'Give him our bearing with your trumpeting,
he'll get the range and lob a boulder.'

                                        'Aye,
he'll smash our timbers and our heads together!'

I would not heed them in my glorying spirit,
415   but let my anger flare and yelled:

                            'Cyclops,
if ever mortal man inquire
how you were put to shame and blinded, tell him
Odysseus, raider of cities, took your eye:
Laertes' son, whose home's on Ithaca!'

420   At this he gave a mighty sob and rumbled:

395–403 The hilltop thrown by Polyphemus lands in front of the ship, causing a huge wave that carries the ship back to the shore. Odysseus uses a long pole to push the boat away from the land.

407–413 The near disaster of Odysseus' boast has frightened the crew. As earlier, in the cave, the men make reasonable appeals.

410 All but stove us in: almost crushed us.

411 Give him...trumpeting: If your shouting tells him our position.

414–419 Odysseus uses the warlike epithet "raider of cities" in his second boast to the Cyclops.

As the epic ends . . .

- The Cyclops tries to prevent Odysseus and his men from escaping.
- The Cyclops prays to Poseidon that Odysseus will never see his home again.
- Odysseus reaches his ships. He and his men hold a feast in honor of Zeus.

What Does It Mean?
Spuming means "foaming."

What Does It Mean?
Sternward means "toward the back of the ship."

Reading Tip
Reread and summarize this account of Odysseus' escape from the land of the Cyclopes.

Reading Check
Why does Odysseus call back to the Cyclops?

'Now comes the weird upon me, spoken of old.
A wizard, grand and wondrous, lived here—Telemus,
a son of Eurymus; great length of days
he had in wizardry among the Cyclopes,
425 and these things he foretold for time to come:
my great eye lost, and at Odysseus' hands.
Always I had in mind some giant, armed
in giant force, would come against me here.
But this, but you—small, pitiful and twiggy—
430 you put me down with wine, you blinded me.
Come back, Odysseus, and I'll treat you well,
praying the god of earthquake to befriend you—
his son I am, for he by his avowal
fathered me, and, if he will, he may
435 heal me of this black wound—he and no other
of all the happy gods or mortal men.'

Few words I shouted in reply to him:
'If I could take your life I would and take
your time away, and hurl you down to hell!
440 The god of earthquake could not heal you there!'

At this he stretched his hands out in his darkness
toward the sky of stars, and prayed Poseidon:

'O hear me, lord, blue girdler of the islands,
if I am thine indeed, and thou art father:
445 grant that Odysseus, raider of cities, never
see his home: Laertes' son, I mean,
who kept his hall on Ithaca. Should destiny
intend that he shall see his roof again
among his family in his father land,
450 far be that day, and dark the years between.
Let him lose all companions, and return
under strange sail to bitter days at home.'

In these words he prayed, and the god heard him.
Now he laid hands upon a bigger stone
455 and wheeled around, titanic for the cast,
to let it fly in the black-prowed vessel's track.
But it fell short, just aft the steering oar,
and whelming seas rose giant above the stone
to bear us onward toward the island.

421 Now comes . . . of old: Now I recall the destiny predicted long ago.

422 Telemus (tĕl'ə-məs)**:** a magician who could predict the future for the Cyclopes.

427–430 Polyphemus is not blind to the irony of being beaten by someone only about one-eighth his size.

432 the god of earthquake: Poseidon (pō-sīd'n).

433 avowal: honest admission.

What Does It Mean?

Blue girdler refers to Poseidon. He rules the bodies of water that girdle, or encircle, the islands.

Reading Tip

Make a list of the details of the curse on Odysseus.

Reading Check

How does the Cyclops try to get revenge on Odysseus?

443–452 Note the details of Polyphemus' curse on Odysseus. As you read on in the *Odyssey*, you'll find out whether the curse comes true.

455 titanic for the cast: drawing on all his enormous strength in preparing to throw.

457 aft: behind.

459 the island: the deserted island where most of Odysseus' men had stayed behind.

460   as we ran in we saw the squadron waiting,
the trim ships drawn up side by side, and all
our troubled friends who waited, looking seaward.
We beached her, grinding keel in the soft sand,
and waded in, ourselves, on the sandy beach.

465   Then we unloaded all the Cyclops' flock
to make division, share and share alike,
only my fighters voted that my ram,
the prize of all, should go to me. I slew him
by the seaside and burnt his long thighbones

470   to Zeus beyond the stormcloud, Cronus' son,
who rules the world. But Zeus <u>disdained</u> my offering;
destruction for my ships he had in store
and death for those who sailed them, my companions.
Now all day long until the sun went down

475   we made our feast on mutton and sweet wine,
till after sunset in the gathering dark
we went to sleep above the wash of ripples.

When the young Dawn with fingertips of rose
touched the world, I roused the men, gave orders

480   to man the ships, cast off the mooring lines;
and filing in to sit beside the rowlocks
oarsmen in line dipped oars in the gray sea.
So we moved out, sad in the vast offing,
having our precious lives, but not our friends."

Pause & Reflect

WORDS TO KNOW

disdain (dĭs-dān′) *v.* to refuse or reject scornfully

483 in the vast offing: toward the open sea.

1. What almost prevents the men from escaping in their ship? **(Clarify)**

_____

_____

_____

2. Do you think it was wise for Odysseus to reveal his name to the Cyclops? **(Evaluate)**

_____

_____

_____

_____

MARK IT UP **3.** Polyphemus tries to get revenge on Odysseus by praying to Poseidon. What does the Cyclops want? Circle phrases in the boxed passage on page 280 that tell the answer. **(Clarify)**

CHALLENGE

As an **epic hero,** Odysseus is portrayed by Homer as strong, brave, and clever—almost superhuman. In your judgment, what weaknesses, if any, does Odysseus have? Box passages in the poem that support your judgment. **(Making Judgments)**

Active Reading SkillBuilder

Predicting

Predicting is the skill that helps readers use clues in a text, along with their prior
knowledge and experience, to make reasonable guesses about what will happen
later in a story. Good readers make and revise predictions as they read. While
reading Book Nine from the *Odyssey*, look for clues that seem to foreshadow future
events. Write down the clues you find and your predictions.

Book 9: New Coasts and Poseidon's Son		
Lines	**Clue**	**Prediction**

Literary Analysis SkillBuilder

Epic Hero

The larger-than-life central figure or "superhero" of an epic story is known as the **epic hero.** Usually a male figure, he is a person of imposing stature who stands for the ideals of a nation or race. He performs deeds of great valor that require superhuman courage. Sometimes he is assisted by supernatural forces.

   Use the chart to evaluate the extent to which Odysseus acts like an epic hero. In the first column, list Odysseus' larger-than-life qualities and actions. In the second column, list Odysseus' human weaknesses and unwise actions.

Heroic Qualities of Odysseus	Weaknesses of Odysseus

Follow Up: In what ways do you think Odysseus' character needs improvement?

Words to Know SkillBuilder

Words to Know

adversary	avenge	entreat	guile	ponderous
appalled	disdain	formidable	indifferent	whim

A. Each of the following sentences suggests a word in the word list. The word itself is hidden in the sentence. Underline the hidden word and then write it on the line. An example, using another word from the epic poem, has been done for you.

Example: He's not only fierce, he's huge! His doctor must have put him <u>on ster</u>oids or another muscle-building drug!

monster

I must plead with you not to give the children treats after they have brushed their teeth. Please do as I ask!

(1) _____

When I saw him, I had an urge to call out, "Hey, good-looking!" Then I did it without stopping to think. What came over me?

(2) _____

Although my mother is now in heaven, George will pay for what he did to her. I swear, I'll make sure of that!

(3) _____

Don't stand by unconcerned while evil triumphs. Although types of sin differ, entirely too many people fail to realize that just not caring can be wicked in itself.

(4) _____

B. Decide which word from the word list belongs in each numbered blank. Then write the word on the blank line on the right.

When I learned what my foe was called
I must confess, I was (1).
It scared me that "Bone-Crushing Harry"
Was to be my (2),
For it seemed a clue to me
Of how (3) he'd be.

(1) _____

(2) _____

You must be nuts! No. I (4)
Your plan of strolling in the rain.

(3) _____

Elephants never perform a ballet
For, as the wisest of elephants say,
Leaping and twirling are part of the dance,
And (5) elephants haven't a chance.

(4) _____

Her (6) is so successful; she's so sneaky and so clever,
That I fall for every trick she thinks of, whatsoever.

(5) _____

C. Write the speech that Polyphemus might give to inspire the Cyclopes to help him get revenge on Odysseus. Use at least **five** of the Words to Know in the speech.

(6) _____

THE TRAGEDY OF
ROMEO + JULIET

Drama by WILLIAM SHAKESPEARE

Before You Read

Connect to Your Life

When two people fall in love, they may have obstacles to overcome. Make a list of some difficulties a couple may face in finding happiness together.

_____

_____

_____

_____

_____

_____

_____

_____

Key to the Play

WHAT YOU NEED TO KNOW At the time when this play takes place, many European marriages were arranged by families for social and economic reasons. Because life spans were shorter than they are today, people married at a young age. Romantic love was not generally viewed as the basis for a sound marriage.

Reading Tips

Everyone finds it difficult to read a Shakespearean drama for the first time. Shakespeare's language is poetic and very rich in meaning. The following strategies may help:

- Try to restate sentences or passages in your own words. When you come across a sentence with unusual word order, try to put the words in a more familiar one.

- Use the Guide for Reading, beginning on page 331, to help you understand unfamiliar words and difficult lines and passages.

- Read some of the lines and passages aloud a few times. When you do so, remember that you are speaking in someone else's voice—a character in this play. Try to **visualize** the character. What would he or she look like and sound like? What words or phrases would he or she emphasize?

from

The Tragedy of

ROMEO +

PREVIEW   This book includes Scenes 1–3 from Act One of Shakespeare's *Romeo and Juliet.* Shakespeare wrote this timeless **drama** in the 1590s. It tells the story of two teenagers who dare to risk everything for love. They live in a society torn apart by violence. In this tense setting, Shakespeare explores which force is stronger—love or hate.

The Montagues

Lord Montague (män'tə-gyo͞o)

Lady Montague

Romeo, son of Montague

Benvolio (běn-vō'lē-ō), nephew of Montague and friend of Romeo

Balthasar (bäl'thə-sär'), servant to Romeo

Abram, servant to Montague

The Capulets

Lord Capulet (kăp'yo͞o-lět')

Lady Capulet

Juliet, daughter of Capulet

Tybalt (tĭb'əlt), nephew of Lady Capulet

Nurse to Juliet

Peter, servant to Juliet's Nurse

Sampson

Gregory

An old man of the Capulet family

Juliet
WILLIAM SHAKESPEARE

OTHERS

Prince Escalus (ĕs'kə-ləs), ruler of Verona

Mercutio (mĕr-kyōō'shō), kinsman of the Prince and friend of Romeo

Friar Laurence, a Franciscan priest

Friar John, another Franciscan priest

Count Paris, a young nobleman, kinsman of the Prince

Apothecary (ə-păth'ə-kĕr'ē)

Page to Paris

Chief Watchman

Three Musicians

An Officer

Citizens of Verona, Gentlemen and Gentlewomen of both houses, Maskers, Torchbearers, Pages, Guards, Watchmen, Servants, and Attendants.

TIME   The 14th century

PLACE   Verona (və-rō'nə); Mantua (măn'chōō-ə) in northern Italy

The Prologue

PREVIEW The CHORUS is one actor who serves as a narrator. This actor enters from the back of the stage to introduce and explain the theme of the play. The Chorus "hooks" the audience's interest by telling people just enough to quiet them down and make them eager for the play to begin. In this prologue, or preview, the narrator explains that the play will be about a feud between two families (the Capulets and the Montagues). This feud will exact a terrible cost on the two families before it is ended.

> **FOCUS**
>
> Read to find out about the feud, or long-standing quarrel, between the two families.
>
> **MARK IT UP** Circle details that tell you about this conflict. An example is highlighted.

[*Enter* Chorus.]

Chorus. Two households, both alike in dignity,
    In fair Verona, where we lay our scene,
    From ancient grudge break to new mutiny,
    Where civil blood makes civil hands unclean.
5   From forth the fatal loins of these two foes,
    A pair of star-crossed lovers take their life,
    Whose misadventured piteous overthrows
    Doth with their death bury their parents' strife.
    The fearful passage of their death-marked love,
10   And the continuance of their parents' rage,
    Which, but their children's end, naught could remove,
    Is now the two hours' traffic of our stage,
    The which if you with patient ears attend,
    What here shall miss, our toil shall strive to mend.

[*Exit.*]

Pause & Reflect

Use this guide for help with unfamiliar words and difficult passages.

As the play begins . . .

- The Chorus tells the plot of the play, which takes place in Verona, Italy.
- Two noble families will fight, and this will lead to the death of the two young lovers.

3–4 ancient . . . unclean: A new outbreak of fighting **(mutiny)** between families has caused the citizens of Verona to have one another's blood on their hands.

6 star-crossed: doomed. The position of the stars when the lovers were born was not favorable. In Shakespeare's day, people took astrology very seriously, believing that the position of the planets might bring about certain events.

11 but: except for; **naught:** nothing.

12 two hours' . . . stage: the action that will take place on the stage during the next two hours.

14 What . . . mend: We will fill in the details that have been left out of the prologue.

Pause **&** Reflect

1. Review the details you circled. Describe the conflict between the two families. **(Infer)**

_____

_____

_____

2. What brings the feud to an end? **(Cause and Effect)**

_____

_____

_____

_____

_____

_____

Act One

SCENE 1 *A public square in Verona.*

PREVIEW As the scene opens, two Capulet servants walk across the stage joking and bragging. When they happen to meet servants from the rival house of Montague, a quarrel begins that grows into an ugly street fight. Finally the ruler of Verona, Prince Escalus, appears. He is angry about the violence in his city and warns that the next offenders will be put to death. The crowd fades away, and the stage is set for the entrance of Romeo, the son of the head of the Montague family. Romeo, lovesick and sad, talks about his love for Rosaline and her cruelty in refusing to love him back.

> **FOCUS**
>
> Read to find out about the street fight between the Capulets and the Montagues.
>
> MARK IT UP Underline details that help you understand how this fight begins and ends.

[*Enter* Sampson *and* Gregory, *servants of the house of* Capulet, *armed with swords and bucklers (shields).*]

Sampson. Gregory, on my word, we'll not carry coals.

Gregory. No, for then we should be colliers.

Sampson. I mean, an we be in choler, we'll draw.

Gregory. Ay, while you live, draw your neck out of
5   collar.

Sampson. I strike quickly, being moved.

Gregory. But thou art not quickly moved to strike.

Sampson. A dog of the house of Montague moves me.

Gregory. To move is to stir, and to be valiant is
10   to stand. Therefore, if thou art moved, thou runnest
away.

Sampson. A dog of that house shall move me to stand.
I will take the wall of any man or maid of
Montague's.

15   **Gregory.** That shows thee a weak slave, for the weakest
goes to the wall.

✎ ▲MARK IT UP WORD POWER

✎ ▲MARK IT UP WORD POWER

Mark words that you'd like to add to your **Personal Word List.** After reading, you can record the words and their meanings beginning on page 402.

As the play continues . . .

- Servants of two of Verona's noble families, the Capulets and the Montagues, start to fight.
- Benvolio tries to stop them.
- Tybalt, a Montague, insults Benvolio, a Capulet, and the fighting escalates.
- Prince Escalus arrives and gives a warning to Montague and Capulet.

Reading Tip

With a partner, paraphrase the opening lines of the play. This will help you understand Shakespeare's humor. For example, the first line can be paraphrased as "We won't put up with being insulted," and the second line means "No, because then we would not be servants, but coal dealers."

1–5 we'll not carry coals: We won't stand to be insulted. (Those involved in the dirty work of hauling coal were often the targets of jokes and insults.) Here the comic characters Gregory and Sampson are bragging about how brave they are. Their boasts include several bad jokes based on words that sound alike: *collier* means "coal dealer"; *in choler* means "angry"; *collar* refers to a hangman's noose.
6–12 Sampson uses the word *moved* to mean "provoke"; Gregory responds by playing with various meanings of the word to tease Sampson.

English Learner Support
LANGUAGE

Insults Here, the word *dog* is an insulting word applied to people whom one does not like. Sampson uses it to refer to the Montagues.

13 take the wall: walk nearest to the wall. People of higher rank had the privilege of walking closer to the wall, to avoid any water or garbage that might be in the street.

Sampson. 'Tis true; and therefore women, being the weaker vessels, are ever thrust to the wall. Therefore I will push Montague's men from the wall and thrust his maids to the wall.

20

Gregory. The quarrel is between our masters and us their men.

Sampson. 'Tis all one. I will show myself a tyrant. When I have fought with the men, I will be cruel with the maids: I will cut off their heads.

25

Gregory. The heads of the maids?

Sampson. Ay, the heads of the maids, or their maidenheads. Take it in what sense thou wilt.

Gregory. They must take it in sense that feel it.

30

Sampson. Me they shall feel while I am able to stand; and 'tis known I am a pretty piece of flesh.

Gregory. 'Tis well thou art not fish; if thou hadst, thou hadst been poor-John. Draw thy tool! Here comes two of the house of Montagues.

[*Enter* Abram *and* Balthasar, *servants to the* Montagues.]

35

Sampson. My naked weapon is out. Quarrel! I will back thee.

Gregory. How? turn thy back and run?

Sampson. Fear me not.

Gregory. No, marry. I fear thee!

40

Sampson. Let us take the law of our sides; let them begin.

Gregory. I will frown as I pass by, and let them take it as they list.

Sampson. Nay, as they dare. I will bite my thumb at

45

them; which is disgrace to them, if they bear it.

Abram. Do you bite your thumb at us, sir?

Sampson. I do bite my thumb, sir.

Abram. Do you bite your thumb at us, sir?

Sampson. [*Aside to* Gregory] Is the law of our side if

50

I say ay?

Gregory. [*Aside to* Sampson] No.

17–28 Sampson's tough talk includes boasts about his ability to overpower women.

✎ **JOT IT DOWN** | **Reread Lines 21–22**

According to Gregory, who is involved in the quarrel between the Capulets and the Montagues? **(Clarify)**

_____

_____

_____

---

33 poor-John: a salted fish, considered fit only for poor people to eat.

35 During the next few speeches in this comic scene, watch what happens when the foolish, boastful servants actually meet their rivals face to face.

39 marry: a short form of "by the Virgin Mary" and so a mild swear word.

40–51 Gregory and Sampson decide to pick a fight by insulting the Montague servants with a rude gesture **(bite my thumb)**. To appreciate the humor in this scene, think about what the servants say openly and what they actually do.

49 Aside: privately, in a way that keeps the other characters from hearing what is said. Think of it as a whisper that the audience overhears.

What Does It Mean?

Draw thy tool means "Take out your weapon."

More About . . .

SHAKESPEARE'S COMIC CHARACTERS
Shakespeare's comic characters are known for their crude jokes and their rude language and gestures. (The nurse in Scene 3 is another example of a comic character in this selection.) Here, two of the servants of the Capulet family brag to each other in a crude way about what they will do if they meet anyone who is part of the Montague family. When they actually meet two of the Montague servants, they are not as brave as they pretended to be.

✔ Reading Check

Why does Sampson want to start a fight with the Montagues?

Sampson. No, sir, I do not bite my thumb at you, sir;
but I bite my thumb, sir.

Gregory. Do you quarrel, sir?

55 **Abram.** Quarrel, sir? No, sir.

Sampson. But if you do, sir, I am for you. I serve as
good a man as you.

Abram. No better.

Sampson. Well, sir.

[*Enter* Benvolio, *nephew of* Montague *and first cousin
of* Romeo.]

60 **Gregory.** [*Aside to* Sampson] Say "better." Here comes
one of my master's kinsmen.

Sampson. Yes, better, sir.

Abram. You lie.

Sampson. Draw, if you be men. Gregory, remember
65 thy swashing blow.

[*They fight.*]

Benvolio. Part, fools! [*Beats down their swords.*] Put up
your swords. You know not what you do.

[*Enter* Tybalt, *hot-headed nephew of* Lady Capulet
and first cousin of Juliet.]

Tybalt. What, art thou drawn among these heartless hinds?
Turn thee, Benvolio! look upon thy death.

70 **Benvolio.** I do but keep the peace. Put up thy sword,
Or manage it to part these men with me.

Tybalt. What, drawn, and talk of peace? I hate the word
As I hate hell, all Montagues, and thee.
Have at thee, coward!

[*They fight.*]

[*Enter several of both houses, who join the fray; then
enter* Citizens *and* Peace Officers, *with clubs.*]

75 **Officer.** Clubs, bills, and partisans! Strike! beat them
down!

Citizens. Down with the Capulets! Down with the
Montagues!

[*Enter old* Capulet *and* Lady Capulet.]

Capulet. What noise is this? Give me my long sword,
80 ho!

60–65 From the corner of his eye, Gregory can see Tybalt, a Capulet, arriving on the scene. With help on the way, Gregory's interest in fighting suddenly returns. He is told by Sampson to use **swashing,** or smashing, blows.

68 heartless hinds: cowardly servants.

68–74 Tybalt misunderstands that Benvolio is trying to stop the fight.

72 drawn . . . peace: You have your sword out, and yet you have the nerve to talk of peace?
74 Have at thee: Defend yourself.

75 bills, and partisans: spears.

✔ **Reading Check**
What are the servants arguing about?

🖉 | **JOT IT DOWN**   Reread Lines 66–70

Think about how Benvolio and Tybalt are different. How would you describe this contrast? (**Compare and Contrast**)

_____

_____

_____

English Learner Support
VOCABULARY

Idiom *Put up your swords* means "Put away your swords."

🖉 | **JOT IT DOWN**   Reread Lines 72–74

Tybalt makes the quarrel between the servants worse by

_____

_____

_____

(Cause and Effect)

What Does It Mean?
Here, *drawn* means "with your sword drawn from its sheath."

Reading Tip
Write a headline for the street fight in this scene.

Lady Capulet. A crutch, a crutch! Why call you for
a sword?

Capulet. My sword, I say! Old Montague is come
And flourishes his blade in spite of me.

[*Enter old* Montague *and* Lady Montague.]

85 **Montague.** Thou villain Capulet!—Hold me not, let
me go.

Lady Montague. Thou shalt not stir one foot to seek
a foe.

[*Enter* Prince Escalus, *with attendants. At first no one
hears him.*]

Prince. Rebellious subjects, enemies to peace,
90 Profaners of this neighbor-stained steel—
Will they not hear? What, ho! you men, you beasts,
That quench the fire of your pernicious rage
With purple fountains issuing from your veins!
On pain of torture, from those bloody hands
95 Throw your mistempered weapons to the ground
And hear the sentence of your moved prince.
Three civil brawls, bred of an airy word
By thee, old Capulet, and Montague,
Have thrice disturbed the quiet of our streets
100 And made Verona's ancient citizens
Cast by their grave beseeming ornaments
To wield old partisans, in hands as old,
Cankered with peace, to part your cankered hate.
If ever you disturb our streets again,
105 Your lives shall pay the forfeit of the peace.
For this time all the rest depart away.
You, Capulet, shall go along with me;
And, Montague, come you this afternoon,
To know our farther pleasure in this case,
110 To old Freetown, our common judgment place.
Once more, on pain of death, all men depart.

[*Exeunt all but* Montague, Lady Montague, *and*
Benvolio.]

Pause & Reflect

81–88 A crutch . . . sword: You need a crutch more than a sword.

89–96 The Prince is furious about the street fighting caused by the feud. He commands all the men to put down their weapons and pay attention.
92 pernicious: destructive.

97–103 Three . . . hate: The Prince holds Capulet and Montague responsible for three recent street fights, probably started by an offhand remark or insult **(airy word)**. He warns the old men that they will be put to death if any more fights occur.

103 Cankered with peace means "rusted from lack of use"; in the phrase "cankered hate," *cankered* means "diseased or infected."

Exeunt *(Latin):* they leave. When one person leaves the stage, the direction is Exit.

Reading Tip
Compare the responses of Lady Capulet and Lady Montague when their husbands act like they are going to start fighting.

✔ Reading Check
What does Prince Escalus say will happen if Montague and Capulet ever disturb the peace again?

Pause & Reflect

1. Review the details you marked. The street fight between the Capulets and the Montagues begins when _____
_____
_____
_____ .
It ends because _____
_____
_____
_____ .
(Cause and Effect)

2. Circle the name of the character below who is most to blame for the street fight. **(Clarify)**

   Benvolio   Tybalt

   the Prince   Lady Montague

MARK IT UP 3. Review the boxed passage on page 338. Circle any details that help you understand how violent the feud is. **(Evaluate)**

FOCUS

Read to find out what Romeo is like at the beginning
of the play.

MARK IT UP Circle details that help you form
impressions of him.

Montague. Who set this ancient quarrel new abroach?
Speak, nephew, were you by when it began?

Benvolio. Here were the servants of your adversary
115   And yours, close fighting ere I did approach.
I drew to part them. In the instant came
The fiery Tybalt, with his sword prepared;
Which, as he breathed defiance to my ears,
He swung about his head and cut the winds,
120   Who, nothing hurt withal, hissed him in scorn.
While we were interchanging thrusts and blows,
Came more and more, and fought on part and part,
Till the Prince came, who parted either part.

Lady Montague. O, where is Romeo? Saw you him today?
125   Right glad I am he was not at this fray.

Benvolio. Madam, an hour before the worshiped sun
Peered forth the golden window of the East,
A troubled mind drave me to walk abroad,
Where, underneath the grove of sycamore
130   That westward rooteth from the city's side,
So early walking did I see your son.
Towards him I made, but he was ware of me
And stole into the covert of the wood.
I—measuring his affections by my own,
135   Which then most sought where most might not be
found,
Being one too many by my weary self—
Pursued my humor, not pursuing his,
And gladly shunned who gladly fled from me.

Montague. Many a morning hath he there been seen,
140   With tears augmenting the fresh morning's dew,
Adding to clouds more clouds with his deep sighs;
But all so soon as the all-cheering sun
Should in the farthest East begin to draw
The shady curtains from Aurora's bed,

112 Who . . . abroach: Who reopened this old argument?

114 adversary: enemy.

115 ere: before.

120 withal: by this.

122 on part and part: some on one side, some on the other.

125 fray: fight.

128 drave: drove.

130 rooteth: grows.

132–138 made: moved; **covert:** covering. Romeo saw Benvolio coming toward him and hid in the woods. Benvolio decided to respect Romeo's privacy and went away. The word *humor* in line 137 means "whim" or "mood."

139–150 Romeo has been wandering through the woods at night, often in tears. At daybreak he returns home and locks himself in his darkened room. Montague is deeply concerned about his son's behavior and feels he needs guidance. **142–144** The sun is pictured as waking up Aurora, the goddess of the dawn.

As the play continues . . .

• Lord and Lady Montague talk with Benvolio about their son Romeo and his strange behavior.

• Romeo enters and tells Benvolio what is bothering him.

English Learner Support

Diction When Lady Montague asks Benvolio, "Saw you him today?" she means, "Have you seen Romeo today?"

145 Away from light steals home my heavy son
And private in his chamber pens himself,
Shuts up his windows, locks fair daylight out,
And makes himself an artificial night.
Black and portentous must this humor prove
150 Unless good counsel may the cause remove.

Benvolio. My noble uncle, do you know the cause?

Montague. I neither know it nor can learn of him.

Benvolio. Have you importuned him by any means?

Montague. Both by myself and many other friends;
155 But he, his own affections' counselor,
Is to himself—I will not say how true—
But to himself so secret and so close,
So far from sounding and discovery,
As is the bud bit with an envious worm
160 Ere he can spread his sweet leaves to the air
Or dedicate his beauty to the sun.

> Could we but learn from whence his sorrows grow,
> We would as willingly give cure as know.

[*Enter* Romeo *lost in thought.*]

Benvolio. See, where he comes. So please you step aside,
165 I'll know his grievance, or be much denied.

Montague. I would thou wert so happy by thy stay
To hear true shrift. Come, madam, let's away.

[*Exeunt* Montague *and* Lady.]

Benvolio. Good morrow, cousin.

Romeo.   Is the day so young?

170 **Benvolio.** But new struck nine.

Romeo.   Ay me! sad hours seem long.
Was that my father that went hence so fast?

> **Benvolio.** It was. What sadness lengthens Romeo's hours?
>
> **Romeo.** Not having that which having makes them short.
>
> 175 **Benvolio.** In love?
>
> **Romeo.** Out—
>
> **Benvolio.** Of love?
>
> **Romeo.** Out of her favor where I am in love.

Benvolio. Alas that love, so gentle in his view,
180 Should be so tyrannous and rough in proof!

145 heavy: sad.

149 black and portentous . . . prove: This state of mind (**humor**) will turn out to be harmful and threatening.

153 importuned: demanded.

155 his own affections' counselor: Romeo keeps to himself.

158–163 So far from . . . know: Finding out what Romeo is thinking is nearly impossible. Montague compares his son to a young bud destroyed by the bite of an envious worm. He wants to find out what is bothering Romeo so he can help him.

167 shrift: confession.

168 cousin: any relative or close friend. The informal version is **coz.**

179–182 love: refers to Cupid, the god of love. Cupid is pictured as a blind boy with wings and a bow and arrow. Anyone hit by one of his arrows falls in love instantly. Since he is blind, love is blind. He looks gentle, but in reality he can be a harsh master.

✎ JOT IT DOWN **Reread Lines 162–163**

What kind of a father is Montague? **(Infer)**

_____

_____

_____

✔ Reading Check

What does Benvolio say he will find out for Lord and Lady Montague?

✎ MARK IT UP **Reread Lines 173–178**

Circle the line that tells why Romeo is so depressed. **(Clarify)**

Romeo. Alas that love, whose view is muffled still,
Should without eyes see pathways to his will!
Where shall we dine?—O me! What fray was
here?—
Yet tell me not, for I have heard it all.

185 Here's much to do with hate, but more with love.
Why then, O brawling love! O loving hate!

O anything, of nothing first create!
O heavy lightness! serious vanity!
Misshapen chaos of well-seeming forms!
190 Feather of lead, bright smoke, cold fire, sick health!
    Still-waking sleep, that is not what it is!
This love feel I, that feel no love in this.
Dost thou not laugh?

Benvolio.   No, coz, I rather weep.

195 **Romeo.** Good heart, at what?

Benvolio. At thy good heart's oppression.

Romeo. Why, such is love's transgression.

Griefs of mine own lie heavy in my breast,
Which thou wilt propagate, to have it prest
200 With more of thine. This love that thou hast shown
Doth add more grief to too much of mine own.
Love is a smoke raised with the fume of sighs;
Being purged, a fire sparkling in lovers' eyes;
Being vexed, a sea nourished with lovers' tears.
205 What is it else? A madness most discreet,
A choking gall, and a preserving sweet.
Farewell, my coz.

Benvolio.   Soft! I will go along.

An if you leave me so, you do me wrong.

210 **Romeo.** Tut! I have lost myself; I am not here:

This is not Romeo, he's some other where.

Benvolio. Tell me in sadness, who is that you love?

Romeo. What, shall I groan and tell thee?

Benvolio.   Groan? Why, no;
215 But sadly tell me who.

Romeo. Bid a sick man in sadness make his will.
Ah, word ill urged to one that is so ill!

183 Romeo notices the damage caused by the street fight.

185–193 Romeo, confused and upset, tries to describe his feelings about hopeless love in phrases like "loving hate."

194–201 Benvolio expresses his sympathy for Romeo. Romeo replies that this is one more problem caused by love. He now feels worse than before because he must carry the weight of Benvolio's sympathy along with his own grief.

199 propagate: increase.

Reading Tip

Is Romeo happy or sad in his love? Circle four or five words that clearly show how he is feeling.

203 purged: cleansed (of the smoke).
204 vexed: troubled.

206 a choking gall: a bitter fluid.

208 Soft: Wait a minute.
209 An if: if.

English Learner Support

LANGUAGE

Changes in Meaning In Shakespeare's time, the word *sad* was used to mean "serious." Today, *sad* means unhappy.

212 sadness: seriousness.

JOT IT DOWN **Reread Line 211**

How would you **paraphrase**—or put in your own words—this line?

_____

_____

_____

In sadness, cousin, I do love a woman.

Benvolio. I aimed so near when I supposed you loved.

220 **Romeo.** A right good markman! And she's fair I love.

Benvolio. A right fair mark, fair coz, is soonest hit.

Romeo. Well, in that hit you miss. She'll not be hit
With Cupid's arrow. She hath Dian's wit,
And, in strong proof of chastity well armed,
225 From Love's weak childish bow she lives unharmed.
She will not stay the siege of loving terms,
Nor bide the encounter of assailing eyes,
Nor ope her lap to saint-seducing gold.
O, she is rich in beauty; only poor
230 That, when she dies, with beauty dies her store.

Benvolio. Then she hath sworn that she will still live
chaste?

Romeo. She hath, and in that sparing makes huge waste;
For beauty, starved with her severity,
235 Cuts beauty off from all posterity.
She is too fair, too wise, wisely too fair,
To merit bliss by making me despair.
She hath forsworn to love, and in that vow
Do I live dead that live to tell it now.

240 **Benvolio.** Be ruled by me: forget to think of her.

Romeo. O, teach me how I should forget to think!

Benvolio. By giving liberty unto thine eyes:
Examine other beauties.

Romeo.   'Tis the way
245 To call hers (exquisite) in question more.
These happy masks that kiss fair ladies' brows,
Being black, puts us in mind they hide the fair.
He that is strucken blind cannot forget
The precious treasure of his eyesight lost.
250 Show me a mistress that is passing fair,
What doth her beauty serve but as a note
Where I may read who passed that passing fair?
Farewell. Thou canst not teach me to forget.

Benvolio. I'll pay that doctrine, or else die in debt.

[*Exeunt.*]

Pause & Reflect

218–219 Romeo seems unaware of how foolish his dramatic confession sounds. Notice that Romeo does not tell the name of his love. Benvolio responds with appropriate but gentle mockery.

219–222 Romeo and Benvolio talk of love in terms of archery, another reference to Cupid and his love arrows.

222–225 She'll . . . unharmed: The girl isn't interested in falling in love. She is like Diana, the goddess of chastity, the moon, and the hunt, who avoided Cupid's arrows. She intends to stay single rather than get married.

226–228 She is unmoved by Romeo's declaration of love, his adoring looks, and his wealth.

231–235 Since she has vowed to remain chaste, she will die without children, and her beauty will not be passed on to future generations **(posterity).**

237–238 To merit . . . despair: The girl will reach heaven **(bliss)** by being chaste, which causes Romeo **despair,** or hopelessness. **forsworn to:** sworn not to.

244–245 'Tis . . . more: That would only make me appreciate my own love's beauty more.

246 Masks were worn by Elizabethan women to protect their complexions from the sun.

254 I'll pay . . . debt: I'll convince you you're wrong, or die trying.

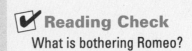

Reading Check
What is bothering Romeo?

Reading Check
What does Benvolio propose as the cure to Romeo's problem? Why doesn't Romeo think Benvolio's plan will work?

Pause & Reflect

1. Circle any of the following words that match your impressions of Romeo. **(Evaluate)**

   merry   sad   hopeful

   lovesick   faithful

2. What problem does Romeo have with the woman he loves? **(Infer)**

   _____

   _____

   _____

   _____

3. How would you rate Benvolio as a friend to Romeo? **(Evaluate)**

   _____

   _____

   _____

CHALLENGE
What have you learned about Romeo's views about love? Highlight passages that show these views. **(Character)**

SCENE 2 *A street near the Capulet house.*

PREVIEW This scene opens with Count Paris, a young nobleman, asking Capulet for permission to marry his daughter, Juliet. Capulet says that Juliet is too young but gives Paris permission to court her and try to win her favor. He also invites Paris to a party he is giving that night. Romeo finds out about the party and discovers that Rosaline, the girl who rejected him, will be present. Benvolio urges Romeo to go to the party to see how Rosaline compares with the other women.

FOCUS

Read to find out how Capulet replies to Paris's request to marry Juliet.

MARK IT UP Underline details that help you understand how Capulet feels about his daughter and about Paris's request.

[*Enter* Capulet *with* Paris, *a kinsman of the* Prince, *and* Servant.]

Capulet. But Montague is bound as well as I,
In penalty alike; and 'tis not hard, I think,
For men so old as we to keep the peace.

Paris. Of honorable reckoning are you both,
5 And pity 'tis you lived at odds so long.
But now, my lord, what say you to my suit?

Capulet. But saying o'er what I have said before:
My child is yet a stranger in the world,
She hath not seen the change of fourteen years;
10 Let two more summers wither in their pride
Ere we may think her ripe to be a bride.

Paris. Younger than she are happy mothers made.

Capulet. And too soon marred are those so early made.
The earth hath swallowed all my hopes but she;
15 She is the hopeful lady of my earth.
But woo her, gentle Paris, get her heart;
My will to her consent is but a part.
An she agree, within her scope of choice
Lies my consent and fair according voice.
20 This night I hold an old accustomed feast,
Whereto I have invited many a guest,

As the play continues . . .

- The setting changes, and we find Count Paris and Lord Capulet together.
- Paris wants to marry Juliet, Capulet's daughter.
- Capulet invites Paris to a party so he can meet Juliet.

1 bound: obligated.

4 reckoning: reputation.

6 what say . . . suit: Paris is asking for Capulet's response to his proposal to marry Juliet.

7 o'er: over; again.

8–13 My child . . . made: Capulet repeats his claim that Juliet, still thirteen, is too young for marriage. He further argues that girls are hurt by becoming mothers too soon.

READ ALOUD Lines 9–11

Listen to the rhythm of these lines. Notice the age Capulet wants Juliet to be before she gets married.

14 The earth . . . she: All my children are dead except Juliet.

16 woo her: try to win her affection.

18–19 An . . . voice: I will give my approval to the one she chooses. The word *an* means "if."

20 old accustomed feast: a traditional or annual party.

Reading Tip

As you read this scene, write any questions you have in the margins. After you have finished reading, discuss your questions with a partner.

Such as I love, and you among the store,
One more, most welcome, makes my number more.
At my poor house look to behold this night

25 Earth-treading stars that make dark heaven light.
Such comfort as do lusty young men feel
When well-appareled April on the heel
Of limping Winter treads, even such delight
Among fresh female buds shall you this night

30 Inherit at my house. Hear all, all see,
And like her most whose merit most shall be;
Which, on more view of many, mine, being one,
May stand in number, though in reck'ning none.
Come, go with me. [*To* Servant, *giving him a paper.*]

35   Go, sirrah, trudge about
Through fair Verona; find those persons out
Whose names are written there, and to them say,
My house and welcome on their pleasure stay.

[*Exeunt* Capulet *and* Paris.]

Pause & Reflect

FOCUS

Read to find out how Romeo and Benvolio learn
about Capulet's party.

Servant. Find them out whose names are written here!

40 It is written that the shoemaker should meddle with
his yard and the tailor with his last, the fisher with
his pencil and the painter with his nets; but I am
sent to find those persons whose names are here
writ, and can never find what names the writing

45 person hath here writ. I must to the learned. In
good time!

[*Enter* Benvolio *and* Romeo.]

25 **Earth-treading stars:** beautiful, dazzling ladies.

29–33 **Among . . . none:** Tonight at the party you will witness **(inherit)** the loveliest young girls in Verona, including Juliet. When you see all of them together, your opinion of Juliet may change.

35 **sirrah:** a term used to address a servant.

38 **My house . . . stay:** My house and my welcome wait for their pleasure.

39–42 The servant is bewildered and frustrated because he has been asked to read—a skill he does not have. He confuses the craftsmen and their tools, tapping a typical source of humor for Elizabethan clowns, then goes off to seek help.The word *yard* means "yardstick," a tailor's tool; the word *last* means "a form shaped like a human foot and used in making or repairing shoes."

45–46 **In good time:** What luck; he is referring to the arrival of Romeo and Benvolio, who look like men who can read.

Pause **&** Reflect

1. Capulet tells Paris that Juliet is _____
   _____
   to get married but allows Paris _____
   _____
   _____
   _____.
   (Clarify)

2. Review the details you underlined as you read. Write down some words that describe Capulet's feelings for his daughter, Juliet. **(Infer)**
   _____
   _____
   _____

As the play continues . . .

- The servant cannot read and does not know what to do with the list of names.
- He asks Romeo and Benvolio for help.
- Benvolio and Romeo decide that they will go to the party.

Benvolio. Tut, man, one fire burns out another's
      burning;
    One pain is lessened by another's anguish;
50   Turn giddy, and be holp by backward turning;
    One desperate grief cures with another's languish.
    Take thou some new infection to thy eye,
    And the rank poison of the old will die.

Romeo. Your plantain leaf is excellent for that.

55 **Benvolio.** For what, I pray thee?

Romeo.   For your broken shin.

Benvolio. Why, Romeo, art thou mad?

Romeo. Not mad, but bound more than a madman is;
    Shut up in prison, kept without my food,
60   Whipped and tormented and—God-den, good
      fellow.

Servant. God gi' go-den. I pray, sir, can you (read?)

Romeo. Ay, mine own fortune in my misery.

Servant. Perhaps you have learned it without book.
65   But I pray, can you read anything you see?

Romeo. Ay, if I know the letters and the language.

Servant. Ye say honestly. Rest you merry!

[Romeo's *joking goes over the clown's head. He
concludes that* Romeo *cannot read and prepares to
seek someone who can.*]

Romeo. Stay, fellow; I can read.   [*He reads.*]

    "Signior Martino and his wife and daughters;
70   County Anselmo and his beauteous sisters;
    The lady widow of Vitruvio;
    Signior Placentio and his lovely nieces;
    Mercutio and his brother Valentine;
    Mine uncle Capulet, his wife, and daughters;
75   My fair niece Rosaline and Livia;
    Signior Valentio and his cousin Tybalt;
    Lucio and the lively Helena."
[*Gives back the paper.*]

    A fair assembly. Whither should they come?

Servant. Up.

47–53 Tut, man . . . die: Benvolio is still trying to convince Romeo that the best way he can be helped (**holp**) in his love for Rosaline is to find someone else. Notice that he compares love to a disease that can only be cured by another disease.

54 plantain leaf: a leaf applied to minor wounds to make them stop bleeding.

58–61 Romeo is giving Benvolio a dismal picture of how he feels when he is interrupted by Capulet's servant. **God-den:** good evening.

62 God gi' go-den: God give you a good evening.

67 Rest you merry: Stay happy; a polite form of *goodbye.*

75 Notice that Romeo's beloved Rosaline, a Capulet, is invited to the party. (This is the first time in the play that her name is mentioned.) Mercutio, a friend of both Romeo and the Capulets, is also invited.

78 Whither: where.

◢ JOT IT DOWN **Reread Line 62**

What does the servant ask Romeo to do? **(Clarify)**

_____

_____

_____

More About . . .
READING DURING SHAKESPEARE'S TIME
The play is set in a time when many people did not know how to (read.) Servants had little chance of getting educated. Romeo and Benvolio are from the upper class, so they have had the opportunity to learn how to read.

English Learner Support
VOCABULARY

Idiom The highlighted phrase means that the joke is beyond the clown's (servant's) understanding.

80 **Romeo.** Whither?

Servant. To supper, to our house.

Romeo. Whose house?

Servant. My master's.

Romeo. Indeed I should have asked you that before.

85 **Servant.** Now I'll tell you without asking. My master is
the great rich Capulet; and if you be not of the
house of Montagues, I pray come and crush a cup of
wine. Rest you merry!
[*Exit.*]

Benvolio. At this same ancient feast of Capulet's
90 Sups the fair Rosaline whom thou so lovest,
With all the admired beauties of Verona.
Go thither, and with unattainted eye
Compare her face with some that I shall show,
And I will make thee think thy swan a crow.

95 **Romeo.** When the devout religion of mine eye
Maintains such falsehood, then turn tears to fires;
And these, who, often drowned, could never die,
Transparent heretics, be burnt for liars!
One fairer than my love? The all-seeing sun
100 Ne'er saw her match since first the world begun.

Benvolio. Tut! you saw her fair, none else being by,
Herself poised with herself in either eye;
But in that crystal scales let there be weighed
Your lady's love against some other maid
105 That I will show you shining at this feast,
And she shall scant show well that now shows best.

Romeo. I'll go along, no such sight to be shown,
But to rejoice in splendor of mine own.

[*Exeunt.*]

Pause **&** *Reflect*

87–88 crush a cup of wine: slang for "drink some wine."

92–94 Go . . . crow: Go to the party and, with unbiased eyes, compare Rosaline with the other beautiful girls.

95–98 When . . . liars: If the love I have for Rosaline, which is like a religion, changes because of such lies (that others could be more beautiful), let my tears be turned to fire and my eyes be burned. To Romeo, Rosaline is like a goddess, or a divine person whom he worships.

101–106 Tut . . . best: You've seen Rosaline alone; now compare her with some other girls.

106 scant: scarcely.

107–108 Romeo agrees to go to the party, but only to see Rosaline.

Pause & Reflect

1. How do Romeo and Benvolio find out about Capulet's party? **(Cause and Effect)**

_____

_____

_____

MARK IT UP 2. Review the boxed passage on page 354. Circle the line that tells how Benvolio thinks Rosaline will compare with the other girls at Capulet's party. **(Clarify)**

3. If you were in Romeo's position, would you go to a party given by Capulet, your family's enemy? Why or why not? **(Connect)**

_____

_____

_____

_____

CHALLENGE

Review lines 47–53 in Scene 2. What message about love does Benvolio share with Romeo? How do his metaphors, or comparisons, help convey that message? **(Infer)**

SCENE 3 *Capulet's house.*

PREVIEW In this scene, you will meet Juliet, her mother, and her nurse. The Nurse, a merry and slightly crude servant, has been in charge of Juliet since her birth. Once she starts talking, she can't stop. Just before the party, Juliet's mother asks if Juliet has thought about getting married. Lady Capulet is trying to convince her daughter that Paris would make a good husband.

FOCUS

Read to find out about Juliet and her relationship with her mother and the Nurse.

MARK IT UP Circle details that help you understand Juliet's attitude toward her mother.

[*Enter* Lady Capulet *and* Nurse.]

Lady Capulet. Nurse, where's my daughter? Call her forth to me.

Nurse. Now, by my maidenhead at twelve year old, I bade her come. What, lamb! what, ladybird!

5   God forbid! Where's this girl? What, Juliet!

[*Enter* Juliet.]

Juliet. How now? Who calls?

Nurse. Your mother.

Juliet. Madam, I am here. What is your will?

Lady Capulet. This is the matter—Nurse, give leave
10   awhile,
We must talk in secret. Nurse, come back again;
I have remembered me, thou's hear our counsel.
Thou knowest my daughter's of a pretty age.

Nurse. Faith, I can tell her age unto an hour.

15 **Lady Capulet.** She's not fourteen.

Nurse.   I'll lay fourteen of my teeth—
And yet, to my teen be it spoken, I have but four—
She's not fourteen. How long is it now
To Lammastide?

20 **Lady Capulet.** A fortnight and odd days.

English Learner Support
VOCABULARY

Idiom *To be in charge of* means "to be responsible for."

As the play continues . . .

- Lady Capulet, Juliet, and Juliet's nurse are introduced.
- The nurse remembers a story from Juliet's childhood.
- Lady Capulet tells Juliet about Paris's marriage offer.
- Both Lady Capulet and the nurse praise Paris, and Juliet agrees to consider his offer.

4–5 What: a call like "Hey, where are you?"

9–13 give leave . . . counsel: Lady Capulet seems flustered or nervous. First she tells the Nurse to leave, then she remembers that the Nurse knows Juliet as well as anyone and asks her to stay and listen. **of a pretty age:** of an attractive age, ready for marriage.

17 teen: sorrow.

19 Lammastide: August 1, a religious feast day and the day after Juliet's birthday. The feast day is now a little more than two weeks **(a fortnight)** away.

Nurse. Even or odd, of all days in the year,
    Come Lammas Eve at night shall she be fourteen.
    Susan and she (God rest all Christian souls!)
    Were of an age. Well, Susan is with God;
25   She was too good for me. But, as I said,
    On Lammas Eve at night shall she be fourteen;
    That shall she, marry; I remember it well.
    'Tis since the earthquake now eleven years;
    And she was weaned (I never shall forget it),
30   Of all the days of the year, upon that day.
    For I had then laid wormwood to my dug,
    Sitting in the sun under the dovehouse wall.
    My lord and you were then at Mantua—
    Nay, I do bear a brain—But, as I said,
35   When it did taste the wormwood on the nipple
    Of my dug and felt it bitter, pretty fool,
    To see it tetchy and fall out with the dug!
    Shake, quoth the dovehouse! 'Twas no need, I trow,
    To bid me trudge.
40   And since that time it is eleven years,
    For then she could stand alone; nay, by the rood,
    She could have run and waddled all about;

    For even the day before, she broke her brow;
    And then my husband (God be with his soul!
45   'A was a merry man) took up the child.
    "Yea," quoth he, "dost thou fall upon thy face?
    Thou wilt fall backward when thou has more wit,
    Wilt thou not, Jule?" And, by my holidam,
    The pretty wretch left crying, and said "Ay."

50   To see now how a jest shall come about!
    I warrant, an I should live a thousand years,
    I never should forget it. "Wilt thou not, Jule?"
      quoth he,
    And, pretty fool, it stinted, and said "Ay."

55 **Lady Capulet.** Enough of this. I pray thee hold thy peace.

    Nurse. Yes, madam. Yet I cannot choose but laugh
    To think it should leave crying and say "Ay."
    And yet, I warrant, it had upon its brow
    A bump as big as a young cock'rel's stone;
60   A perilous knock; and it cried bitterly.

21–54 The Nurse now begins to babble on about various memories of Juliet's childhood. She talks of Susan, who was the same age as Juliet. Susan probably died in infancy, allowing for the Nurse to become a wet nurse to (breast-feed) Juliet. She remembers an earthquake that happened on the day she stopped breast-feeding Juliet **(she was weaned).**

31 laid wormwood to my dug: applied wormwood, a plant with a bitter taste, to her breast in order to discourage the child from breast-feeding.

32 dovehouse: a house, often raised on a pole, for pigeons.

37 tetchy: touchy; cranky.

38–39 Shake . . . trudge: When the dovehouse shook, I knew enough to leave.

41 by the rood: The rood is the cross on which Christ was crucified. The expression means something like "by God."

43 broke her brow: hurt her forehead.

46–54 "Yea" . . . "Ay": To quiet Juliet after her fall, the Nurse's husband makes a crude joke, asking the baby whether she'll fall the other way (on her back) when she's older. Although at three Juliet doesn't understand the question, she stops crying **(stinted)** and innocently answers, "Yes." The Nurse finds this story so funny, she can't stop retelling it. The phrase **by my holidam** means "by my holiness" or "by my holy lady"—a mild oath.

56–63 The Nurse is one of Shakespeare's most famous comic characters. One of her comic traits is that she can't stop talking. Even after Lady Capulet has told her to be quiet, she repeats her story about Juliet as a toddler.

English Learner Support

LANGUAGE

Pronoun During this time, people sometimes referred to infants or babies as "it."

JOT IT DOWN Reread Lines 43–49

How would you feel if someone told stories about you as a baby? **(Connect)**

_____

_____

_____

"Yea," quoth my husband, "fallst upon thy face?
Thou wilt fall backward when thou comest to age,
Wilt thou not, Jule?" It stinted, and said "Ay."

Juliet. And stint thou too, I pray thee, nurse, say I.

65 **Nurse.** Peace, I have done. God mark thee to his grace!
Thou wast the prettiest babe that e'er I nursed.
An I might live to see thee married once,
I have my wish.

Lady Capulet. Marry, that "marry" is the very theme
70 I came to talk of. Tell me, daughter Juliet,
How stands your disposition to be married?

Juliet. It is an honor that I dream not of.

Nurse. An honor? Were not I thine only nurse,
I would say thou hadst sucked wisdom from thy teat.

75 **Lady Capulet.** Well, think of marriage now. Younger
    than you,
Here in Verona, ladies of esteem,
Are made already mothers. By my count,
I was your mother much upon these years
80 That you are now a maid. Thus then in brief:
The valiant Paris seeks you for his love.

Nurse. A man, young lady! lady, such a man
As all the world—why he's a man of wax.

Lady Capulet. Verona's summer hath not such a
85 flower.

Nurse. Nay, he's a flower, in faith—a very flower.

Lady Capulet. What say you? Can you love the
    gentleman?
This night you shall behold him at our feast.
90 Read o'er the volume of young Paris' face,
And find delight writ there with beauty's pen;
Examine every several lineament,
And see how one another lends content;
And what obscured in this fair volume lies
95 Find written in the margent of his eyes.
This precious book of love, this unbound lover,
To beautify him only lacks a cover.
The fish lives in the sea, and 'tis much pride
For fair without the fair within to hide.

66 e'er: ever.

67 An: if.

69 Lady Capulet uses the word **marry** in two different senses. The first **marry** means "by the Virgin Mary"; the second means "to wed."

79–80 I was . . . maid: I was your mother at about your age, yet you are still unmarried.

83 a man of wax: a man so perfect he could be a wax statue. Sculptors used to use wax figures as models for their works.

90–97 Read . . . cover: Lady Capulet uses an extended metaphor that compares Paris to a book that Juliet should read. Look for the similarities she points out.

92 several lineament: separate feature. Lady Capulet points out how each of Paris' features makes the others look even better.

95 margent . . . eyes: She compares Paris' eyes to the margin of the page of a book where notes are written that explain the content.

96–99 This . . . hide: This beautiful book (Paris) only needs a cover (wife) to become even better. He may be hiding even more wonderful qualities inside.

✏️ **JOT IT DOWN** **Reread Lines 75–81**

How does Lady Capulet's view of early marriage differ from her husband's?
(Compare and Contrast)

_____

_____

_____

✏️ **JOT IT DOWN** **Reread Line 83**

Write down a modern word or phrase that you might use to update "a man of wax."
(Connect)

_____

_____

_____

☑️ **Reading Check**

What does Lady Capulet want her daughter to do at the party that evening?

100 That book in many's eyes doth share the glory,
That in gold clasps locks in the golden story;
So shall you share all that he doth possess,
By having him making yourself no less.

Nurse. No less? Nay, bigger! Women grow by men.

105 **Lady Capulet.** Speak briefly, can you like of Paris' love?

Juliet. I'll look to like, if looking liking move;
But no more deep will I endart mine eye
Than your consent gives strength to make it fly.

[*Enter a* Servingman.]

Servingman. Madam, the guests are come, supper served
110 up, you called, my young lady asked for, the nurse
cursed in the pantry, and everything in extremity. I
must hence to wait. I beseech you follow straight.

Lady Capulet. We follow thee. [*Exit* Servingman.]
Juliet, the County stays.

115 **Nurse.** Go, girl, seek happy nights to happy days.
[*Exeunt.*]

Pause & *Reflect*

104 The Nurse can't resist one of her earthy comments. She notes that women get bigger (pregnant) when they marry.

106–108 **I'll look . . . move:** Juliet's playful answer means "I'll look at him with the intention of liking him, if simply looking can make me like him." In the next two lines, Juliet says that she will look over Paris (**endart mine eye**) only as far as her mother wishes.

111 **extremity:** confusion. The servant is upset because everything is happening at once, and he can't handle it. **straight:** immediately.

114 **the County stays:** Count Paris is waiting for you.

Reading Tip

Use a word web to gather words that describe the nurse. Use another for Juliet.

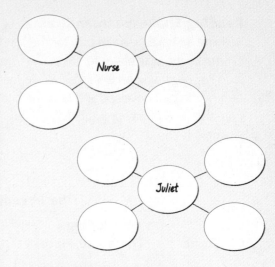

Pause & Reflect

1. Review the details that you circled as you read. What can you tell about Juliet's attitude toward her mother? **(Infer)**

_____

_____

_____

2. How would you feel if your parents set up a blind date for you in hope that it might lead to marriage? **(Connect)**

_____

_____

_____

CHALLENGE

In the first part of this play, Shakespeare introduces the **protagonists,** or main characters, Romeo and Juliet. Review the first three scenes of the play and use one color highlighter to mark important details about Romeo. Use another color to mark important details about Juliet. Based on what you've learned so far, what do you think their meeting will be like? **(Predict)**

Active Reading SkillBuilder

Reading Shakespearean Drama

Reading a Shakespearean play for the first time is not easy. Keeping track of events can make the play easier to follow. *The Tragedy of Romeo and Juliet* takes place in six days, beginning on a Sunday. While reading the play, use the chart to keep track of how the plot develops and how the characters relate to one another. Be sure to note the time of day or hours passed, the setting, and a summary of the plot. An example is shown.

	The Tragedy of Romeo and Juliet: Act One	
Scene	**Setting (Time and Place)**	**Plot Summary**
Scene 1	*early morning; a street in Verona*	*A fight starts between the Capulets and the Montagues. The Prince stops the fight. Romeo tells Benvolio about his hopeless love.*
Scene 2		
Scene 3		
Scene 4		
Scene 5		

Literary Analysis SkillBuilder

Blank Verse

Blank verse consists of unrhymed lines of iambic pentameter, in which a typical line has five unstressed syllables, each followed by a stressed syllable. Because the rhythms of blank verse are closest to those of natural speech, it is particularly suited for drama. Blank verse can contain variations, which give the lines the flow and sound of spoken English. On the chart, write three lines of blank verse from Act One. Mark the unstressed (˘) and stressed (´) syllables. An example is shown.

Scene 2   Line 10
˘ ´ ˘ ´ ˘ ´ ˘ ´ ˘ ´ Let two more summers wither in their pride

Scene_____   Line _____

Scene_____   Line _____

Scene_____   Line _____

Follow Up: How well do you think the passage captures the sound of spoken English? How does this sound affect the meaning?

Academic and Informational Reading

In this section, you will find strategies to help you read different kinds of informational materials. The examples here range from a magazine article you read for fun to textbooks and maps you read for information. Using the tips given with each type of material will help you become a more effective reader of the many texts you come across every day.

Reading a Magazine Article

A magazine article is designed to catch and hold your interest. You will get the most from your reading if you recognize the format of a magazine page and learn how to use its special features. Look at the sample magazine article as you read each strategy below.

A Read the **title** to get an idea of what the article is about. Scan any other **headings** to see how information in the article is organized.

B As you read, notice any **quotations.** Who is quoted? Is the person a reliable source on the subject?

C Notice information set in special type, such as **italics** or **boldface.** For example, look at the quotation in the article that is set in italic boldface.

D Study **visuals,** such as charts, graphs, pictures, maps, photographs, and captions. Visuals bring the topic to life.

E Pay attention to **bulleted lists.** Bullets often highlight or summarize important information.

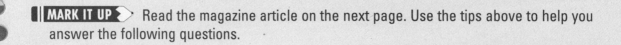 **MARK IT UP** Read the magazine article on the next page. Use the tips above to help you answer the following questions.

1. What is this article about? _____

_____

_____

2. Who explains what "echo boomers" are? Underline the name of the person who is quoted.

3. Circle the quotation that is set off in large italic type.

4. Draw a star next to a visual that shows what a typical echo boomer might look like.

5. Draw a box around the bulleted list that profiles echo boomers.

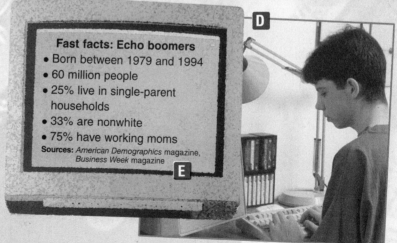

A # Advertisers Want Young Adults' Attention—and Money

by Chantal Kurczewsk

If you were born between 1979 and 1994, you are part of what is the largest teen population in U.S. history. Advertisers want to know what you like and dislike—and they are spending millions of dollars to find out.

B "There's no one name for this group of people," explains advertising executive Adele Worman. "Sometimes they're called the echo boomers, because they're mostly children of baby boomers." The baby boom generation is made up of people born between 1946 and 1964. "Other people call them Generation Y, because the generation right before them was nicknamed Generation X," Worman continues. "The 1979-to-1994 group is also called the Millennium Generation."

Echo boomers are savvy about technology: "They will surf the Internet to compare prices before they buy something," says demographer Evan Mulligan. Mulligan makes his living by compiling statistical information about this group. "Echo boomers tend to be skilled at collecting information and comfortable making decisions."

They also shoulder a great deal of responsibility. "In most cases, both parents work full-time," Mulligan explains. "That means that echo boomers are used to taking care of themselves, earning their own money, and maybe doing some of the family grocery shopping."

The echo boomers' buying power will increase steadily in the future.

"Four million new drivers will come of age each year until 2010," Worman says. "Think about how many cars those new drivers or their parents will buy."

C *"Echo boomers are used to taking care of themselves."*

D

Fast facts: Echo boomers
- Born between 1979 and 1994
- 60 million people
- 25% live in single-parent households
- 33% are nonwhite
- 75% have working moms

Sources: *American Demographics* magazine, *Business Week* magazine **E**

Reading a Textbook

The first page of a textbook lesson introduces you to a particular topic. The page also provides important information that will guide you through the rest of the lesson. Look at the sample textbook page as you read each strategy below.

A Preview the **title** and other **headings** to find out the lesson's main topic and related subtopics.

B Read the list of **key ideas** or **objectives** near the title. Keep these in mind as you read. They will help you set a purpose for your reading.

C Look for a list of terms or **vocabulary words** at the start of each lesson. These words will be identified and defined thoughout the lesson.

D Study **visuals,** such as photographs, illustrations, charts, maps, and time lines. Read the **captions.** Visuals can help the topic come alive.

MARK IT UP Read the sample textbook page. Then use the strategies above to help you answer the following questions.

1. What is the topic of this lesson? _____

   _____

2. Draw a box around the lesson's key idea.

3. (a) Circle the list of vocabulary words that will be defined in this lesson.

   (b) Underline one boldfaced vocabulary word in the text.

4. Put a star next to the visuals that show you the shape of a shield volcano.

5. Taking notes in the form of a graphic organizer can help you understand new ideas and terms. Use information in this lesson to complete the chart.

Characteristics of Volcanoes

Shield Volcanoes	Cinder Cones
broad bases	cone shaped
gently sloping sides	

9.3

A Volcanic Landforms

The term *volcano* refers not only to a volcanic vent, but also to the landform that develops as the materials from a volcanic eruption harden. The shape and structure of a volcano are determined by the nature of its eruptions and the materials it ejects.

A Shield Volcanoes

Because of its low viscosity, basaltic lava tends to flow long distances before hardening. In some cases, the lava builds up in layers, forming **shield volcanoes** with broad bases and gently sloping sides. The broad base of a shield volcano can support a mountain of enormous height. For example, Mauna Loa, a volcano on the island of Hawaii, rises 4170 meters above sea level and its base is 5000 meters below sea level; thus, its total height is 9170 meters.

Because shield volcanoes discharge basaltic lavas, they tend to be less explosive than other types of volcanoes. Basaltic lava flows, however, may be frequent and copious, causing damage to homes, highways, and other property.

Cinder Cones

A **cinder cone,** perhaps the simplest type of volcano, forms when molten lava is thrown into the air from a vent. As it falls, the lava breaks into fragments that harden before hitting the ground. These fragments accumulate, forming a cone-shaped mound with an oval base. Cinder cones, which tend to be smaller than other types of volcanoes, typically form in groups and on the sides of larger volcanoes.

D MAUNA LOA is a shield volcano on the island of Hawaii.

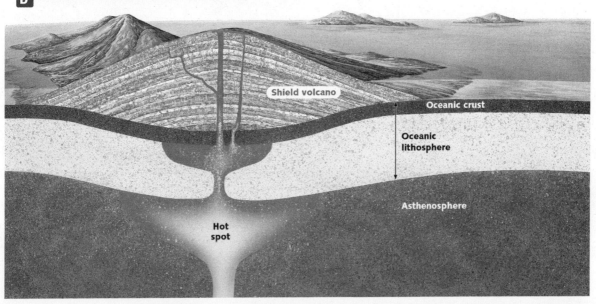

Shield volcano

Oceanic crust

Oceanic lithosphere

Asthenosphere

Hot spot

Reading a Table

Tables hold a lot of information in an organized way. These tips can help you read a table quickly and accurately. Look at the example as you read each strategy in this list.

A Read the **title** to find out the content of the table.

B the **introduction** to get a general overview of the information included in the table.

C Look at the **heading** of each row and column. To find specific information, locate the place where a row and column intersect.

A Sports-Related Injuries

B This table shows the number of sports-related injuries treated in a hospital emergency room in one year.

C

Related sport	Number of injuries
basketball	56
football	34
skating/hockey	22
track and field	10
other	28

MARK IT UP Answer the following questions using the table of sports injuries.

1. Which sport has the highest number of injuries requiring emergency room treatment? Circle the answer on the table.

2. What period of time is covered by the table? _____

_____

3. What sports might be in the "other" category? _____

_____

_____

Reading a Map

To read a map correctly, you have to identify and understand its elements. Look at the example below as you read each strategy in this list.

A Read the **title** to find out what the map shows.

B Study the **legend,** or **key,** to find out what symbols and colors are used on the map and what they stand for.

C Look at **geographic labels** to understand specific places on the map.

D Look at the **scale** to understand how distance is represented on the map.

E Look at the **compass rose,** or **pointer,** to determine direction.

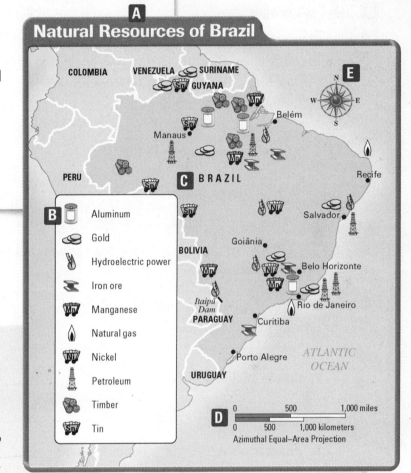

A Natural Resources of Brazil

B Legend:
- Aluminum
- Gold
- Hydroelectric power
- Iron ore
- Manganese
- Natural gas
- Nickel
- Petroleum
- Timber
- Tin

D 0 500 1,000 miles / 0 500 1,000 kilometers / Azimuthal Equal–Area Projection

| **MARK IT UP** | Use the map to answer the following questions. |

1. What is the purpose of this map?

_____

_____

2. What natural resources are found near the town of Salvador? _____

_____

3. Circle the symbol for tin each time it is used on the map.

4. Draw a straight line from Salvador to Rio de Janeiro. About how far apart in miles are these cities? _____

5. What is a city in the north of Brazil? _____

_____

Reading a Diagram

Diagrams combine pictures with a few words to provide a lot of information. Look at the example on the opposite page as you read each of the following strategies.

A Look at the **title** to get a quick idea of what the diagram is about.

B Study the **images** closely to understand each part of the diagram.

C Look at the **captions** and the **labels** for more information.

MARK IT UP Study the diagram, then answer the following questions using the strategies above.

1. What does the diagram illustrate? _____

   _____

2. How is the bottom of the pot heated? _____

   _____

3. How are objects near the burner heated? _____

   _____

4. What is the form of heat represented by the two circles of thick arrows in the center of the diagram? _____

   _____

5. Circle the parts of the diagram that show how heat moves by conduction.

Heat Transfer: Radiation, Conduction, and Convection

How Does Heat Energy Move?

Heat energy is transferred through the atmosphere in three basic ways. *Radiation* is the transfer of heat energy in the form of visible light. *Conduction* is the transfer of heat energy through collisions of the atoms and molecules of a substance, and *convection* is the transfer of heat energy in a liquid or gas through the motion of the liquid or gas caused by differences in density. All three forms of heat transfer occur when water is heated, as illustrated in the diagram below.

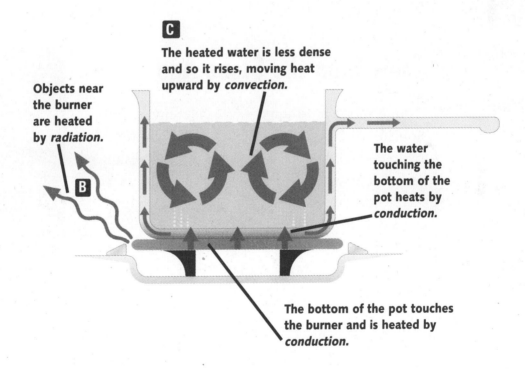

C

The heated water is less dense and so it rises, moving heat upward by *convection.*

Objects near the burner are heated by *radiation.*

B

The water touching the bottom of the pot heats by *conduction.*

The bottom of the pot touches the burner and is heated by *conduction.*

Main Idea and Supporting Details

The *main idea* in a paragraph is its most important point. *Details* in the paragraph support the main idea. Identifying the main idea will help you focus on the main message the writer wants to communicate. Use the following strategies to help you identify a paragraph's main idea and supporting details.

- Look for the **main idea,** which is often the first sentence in a paragraph.

- Use the main idea to help you **summarize** the point of the paragraph.

- Identify specific **details,** including facts and examples, that **support** the main idea.

Tools from the Stone Age

Main idea ——— Some of the most impressive achievements in human history took place during the prehistoric period called the Stone Age. These accomplishments included the invention of tools and pottery as well

Details —— as the development of farming. Stone chopping tools date from the early Stone Age—2.5 million to 8000 B.C. Polished tools, pottery, and agriculture were developed during the late Stone Age— 8000 to 3000 B.C.

MARK IT UP ⟩ Read the following paragraph. Circle the main idea. Then underline and number three details that support the main idea.

Cro-Magnons, a group of prehistoric humans, used survival skills to help their population grow and thrive. They studied animals' habits, and scientists believe that they planned their hunts carefully. Cro-Magnons also developed advanced language skills, which improved their ability to cooperate and plan.

Problem and Solution

Does the proposed solution to a problem make sense? In order to decide, you need to look at each part of the text. Use the following strategies to read the text below.

- Look at the beginning or middle of a paragraph to find the **statement of the problem.**

- Find **details** that explain the problem and tell why it is important.

- Look for the **proposed solution.**

- Identify the **supporting details** for the proposed solution.

- Think about whether the solution is a good one.

Testing Center Gets A+ *by Todd Archer*

Problem — Students at our school must take make-up tests in noisy, distracting environments.

Explanation of problem — When students come back to school after being sick, they have to make up tests during class time and are distracted by their teachers and classmates. So they miss yet another class.

Our school needs to establish a special area for taking make-up tests. There are many reasons a testing center is necessary. On any given day, an average of 4 percent of the students in our school are absent. Many of these students have tests to make up when they return. That means that make-up tests happen dozens of times every day.

Creating a testing center would not require more money or additional staff. The tables at the north end of the library would be ideal. A teacher or another faculty member could administer the tests.

A testing center would show students and parents that our school takes exams seriously.

MARK IT UP Use the text and strategies above to answer these questions.

1. Underline the proposed solution.

2. Circle at least one reason that supports this solution.

3. Do you think the solution is a good one? Explain why or why not. _____

_____

Sequence

Sequence is the order in which events happen. Whether you read a story or a social studies lesson, it is important for you to understand *when* things happen in relation to one another. The tips below can help you identify sequence in any type of text.

- Look for the **main steps** or **events** in the sequence.

- Look for **words and phrases that signal time,** such as *later, in a year,* and *in 202 B.C.*

- Look for **words and phrases that signal order,** such as *first, afterward,* and *before then.*

MARK IT UP ⟩ Read the passage about China on the next page. Then use the information from the article and the tips above to answer the questions.

1. Underline two words or phrases that signal time.

2. Circle two words or phrases that signal order.

3. A time line can help you identify and understand a sequence of events. Use the information from the passage to complete this time line.

China's Dynasties

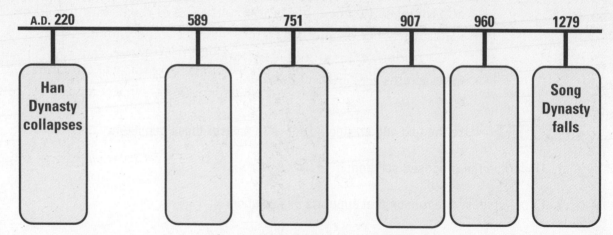

A.D. 220	589	751	907	960	1279
Han Dynasty collapses					Song Dynasty falls

China's Dynasties, 202 B.C. to A.D. 1279

The Han Dynasty ruled China from 202 B.C. to A.D. 220. (A dynasty is a series of rulers from a single family.) For more than 350 years after the Han Dynasty collapsed, no emperor was able to unite northern and southern China. Then in 589, Emperor Sui Wendi created a strong central government and laid the foundation for a golden age of China under the Tang and Song Dynasties. Literature, poetry, architecture, sculpture, painting, and dance all flourished during this period.

The Tang Dynasty ruled China for almost 300 years, from 618 to 907. The first important Tang emperor, Tang Taizong, held the throne from 627 to 649. During his reign, China regained its northern and western lands. After 660 or so, the real power in China was Empress Wu Zhao, although a series of weak emperors actually sat on the throne. By 690, Wu Zhao had become emperor in her own right, the only woman to hold that title; by the mid-700s, the Tang emperors began losing control over their huge empire. Arab armies defeated the Chinese on their far western frontier in 751. For the next 150 years, China suffered attacks on its borders and internal rebellions. Then in 907, Chinese rebels burned the capital city of Chang'an and murdered the child emperor, ending the Tang Dynasty.

Much of China was reunited in 960 under the first Song emperor, Song Taizu. However, in the early 1100s, the Song lost all of northern China to the Jurchen people. The Song established a new capital in the coastal city of Hangzhou, where they continued to rule from 1127 to 1279. During this century and a half, southern China became a prosperous trading center.

A ceramic sculpture from the Han Dynasty

Cause and Effect

A *cause* is an event that brings about another event. An *effect* is something that happens as a result of the first event. Identifying causes and effects helps you understand how events are related. Use the tips below to find causes and effects in any kind of reading.

- Look for an action or event that answers the question "What happened?" This is the **effect**.

- Look for an action or event that answers the question "Why did it happen?" This is the **cause**.

- Look for words or phrases that **signal** causes and effects, such as *because, as a result, therefore, consequently,* and *since.*

MARK IT UP Read the cause-and-effect passage on the next page. Then use the tips above to help you answer the following questions.

1. Circle words in the passage that signal causes and effects. The first one is done for you.

2. Sometimes a cause has more than one effect. Underline two changes that may have resulted from the presence of volcanic dust in the air.

3. Complete the following diagram to identify three effects of the main cause described in the passage.

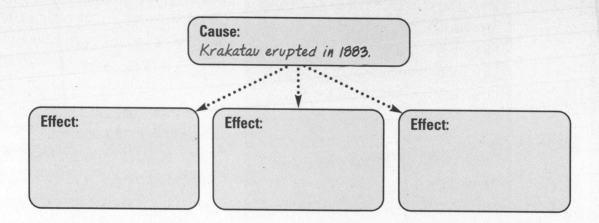

Cause:
Krakatau erupted in 1883.

Effect:

Effect:

Effect:

Krakatau: Disaster with World-Wide Results

In 1883, the massive explosion of a volcano called Krakatau resulted in tens of thousands of deaths as well as long-term changes in climate conditions.

Krakatau, also called Krakatoa, takes up much of a small island called Rakata. Part of the country of Indonesia, Rakata lies between the islands of Java and Sumatra in the Indian Ocean. Until 1883, Krakatau was a huge volcano, with a height of about 6,000 feet above sea level.

At 10:00 A.M. on August 27, 1883, a huge eruption destroyed most of Krakatau. As a result of the explosion, volcanic ash spewed into the air as high as 50 miles above the volcano.

The effects of the explosion were immediate and deadly. The blast caused nearly five cubic miles of rock fragments to be released into the air. In the region of the blast, the sun was not visible for the next two and a half days. Burning ash and rocks killed thousands. Tidal waves up to 120 feet high struck Java and Sumatra. Because of the ash, rocks, and waves, about 36,000 people lost their lives.

The destruction at Krakatau had effects around the world. People in Australia, more than 2,000 miles away, heard the boom. Weather forecasters all over the planet detected sudden increases in atmospheric pressure. A series of tidal waves resulting from the blast reached as far as Hawaii and South America. Volcanic dust from Krakatau became part of Earth's atmosphere and created unusually beautiful sunsets in the Northern Hemisphere for about three years afterwards. Some scientists believe that dust from Krakatau may have been the reason for a five-year drop in global temperatures.

Comparison and Contrast

Comparing two things means showing how they are the same. *Contrasting* two things means showing how they are different. Comparisons and contrasts are often used in science and history books to make a subject clearer. Use these tips to help you understand comparison and contrast in reading assignments, such as the article on the opposite page.

- Look for **direct statements** of comparison and contrast: "These things are similar because . . . " or "One major difference is. . . ."

- Pay attention to **words and phrases that signal comparisons,** such as *also, both, is the same as,* and *in the same way.*

- Notice **words and phrases that signal contrasts.** Some of these are *however, still, but,* and *in contrast.*

MARK IT UP Read the essay on the next page. Then use the information from the essay and the reading tips above to answer the questions.

1. Circle the words and phrases that signal comparisons. A sample has been done for you.

2. Underline the words and phrases that signal contrasts. A sample has been done for you.

3. A Venn diagram shows how two subjects are similar and how they are different. Complete this diagram, which uses information from the essay to compare and contrast the governments of Rome and the United States. Add at least one similarity to the middle part of the diagram. Add at least one difference in each outer circle.

GOVERNMENT OF ROME

the Twelve Tables

BOTH

based on a code of laws

GOVERNMENT OF U.S.

the Constitution

Forms of Republican Government: Rome and the United States

After fighting the Revolutionary War, Americans were faced with the task of creating a new government. The vision of the new nation as a republic —a government in which citizens rule through their elected representatives— was based on the republic of ancient Rome. The republican governments of Rome and the United States have both similarities and differences.

The guiding principles of the government of Rome were the Twelve Tables, a list of legal rules. Only adult male landowners could be citizens, and only they could vote. The legislative branch was divided into three houses: a 300-member Senate chosen from the aristocracy, a Centuriate Assembly of citizen-soldiers, and a Tribal Assembly of general citizens. The judicial branch consisted of eight judges chosen by the Centuriate Assembly for one-year terms.

(Like) the republic of Rome, the government of the United States is based on a code of laws, the U.S. Constitution, which gives its citizens the right to select their leaders. However, U.S. citizens now include all native-born or naturalized persons, not just adult male landowners, as in Rome. The U.S. government also consists of an executive, a judicial, and a legislative branch. In contrast to the Roman executive consuls, the U.S. executive is one person—a president elected by citizens for a four-year term. The legislative branch includes only two houses compared with Rome's three —a 100-member Senate elected by the people for six-year terms and a House of Representatives elected for two-year terms. However, while Roman judges were appointed by the Assembly for a term of only one year, the nine members of the U.S. judicial branch, the Supreme Court, are appointed by the president for life.

Comparison

Contrast

Argument

An *argument* is an opinion that is backed up with reasons and facts. After you carefully read an opinion and the reasons and facts that support it, you will be able to decide if the opinion makes sense. As you read these tips, look at the sample argument on the right.

- Look for words or phrases that **signal an opinion,** such as *I believe, I think, in my opinion.*

- Identify reasons, facts, or expert opinions that **support** the argument.

- Ask yourself if the argument and the reasons that back it up **make sense.**

- Look for **errors in reasoning,** such as overgeneralizations, that may affect the argument.

MARK IT UP Read the argument on the following page. Then use the strategies above to help you answer the following questions.

1. Circle any words that signal an opinion.

2. Underline the words or phrases that signal the writer's opinion.

3. The writer presents both sides of the argument. Fill in the chart below to show the two sides. One reason has been provided for you.

Reasons for Use at School	Reasons Against Use at School
1. Students will be safer.	

A Needed Compromise

By Tamia Kierney-Smith

It is time for the administration to revise the cell phone policy at Jefferson High School and allow students to use cell phones during the lunch period. Currently, cell phones may not be used at any time. As a result, students are forced to leave campus during lunch if they wish to talk on the phone. This situation creates many problems.

First, students who leave the school building during lunch must hurry back for afternoon classes and are often late. They also risk injury when crossing McKinny Avenue to get to the mall. The road can be quite busy and dangerous.

These problems would largely be solved if students were allowed to use cell phones during their lunch period. Students would be safer if they remained in the building, and fewer would be late to class. Finally, students would be more likely to eat a healthful and leisurely lunch if they remained at school. The fast food restaurants in the mall serve greasy, non-nutritious food.

Some teachers disagree with my views. They argue that many high school students would abuse such a policy. They feel strongly that students would continue lunch conversations in the halls and classrooms. They also think that cell phone loss and theft would be a problem.

I would argue that high school students can be responsible. The more opportunities we are given to exercise responsibility, the sooner we will become responsible adults. I also think that making rules based on anticipated problems is unfair. I hope the administration will at least consider my proposal to allow students at Jefferson High School to use cell phones during the lunch period.

Social Studies

Social studies class becomes easier when you understand how your textbook's words, pictures, and maps work together to give you information. Following these tips can make you a better reader of social studies lessons. As you read the tips, look at the sample lesson on the right-hand page.

A Read the **title** of the lesson and other **headings** to find out what the lesson is about. Smaller headings may introduce subtopics that are related to the main topic.

B Read the **main ideas** or **objectives** listed on the first page of the lesson. These items summarize the lesson and help set a purpose for your reading.

C Look at the **vocabulary terms** listed on the lesson's first page. These terms will later be boldfaced or underlined, and defined in the text.

D Notice **how information is organized.** In social studies lessons, ideas are often presented using sequence, cause and effect, comparison and contrast, and main idea and supporting details.

E Carefully examine **visuals** such as art, maps, charts, bulleted lists, time lines, or diagrams. Think about how the visuals and the text are related.

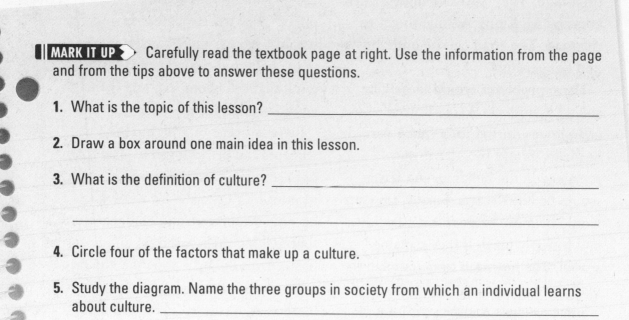

MARK IT UP Carefully read the textbook page at right. Use the information from the page and from the tips above to answer these questions.

1. What is the topic of this lesson? _____

2. Draw a box around one main idea in this lesson.

3. What is the definition of culture? _____

_____

4. Circle four of the factors that make up a culture.

5. Study the diagram. Name the three groups in society from which an individual learns about culture. _____

_____

The Elements of Culture

A

B Main Ideas

• Human beings are members of social groups with shared and unique sets of behaviors and attitudes.

• Language and religion are two very important aspects of culture.

C Places & Terms

culture	cultural hearth
society	acculturation
ethnic group	dialect
innovation	religion
diffusion	

BASICS

A HUMAN PERSPECTIVE In an article titled "The 100% American," anthropologist Ralph Linton described how a typical American, in eating breakfast, had borrowed from other cultures.

> He has coffee, an Abyssinian plant, with cream and sugar. Both the domestication of cows and the idea of milking them originated in the Near East, while sugar was first made in India. . . . As a side dish he may have the egg of a species of bird domesticated in Indo-China, or thin strips of the flesh of an animal domesticated in Eastern Asia.

Borrowing from other cultures is common around the world, even if we are not aware of it.

A Defining Culture

D

What makes us similar to some people in the world but different from most others? The answer is culture. **Culture** is the total of knowledge, attitudes, and behaviors shared by and passed on by the members of a specific group. Culture acts as a blueprint for how a group of people should behave if they want to fit in with the group. It ties us to one group and separates us from other groups—and helps us to solve the problems that all humans face. Culture involves the following factors:

- food and shelter
- education
- religion
- security/protection
- relationships to family and others
- political and social organization
- language
- creative expression

A group that shares a geographic region, a sense of identity, and a culture is called a **society**. Sometimes you will hear the term **ethnic group** used to refer to a specific group that shares a language, customs, and a common heritage. An ethnic group has an identity as a separate group of people within the region where they live. For example, the San peoples—known as the Bushmen of the Kalahari Desert in Africa—live in a specific territory, speak their own language, and have a social organization distinct from other groups living in the region.

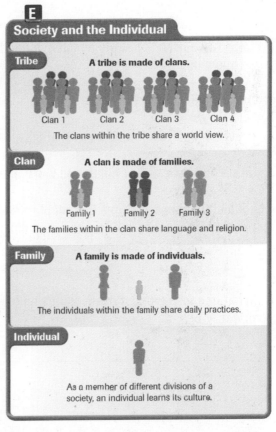

E Society and the Individual

Tribe — A tribe is made of clans.

Clan 1   Clan 2   Clan 3   Clan 4

The clans within the tribe share a world view.

Clan — A clan is made of families.

Family 1   Family 2   Family 3

The families within the clan share language and religion.

Family — A family is made of individuals.

The individuals within the family share daily practices.

Individual

As a member of different divisions of a society, an individual learns its culture.

Science

Reading a science textbook becomes easier when you understand how the explanations, drawings, and special terms work together. Use the strategies below to help you better understand your science textbook. Look at the examples on the opposite page as you read each strategy in this list.

A Preview the **title** and any **headings** to see what scientific concepts you will learn about.

B Read the **key ideas** or **objectives.** These items summarize the lesson and help set a purpose for your reading.

C Read the list of **vocabulary terms** that will be introduced and defined in the lesson.

D Notice the **boldfaced** and **italicized** terms in the text. Look for definitions of these terms.

E Carefully examine any **pictures** or **diagrams.** Read the **captions** to see how the graphics help to illustrate the text.

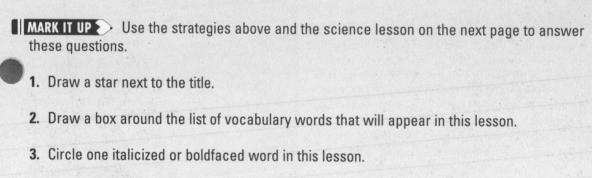

∎MARK IT UP Use the strategies above and the science lesson on the next page to answer these questions.

1. Draw a star next to the title.

2. Draw a box around the list of vocabulary words that will appear in this lesson.

3. Circle one italicized or boldfaced word in this lesson.

4. Look at the diagram at the bottom of the page and read the caption. What scientific process or concept does the diagram illustrate? _____

_____

5. What happens when the sun shines on the ocean or another body of water? Describe one effect. _____

_____

Cycles and the Earth

A **cycle** is a sequence of events that repeats. Some cycles repeat over relatively short periods. Other cycles may occur over millions of years. On Earth, the water cycle, carbon cycle, and energy cycle all work together to maintain a dynamic planet.

A The Water Cycle

Of the many cycles that happen on Earth, the **water cycle** is the one you probably notice most, especially when it rains or snows.

Most of Earth's water is in liquid form in the oceans. When the sun shines on the ocean, or on any body of water, it causes some of the water to evaporate, thus becoming water vapor, the gaseous phase of water. As water vapor rises into the atmosphere, it cools; and when water vapor cools, it condenses to form clouds. As the clouds cool further, rain begins to fall, or, depending on the temperature, it snows.

The rain falls to Earth. If rain flows over the ground and into a body of water, it is called *runoff*. Runoff flows into streams and rivers and eventually back to the sea. Water can also soak into the ground where it might be stored as groundwater in the small spaces between particles of soil, sand, and rock. It moves slowly, but eventually flows back to the ocean.

Some of the water evaporates again quickly or is breathed out by the leaves of plants in a process called **transpiration.** Scientists who study the hydrosphere call these processes **evapotranspiration.**

When water returns to the oceans, one turn of the water cycle is complete. The energy of the Sun drives the water cycle. All Earth's water, whether fresh or salt, has moved through this water cycle millions of times, over millions of years. Water is never created or destroyed—only changed.

1.3

B KEY IDEA

The water cycle, the carbon cycle, and the energy cycle all involve interactions among the four spheres of Earth.

C KEY VOCABULARY

- cycle
- water cycle
- evapotranspiration
- carbon cycle
- energy cycle
- solar energy
- geothermal energy
- tidal energy

E WATER cycles through the Earth system in solid, liquid, and gas forms, but the total amount of water remains relatively constant.

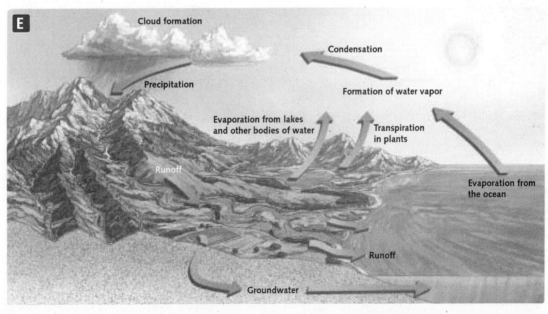

E

Cloud formation

Condensation

Precipitation

Formation of water vapor

Evaporation from lakes and other bodies of water

Transpiration in plants

Evaporation from the ocean

Runoff

Runoff

Groundwater

Mathematics

Reading in mathematics is different from reading in history, literature, or science. A math lesson has few words but instead illustrates math concepts using numbers, symbols, formulas, equations, diagrams, and word problems. Use the following strategies, and the lesson on the next page, to help you better understand your mathematics textbook.

A Scan the **title** and **headings** to see which math concepts you will learn about.

B Read **explanations** carefully. Sometimes a concept is explained in more than one way to make sure you understand it.

C Look for **special features** such as study or technology tips. These provide more help or information.

D Pay attention to **graphic aids** such as diagrams, charts, or tables. Visuals help you picture the information presented in the text.

E Study any **worked-out solutions** to sample problems. These are the key to understanding how to do the homework assignment.

| MARK IT UP ⟩ Use the strategies above and the mathematics lesson on page 391 to answer the following questions.

1. What is the title of the lesson? _____

   _____

2. Circle the formula for finding the area of a square.

3. Draw a star next to the technology tip that appears on the page.

4. Draw a box around the graphic aid that shows you how to calculate the volume of a cube.

5. What is the topic of the real-life word problem? _____

   _____

   _____

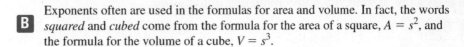

Exponents often are used in the formulas for area and volume. In fact, the words *squared* and *cubed* come from the formula for the area of a square, $A = s^2$, and the formula for the volume of a cube, $V = s^3$.

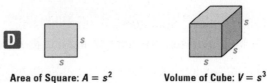

Area of Square: $A = s^2$ **Volume of Cube:** $V = s^3$

Units of area, such as square feet, ft^2, can be written using a second power. Units of volume, such as cubic centimeters, cm^3, can be written using a third power.

EXAMPLE 5 *Making a Table*

You can find the volume of cubes that have edge lengths of 1 inch, 2 inches, 3 inches, 4 inches, and 5 inches by using the formula $V = s^3$.

Edge, s	1	2	3	4	5
s^3	1^3	2^3	3^3	4^3	5^3
Volume, V	1 in.^{3}	8 in.^{3}	27 in.^{3}	64 in.^{3}	125 in.^{3}

EXAMPLE 6 *Finding Volume*

Aquarium

The aquarium has the shape of a cube. Each edge is 2.5 feet long.

a. Find the volume in cubic feet.

b. How many gallons of water will the cubic aquarium hold? Convert to liquid volume, where one cubic foot holds 7.48 gallons.

2.5 ft

2.5 ft

2.5 ft

SOLUTION

a. $V = s^3$ Write formula for volume.

$\quad = 2.5^3$ Substitute 2.5 for s.

$\quad = 15.625$ Evaluate power.

▶ The volume of the aquarium is 15.625 ft^3.

b. $V = 15.625$ ft^3 $(7.48$ gal/1 ft$^3)$ Write conversion factor.

$\quad = 116.875$ gal   Multiply.

▶ A 15.625 cubic foot aquarium will hold 116.875 gallons of water.

STUDENT HELP

▸ **KEYSTROKE HELP**
Your calculator may have a y^x key or a $\wedge$ key that you can use to evaluate powers.

Reading an Application

To get a part-time job, a learner's permit, or to register for classes at the local community center, you will have to fill out an application. Being able to understand the format of an application will help you fill it out correctly. Use the following strategies and the sample on the next page to help you understand any application.

A **Begin at the top.** Scan the application to understand the different sections.

B Look for special **instructions for filling out** the application.

C Note any **request for materials** that must be included with the application.

D Pay attention to **optional sections,** or those **sections you don't have to fill in.**

E Look for difficult or confusing words or abbreviations. Look them up in a dictionary or ask someone what they mean.

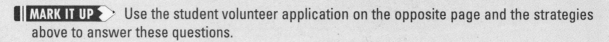 **MARK IT UP** Use the student volunteer application on the opposite page and the strategies above to answer these questions.

1. Underline the part of the application that tells you where to send the application.

2. If you are less than 18 years of age, what other items must you submit with the application?

_____

3. Draw a star next to the section of the application that you do not have to fill out.

4. Circle the section of the application where you describe when you can volunteer.

5. **ASSESSMENT PRACTICE** Circle the letter of the correct answer.
   What should be written in the Reference section of the application?
   A. your name
   B. your skills and interests
   C. the name of a friend, neighbor, relative, or employer
   D. your schedule

A # Greenville Public Library
Student Volunteer Application

Complete and sign the application. Please print or type. Send to Mr. Reid N. Starry, Director, Greenville Public Library, 148 Grove Street, Greenville, OH 44121 **B**

PERSONAL DATA

Name

Address

City   State   Zip

Telephone

Volunteers under 18 years old must obtain parent or guardian permission. (You must be at least 14 to volunteer.) **C**

Age   Current school

Current grade   ☐ 9   ☐ 10   ☐ 11   ☐ 12

VOLUNTEER INFORMATION   (Answers to this section are optional.) **D**

Why do you want to volunteer?

How did you hear about Greenville Public Library's Volunteer Program?

Have you ever previously held a volunteer position?   ☐ Yes   ☐ No

If yes, explain your duties.

SCHEDULE   Indicate days and times you would like to volunteer.

☐ Monday   ☐ Tuesday   ☐ Wednesday   ☐ Thursday   ☐ Friday

☐ Saturday   ☐ Sunday

☐ 9 A.M.–12 P.M.   ☐ 12–3 P.M.   ☐ 3–6 P.M.   ☐ 6–9 P.M.

SKILLS AND INTERESTS   Do you have any computer skills?   ☐ Yes   ☐ No

If yes, explain.

Please check the volunteer duties that interest you most.

☐ assisting with children's programs   ☐ doing clerical work

☐ arranging magazines   ☐ calling patrons with ILLs

☐ setting up for special events   ☐ repairing damaged books

☐ shelving books, DVDs, CDs, videos   ☐ making covers for new books

☐ creating seasonal displays   ☐ maintaining bulletin boards

E ☐ showing the facilities to new patrons   ☐ other

REFERENCE   Provide a personal or a professional reference:

First name

Last name

Telephone

To the best of my knowledge, I certify that the information on this application is true.

Signature

Reading a Public Notice

Public notices can tell you about events in your community and give you valuable information about safety. When you read a public notice, follow these tips. Each tip relates to a specific part of the notice on the opposite page.

A Read the notice's **title,** if it has one. The title often gives the main idea or purpose of the notice.

B See if there is a logo, credit, or other way of telling **who created the notice.**

C Ask yourself, **"Who should read this notice?"** If the information in it might be important to you or someone you know, then you should pay attention to it.

D Look for **instructions**—things the notice is asking or telling you to do.

E Examine **illustrations** or other **graphics** in the notice. Think about how the text and the images are related.

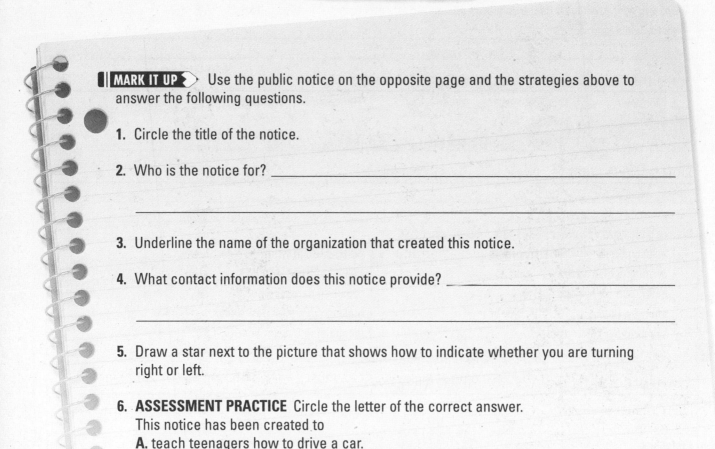

MARK IT UP Use the public notice on the opposite page and the strategies above to answer the following questions.

1. Circle the title of the notice.

2. Who is the notice for? _____

   _____

3. Underline the name of the organization that created this notice.

4. What contact information does this notice provide? _____

   _____

5. Draw a star next to the picture that shows how to indicate whether you are turning right or left.

6. **ASSESSMENT PRACTICE** Circle the letter of the correct answer.
   This notice has been created to
   A. teach teenagers how to drive a car.
   B. inform cyclists about how to ride a bicycle safely.
   C. notify community residents about temporary road closings.
   D. persuade local leaders to create a bike path.

A Rules of the Road for Cyclists

C Follow these rules when you are bicycling in our area.

Be Visible

D **Obey Traffic Signs and Signals:**
They apply to you as well as to drivers.
For example, don't go straight in a lane marked "turn only."

E **Don't Ride Against Traffic:**
Motorists may not see you on the wrong side of the road.

Use Hand Signals:
These let drivers know what you plan to do.
Be polite—and be safer, too!

Ride Defensively

Watch for Vehicles:
Cars and trucks may pull out suddenly.

D **Don't Weave Between Parked Cars:**
Drivers may not see you as you move back into traffic.

Protect Yourself:
Local laws require you to wear a helmet while cycling.
If you are riding at night, your bike must have a headlight and a rear reflector.

Thank you for being a courteous cyclist!

B Buena Vista County Parks Department   (888) 555-1234   www.buenavistacounty.az.gov/parksdept
Para los hispanohablantes, llame por favor a (888) 555-1234.

Reading a Web Page

When you research information for a report or project, you may use the World Wide Web. Once you find the site you want, the strategies below will help you find the facts and details you need. Look at the sample Web page on the right as you read each of the strategies.

A Notice the page's **Web address,** or URL. Write down the Web address if you think you might return to the page at another time or if you need to add it to a list of sources.

B Read the **title** of the page. The title usually tells you what topics the page covers.

C Look for **menu bars** along the top, bottom, or side of the page. These guide you to other parts of the site that may be useful.

D Notice any **links** to other parts of the site or to related pages. Links are often underlined words.

E Many sites have a link that allows you to **contact** the creators with questions or feedback.

F Use a **search feature** to quickly find out whether a certain kind of information you want to locate appears anywhere on the site.

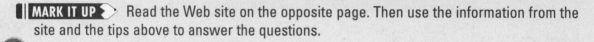 **MARK IT UP** Read the Web site on the opposite page. Then use the information from the site and the tips above to answer the questions.

1. Circle the Web address.

2. Put a check mark next to NASA's search feature.

3. Circle the link you would click on to go to other NASA Web sites.

4. Who is the author of the page? _____

5. **ASSESSMENT PRACTICE** Circle the letter of the correct answer.
   What is the lead story on this Web page about?
   A. employment opportunities with NASA
   B. a new childen's program about space
   C. future plans for exploring Mars
   D. an exhibit of a model spacecraft

L-Net

Back | Forward | Reload | Home | Images | Print | Security | Stop

Location: http://www.nasa.gov/ **A**

June 12, 2001

Text Only Version

NASA's Vision
(*Flash* movie)

"NASA is deeply committed to spreading the unique knowledge that flows from its aeronautics and space research..."

Read NASA Administrator Daniel S. Goldin's welcome letter, bio and speeches.

Welcome to NASA Web

Do you dream of exploring space or working for NASA? If so, avoid black holes and drugs. You decide.

Navigating NASA's Strategic Enterprises

C

Aerospace Technology

Biological and Physical Research

Earth Science

Human Exploration and Development of Space

Space Science

NASA for Kids

More About NASA:

Doing Business with NASA

Educational Resources

Freedom of Information Act

History

Jobs and Internships

NASA Technology Portal

News and Information

Organization and Subject Index

Project Home Pages

Research Opportunities

Scientific and Technical Information

See a Launch

NASA

international SPACE STATION

IT'S ABOUT LIFE ON EARTH

B ### NASA's Starship 2040 Touring US With Vision of Future Passenger Travel

NASA's newest "space" vehicle has docked on Capitol Hill, in Washington, DC, and thrown open its airlocks, inviting the public to tour a passenger spacecraft as it might look a short four decades from now. Although Starship 2040 isn't designed to escape Earth's gravity, NASA's space transportation officials expect the experience to send visitors' imaginations straight into orbit. Housed in a 48-foot trailer, the traveling exhibit is designed to share NASA's vision of what commercial spaceflight might be like within the next 40 years. During the free tour, visitors board the "ship" and move through a fully realized mock-up of the control, passenger and engineering compartments, where they'll gain insight into technologies that eventually will make such an out-of-this-world experience as routine as air travel. The exhibit will bring the future to more locations in the United States in the coming months. (Full Story) (06/12/2001)

today@nasa.gov

Highlights of President's 2002 Budget for NASA **NEW**

Top Search Terms

NASA TV Schedule

See the Space Station

Interested in the latest information NASA has to offer? Then take a look at today@nasa.gov. This on-line newsletter, updated daily, contains the latest news about NASA science and technology.

- NASA's Starship 2040 Touring US With Vision of Future Passenger Travel
- A Change of Seasons on Saturn
- Where no Telescope Has Gone Before

D ### Cool NASA Websites

 Mars Odyssey

 NASA Webcasts

 Space Station People

 Space in My Life

Other Cool NASA Websites

C [Frequently Asked Questions] [Hot Topics] [Multimedia Gallery] [NASA Television] [Text Only Version]
[NASA Privacy Statement, Disclaimer, and Accessibility Certification] [Site Maps]

Author: Bvia Thompson **E**
Responsible NASA Official: Brian Dunbar
Site Maintainer: K.F. Chow
Comments and Questions
Last Updated: June 12, 2001

 SEARCH the NASA web **F**

FIRSTGOV
Your First Click to the U.S. Government

Reading Technical Directions

Reading technical directions will help you understand how to use the products you buy. Use the following tips to help you read a variety of technical directions.

A Look carefully at any **diagrams** or **other images** of the product.

B **Read all the directions** carefully at least once before using the product.

C Notice **headings** or **rules** that separate one section from another.

D Look for **numbers** or **letters** that give the steps in sequence.

E Watch for **warnings** or **notes** with more information.

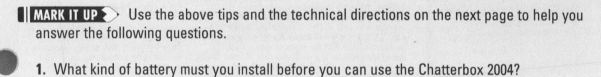 **MARK IT UP** Use the above tips and the technical directions on the next page to help you answer the following questions.

1. What kind of battery must you install before you can use the Chatterbox 2004?

   _____

2. What will happen if you put the battery in backwards? _____

   _____

3. What should you do if the Chatterbox 2004 does not turn on? Circle the answer on the next page.

4. What steps must you follow to turn the device off? Underline them on the next page.

5. **ASSESSMENT PRACTICE** Circle the letter of the correct answer.
   Which of the following do you NOT have to do to set the time and date?
   A. Delete CLOCK.
   B. Highlight PREFERENCES.
   C. Use the UP navigation button.
   D. Go to the MAIN MENU.

Communicator Instructions

Welcome! Here is your user's guide for the Chatterbox 2004. After you follow the instructions for getting started, you will be ready to send messages to an e-mail address, to a pager, or to another personal interactive communicator.

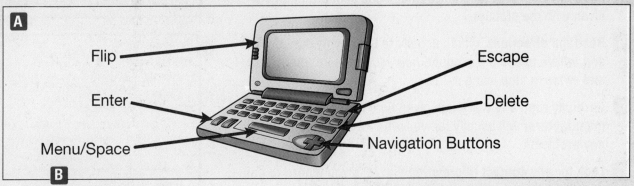

C **A. Installing Batteries**

1. Hold the Chatterbox personal interactive communicator face down.

D 2. Move the slide latch toward the battery door.

3. Now slide the battery door in the direction that the arrow points.

4. Lift the door.

5. Insert a single AA battery in the battery compartment. Make sure the positive (+) and negative (−) markings on the battery match the markings on the diagram in the battery compartment.

6. Replace the battery door cover and lock.

E NOTE: Putting the battery in backwards will erase all messages.

B. Turning the Device On

1. Open the flip.

2. Press any key. The Chatterbox sounds an alert and then displays the Status screen.

3. Using the Status screen, press any key. The MAIN MENU will appear.

4. Select a menu item.

5. If you do not select a menu item, let the Chatterbox go automatically into standby mode.

NOTE: If the Chatterbox does not turn on, refer to Troubleshooting Tips, page 27.

C. Turning the Device Off

1. Go to the MAIN MENU.

2. Press the UP or DOWN navigation button.

3. When you see the highlighted words POWER OFF, press ENTER.

4. Highlight YES.

5. Now press ENTER again.

D. Setting the Time and Date

1. Go to the MAIN MENU.

2. Press the UP or DOWN navigation button to highlight PREFERENCES.

3. Press ENTER.

4. Press the UP navigation button to highlight SET TIME AND DATE and press ENTER.

5. Press the UP or DOWN navigation button to set the correct hour, minutes, and date.

6. Press ENTER to save the settings when you have finished.

Product Information: Directions for Use

Many of the products you buy come with instructions that tell you how to use them correctly. Directions for use may appear on the product itself, on its packaging, or on a separate insert. Learning to read and follow directions for use is important for your safety. As you read each strategy below, look at the sample.

A Read any **headings** to find out what kinds of information are given with the product.

B Read the **directions,** which usually tell you *why, how, when,* and *where* to use the product, *how much* to use, *how often,* and *when* to stop using it.

C Carefully read any **warnings** given with the product. The manufacturer will usually tell you what to do if you experience any problems.

D Look for any **contact information** that tells you where to call or write if you have a question about the product.

AcneAid   **A**

Active Ingredient	**Purpose**
salicylic acid 2%..............	Acne medication

Use for the teatment of acne

C **Warnings**

For external use only.

Flammable, keep away from open fire or flame.

When using this product

- Avoid contact with eyes. If contact occurs, flush immediately with water.
- Do not use with other topical acne medications. Use of this product at the same time may cause skin irritation.
- Discontinue use if extreme peeling, dryness, or irritation occurs.

Keep out of reach of children. If accidentally swallowed, seek immediate medical help or contact a Poison Control Center.

Directions

B
- Clean skin thoroughly before you apply the medication. Wash with warm water.
- Apply a thin layer over the affected area.
- Begin treatment with one application daily. Gradually increase to two or three times daily as needed or if recommended by a doctor.
- Continue treatment as directed until acne symptoms are lessened or eliminated.

Inactive Ingredients: purified water, fragrance, glycerin, sodium citrate, sodium hydroxide, alcohol, aloe gel, methylparaben, propylene glycol

D **For further information,** call the AcneAid hotline at *1-888-555-1234.*

MARK IT UP Read the product directions to help you answer these questions.

1. According to the directions, what should you do first?

_____

_____

2. Put a star next to the active ingredient in AcneAid.

3. What should you do if you accidentally swallow or get AcneAid in your eyes? Circle the answers.

4. Underline the number you can call if you have a question about AcneAid.

5. **ASSESSMENT PRACTICE** Circle the letter of the correct answer.
   What should you do before you apply the medication?
   A. Clean your skin thoroughly.
   B. Heat the medication.
   C. Contact a doctor.
   D. Use another topical acne medication.

Reading a Bus Schedule

Knowing how to read a bus schedule accurately will help you get where you need to go—on time! Look at the example of a bus schedule as you read each tip below.

A Read the **title** to learn what the schedule covers.

B Look for **labels** that show **dates** or **days of the week** to find out how the weekly or daily schedule works.

C Study **place labels** so that you know what stops are listed on the schedule.

D Look for **expressions of time** to know what hours or minutes are listed on the schedule.

E Pay attention to the **organization** of the information. Read across the row to see when a bus will reach each location.

A Bus Route 77: Pine Street   **B** Weekend Mornings—WESTBOUND

C Porter Square Station	Pine & Elm	Mercy Hospital	Westerly Mall	Pine & Aspen	Lakeview Hills Station
5:15 A.M.	5:23 A.M.	5:28 A.M.	5:31 A.M.	5:38 A.M. **D**	5:42 A.M.
6:15	6:23	6:28	6:31	6:38	6:42
7:15	7:23	7:28	7:31	7:38	7:42
7:47	7:55	8:00	8:04	8:11	8:15
8:15	8:23	8:28	8:31	8:38	8:42
8:47	8:55	9:00	9:04	9:11	9:15
E 9:15	9:23	9:28	9:31	9:38	9:42
9:47	9:55	10:00	10:04	10:11	10:15
10:20	10:28	10:33	10:39	10:46	10:52
10:40	10:48	10:53	10:59	11:06	11:12
11:20	11:28	11:33	11:39	11:46	11:52

MARK IT UP > Answer the following questions using the bus schedule and the strategies on this page.

1. Circle the name of one stop on this route.

2. How many buses arrive at Lakeview Hills Station before 9 A.M.? _____

3. If you took the 9:28 A.M. bus from Mercy Hospital, at what time would you arrive at the corner of Pine and Aspen? _____

4. **ASSESSMENT PRACTICE** If you lived near the bus stop at Pine and Elm streets, how many different westbound buses could you catch between 9 and 11 A.M.?
   A. one   **B.** two   **C.** three   **D.** four

Test Preparation Strategies

In this section, you'll find strategies and practice to help you with many different kinds of standardized tests. The strategies apply to questions based on long and short readings as well as questions about charts, graphs, and product labels. You'll also find examples and practice for revising-and-editing tests and writing tests. Applying the strategies to the practice materials and thinking through the answers will help you succeed in many formal testing situations.

Test Preparation Strategies

You can prepare for tests in several ways. First, study and understand the content that will be on the test. Second, learn as many test-taking techniques as you can. These techniques will help you better understand the questions and how to answer them. Following are some general suggestions for preparing for and taking tests. In the next parts, you'll find more detailed suggestions, together with test-taking practice.

Successful Test Taking

 Study Content Throughout the Year

1. **Master the content of your language arts class.** The best way to study for tests is to read, understand, and review the content of your language arts class. Read your daily assignments carefully. Study the notes that you have taken in class. Participate in class discussions. Work with classmates in small groups to help one another learn. You might trade writing assignments and comment on your classmates' work.

2. **Use your textbook for practice.** Your textbook includes many different types of questions. Some may ask you to talk about a story you just read. Others may ask you to figure out what's wrong with a sentence or how to make a paragraph sound better. Try answering these questions out loud and in writing. This type of practice can make taking a test much easier.

3. **Learn how to understand the information in charts, maps, and graphic organizers.** One type of test question may ask you to look at a graphic organizer, such as a spider map, and explain something about the information you see there. Another type of question may ask you to look at a map to find a particular place, such as the Arctic setting of the story "To Build a Fire." You'll find charts, maps, and graphic organizers to study in your literature textbook. You'll also find charts, maps, and graphs in your science, mathematics, and social studies textbooks. When you look at these, ask yourself, What information is being presented and why is it important?

4. **Practice taking tests.** Use copies of tests you have taken in the past or in other classes for practice. Every test has a time limit, so set a timer for 15 or 20 minutes and then begin your practice. Try to finish the test in the time you've given yourself.

☑ Reading Check

In what practical way can your textbooks help you prepare for a test?

---

5. **Talk about test-taking experiences.** After you've taken a classroom test or quiz, talk about it with your teacher and classmates. Which types of questions were the hardest to understand? What made them difficult? Which questions seemed easiest, and why? When you share test-taking techniques with your classmates, everyone can become a successful test taker.

Use Strategies During the Test

1. **Read the directions carefully.** You can't be a successful test taker unless you know exactly what you are expected to do. Look for key words and phrases, such as *circle the best answer, write a paragraph,* or *choose the word that best completes each sentence.*

2. **Learn how to read test questions.** Test questions can sometimes be difficult to figure out. They may include unfamiliar language or be written in an unfamiliar way. Try rephrasing the question in a simpler way using words you understand. Always ask yourself, What type of information does this question want me to provide?

3. **Pay special attention when using a separate answer sheet.** If you accidentally skip a line on an answer sheet, all the rest of your answers may be wrong! Try one or more of the following techniques:

   - Use a ruler on the answer sheet to make sure you are placing your answers on the correct line.

   - After every five answers, check to make sure you're on the right line.

   - Each time you turn a page of the test booklet, check to make sure the number of the question is the same as the number of the answer line on the answer sheet.

   - If the answer sheet has circles, fill them in neatly. A stray pencil mark might cause the scoring machine to count the answer as incorrect.

4. **If you're not sure of the answer, make your best guess.** Unless you've been told that there is a penalty for guessing, choose the answer that you think is likeliest to be correct.

5. **Keep track of the time.** Answering all the questions on a test usually results in a better score. That's why finishing the test is important. Keep track of the time you have left. At the beginning of the test, figure out how many questions you will have to answer by the halfway point in order to finish in the time given.

☑ **Reading Check**
What are at least two good ways to avoid skipping lines on an answer sheet?

Understand Types of Test Questions

Most tests include two types of questions: multiple choice and open-ended. Specific strategies will help you understand and correctly answer each type of question.

A multiple-choice question has two parts. The first part is the question itself, called the stem. The second part is a series of possible answers. Usually four possible answers are provided, and only one of them is correct. Your task is to choose the correct answer. Here are some strategies to help you do just that.

1. Read and think about each question carefully before looking at the possible answers.

2. Pay close attention to key words in the question. For example, look for the word *not,* as in "Which of the following is not a cause of the conflict in this story?"

3. Read and think about all of the possible answers before making your choice.

4. Reduce the number of choices by eliminating any answers you know are incorrect. Then, think about why some of the remaining choices might also be incorrect.

   - If two of the choices are pretty much the same, both are probably wrong.

   - Answers that contain any of the following words are usually incorrect: *always, never, none, all,* and *only.*

5. If you're still unsure about an answer, see if any of the following applies:

   - When one choice is longer and more detailed than the others, it is often the correct answer.

   - When a choice repeats a word that is in the question, it may be the correct answer.

   - When two choices are direct opposites, one of them is likely the correct answer.

   - When one choice includes one or more of the other choices, it is often the correct answer.

   - When a choice includes the word *some* or *often,* it may well be the correct answer.

✔ **Reading Check**
What words in a multiple-choice question probably signal a wrong answer?

- If one of the choices is *All of the above,* make sure that at least two of the other choices seem correct.

- If one of the choices is *None of the above,* make sure that none of the other choices seems correct.

An **open-ended test item** can take many forms. It might ask you to write a word or phrase to complete a sentence. You might be asked to create a chart, draw a map, or fill in a graphic organizer. Sometimes, you will be asked to write one or more paragraphs in response to a writing prompt. Use the following strategies when reading and answering open-ended items:

1. If the item includes directions, read them carefully. Take note of any steps required.

2. Look for key words and phrases in the item as you plan how you will respond. Does the item ask you to identify a cause-and-effect relationship or to compare and contrast two or more things? Are you supposed to provide a sequence of events or make a generalization? Does the item ask you to write an essay in which you state your point of view and then try to persuade others that your view is correct?

3. If you're going to be writing a paragraph or more, plan your answer. Jot down notes and a brief outline of what you want to say before you begin writing.

4. Focus your answer. Don't include everything you can think of, but be sure to include everything the item asks for.

5. If you're creating a chart or drawing a map, make sure your work is as clear as possible.

✔ Reading Check

What are at least three key strategies for answering an open-ended question?

Reading Strategies for Assessment

Find the main idea. Look closely at the title and the first few sentences of the selection. Write what you think this selection will be about.

Notice details and comparisons. Circle the details the author presents about the Fakahatchee Strand. What comparisons does the author make?

Infer meanings. What is a *geyser*?

Reading Test Model
LONG SELECTIONS

DIRECTIONS Here is a selection from *The Orchid Thief,* by Susan Orlean. Read the selection carefully. The notes in the side columns will help you prepare for the kinds of questions that are likely to follow readings like this. You might want to preview the questions on pages 9 and 10 before you begin reading.

"The Fakahatchee Strand" from The Orchid Thief

by Susan Orlean

You would have to want something very badly to go looking for it in the Fakahatchee Strand. The Fakahatchee is a preserve of sixty-three thousand coastal lowland acres in the southwestern corner of Florida, about twenty-five miles south of Naples, in that part of Collier County where satiny lawns and golf courses give way to an ocean of saw grass with edges as sharp as scythes. Part of the Fakahatchee is deep swamp, part is cypress stands, part is wet woods, part is estuarine tidal marsh, and part is parched prairie. The limestone underneath it is six million years old and is capped with hard rock and sand, silt and shell marls, and a grayish-greenish clay. Overall, the Fakahatchee is as flat as a cracker. Ditches and dents fill up fast with oozing groundwater. The woods are dense and lightless. In the open stretches the land unrolls like a smooth grass mat and even small bumps and wrinkles are easy to see. Most of the land is at an elevation of only five or ten feet, and it slopes millimeter by millimeter until it is dead even with the sea. The Fakahatchee has a particular strange and exceptional beauty. The grass prairies in sunlight look like yards of raw silk. The tall, straight palm trunks and the tall, straight cypress trunks shoot up out of the flat land like geysers. It is beautiful the way a Persian carpet is beautiful—thick, intricate, lush, almost monotonous in its richness.

People live in the Fakahatchee and around it, but it is an unmistakably inhospitable place. In 1872 a surveyor made this entry in his field notes: "A pond, surrounded by bay and cypress swamp, impracticable. Pond full of monstrous alligators. Counted fifty and stopped." In fact, the hours I spent in the Fakahatchee retracing Laroche's footsteps were probably the most miserable I have spent in my entire life. The swampy part of the Fakahatchee is hot and wet and buggy and full of cottonmouth snakes and diamondback rattlers and alligators and snapping turtles and poisonous plants and wild hogs and things that stick into you and on you and fly into your nose and eyes. Crossing the swamp is a battle. You can walk through about as easily as you could walk through a car wash. The sinkholes are filled with as much as seven feet of standing water, and around them the air has the slack, drapey weight of wet velvet. Sides of trees look sweaty. Leaves are slick from the humidity. The mud sucks your feet and tries to keep ahold of them; if it fails it will settle for your shoes. The water in the swamp is stained black with tannin from the bark of cypress trees that is so corrosive it can cure leather. Whatever isn't wet in the Fakahatchee is blasted. The sun pounds the treeless prairies. The grass gets so dry that the friction from a car can set it on fire, and the burning grass can engulf the car in flames. The Fakahatchee used to be littered with burned-up cars that had been abandoned by panfried adventurers—a botanist who traveled through in the 1940s recalled in an interview that he was most impressed by the area's variety of squirrels and the number of charred Model T's.

The swamp's stillness and darkness and thickness can rattle your nerves. In 1885 a sailor on a plume-collecting expedition wrote in his diary: "The place looked wild and lonely. About three o'clock it seemed to get on Henry's nerves and we saw him crying, he could not tell us why, he was just plain scared."

Spooky places are usually full of death, but the Fakahatchee is crazy with living things. Birders used to come from as far away as Cuba and leave with enough plumes to decorate thousands of ladies' hats; in the 1800s one group of birders also took home eight tons of birds' eggs. One turn-of-the-

Evaluate quoted information. Would these field notes be a reliable source? Why or why not?

Look for cause-and-effect relationships. What causes cars to catch fire in the Fakahatchee? Circle the cause.

Notice the topic sentences. Key sentences often point to the author's purpose. Circle the topic sentence of the last paragraph.

Make inferences. As you read, ask yourself why things are described as they are. For example, why do you think this area of the swamp is nicknamed the Cathedral?

century traveler wrote that on his journey he found the swamp's abundance marvelous—he caught two hundred pounds of lobsters, which he ate for breakfasts, and stumbled across a rookery where he gathered "quite a supply of cormorant and blue heron eggs, with which I intend to make omelets." That night he had a dinner of fried blue heron and a cabbage-palm heart. In the Fakahatchee there used to be a carpet of lubber grasshoppers so deep that it made driving hazardous, and so many orchids that visitors described their heavy sweet smell as nauseating. On my first walk in the swamp I saw strap lilies and water willows and sumac and bladderwort, and resurrection ferns springing out of a fallen dead tree; I saw oaks and pines and cypress and pop ash and beauty-berry and elderberry and yellow-eyed grass and camphor weed. When I walked in, an owl gave me a lordly look, and when I walked out three tiny alligators skittered across my path. I wandered into a nook in the swamp that was girdled with tall cypress. The rangers call this nook the Cathedral. I closed my eyes and stood in the stillness for a moment hardly breathing, and when I opened my eyes and looked up I saw dozens of bromeliad plants roosting in the branches of almost every tree I could see. The bromeliads were bright red and green and shaped like fright wigs. Some were spider-sized and some were as big as me. The sun shooting through the swamp canopy glanced off their sheeny leaves. Hanging up there on the branches the bromeliads looked not quite like plants. They looked more like a crowd of animals, watching everything that passed their way.

Now answer questions 1 through 6. Base your answers on the passage "The Fakahatchee Strand." Then check yourself by reading through the side column notes.

1 What is the author's purpose for writing about the Fakahatchee Strand?

  A. to show what it is like to be lost there
  B. to point out how unchanged it is
  C. to describe it vividly and fully
  D. to convince people to cultivate the area as farmland

> **Note key words.** The word *purpose* in question 1 tells you what to look for. Avoid answers that identify the purpose of only one part of the selection.

2 Based on this sentence, what is a *geyser?*

  The tall, straight palm trunks and the tall, straight cypress trunks shoot up out of the flat land like geysers.

  E. something that is as flat as a board
  F something that bursts straight out of the ground
  G. something that meanders along the ground
  H. something that hangs straight down to the ground

> **Infer meanings.** Question 2 says that palm and cypress trunks "shoot up out of the flat land." Look for an answer choice with language that is *similar to* this description. Avoid choices with language that is *the opposite of* this description.

3 One major point the author makes is that

  A. the Fakahatchee has a strange and unusual beauty.
  B. people ought to cultivate the rich soil of the Fakahatchee.
  C. the alligators of the Fakahatchee are endangered.
  D. the Fakahatchee is really not a very threatening place.

> **Find main ideas.** This question asks for *one major point.* Watch for answers that are only partially correct or that contain factual errors.

4 The author includes details from the field notes of a surveyor and an interview with a botanist. Such information is likely to be

  E. too subjective to be believable.
  F invalid because it comes from only two authorities.
  G. reliable because it comes from expert observers.
  H. inconclusive because it is outdated.

> **Evaluate quoted information.** Question 4 asks you to judge the usefulness of primary-source material. Has the author quoted from experts on the topic?

5 Which of the following sentences from the selection contains a comparison or contrast?

  A. *You would have to want something very badly to go looking for it in the Fakahatchee Strand.*
  B. *Overall, the Fakahatchee is as flat as a cracker.*
  C. *The sun pounds the treeless prairies.*
  D. *That night he had a dinner of fried blue heron and a cabbage-palm heart.*

> **Note details and comparisons.** Look for an answer that includes two things and a signal word such as *like, as,* or *but.*

Plan your response. Look at what the question asks and plan how to proceed. For this question, you have to first identify the details in the selection that support the author's statement. Then you have to either restate those details in your own words or quote from the selection.

Study the response. Notice how the response includes details and quotations from the selection.

6 One of the author's main points is that the Fakahatchee is "an unmistakably inhospitable place." What information does she use to make her point? Use details from the text to support your conclusion.

Sample short response for question 6:

Although the author shows that the Fakahatchee is "crazy with living things," she points out that it is "an unmistakably inhospitable place" to people. She describes the swamp as "hot and wet and buggy and full of cottonmouth snakes and diamondback rattlers and alligators...." She also notes that the "grass gets so dry that the friction from a car can set it on fire." After reading such details, the reader cannot help but conclude that the Fakahatchee is a deathtrap for humans.

Reading Test Practice
LONG SELECTIONS

DIRECTIONS Now it's time to practice what you've learned about reading test items and choosing the best answers. Read the following selection from Russell Freedman's *Looking Back at Looking Forward: Predicting the Twentieth Century*. Use the side columns to make notes about the important parts of this selection: main ideas, cause and effect, comparisons and contrasts, difficult vocabulary, supporting details, and so on.

from **Looking Back at Looking Forward: Predicting the Twentieth Century**

by Russell Freedman

In the coming century, engineers will control the climate by flicking a switch and turning a dial. Deserts will be transformed into gardens, the polar ice caps will be melted, and the entire earth will enjoy perpetual spring.

Cities in the next century will have skyscrapers a thousand feet tall, boulevards a hundred yards wide, and moving sidewalks for pedestrians. Homes throughout the world will be linked by televised telephones. Trains will speed through pneumatic tubes at a thousand miles an hour, luxury airliners will fly nonstop to any point on earth, and manned spaceships will race off to planets circling distant suns.

The next century? Those predictions were made more than a hundred years ago by the French author Jules Verne, who peered through a keyhole of the future into our own twentieth century with surprising accuracy. As far back as 1865, when passenger-carrying balloons were the most advanced form of aircraft, Verne wrote about a trip to the moon in a rocket-equipped projectile. His story was so convincing that hundreds of people volunteered to ride in the spaceship he had "invented."

While some of Verne's predictions have yet to be realized, many others that seemed fantastic at the time are now established fact. He sent his heroes to the North Pole forty-five years before Robert E. Peary, to the South Pole forty-one years before Roald Amundsen. In an era when city streets were illuminated by gas lamps, he foresaw the widespread use of electricity in everyday life. When oceangoing ships still carried sails, he envisioned an around-the-world voyage in an all-electric submarine. He described airplanes and helicopters when the Wright brothers were still building bicycles. And he wrote about television newscasts before Guglielmo Marconi had even thought of the wireless telegraph.

Verne predicted motion pictures, wirephotos, color photography, recorded books, air conditioners, computers, synthetic materials, condensed foods, prefabricated mass housing, public health programs, air pollution control, and space satellites before any of those things actually existed. He also prophesied guided missiles that could annihilate cities, lethal fallout that could make large areas uninhabitable, and the modern totalitarian state, with its secret police and enforced regimentation.

Verne did not originate what we now call "science fiction." Stories about amazing inventions, discoveries, and journeys go all the way back to ancient times, yet those early tales were usually based more on fantasy than on fact. Verne was the first author to write an entire series of stories dramatizing the scientific and technological accomplishments of an era and predicting the future outcome of those accomplishments. He popularized such stories and established them as a special branch of fiction. For those reasons, he is usually considered the founder of modern science fiction.

When he first started writing his series of "Extraordinary Journeys" during the 1860s, the achievements of explorers, inventors, and scientists were inspiring widespread popular interest in those regions of the earth that were still unmapped and in the powers of science and technology to change people's lives. Verne's novels focusing on these developments became wildly popular. His books were translated into dozens of languages. They were read not only by the young people for whom they were originally intended, but by enthusiastic readers of all ages and in every walk of life. Verne's name became a household word in France and in places like Russia and the United States, where some of his stories take place and where many of the accomplishments he envisioned would, in fact, be realized.

One of Verne's devoted fans was a British youngster named Herbert George Wells, who grew up during the 1870s when Verne was writing some of his best-known stories. During the 1890s, Wells took his place beside the French author as another master of science fiction. Like Verne, he sent his heroes from the earth to the moon. And he predicted many scientific and technological developments, such as television, intercontinental airplanes, air-conditioned cities, and nuclear warfare.

Wells was the first author to write about a time machine, an "invention" that could carry its operator to any point in the future or the past. His short novel *The Time Machine* (1895) describes an imaginary world in the distant future. And he was the first to imagine an invasion of the earth by aliens from another planet. *The War of the Worlds* (1898) describes with hair-raising realism how Martians—superior beings with super-advanced technology—land in England and lay waste to turn-of-the-century London.

Forty years after its publication, the novel was dramatized on the radio by Orson Welles, who changed the setting to New Jersey and presented the story in the form of news flashes and on-the-scene interviews. Welles's broadcast seemed so nightmarishly real that hundreds of listeners panicked and fled into the countryside, seeking places to hide from the invading Martians.

H. G. Wells was often called the "English Jules Verne," a term that made him furious. While he had read Verne's books avidly as a boy, he insisted that there was a world of difference between himself and the French writer. Verne emphatically agreed. Neither man regarded himself as the French or English equivalent of the other.

Verne's aim was to convey scientific and technological information by means of an exciting story. He narrated his heroes' adventures with documentary precision, describing in minute detail the methods they use and the conditions they encounter. Wells, in contrast, gave his imagination a much wider latitude and was not so scrupulous about the factual basis of his stories.

Verne's work dealt with the actual possibilities of invention and discovery. "He wrote and believed and told that this thing or that could be done, which was not at that time done," said Wells in his introduction to his own *Collected Scientific Romances*. "He helped his readers to imagine it done and to realize what fun, excitement, or mischief might ensue. Many of his inventions have 'come true.' But these stories of mine collected here do not pretend to deal with possible things; they are exercises of the imagination in a quite different field."

Verne aimed for absolute realism. He tried to avoid saying anything in his stories that could not be justified by the science of the time. He crammed his stories with technical explanations that made it easier for the reader to accept his imaginative plots. A tale about a trip to the moon was filled with the same attention to detail as a story about a train trip from Paris to Marseilles.

Wells, on the other hand, was less interested in strict scientific realism than in exploring the effects of science and technology on human behavior. He disposed of the scientific machinery and gadgetry quickly in his books, asking the reader to suspend disbelief, if only for a moment, so that he could get on with his story.

In *The Time Machine*, Wells does not offer any explanation of how that machine functions or the manner in which his hero, the Time Traveller, managed to build it. His science fiction tales are not so much about the advance of science as about the reaction of human beings to that advance. *The Time Machine* gave Wells an opportunity to imagine the future evolution of the human race, while *The War of the Worlds* allowed him to speculate on the behavior of humans in the face of utter catastrophe.

After publishing several "scientific romances," as he called his science fiction, Wells turned from the fantastic to the realistic. He began to write satirical novels about contemporary British life, social and political commentary, and, later, popularized accounts of history and science. Verne also wrote popular history, but he remained primarily a writer of science fiction and a prophet of the future until his death in 1905.

Now answer questions 1 through 7 . Base your answers on the excerpt from *Looking Back at Looking Forward*.

1 What is the author's primary purpose for comparing and contrasting the writing of Jules Verne and H. G. Wells?

A. to show that their works did not differ significantly
B. to show in what ways their works differed
C. to convince readers that Verne was the better writer
D. to entertain readers

2 Read this sentence from the passage.

> Deserts will be transformed into gardens, the polar ice caps will be melted, and the entire earth will enjoy perpetual spring.

What does *perpetual* mean?

E. instant
F. constant
G. temporary
H. late

3 The author compares Verne's science fiction "predictions" with

A. what actually occurred during Verne's lifetime
B. similar predictions made by dozens of other science fiction writers
C. what actually occurred during the twentieth century
D. Arthur C. Clarke's predictions

4 In 1938, what caused hundreds of Americans to flee in panic from their cities?

E. a fear of invading Martians
F. a prediction of lethal fallout occurring
G. news that London was under attack
H. the premiere of H. G. Wells's *The Time Machine*

5 Which method of organization does the author primarily use in this excerpt?

A. chronological order

B. spatial order

C. cause-and-effect

D. compare-and-contrast

6 According to Freedman, what made H. G. Wells furious?

E. being confused with Orson Welles

F. being regarded as the English equivalent of Jules Verne

G. not being acknowledged as the inspiration for many new scientific inventions

H. being unable to prevent the changes Orson Welles made to *The War of the Worlds*

7 Based on what you have read in this essay, was H. G. Wells an "English Jules Verne"? Use details and information from the piece to support your answer.

_____

_____

_____

_____

_____

_____

_____

_____

_____

_____

_____

_____

THINKING IT THROUGH

The notes in the side columns will help you think through your answers. See the key at the bottom of the page.

1 What is the author's primary purpose for comparing and contrasting the writing of Jules Verne and H. G. Wells?

A. to show that their works did not differ significantly
B. to show in what ways their works differed
C. to convince readers that Verne was the better writer
D. to entertain readers

> Look at both A and B. Notice that these two answers are exact opposites. That's a clue that one of them is probably the correct answer.

2 Read this sentence from the passage.

> **Deserts will be transformed into gardens, the polar ice caps will be melted, and the entire earth will enjoy perpetual spring.**

What does *perpetual* mean?

E. instant
F. constant
G. temporary
H. late

> Eliminate answers that don't fit the context of the sentence. Examine each of the four choices. Does the sentence say that the change will be instant? temporary? late? *Constant* is the only choice that makes sense.

3 The author compares Verne's science fiction "predictions" with

A. what actually occurred during Verne's lifetime
B. similar predictions made by dozens of other science fiction writers
C. what actually occurred during the twentieth century
D. Arthur C. Clarke's predictions

> Skim the reading looking for the key word *predictions*. Reread that section closely to get the the answer.

4 In 1938, what caused hundreds of Americans to flee in panic from their cities?

E. a fear of invading Martians
F. a prediction of lethal fallout occurring
G. news that London was under attack
H. the premiere of H. G. Wells's *The Time Machine*

> Eliminate answers that just don't make sense. Choice F talks about fallout, but nuclear weapons would not be invented until the middle 1940s. Choice G is unlikely because London is too far away for Americans to feel threatened by an attack there. Choice H is easily eliminated. Would Americans really flee their cities just because of a movie premiere?

Answers:
1.B, 2.F, 3.C, 4.E

5 Which method of organization does the author primarily use in this excerpt?

A. chronological order

B. spatial order

C. cause-and-effect

D. compare-and-contrast

6 According to Freedman, what made H. G. Wells furious?

E. being confused with Orson Welles

F. being regarded as the English equivalent of Jules Verne

G. not being acknowledged as the inspiration for many new scientific inventions

H. being unable to prevent the changes Orson Welles made to *The War of the Worlds*

7 Based on what you have read in this essay, was H. G. Wells an "English Jules Verne"? Use details and information from the piece to support your answer.

Based on the information provided by Russell Freedman, it would be a mistake to characterize Wells as an "English Jules Verne." According to Freedman, Verne wrote "to convey scientific and technological information by means of an exciting story." Wells, on the other hand, was more interested in "exploring the effects of science and technology on human behavior." The two writers' aims differed significantly, and consequently, their works differed as well. What's more, as Freedman notes, "Neither man regarded himself as the French or English equivalent of the other."

Reading Test Model
SHORT SELECTIONS

DIRECTIONS This reading selection is just two paragraphs long. The strategies you have just used can also help you with this shorter selection. As you read the selection, respond to the notes in the side column.

When you've finished reading, you'll find two multiple-choice questions. Again, use the side column notes to help you understand what each question is asking for and why each answer is the correct one.

Sunken Treasure

Two seventeenth-century Spanish ships, the *Atocha* and the *Margarita*, were the source of one of the richest sunken treasures ever found. In 1622, they were headed from America to Spain, loaded with half a billion dollars in gold, silver, and jewels. They never reached their destination. Both ships sank off the coast of Florida during a hurricane. Their precious cargo was scattered over the ocean floor.

For centuries no one could find the ships or their treasure. Finally, in 1985, a team of divers got lucky. In addition to the treasure, they recovered tools, weapons, tableware, and navigational equipment. Although not gold, these everyday objects were of great value to historians.

1. What is the main idea of the passage?
   A. Spanish ships carried valuable riches.
   B. Vacationers can find treasure on beaches.
   C. Two sunken Spanish ships were found, and their valuable shipments recovered.
   D. To historians, everyday objects are as valuable as gold.

2. Which word is closest in meaning to the word *cargo* in the first paragraph?
   E. mail
   F. contents
   G. tools
   H. jewels

Read the title. What does the title tell you the graph is about?

Read the key. What do the different bars represent?

Read the labels. Which labels are on the horizontal axis? Which are on the vertical axis? What conclusions can you draw from analyzing this graph?

Answer Strategies

Find the key word. The word *LEAST* is the key to this answer. Look for the smallest number of tickets sold.

Analyze the graph and draw conclusions. Read the graph for increases over time.

Understand the key words. The key words in this question are *twice as popular.* Look for gains that are double over time.

DIRECTIONS Some test questions ask you to analyze a visual rather than read a passage. Analyze this graph and answer the questions that follow.

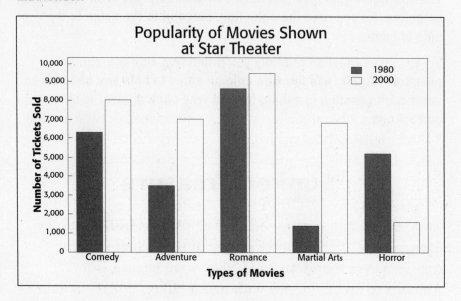

3 If you owned Star Theater in 2001, which type of movie would you be LEAST likely to show?

A. comedy

B. romance

C. martial arts

D. horror

4 Which type of movie gained most in popularity between 1980 and 2000?

E. comedy

F. adventure

G. romance

H. martial arts

5 Which type of movie was twice as popular in 2000 as it was in 1980?

A. adventure

B. romance

C. martial arts

D. horror

Reading Test Practice
SHORT SELECTIONS

DIRECTIONS Use the following to practice your skills. Read the paragraph about the Hubble Space Telescope and circle the key ideas. Then answer the multiple-choice questions that follow.

The Hubble Space Telescope

In 1990, the National Aeronautics and Space Administration (NASA) launched an orbiting observatory called the Hubble Space Telescope. This gigantic reflecting telescope spans 94 inches across. What makes the Hubble special is that it orbits 380 miles above Earth, capturing its images from beyond the distorting effects of Earth's atmosphere. Controlled by radio, it observes and records data, transmitting images of the far reaches of the universe. The Hubble relies largely on four instruments, three of which are cameras of various kinds. The fourth, called a spectrograph, analyzes the light emitted by distant stars. Although a remarkable feat of engineering, the Hubble has required at least two shuttle visits by NASA repair crews to get the telescope running properly.

1 To find out how large the telescope is, what is the BEST way to read this passage?

    A. slowly, paying attention to every detail

    B. several times in order to get the facts straight

    C. quickly, scanning for a specific detail

    D. once through slowly, to get the main ideas

2 Which is the closest in meaning to the word *emitted?*

    E. sent

    F. destroyed

    G. measured

    H. buried

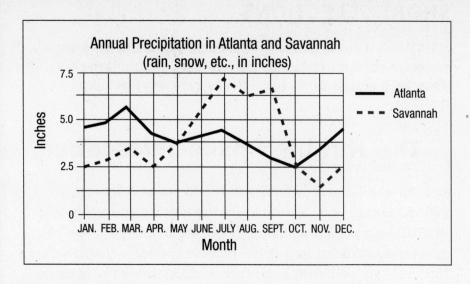

Annual Precipitation in Atlanta and Savannah (rain, snow, etc., in inches)

DIRECTIONS Use the graph to answer questions 3, 4, and 5.

3 According to the graph, in what month is the precipitation greatest in Savannah?

A. March

B. June

C. July

D. September

4 If you want to avoid rain and snow, when is the BEST time to visit Atlanta?

E. March

F. May

G. October

H. November

5 If the average temperature in the summer is approximately the same in Savannah and Atlanta, which of the following would MOST LIKELY explain the amount of precipitation in Savannah during the summer months?

A. population density

B. coastal influence

C. higher elevation

D. southern location

THINKING IT THROUGH

The notes in the side columns will help you think through your answers. Check the key at the bottom of the page. How well did you do?

1 To find out how large the telescope is, what is the BEST way to read this passage?

    A. slowly, paying attention to every detail
    B. several times in order to get the facts straight
    C. quickly, scanning for a specific detail
    D. once through slowly, to get the main ideas

> The key words are *BEST way*. Think of how you would read to find a very specific piece of information.

2 Which is the closest in meaning to the word *emitted*?

    E. sent
    F. destroyed
    G. measured
    H. buried

> Substitute each of the answer choices for the word *emitted* as you reread the sentence. Only one of the choices makes sense in the context of the sentence and of the paragraph.

3 According to the graph, in what month is the precipitation greatest in Savannah?

    A. March
    B. June
    C. July
    D. September

> Identify which line marks the level of precipitation for Savannah. Look for the month when that line marks the highest point.

4 If you want to avoid rain and snow, when is the BEST time to visit Atlanta?

    E. March
    F. May
    G. October
    H. November

> Look for the line that represents Atlanta. Then look for the lowest point on that line to find the time of least precipitation.

5 If the average temperature in the summer is approximately the same in Savannah and Atlanta, which of the following would MOST LIKELY explain the amount of precipitation in Savannah during the summer months?

    A. population density
    B. coastal influence
    C. higher elevation
    D. southern location

> The key words are *MOST LIKELY*. Think about cause-and-effect relationships and about what is most likely to cause rain. Which choice is most associated with greater moisture in the air?

Answers: 1.C, 2.E, 3.C, 4.G, 5.B

Functional Reading Test Model

DIRECTIONS Study the following nutrition label from a can of albacore tuna. Then answer the questions that follow.

Reading Strategies for Assessment

Examine the structure. Circle the four parts of this label.

Consider type style. Why are some words boldfaced?

Nutrition Facts

Serv. Size 1/4 cup (56g)
Servings about 2

Amount Per Serving

Calories 65   Fat Calories 0

Amount/Serving	% DV*
Total Fat 0.5g	1%
Sat. Fat 0g	0%
Cholest. 30 mg	10%
Sodium 150 mg	6%
Total Carb. 0g	0%
Fiber 0g	0%
Sugars 0g	
Protein 15g	30%

Vitamin A 0%	•	Vitamin C 0%
Calcium 0%	•	Iron 6%

*Percent Daily Values (DV) are based on a 2,000 calorie diet.

Answer Strategies

> Note that the label lists amount per serving. This can has two servings, so you must double the calories for one serving.

1 How many calories does this can of tuna contain?

   A. 65

   B. 32

   C. 130

   D. 120

> The %DV column is the percentage of the Daily Value. You must double the percentage in one serving.

2 If you eat the whole can of tuna, what percentage of the Daily Value of protein will you consume?

   E. 15%

   F. 60%

   G. 30%

   H. 45%

> The label clearly states that the %DV for calcium is 0%.

3 If you wish to add calcium to your diet, should you choose tuna?

   A. Yes, because tuna is low in fat.

   B. No, because the %DV for calcium is 0%.

   C. Yes, because tuna is low in fiber.

   D. No, because tuna has no Vitamin A or C.

Answers: 1.C, 2.F, 3.B

Functional Reading Test Practice

DIRECTIONS Study the directions for buying a transit card below. Circle the information you think is the most important. Answer the multiple-choice questions that follow.

Transit Card

One-way fare $1.50. Fare with transfer (2 more rides within 2 hours) $1.80

Press A **Buying Card**	Press B **Checking Value**	Press C **Adding Value**
1. Insert EXACT amount you want on card in bills or coins ($1.50 to $91). To stop, press CANCEL 2. Press VEND and take card.	1. Insert Transit Card in slot; remaining value appears in display window. **$3.60** 2. Press CANCEL and take card.	1. Insert Transit Card in slot; see remaining value. 2. Insert EXACT amount you want to add on card in bills or coins (5¢ minimum); maximum card value $100. To stop, press CANCEL 3. Press VEND and take card.

Transit card can pay for up to 7 full-fare rides at once (each person inserts separately). Card is good on buses and trains.

Transit Card Fares
Minimum Purchase: $1.50
Minimum Recharge: 5¢
Card Deducts These Fares:
One ride (full-fare) $1.50
1st transfer in two hours: 30¢
2nd transfer in two hours: FREE

Reduced fare riders
Fare: 75 cents Transfer: 15¢
Ages 7–11
Permit required for Grade and High School students, Seniors, Disabled

See Customer Assistance in station for entry if paying in coins or push Call Button near turnstile if needed.

1 You need to make a roundtrip by bus. You will need to transfer to another bus to reach your destination. How much money will you need to put on a transit card?

A. $1.80
B. $1.50
C. $3.00
D. $3.60

2 You are a high school student who takes the train to school. How much must you put on your transit card to get to school and back home every day for a week?

E. $5.00

F. $7.50

G. $15.00

H. $10.00

3 You want to know how much money remains on the transit card you own. What can you do?

A. ask the person at the transit station

B. press A and insert your card into the slot

C. call the bus company

D. press B and insert your card into the slot

4 Your card has $2.50 left on it. How much value do you need to add to make two roundtrips?

E. $2.50

F. $3.50

G. $3.00

H. $4.50

THINKING IT THROUGH

The notes in the side columns will help you think through your answers. Check the key at the bottom of the page. How well did you do?

1 You need to make a roundtrip by bus. You will need to transfer to another bus to reach your destination. How much money will you need to put on a transit card?

A. $1.80
B. $1.50
C. $3.00
D. $3.60

> You need to make a transfer to reach and return from your destination, so you need to double the one-way-with-transfer fare.

2 You are a high school student who takes the train to school. How much must you put on your transit card to get to school and back home every day for a week?

E. $5.00
F. $7.50
G. $15.00
H. $10.00

> As a student, you qualify for a reduced fare of 75¢. You don't need a transfer, so you will have one roundtrip every day for five days.

3 You want to know how much money remains on the transit card you own. What can you do?

A. ask the person at the transit station
B. press A and insert your card into the slot
C. call the bus company
D. press B and insert your card into the slot

> You need to read the instructions for Checking Value.

4 Your card has $2.50 left on it. How much value do you need to add to make two roundtrips?

E. $2.50
F. $3.50
G. $3.00
H. $4.50

> A single fare is $1.50, so a roundtrip is $3.00. You will need $6.00 minus the $2.50 you already have.

Revising-and-Editing Test Model

Reading Strategies for Assessment

Watch for common errors. Revising-and-editing test questions often focus on typical errors such as punctuation, spelling, and capitalization errors; incomplete sentences; and missing or misplaced information.

DIRECTIONS Read the following paragraph carefully. Then answer the multiple-choice questions that follow. After answering the questions, read the material in the side column to check your answer strategies.

¹On January 4, 2001, I sat in the doctor's office waiting for the news. ²When my parents and the doctor came back into the room. ³I could tell by they're expressions that the news wasn't too bad. ⁴Finally, they gave me all of the information that I had been asking for. ⁵I felt as if a weight had been lifted off my shoulders. ⁶My parents said we should stop by my grandparents house on the way home and tell them the news. ⁷I had caught a disease that is serious, but can be treated with medicine. ⁸Thank goodness dr. perez has so much experience!

Answer Strategies

Punctuating Dates In dates, use a comma between the day of the month and the year.
For help, see Pupil Edition, p. 1201* Grammar, Usage, and Mechanics Book, p. 181

1 What is the correct way to write the date in sentence 1?

   A. January, 4, 2001

   B. January 4, 2001

   C. January/4/2001

   D. January 4th 2001

Complete Sentences A sentence must express a complete thought.
For help, see Pupil Edition, p. 1197 Grammar, Usage, and Mechanics Book, p. 85

2 Which sentence in the paragraph is a fragment?

   E. sentence 2

   F. sentence 5

   G. sentence 6

   H. sentence 8

Kinds of Sentences Check the Grammar Handbook on p. 1196 to review the kinds of sentences. Because the last sentence ends with an exclamation point, you can eliminate choices A and B. None of the sentences in the paragraph give a command.
For help, see Pupil Edition, p. 1196 Grammar, Usage, and Mechanics Book, p. 34

3 What types of sentences does this paragraph include?

   A. declarative and imperative

   B. imperative and interrogative

   C. imperative and exclamatory

   D. declarative and exclamatory

Answers: 1.B, 2.E, 3.D

*Pages listed are for the Grammar Handbook in The Language of Literature Pupil Edition and the Grammar, Usage, and Mechanics Book.

4 Which of the following is the correct way to write the first part of sentence 3?

   E. I could tell by there expressions
   F. I could tell by theyre expressions
   G. I could tell by their expressions
   H. I could tell by thier expressions

5 In sentence 4, what is the function of *information* in the phrase *of the information?*

   A. object of a preposition
   B. indirect object
   C. direct object
   D. subject

6 What is the correct spelling of *grandparents* in sentence 6?

   E. grandparent's
   F. grandparent's'
   G. grandparents'
   H. grandparents

7 Where would you add supporting details about the writer's disease?

   A. in sentence 2
   B. in sentence 3
   C. in sentence 5
   D. in sentence 7

8 What is the correct capitalization in sentence 8?

   E. dr. Perez
   F. Dr. Perez
   G. Dr. perez
   H. DR. Perez

Answers: 4.G, 5.A, 6.G, 7.D, 8.F

Revising-and-Editing Test Practice

DIRECTIONS Read the following paragraph carefully. As you read, circle each error you find and identify the error in the side column— for example, *misspelled word* or *not a complete sentence.* When you have finished, circle the letter of the correct choice for each question that follows.

¹Have you ever seen the destructive effects of gypsy moths? ²During a gypsy moth infestation six years ago. ³The moths did severe damage to trees. ⁴The caterpillars are huge furry and indestructible. ⁵These creatures look harmless, but they're not. ⁶One way to try to save the trees is to put a tape of sticky gel around the trunks. ⁷This remedy is sometimes worser for the trees than the caterpillars, though. ⁸This prevents the caterpillars from climbing the trees to get their food.

1 Which sentence in this paragraph is a sentence fragment?

A. sentence 1

B. sentence 2

C. sentence 5

D. sentence 6

2 Which change would MOST improve the logical organization of the paragraph?

E. Move sentence 1 to the end of the paragraph.

F. Place sentence 5 before sentence 4.

G. Place sentence 8 before sentence 7.

H. Delete sentence 8.

3 To gather details missing from this paragraph about how gypsy moths destroy trees, which resource would you consult?

A. an encyclopedia

B. an atlas

C. a dictionary

D. a periodical

4 Which change should be made to sentence 4?

   E. Add a colon after *are*.

   F. Add commas after *are* and *huge*.

   G. Add commas after *huge* and *furry*.

   H. Add a semicolon after *are* and commas after *huge* and *furry*.

5 In sentence 6, what part of speech is the phrase *to put a tape of sticky gel around the trunks*?

   A. subject

   B. predicate nominative

   C. direct object

   D. predicate

6 What is the antecedent of *This* in sentence 8?

   E. caterpillars

   F. remedy

   G. trunks

   H. tape

7 What is the correct form of the comparative adjective in sentence 7?

   A. worst

   B. more worse

   C. worse

   D. worsest

THINKING IT THROUGH

DIRECTIONS Use the notes in the side column to help you understand why some answers are correct and others are not. See the answer key on the next page. How well did you do?

Examine each answer choice. Look for a group of words that does not express a complete thought.
For help, see Pupil Edition, pp. 1197, 1204*
Grammar, Usage, and Mechanics Book, p. 85

1 Which sentence in this paragraph is a sentence fragment?

   A. sentence 1

   B. sentence 2

   C. sentence 5

   D. sentence 6

Look for sentences that belong together because they show clear cause and effect.

2 Which change would MOST improve the logical organization of the paragraph?

   E. Move sentence 1 to the end of the paragraph.

   F. Place sentence 5 before sentence 4.

   G. Place sentence 8 before sentence 7.

   H. Delete sentence 8.

Use the process of elimination. An encyclopedia gives information about many subjects. An atlas shows geography. A dictionary gives word meanings. A periodical is a magazine and could be about anything.

3 To gather details missing from this paragraph about how gypsy moths destroy trees, which resource would you consult?

   A. an encyclopedia

   B. an atlas

   C. a dictionary

   D. a periodical

Remember that items in a series must be separated by commas.
For help, see Pupil Edition, p. 1201

4 Which change should be made to sentence 4?

   E. Add a colon after *are*.

   F. Add commas after *are* and *huge*.

   G. Add commas after *huge* and *furry*.

   H. Add a semicolon after *are* and commas after *huge* and *furry*.

*Pages listed are for the Grammar Handbook in *The Language of Literature* Pupil Edition and the *Grammar, Usage, and Mechanics Book*.

5 In sentence 6, what part of speech is the phrase *to put a tape of sticky gel around the trunks*?

A. subject
B. predicate nominative
C. direct object
D. predicate

Find the subject and verb of the sentence and then examine the answer choices. A predicate nominative follows and completes the meaning of the linking verb *is*. A direct object always follows an action verb.
For help, see Pupil Edition, p. 1212

6 What is the antecedent of *This* in sentence 8?

E. caterpillars
F. remedy
G. trunks
H. tape

Remember that an antecedent is the word for which a pronoun stands, so look for a noun that makes sense in the sentence.
For help, see Pupil Edition, p. 1181 Grammar, Usage, and Mechanics Book, p. 139

7 What is the correct form of the comparative adjective in sentence 7?

A. worst
B. more worse
C. worse
D. worsest

Irregular comparisons are tricky and must be memorized. The comparative and superlative forms of *bad* are *worse* and *worst*.
For help, see Pupil Edition, p. 1187 Grammar, Usage, and Mechanics Book, p. 157

Answers:
1.B, 2.G, 3.A, 4.G, 5.B, 6.F, 7.C

Writing Test Model

DIRECTIONS Many tests ask you to write an essay in response to a writing prompt. A writing prompt is a brief statement that describes a writing situation. Some writing prompts ask you to explain what, why, or how. Others ask you to convince someone about something.

As you analyze the following writing prompts, read and respond to the notes in the side column. Then look at the response to each prompt. The notes in the side column will help you understand why each response is considered strong.

Prompt A

Home schooling is more popular than ever before. Taught at home by their parents, teens may learn from textbooks or from field trips and other real-life situations. Some people say home schooling protects teens from the possible dangers and distractions at school. Others argue that home-schooled teens receive an inferior education and don't learn how to socialize with their peers.

What is your opinion about home schooling? Write a letter to the editor of your community newspaper stating your opinion. Be sure to provide support for your argument.

Analyzing the Prompt

Find the main idea. These first two sentences introduce and define the subject of the prompt. Restate the subject in your own words.

Understand what's expected of you. What is the purpose of your response? What form will your response take? In addition to stating your opinion, what else must you do?

Answer Strategies

Clearly state your opinion in the opening paragraph. This writer is in favor of home schooling.

Include effective transitional words and phrases. Such words and phrases as *the first reason, another reason,* and *finally* help the reader follow your reasoning.

Develop your argument with strong reasons and specific details. The writer gives three reasons for her support of home schooling. Look for the details that support those reasons.

Strong Response

As a ninth grader in a public school, I am concerned about today's classroom conditions. While I agree that the lessons learned in school are valuable, many kids would do better in a home schooling situation. I believe the benefits would outweigh the costs.

The first reason I support home schooling is that it allows parents the freedom to teach what they want to. Parents know their kids better than anyone else. Parents don't have to rely only on textbooks. They can create real-life learning experiences built around their children's natural interests. This means that children will want to learn.

Home schooling works for another reason. Parents can teach kids at their own pace. It is no secret that many of today's classrooms are overcrowded. Kids with learning problems and kids who excel often get lost in the crowd. Low-achieving students become frustrated and they decide they don't like learning. High-performance kids often become bored because the class is moving too slowly. With home schooling, parents can provide individualized attention.

Finally, I think one of the best arguments for home schooling is that it prevents kids from having to deal with peer pressure. Many kids aren't strong enough to turn away from the influence of other students. Home schooling gives those kids more time to develop the skills they need to become strong and healthy adults. Although some might say that school gives kids the skills necessary to deal with the pressures of drugs and violence, I disagree. I think parents can teach these lessons better at home.

At first glance, home schooling seems like an unfair solution, but it is not. Kids do better when they learn at their own pace in a calm, safe environment. They should be protected while they're young, so that they will grow into healthy, productive adults. I think the lessons learned in school can be learned just as well at home.

Keep your audience in mind. The writer has used language and sentence structures that are appropriate for the readers of a community newspaper.

Don't ignore opposing views. The writer addresses the views of those who disagree with her.

Restate your opinion in the concluding paragraph. The writer repeats her main points in the last paragraph.

Analyzing the Prompt

Find the main idea. What is the topic of this writing prompt? Restate it in your own words.

Understand what's expected of you. Your response will have two parts. What are they?

Answer Strategies

Set the scene. The writer uses colorful language to set the scene for his readers.

State your topic clearly. What does the writer love?

Signal the order of events. Notice how this writer uses words and phrases that indicate time order.

Include significant details. The details about the writer's grandmother and his best friend help him support his topic.

Restate your main idea. He ends with a reminder of his main idea.

Prompt B

Everyone has something he or she loves to do— a favorite activity or way to spend time.

Think about something you love to do. Identify what this is and explain why you love it.

Strong Response

Picture this: it's early in the morning—so early that only the birds are awake. You get up and open the back door to get a sense of the weather. As soon as you do, you have to shade your eyes from the sun's glare and the breeze makes you shiver. What would you do next? For me, the answer is simple: go for a run. Running outdoors in the morning is the thing I love to do most.

There's nothing quite like the feeling of running on a cool, sunny morning. At first, my limbs feel heavy. As I drag myself forward, each footfall jars my whole body. Gradually, though, I get lighter and lighter. Pretty soon, maybe after about a mile, I feel like I'm flying. Meanwhile, the clean morning air and cool breeze keep me comfortable. (Just a few hours later in the day, the air gets too hot for a run. Later still, it becomes too polluted.)

Pushing myself to run faster, I revel in my body's strength and energy and in how lucky I am to be able to do this. My grandmother uses a wheelchair to get around. My best friend can't run because of her asthma. There was even a time when I was so out of shape that I could barely do a mile myself. Now I do four miles, four times a week, and I feel grateful every time I finish them.

Writing Test Practice

DIRECTIONS Read the following writing prompt. Using the strategies you've learned in this Test Preparation Guide, analyze the prompt, plan your response, and then write an essay explaining your position.

Prompt C

Movies are given ratings by the Motion Picture Association of America. A movie may be rated G (general audiences), PG-13 (may be unsuitable for children under 13), or R (under 17 not admitted without a parent). Some people believe movies should not be rated. Others say that ratings must remain in place to warn children and parents of a movie's content.

What is your position concerning movie ratings? Write an essay in which you state and provide support for your position.

Scoring Rubrics

DIRECTIONS Use the following checklist to see whether you have written a strong persuasive essay. You will have succeeded if you can check nearly all of the items.

The Prompt

☐ My response meets all the requirements stated in the prompt. I have stated my position clearly and supported it with details. I raised and responded to opposing arguments.

☐ I addressed the audience appropriately.

☐ My essay fits the type of writing suggested in the prompt (letter to the editor, article for the school paper, and so on).

Reasons

☐ The reasons I offer really support my position.

☐ My audience will find the reasons convincing.

☐ I have stated my reasons clearly.

☐ I have given at least three reasons.

☐ I have supported my reasons with sufficient facts, examples, quotations, and other details.

☐ I have presented and responded to opposing arguments.

☐ My reasoning is sound. I have avoided faulty logic.

Order and Arrangement

☐ I have included a strong introduction.

☐ I have included a strong conclusion.

☐ The reasons are arranged in a logical order.

Word Choice

☐ The language of my essay is appropriate for my audience.

☐ I have used precise, vivid words and persuasive language.

Fluency

☐ I have used sentences of varying lengths and structures.

☐ I have connected ideas with transitions and other devices.

☐ I have used correct spelling, punctuation, and grammar.

Personal Word List

Use these pages to build your personal vocabulary. As you read the selections, take time to mark unfamiliar words. These should be words that seem interesting or important enough to add to your permanent vocabulary. After reading, look up the meanings of these words and record the information below. For each word, write a sentence that shows its correct use.

Review your list from time to time. Try to put these words into use in your writing and conversation.

Word: _____

Selection: _____

Page/Line: _____ / _____

Part of Speech: _____

Definition: _____

_____

Sentence: _____

_____

Word: _____

Selection: _____

Page/Line: _____ / _____

Part of Speech: _____

Definition: _____

_____

Sentence: _____

_____

Word: _____

Selection: _____

Page/Line: _____ / _____

Part of Speech: _____

Definition: _____

_____

_____

Sentence: _____

_____

Word: _____

Selection: _____

Page/Line: _____ / _____

Part of Speech: _____

Definition: _____

_____

_____

Sentence: _____

_____

Word: _____

Selection: _____

Page/Line: _____ / _____

Part of Speech: _____

Definition: _____

_____

_____

Sentence: _____

_____

Word: _____

Selection: _____

Page/Line: _____ / _____

Part of Speech: _____

Definition: _____

_____

_____

Sentence: _____

_____

Word:_____

Selection: _____

Page/Line: _____ / _____

Part of Speech: _____

Definition: _____

_____

_____

Sentence: _____

_____

Word:_____

Selection: _____

Page/Line: _____ / _____

Part of Speech: _____

Definition: _____

_____

_____

Sentence: _____

_____

Word:_____

Selection: _____

Page/Line: _____ / _____

Part of Speech: _____

Definition: _____

_____

_____

Sentence: _____

_____

Word:_____

Selection: _____

Page/Line: _____ / _____

Part of Speech: _____

Definition: _____

_____

_____

Sentence: _____

_____

Word:_____

Selection: _____

Page/Line: _____ / _____

Part of Speech: _____

Definition: _____

_____

_____

Sentence: _____

_____

Word:_____

Selection: _____

Page/Line: _____ / _____

Part of Speech: _____

Definition: _____

_____

_____

Sentence: _____

_____

Word:_____

Selection: _____

Page/Line: _____ / _____

Part of Speech: _____

Definition: _____

_____

_____

Sentence: _____

_____

Word:_____

Selection: _____

Page/Line: _____ / _____

Part of Speech: _____

Definition: _____

_____

_____

Sentence: _____

_____

Personal Word List (continued)

Word:_____

Selection: _____

Page/Line: _____ / _____

Part of Speech: _____

Definition: _____

_____

_____

Sentence: _____

_____

Word:_____

Selection: _____

Page/Line: _____ / _____

Part of Speech: _____

Definition: _____

_____

_____

Sentence: _____

_____

Word:_____

Selection: _____

Page/Line: _____ / _____

Part of Speech: _____

Definition: _____

_____

_____

Sentence: _____

_____

Word:_____

Selection: _____

Page/Line: _____ / _____

Part of Speech: _____

Definition: _____

_____

_____

Sentence: _____

_____

Word:_____

Selection: _____

Page/Line: _____ / _____

Part of Speech: _____

Definition: _____

_____

_____

Sentence: _____

_____

Word:_____

Selection: _____

Page/Line: _____ / _____

Part of Speech: _____

Definition: _____

_____

_____

Sentence: _____

_____

Word:_____

Selection: _____

Page/Line: _____ / _____

Part of Speech: _____

Definition: _____

_____

_____

Sentence: _____

_____

Word:_____

Selection: _____

Page/Line: _____ / _____

Part of Speech: _____

Definition: _____

_____

_____

Sentence: _____

_____

Word:_____

Selection: _____

Page/Line: _____ / _____

Part of Speech: _____

Definition: _____

_____

_____

Sentence: _____

_____

Word:_____

Selection: _____

Page/Line: _____ / _____

Part of Speech: _____

Definition: _____

_____

_____

Sentence: _____

_____

Word:_____

Selection: _____

Page/Line: _____ / _____

Part of Speech: _____

Definition: _____

_____

_____

Sentence: _____

_____

Word:_____

Selection: _____

Page/Line: _____ / _____

Part of Speech: _____

Definition: _____

_____

_____

Sentence: _____

_____

Word:_____

Selection: _____

Page/Line: _____ / _____

Part of Speech: _____

Definition: _____

_____

_____

Sentence: _____

_____

Word:_____

Selection: _____

Page/Line: _____ / _____

Part of Speech: _____

Definition: _____

_____

_____

Sentence: _____

_____

Word:_____

Selection: _____

Page/Line: _____ / _____

Part of Speech: _____

Definition: _____

_____

_____

Sentence: _____

_____

Word:_____

Selection: _____

Page/Line: _____ / _____

Part of Speech: _____

Definition: _____

_____

_____

Sentence: _____

_____

Personal Word List (continued)

Word:_____

Selection: _____

Page/Line: _____ / _____

Part of Speech: _____

Definition: _____

_____

_____

Sentence: _____

_____

Word:_____

Selection: _____

Page/Line: _____ / _____

Part of Speech: _____

Definition: _____

_____

_____

Sentence: _____

_____

Word:_____

Selection: _____

Page/Line: _____ / _____

Part of Speech: _____

Definition: _____

_____

_____

Sentence: _____

_____

Word:_____

Selection: _____

Page/Line: _____ / _____

Part of Speech: _____

Definition: _____

_____

_____

Sentence: _____

_____

Word:_____

Selection: _____

Page/Line: _____ / _____

Part of Speech: _____

Definition: _____

_____

_____

Sentence: _____

_____

Word:_____

Selection: _____

Page/Line: _____ / _____

Part of Speech: _____

Definition: _____

_____

_____

Sentence: _____

_____

Word:_____

Selection: _____

Page/Line: _____ / _____

Part of Speech: _____

Definition: _____

_____

_____

Sentence: _____

_____

Word:_____

Selection: _____

Page/Line: _____ / _____

Part of Speech: _____

Definition: _____

_____

_____

Sentence: _____

_____

Word: _____

Selection: _____

Page/Line: _____ / _____

Part of Speech: _____

Definition: _____

_____

_____

Sentence: _____

_____

Word: _____

Selection: _____

Page/Line: _____ / _____

Part of Speech: _____

Definition: _____

_____

_____

Sentence: _____

_____

Word: _____

Selection: _____

Page/Line: _____ / _____

Part of Speech: _____

Definition: _____

_____

_____

Sentence: _____

_____

Word: _____

Selection: _____

Page/Line: _____ / _____

Part of Speech: _____

Definition: _____

_____

_____

Sentence: _____

_____

Word: _____

Selection: _____

Page/Line: _____ / _____

Part of Speech: _____

Definition: _____

_____

_____

Sentence: _____

_____

Word: _____

Selection: _____

Page/Line: _____ / _____

Part of Speech: _____

Definition: _____

_____

_____

Sentence: _____

_____

Word: _____

Selection: _____

Page/Line: _____ / _____

Part of Speech: _____

Definition: _____

_____

_____

Sentence: _____

_____

Word: _____

Selection: _____

Page/Line: _____ / _____

Part of Speech: _____

Definition: _____

_____

_____

Sentence: _____

_____

Personal Word List (continued)

Word:_____

Selection: _____

Page/Line: _____ / _____

Part of Speech: _____

Definition: _____

_____

_____

Sentence: _____

_____

Word:_____

Selection: _____

Page/Line: _____ / _____

Part of Speech: _____

Definition: _____

_____

_____

Sentence: _____

_____

Word:_____

Selection: _____

Page/Line: _____ / _____

Part of Speech: _____

Definition: _____

_____

_____

Sentence: _____

_____

Word:_____

Selection: _____

Page/Line: _____ / _____

Part of Speech: _____

Definition: _____

_____

_____

Sentence: _____

_____

Word:_____

Selection: _____

Page/Line: _____ / _____

Part of Speech: _____

Definition: _____

_____

_____

Sentence: _____

_____

Word:_____

Selection: _____

Page/Line: _____ / _____

Part of Speech: _____

Definition: _____

_____

_____

Sentence: _____

_____

Word:_____

Selection: _____

Page/Line: _____ / _____

Part of Speech: _____

Definition: _____

_____

_____

Sentence: _____

_____

Word:_____

Selection: _____

Page/Line: _____ / _____

Part of Speech: _____

Definition: _____

_____

_____

Sentence: _____

_____

Word:_____

Selection: _____

Page/Line: _____ / _____

Part of Speech: _____

Definition: _____

_____

_____

Sentence: _____

_____

Word:_____

Selection: _____

Page/Line: _____ / _____

Part of Speech: _____

Definition: _____

_____

_____

Sentence: _____

_____

Word:_____

Selection: _____

Page/Line: _____ / _____

Part of Speech: _____

Definition: _____

_____

_____

Sentence: _____

_____

Word:_____

Selection: _____

Page/Line: _____ / _____

Part of Speech: _____

Definition: _____

_____

_____

Sentence: _____

_____

Word:_____

Selection: _____

Page/Line: _____ / _____

Part of Speech: _____

Definition: _____

_____

_____

Sentence: _____

_____

Word:_____

Selection: _____

Page/Line: _____ / _____

Part of Speech: _____

Definition: _____

_____

_____

Sentence: _____

_____

Word:_____

Selection: _____

Page/Line: _____ / _____

Part of Speech: _____

Definition: _____

_____

_____

Sentence: _____

_____

Word:_____

Selection: _____

Page/Line: _____ / _____

Part of Speech: _____

Definition: _____

_____

_____

Sentence: _____

_____

Personal Word List (continued)

Word:_____

Selection: _____

Page/Line: _____ / _____

Part of Speech: _____

Definition: _____

_____

_____

Sentence: _____

_____

Word:_____

Selection: _____

Page/Line: _____ / _____

Part of Speech: _____

Definition: _____

_____

_____

Sentence: _____

_____

Word:_____

Selection: _____

Page/Line: _____ / _____

Part of Speech: _____

Definition: _____

_____

_____

Sentence: _____

_____

Word:_____

Selection: _____

Page/Line: _____ / _____

Part of Speech: _____

Definition: _____

_____

_____

Sentence: _____

_____

Word:_____

Selection: _____

Page/Line: _____ / _____

Part of Speech: _____

Definition: _____

_____

_____

Sentence: _____

_____

Word:_____

Selection: _____

Page/Line: _____ / _____

Part of Speech: _____

Definition: _____

_____

_____

Sentence: _____

_____

Word:_____

Selection: _____

Page/Line: _____ / _____

Part of Speech: _____

Definition: _____

_____

_____

Sentence: _____

_____

Word:_____

Selection: _____

Page/Line: _____ / _____

Part of Speech: _____

Definition: _____

_____

_____

Sentence: _____

_____

Word:_____

Selection: _____

Page/Line: _____ / _____

Part of Speech: _____

Definition: _____

_____

_____

Sentence: _____

_____

Word:_____

Selection: _____

Page/Line: _____ / _____

Part of Speech: _____

Definition: _____

_____

_____

Sentence: _____

_____

Word:_____

Selection: _____

Page/Line: _____ / _____

Part of Speech: _____

Definition: _____

_____

_____

Sentence: _____

_____

Word:_____

Selection: _____

Page/Line: _____ / _____

Part of Speech: _____

Definition: _____

_____

_____

Sentence: _____

_____

Word:_____

Selection: _____

Page/Line: _____ / _____

Part of Speech: _____

Definition: _____

_____

_____

Sentence: _____

_____

Word:_____

Selection: _____

Page/Line: _____ / _____

Part of Speech: _____

Definition: _____

_____

_____

Sentence: _____

_____

Word:_____

Selection: _____

Page/Line: _____ / _____

Part of Speech: _____

Definition: _____

_____

_____

Sentence: _____

_____

Word:_____

Selection: _____

Page/Line: _____ / _____

Part of Speech: _____

Definition: _____

_____

_____

Sentence: _____

_____

Personal Word List (continued)

Word:_____

Selection: _____

Page/Line: _____ / _____

Part of Speech: _____

Definition: _____

_____

_____

Sentence: _____

_____

Word:_____

Selection: _____

Page/Line: _____ / _____

Part of Speech: _____

Definition: _____

_____

_____

Sentence: _____

_____

Word:_____

Selection: _____

Page/Line: _____ / _____

Part of Speech: _____

Definition: _____

_____

_____

Sentence: _____

_____

Word:_____

Selection: _____

Page/Line: _____ / _____

Part of Speech: _____

Definition: _____

_____

_____

Sentence: _____

_____

Word:_____

Selection: _____

Page/Line: _____ / _____

Part of Speech: _____

Definition: _____

_____

_____

Sentence: _____

_____

Word:_____

Selection: _____

Page/Line: _____ / _____

Part of Speech: _____

Definition: _____

_____

_____

Sentence: _____

_____

Word:_____

Selection: _____

Page/Line: _____ / _____

Part of Speech: _____

Definition: _____

_____

_____

Sentence: _____

_____

Word:_____

Selection: _____

Page/Line: _____ / _____

Part of Speech: _____

Definition: _____

_____

_____

Sentence: _____

_____

Word:_____

Selection: _____

Page/Line: _____ / _____

Part of Speech: _____

Definition: _____

_____

_____

Sentence: _____

_____

Word:_____

Selection: _____

Page/Line: _____ / _____

Part of Speech: _____

Definition: _____

_____

_____

Sentence: _____

_____

Word:_____

Selection: _____

Page/Line: _____ / _____

Part of Speech: _____

Definition: _____

_____

_____

Sentence: _____

_____

Word:_____

Selection: _____

Page/Line: _____ / _____

Part of Speech: _____

Definition: _____

_____

_____

Sentence: _____

_____

Word:_____

Selection: _____

Page/Line: _____ / _____

Part of Speech: _____

Definition: _____

_____

_____

Sentence: _____

_____

Word:_____

Selection: _____

Page/Line: _____ / _____

Part of Speech: _____

Definition: _____

_____

_____

Sentence: _____

_____

Word:_____

Selection: _____

Page/Line: _____ / _____

Part of Speech: _____

Definition: _____

_____

_____

Sentence: _____

_____

Word:_____

Selection: _____

Page/Line: _____ / _____

Part of Speech: _____

Definition: _____

_____

_____

Sentence: _____

_____

Personal Word List (continued)

Word:_____

Selection: _____

Page/Line: _____ / _____

Part of Speech: _____

Definition: _____

_____

Sentence: _____

_____

Word:_____

Selection: _____

Page/Line: _____ / _____

Part of Speech: _____

Definition: _____

_____

Sentence: _____

_____

Word:_____

Selection: _____

Page/Line: _____ / _____

Part of Speech: _____

Definition: _____

_____

Sentence: _____

_____

Word:_____

Selection: _____

Page/Line: _____ / _____

Part of Speech: _____

Definition: _____

_____

Sentence: _____

Word:_____

Selection: _____

Page/Line: _____ / _____

Part of Speech: _____

Definition: _____

_____

Sentence: _____

_____

Word:_____

Selection: _____

Page/Line: _____ / _____

Part of Speech: _____

Definition: _____

_____

Sentence: _____

_____

Word:_____

Selection: _____

Page/Line: _____ / _____

Part of Speech: _____

Definition: _____

_____

Sentence: _____

_____

Word:_____

Selection: _____

Page/Line: _____ / _____

Part of Speech: _____

Definition: _____

_____

Sentence: _____

Word:_____

Selection: _____

Page/Line: _____ / _____

Part of Speech: _____

Definition: _____

_____

_____

Sentence: _____

_____

Word:_____

Selection: _____

Page/Line: _____ / _____

Part of Speech: _____

Definition: _____

_____

_____

Sentence: _____

_____

Word:_____

Selection: _____

Page/Line: _____ / _____

Part of Speech: _____

Definition: _____

_____

_____

Sentence: _____

_____

Word:_____

Selection: _____

Page/Line: _____ / _____

Part of Speech: _____

Definition: _____

_____

_____

Sentence: _____

_____

Word:_____

Selection: _____

Page/Line: _____ / _____

Part of Speech: _____

Definition: _____

_____

_____

Sentence: _____

_____

Word:_____

Selection: _____

Page/Line: _____ / _____

Part of Speech: _____

Definition: _____

_____

_____

Sentence: _____

_____

Word:_____

Selection: _____

Page/Line: _____ / _____

Part of Speech: _____

Definition: _____

_____

_____

Sentence: _____

_____

Word:_____

Selection: _____

Page/Line: _____ / _____

Part of Speech: _____

Definition: _____

_____

_____

Sentence: _____

_____

Personal Word List (continued)

Word:_____

Selection: _____

Page/Line: _____ / _____

Part of Speech: _____

Definition: _____

_____

_____

Sentence: _____

_____

Word:_____

Selection: _____

Page/Line: _____ / _____

Part of Speech: _____

Definition: _____

_____

_____

Sentence: _____

_____

Word:_____

Selection: _____

Page/Line: _____ / _____

Part of Speech: _____

Definition: _____

_____

_____

Sentence: _____

_____

Word:_____

Selection: _____

Page/Line: _____ / _____

Part of Speech: _____

Definition: _____

_____

_____

Sentence: _____

_____

Word:_____

Selection: _____

Page/Line: _____ / _____

Part of Speech: _____

Definition: _____

_____

_____

Sentence: _____

_____

Word:_____

Selection: _____

Page/Line: _____ / _____

Part of Speech: _____

Definition: _____

_____

_____

Sentence: _____

_____

Word:_____

Selection: _____

Page/Line: _____ / _____

Part of Speech: _____

Definition: _____

_____

_____

Sentence: _____

_____

Word:_____

Selection: _____

Page/Line: _____ / _____

Part of Speech: _____

Definition: _____

_____

_____

Sentence: _____

_____

Word:_____

Selection: _____

Page/Line: _____ / _____

Part of Speech: _____

Definition: _____

_____

_____

Sentence: _____

_____

Word:_____

Selection: _____

Page/Line: _____ / _____

Part of Speech: _____

Definition: _____

_____

_____

Sentence: _____

_____

Word:_____

Selection: _____

Page/Line: _____ / _____

Part of Speech: _____

Definition: _____

_____

_____

Sentence: _____

_____

Word:_____

Selection: _____

Page/Line: _____ / _____

Part of Speech: _____

Definition: _____

_____

_____

Sentence: _____

_____

Word:_____

Selection: _____

Page/Line: _____ / _____

Part of Speech: _____

Definition: _____

_____

_____

Sentence: _____

_____

Word:_____

Selection: _____

Page/Line: _____ / _____

Part of Speech: _____

Definition: _____

_____

_____

Sentence: _____

_____

Word:_____

Selection: _____

Page/Line: _____ / _____

Part of Speech: _____

Definition: _____

_____

_____

Sentence: _____

_____

Word:_____

Selection: _____

Page/Line: _____ / _____

Part of Speech: _____

Definition: _____

_____

_____

Sentence: _____

_____

Personal Word List (continued)

Word:_____

Selection: _____

Page/Line: _____ / _____

Part of Speech: _____

Definition: _____

_____

_____

Sentence: _____

_____

Word:_____

Selection: _____

Page/Line: _____ / _____

Part of Speech: _____

Definition: _____

_____

_____

Sentence: _____

_____

Word:_____

Selection: _____

Page/Line: _____ / _____

Part of Speech: _____

Definition: _____

_____

_____

Sentence: _____

_____

Word:_____

Selection: _____

Page/Line: _____ / _____

Part of Speech: _____

Definition: _____

_____

_____

Sentence: _____

_____

Word:_____

Selection: _____

Page/Line: _____ / _____

Part of Speech: _____

Definition: _____

_____

Sentence: _____

_____

Word:_____

Selection: _____

Page/Line: _____ / _____

Part of Speech: _____

Definition: _____

_____

Sentence: _____

_____

Word:_____

Selection: _____

Page/Line: _____ / _____

Part of Speech: _____

Definition: _____

_____

Sentence: _____

_____

Word:_____

Selection: _____

Page/Line: _____ / _____

Part of Speech: _____

Definition: _____

_____

_____

Sentence: _____

_____

Word:_____

Selection: _____

Page/Line: _____ / _____

Part of Speech: _____

Definition: _____

_____

_____

Sentence: _____

_____

Word:_____

Selection: _____

Page/Line: _____ / _____

Part of Speech: _____

Definition: _____

_____

_____

Sentence: _____

_____

Word:_____

Selection: _____

Page/Line: _____ / _____

Part of Speech: _____

Definition: _____

_____

_____

Sentence: _____

_____

Word:_____

Selection: _____

Page/Line: _____ / _____

Part of Speech: _____

Definition: _____

_____

_____

Sentence: _____

_____

Word:_____

Selection: _____

Page/Line: _____ / _____

Part of Speech: _____

Definition: _____

_____

_____

Sentence: _____

_____

Word:_____

Selection: _____

Page/Line: _____ / _____

Part of Speech: _____

Definition: _____

_____

_____

Sentence: _____

_____

Word:_____

Selection: _____

Page/Line: _____ / _____

Part of Speech: _____

Definition: _____

_____

_____

Sentence: _____

_____

Word:_____

Selection: _____

Page/Line: _____ / _____

Part of Speech: _____

Definition: _____

_____

_____

Sentence: _____

_____

Acknowledgments

Arte Público Press: "A Voice," from *Communion* by Pat Mora (Houston: Arte Público Press—University of Houston, 1991). Copyright © 1991 by Pat Mora. Reprinted with permission from the publisher, Arte Público Press.

Susan Bergholz Literary Services: Excerpt from the Introduction to *The House on Mango Street* by Sandra Cisneros. Copyright © 1984 by Sandra Cisneros. Published by Alfred A. Knopf, a division of Random House, Inc., New York. Reprinted by permission of Susan Bergholz Literary Services, New York. All rights reserved.

Brandt & Hochman Literary Agents: "The Most Dangerous Game" by Richard Connell. Copyright © 1924 by Richard Connell. Copyright renewed © 1952 by Louise Fox Connell. Reprinted by permission of Brandt & Hochman Literary Agents, Inc.

City News Publishing: "Glory and Hope" by Nelson Mandela, from *Vital Speeches of the Day,* Vol. LX, No. 16 (1 June 1994), page 486. Reprinted by permission of City News Publishing Company, Inc.

Eugenia Collier: "Marigolds" by Eugenia Collier, originally published in *Negro Digest,* November 1969. Copyright © 1994 by Eugenia Collier. Reprinted by permission of the author.

Farrar, Straus & Giroux: Excerpts from *The Odyssey* by Homer, translated by Robert Fitzgerald. Translation copyright © 1961, renewed © 1989 by Benedict R. C. Fitzgerald on behalf of the Fitzgerald children. This edition © 1998 by Farrar, Straus & Giroux, Inc. Reprinted by permission of Farrar, Straus & Giroux, LLC.

Grove/Atlantic: "The Journey," from *Dream Work* by Mary Oliver. Copyright © 1986 by Mary Oliver. Used by permission of Grove/Atlantic, Inc., and the author.

Harcourt: "The Necklace" by Guy de Maupassant, from *Adventures in Reading, Laureate Edition, Grade 9.* Copyright © 1963 by Harcourt Brace & Company and renewed 1991 by Deborah Jean Lodge, Alice Lodge, Jeanne M. Shutes, Jessica Sand, Lydia Winderman, Florence F. Potell, and Mary Rivers Bowman. Reprinted by permission of the publisher.

HarperCollins Publishers: Excerpt from *Black Boy* by Richard Wright. Copyright 1937, 1942, 1944, 1945 by Richard Wright. Copyright renewed 1973 by Ellen Wright. Reprinted by permission of HarperCollins Publishers, Inc.

James Hurst: "The Scarlet Ibis" by James Hurst. Copyright © 1960 by *The Atlantic Monthly* and renewed 1988 by James Hurst. Reprinted by permission of James Hurst.

W. W. Norton & Company: Excerpt from *The Perfect Storm* by Sebastian Junger. Copyright © 1997 by Sebastian Junger. Reprinted by permission of W. W. Norton & Company, Inc.

Random House: "O What Is That Sound," from *W. H. Auden: The Collected Poems* by W. H. Auden. Copyright © 1976 by Edward Mendelson, William Meredith, and Monroe K. Spears, Executors of the Estate of W. H. Auden. Used by permission of Random House, Inc.

"A Christmas Memory" by Truman Capote. Copyright © 1956 by Truman Capote. Used by permission of Random House, Inc.

Excerpt from *I Know Why the Caged Bird Sings* by Maya Angelou. Copyright © 1969 and renewed 1997 by Maya Angelou. Used by permission of Random House, Inc.

Excerpt from *The Orchid Thief* by Susan Orlean. Copyright © 1998 by Susan Orlean. Used by permission of Random House, Inc.

Scribner: Excerpt from *Angela's Ashes: A Memoir* by Frank McCourt. Copyright © 1996 by Frank McCourt. Reprinted with the permission of Scribner, a division of Simon & Schuster Adult Publishing Group.

Simon & Schuster Children's Publishing Division: Excerpt from "Looking Back at Looking Forward: Predicting the Twentieth Century" by Russell Freedman, from *The Century That Was: Reflections on the Last One Hundred Years,* edited and with an introduction by James Cross Giblin. Copyright © 2000 by Russell Freedman. Reprinted by permission of Atheneum Books for Young Readers, an imprint of Simon & Schuster Children's Publishing Division.

Writers House: "I Have a Dream" by Martin Luther King, Jr. Copyright © 1963 by Martin Luther King, Jr. Copyright renewed 1991 by the Estate of Martin Luther King. Reprinted by arrangement with the Heirs to the Estate of Martin Luther King, Jr., c/o Writers House, LLC, as agent for the proprietor.

Cover

Illustration copyright © 1998 Michael Steirnagle.